Exploring CQRS and Event Sourcing

A journey into high scalability, availability, and maintainability with Windows Azure

Exploring CQRS and Event Sourcing

A journey into high scalability, availability, and maintainability with Windows Azure

Dominic Betts
Julián Domínguez
Grigori Melnik
Fernando Simonazzi
Mani Subramanian

978-1-62114-017-7

This document is provided "as-is". Information and views expressed in this document, including URL and other Internet Web site references, may change without notice.

Some examples depicted herein are provided for illustration only and are fictitious. No real association or connection is intended or should be inferred.

This document does not provide you with any legal rights to any intellectual property in any Microsoft product. You may copy and use this document for your internal, reference purposes. You may modify this document for your internal, reference purposes

© 2012 Microsoft. All rights reserved.

Microsoft, MSDN, SQL Azure, SQL Server, Visual Studio, Windows, and Windows Azure are trademarks of the Microsoft group of companies. All other trademarks are property of their respective owners.

Contents

What other readers are saying about this guide — xvii

Foreword by Greg Young — xxi

Preface — xxiii
   Why we created this guidance now — xxiii
   How is this guidance structured? — xxiii
   A CQRS journey — xxiv
      CQRS reference — xxv
      Tales from the trenches — xxv
         A CQRS journey — xxv
         CQRS reference — xxvi
         Tales from the trenches — xxvi
      Selecting the domain for the RI — xxvi
      Arrow legend — xxvii
   Where to go for more information — xxviii

The Crew — xxix

Journey 1: Our Domain: Conference Management System — 1
   The Contoso Corporation — 1
   Who is coming with us on the journey? — 2
   The Contoso Conference Management System — 3
      Overview of the system — 3
         Selling seats for a conference — 4
         Creating a conference — 4
      Nonfunctional requirements — 4
         Scalability — 4
         Flexibility — 5
   Beginning the journey — 5
   More information — 5

Journey 2: Decomposing the Domain 7
Definitions used in this chapter 7
Bounded contexts in the conference management system 8
Bounded contexts not included 9
The context map for the Contoso Conference Management System 10
Why did we choose these bounded contexts? 11
More information 11

Journey 3: Orders and Registrations Bounded Context 13
A description of the bounded context 13
Working definitions for this chapter 14
Domain definitions (ubiquitous language) 15
Requirements for creating orders 17
Architecture 18
Patterns and concepts 18
Validation 23
Transaction boundaries 24
Concurrency 25
Aggregates and aggregate roots 25
Implementation details 25
High-level architecture 26
1. Querying the read model 27
2. Issuing commands 28
3. Handling commands 28
4. Initiating business logic in the domain 29
5. Persisting the changes 29
6. Polling the read model 29
Inside the write model 31
Aggregates 31
Aggregates and process managers 34
Infrastructure 40
Using the Windows Azure Service Bus 42
Delivering a command to a single recipient 44
Why have separate CommandBus and EventBus classes? 48
How scalable is this approach? 48
How robust is this approach? 48
What is the granularity of a topic and a subscription? 48
How are commands and events serialized? 49
Impact on testing 49
Summary 52
More information 52

Journey 4: Extending and Enhancing the Orders and Registrations Bounded Context — 53
Changes to the bounded context — 53
Working definitions for this chapter — 53
User stories — 54
Implement a login using a record locator — 54
Tell the registrant how much time remains to complete an order — 55
Enable a registrant to create an order that includes multiple seat types — 55
Architecture — 55
Patterns and concepts — 56
Record locators — 56
Querying the read side — 56
Storing denormalized views in a database — 57
Making information about partially fulfilled orders available to the read side — 60
CQRS command validation — 61
The countdown timer and the read model — 62
Implementation details — 62
The order access code record locator — 63
The countdown timer — 64
Using ASP.NET MVC validation for commands — 66
Pushing changes to the read side — 69
Querying the read side — 72
Refactoring the SeatsAvailability aggregate — 73
The AddSeats method — 74
Impact on testing — 74
Acceptance tests and the domain expert — 74
Defining acceptance tests using SpecFlow features — 74
Making the tests executable — 76
Using tests to help developers understand message flows — 81
A journey into code comprehension: A tale of pain, relief, and learning — 83
Testing is important — 83
Domain tests — 84
The other side of the coin — 86
Summary — 90
More information — 90

Journey 5: Preparing for the V1 Release — 91
The Contoso Conference Management System V1 release — 91
Working definitions for this chapter — 91
User stories — 92
Ubiquitous language definitions — 92
Conference Management bounded context user stories — 92
Ordering and Registration bounded context user stories — 92

Architecture	93
Conference Management bounded context	97
Patterns and concepts	97
Event sourcing	97
Identifying aggregates	98
Task-based UI	99
CRUD	101
Integration between bounded contexts	101
Pushing changes from the Conference Management bounded context	102
Pushing changes to the Conference Management bounded context	104
Choosing when to update the read-side data	105
Distributed transactions and event sourcing	105
Autonomy versus authority	105
Favoring autonomy	106
Favoring authority	106
Choosing between autonomy and authority	106
Approaches to implementing the read side	107
Eventual consistency	107
Implementation details	108
The Conference Management bounded context	108
Integration with the Orders and Registration bounded context	108
The Payments bounded context	109
Integration with online payment services, eventual consistency, and command validation	111
Event sourcing	113
Raising events when the state of an aggregate changes	113
Persisting events to the event store	117
Replaying events to rebuild state	118
Issues with the simple event store implementation	120
Windows Azure table storage-based event store	120
Calculating totals	122
Impact on testing	123
Timing issues	123
Involving the domain expert	123
Summary	124
More information	124
Journey 6: Versioning Our System	**125**
Working definitions for this chapter	125
User stories	126
No down time upgrade	126
Display remaining seat quantities	126
Handle zero-cost seats	126
Architecture	126

Patterns and concepts 127
Handling changes to events definitions 128
Mapping/filtering event messages in the infrastructure 128
Handling multiple message versions in the aggregates 128
Honoring message idempotency 128
Avoid processing events multiple times 129
Persisting integration events 131
Message ordering 133
Implementation details 133
Adding support for zero-cost orders 134
Changes to the RegistrationProcessManager class 134
Changes to the UI 134
Data migration 136
Displaying remaining seats in the UI 138
Adding information about remaining seat quantities
to the read model 138
Modifying the UI to display remaining seat quantities 140
Data migration 140
De-duplicating command messages 141
Guaranteeing message ordering 142
Persisting events from the Conference Management
bounded context 146
Adding additional metadata to the messages 146
Capturing and persisting messages to the message log 146
Data migration 148
Migrating from V1 to V2 150
Generating past log messages for the Conference
Management bounded context 151
Migrating the event sourcing events 151
Rebuilding the read models 151
Impact on testing 151
SpecFlow revisited 152
Discovering a bug during the migration 155
Summary 155
More information 155

Journey 7: Adding Resilience and Optimizing Performance 157
Working definitions for this chapter 157
Architecture 158
Adding resilience 159
Making the system resilient when an event is reprocessed 161
Ensuring that commands are always sent 161
Optimizing performance 162
UI flow before optimization 162
Optimizing the UI 163
UI optimization 1 164
UI optimization 2 165

Optimizing the infrastructure	165
Sending and receiving commands and events asynchronously	165
Optimizing command processing	166
Using snapshots with event sourcing	166
Publishing events in parallel	167
Filtering messages in subscriptions	167
Creating a dedicated receiver for the SeatsAvailability aggregate	167
Caching conference information	167
Partitioning the Service Bus	168
Other optimizations	168
Further changes that would improve performance	169
Further changes that would enhance scalability	171
No down-time migration	172
Rebuilding the read models	173
Implementation details	174
Hardening the RegistrationProcessManager class	174
Detecting out-of-order SeatsReserved events	175
Detecting duplicate OrderPlaced events	178
Creating a pseudo transaction when the RegistrationProcessManager class saves its state and sends a command	178
Optimizing the UI flow	181
Receiving, completing, and sending messages asynchronously	186
Receiving messages asynchronously	186
Completing messages asynchronously	186
Sending messages asynchronously	186
Handling commands synchronously and in-process	186
Implementing snapshots with the memento pattern	189
Publishing events in parallel	191
Filtering messages in subscriptions	192
Creating a dedicated SessionSubscriptionReceiver instance for the SeatsAvailability aggregate	193
Caching read-model data	194
Using multiple topics to partition the service bus	195
Other optimizing and hardening changes	196
Sequential GUIDs	196
Asynchronous ASP.NET MVC controllers.	198
Using prefetch with Windows Azure Service Bus	198
Accepting multiple sessions in parallel	199
Adding an optimistic concurrency check	199
Adding a time-to-live value to the MakeSeatReservation command	199
Reducing the number of round-trips to the database	199

Impact on testing	200
Integration tests	200
User interface tests	200
Summary	200
More information	200

Journey 8: Epilogue: Lessons Learned — 201

What did we learn?	201
Performance matters	201
Implementing a message-driven system is far from simple	202
The cloud has challenges	203
CQRS is different	204
Event sourcing and transaction logging	205
Involving the domain expert	206
When to use CQRS	206
What would we do differently if we started over?	207
Start with a solid infrastructure for messaging and persistence	207
Leverage the capabilities of the infrastructure more	207
Adopt a more systematic approach to implementing process managers	208
Partition the application differently	208
Organize the development team differently	208
Evaluate how appropriate the domain and the bounded contexts are for the CQRS pattern	208
Plan for performance	208
Think about the UI differently	209
Explore some additional benefits of event sourcing	209
Explore the issues associated with integrating bounded contexts	210
More information	210

Reference 1: CQRS in Context — 211

What is domain-driven design?	212
Domain-driven design: concepts and terminology	212
Domain model	213
Ubiquitous language	213
Entities, value objects, and services	214
Aggregates and aggregate roots	215
Bounded contexts	215
Anti-corruption layers	217
Context maps	218
Bounded contexts and multiple architectures	218
Bounded contexts and multiple development teams	219
Maintaining multiple bounded contexts	220
CQRS and DDD	220
More information	221

Reference 2: Introducing the Command Query Responsibility Segregation Pattern — **223**
- What is CQRS? — 223
  - Read and write sides — 225
- CQRS and domain-driven design — 227
- Introducing commands, events, and messages — 228
- Why should I use CQRS? — 230
  - Scalability — 230
  - Reduced complexity — 231
  - Flexibility — 231
  - Focus on the business — 232
  - Facilitates building task-based UIs — 232
- Barriers to adopting the CQRS pattern — 232
- When should I use CQRS? — 232
  - Collaborative domains — 233
  - Stale data — 233
  - Moving to the cloud — 234
- When should I avoid CQRS? — 234
- Summary — 234
- More information — 234

Reference 3: Introducing Event Sourcing — **235**
- What is event sourcing? — 236
  - Comparing using an ORM layer with event sourcing — 236
- Why should I use event sourcing? — 240
- Event sourcing concerns — 242
- CQRS/ES — 243
- Standalone event sourcing — 245
- Event stores — 245
  - Basic requirements — 245
  - Underlying storage — 245
  - Performance, scalability, and consistency — 245
- More information — 246

Reference 4: A CQRS and ES Deep Dive — **247**
- Introduction — 247
  - Read models and write models — 247
  - Commands and data transfer objects — 247
  - Domain-driven design (DDD) and aggregates — 248
  - Data and normalization — 248
  - Events and event sourcing — 248
  - Eventual consistency — 248
- Defining aggregates in the domain model — 249
  - Aggregates and object-relational mapping layers — 249
  - Aggregates and event sourcing — 250

Commands and command handlers	252
Commands	253
Example code	253
Command handlers	254
Commands and optimistic concurrency	256
Events and event handlers	256
Events and intent	256
How to model intent	258
Events	259
Sample Code	259
Event handlers	260
Sample code	260
Embracing eventual consistency	261
Eventual consistency and CQRS	263
Optimizing the read-side	266
Optimizing the write side	267
Concurrency and aggregates	267
Messaging and CQRS	268
Messaging considerations	268
Duplicate messages	268
Lost messages	269
Out-of-order messages	269
Unprocessed messages	269
Event versioning	269
Redundant events	270
New event types	270
Changing existing event definitions	270
Task-based UIs	271
Taking advantage of Windows Azure	272
Scaling out using multiple role instances	273
Implementing an event store using Windows Azure table storage	273
Persisting events	274
Retrieving events	275
Publishing events	276
Implementing a messaging infrastructure using the Windows Azure Service Bus	278
A word of warning	279
More information	279
Reference 5: Communicating Between Bounded Contexts	**281**
Introduction	281
Context maps	281
The anti-corruption layer	281

Integration with legacy systems	282
Reading the database	282
Generating events from the database	282
Modifying the legacy systems	282
Implications for event sourcing	282
More information	283
Reference 6: A Saga on Sagas	**285**
Clarifying the terminology	285
Process Manager	286
Messages and CQRS	286
What is a process manager?	286
When should I use a process manager?	290
When should I not use a process manager?	290
Sagas and CQRS	290
More information	290
Reference 7: Technologies Used in the Reference Implementation	**291**
Windows Azure Service Bus	291
Queues	292
Topics and Subscriptions	293
Useful API features	294
Reading messages	294
Sending messages	294
Expiring messages	294
Delayed message processing	294
Serializing messages	295
Further information	295
Unity Application Block	296
Further information	296
More information	296
Tales from the Trenches	**297**
Twilio	**297**
Product overview	297
Lessons learned	297
Separating reads and writes	297
Designing for high availability	297
Idempotency	298
No-downtime deployments	298
Performance	298
References	299
More information	299

Tales from the Trenches: Lokad Hub — 300
- Project overview — 300
- Lessons learned — 300
  - Benefits of DDD — 301
  - Reducing dependencies — 301
  - Using sagas — 301
  - Testing and documentation — 301
  - Migration to ES — 301
  - Using projections — 301
  - Event sourcing — 301
  - Infrastructure — 302
- References — 302
- More information — 302

Tales from the Trenches: DDD/CQRS for large financial company — 303
- Project overview — 303
- Lessons learned — 304
  - Query performance — 304
  - Commands — 304
  - Working with legacy databases — 304
  - Using an Inversion of Control (IoC) container — 304
  - Key lessons learned — 305
- More information — 305

Tales from the Trenches: Digital Marketing — 306
  - Single Responsibility of Objects — 309
- More information — 309

Tales from the Trenches: TOPAZ Technologies — 310
- What did we hope to accomplish by using CQRS/ES? — 310
- What were the biggest challenges and how did we overcome them? — 310
- What were the most important lessons learned? — 311
- With hindsight, what would we have done differently? — 311
- Further information — 311
- More information — 311

Tales from the Trenches: eMoney Nexus — 312
- eMoney Nexus: Some CQRS lessons — 312
- About eMoney & the Nexus — 312
- System overview — 313
- The evolution of the system — 314
- Lessons learned — 320
- Making it better — 321

Appendix 1: Release Notes — 323
  System evolution — 323
  Building and running the sample code (RI) — 323
  Prerequisites — 324
  Obtaining the code — 325
  Creating the databases — 325
    SQL Express Database — 325
    Windows Azure SQL Database instance — 325
  Creating the Settings.xml File — 327
  Building the RI — 327
    Build Configurations — 328
      Release — 328
      Debug — 328
      DebugLocal — 328
  Running the RI — 328
    Scenario 1. Local Web Server, SQL Event Bus, SQL Event Store — 328
    Scenario 2. Local Web Server, Windows Azure Service Bus, Table Storage Event Store — 329
    Scenario 3. Compute Emulator, SQL Event Bus, SQL Event Store — 329
    Scenario 4. Compute Emulator, Windows Azure Service Bus, Table Storage Event Store — 329
    Scenario 5. Windows Azure, Windows Azure Service Bus, Table Storage Event Store — 329
  Running the Tests — 329
    Running the Unit and Integration Tests — 329
    Running the Acceptance Tests — 330
  Known issues — 330
  More information — 330

Appendix 2: Migrations — 331
  Migrating from the V1 to the V2 release — 331
    Running the migration program to migrate the data — 331
      If the data migration fails — 332
  Migrating from the V2 to the V3 Release — 333
  More information — 333

Index — 335

What other readers are saying about this guide

This is another excellent guide from the patterns & practices team—real software engineering with no comforting illusions taken or offered. This guide provides a detailed journal of the practitioners implementing a real production system using the CQRS and Event Sourcing patterns, and also highlights the tradeoffs and teaches the principles that underlie them. The topics presented are relevant and useful, especially if you are building highly scalable Windows Azure applications. You'll be both challenged and inspired!

—*Scott Guthrie, Corporate Vice-President, Azure App Platform, Microsoft*

Having participated and co-authored various guides from patterns & practices, the "CQRS Journey" follows the same walkthrough, scenario-based style, but adding even more fresh empirical content. It's a true testament of a skilled development team without previous CQRS experience, going through the journey of implementing a complex system and documenting their adventures and lessons learnt in this diary. If I had to recommend to someone where to start with CQRS, I would definitely point them to this guide.

—*Matias Woloski, CTO, Auth10 LLC*

The "CQRS Journey" guide is an excellent resource for developers who want to begin developing a CQRS system or convert their current system. It's a true "trial by fire" approach to the concepts and implementation hurdles that a team would encounter when adopting CQRS. I would recommend reading it twice as I picked up even more lessons the second time through.

—*Dan Piessens, Lead Software Architect, Zywave*

I think it's a really big step in communication with the developer community. You not only share your development experience with a broad audience (which is very valuable by itself) but you're also open for learning from the community. While working on real projects it's difficult to stop, find some time to structure your knowledge, prepare it in the form understandable for others. It's very cool that you found time and resources for such educational effort, I really appreciate this.

—*Ksenia Mukhortova, Business Applications Developer, Intel*

I'm very excited about A CQRS Journey for a number of reasons. It explores, with an even hand and a fair mind, a topic where opinions are both diverse and numerous. True to its name, the guide captures the progression of learning. Conclusions are not simply stated; they arrive as a result of experience. Additionally, the project embraced a passionate community with a spirit of inclusion and transparency. The result is friendly-to-read guidance that is both diligent in execution and rigorous in its research.

—*Christopher Bennage, Software Development Engineer, Microsoft*

The journey project used Windows Azure SQL Database (backing write & read models), Service Bus (for reliable messaging), and Tables (for event store). Production-quality, scalable cloud services that can be provisioned on-demand with a few mouse-clicks (or API calls) can turn some tough infrastructure problems into trivial ones.

—*Bill Wilder, MVP, Independent Consultant*

Perhaps the best lessons out of this guidance will be just how easy it is to work with Microsoft now that they are embracing more community and open source.

—*Adam Dymitruk, Systems Architect*

The work that patterns & practices is doing here is very important as it is packaging the concepts in a digestible fashion and helping developers to wade through the ambiguities of CQRS. The real world experiences captured within the journey project will be invaluable to folks looking at applying CQRS within their application development"

—*Glenn Block, Senior Program Manager, Microsoft, Windows Azure SDK for Node.js, Organizer at ALT.NET Seattle Chapter*

The p&p team's dedication and hard work go hand-in-hand with the very high level of competency present on the team. Their attention to detail, insistence on clarity, and open collaboration with the community all led to the creation of material representing enormous value to consumers of the guidance. I definitely plan on referencing this material and code in future engagements because I think my clients will derive many benefits from it–a win-win for everyone!

—*Josh Elster, Principal, Liquid Electron*

CQRS is a very important pattern, and a tool that any cloud developer should have in his or her toolbelt. It is particularly well-suited for the cloud since it allows for the implementation of massively scalable solutions based on simple, common patterns (like queues, event handlers, and view models, to name a few). Like all patterns, there are several concrete, correct ways of implementing CQRS. A journey of the type undertaken by Microsoft's patterns & practices team is a great way to explore the different options, tradeoffs, and even possible mistakes one can make along the way, and accelerate one's learning of the CQRS pattern.

—*Shy Cohen, Principal, Shy Cohen Consulting*

patterns & practices assembled many of the active and key people in the CQRS community to join them on the their journey with CQRS and along the way discovered confusing terminology and concepts that created opportunities for leaders in the community to bring clarity to a broad audience. The material produced is influenced from the results of building a real world application and expresses the experiences from advisors and the patterns & practices team during the development process. By request from the community to allow outside contributions, everything has been open sourced on GitHub. Anyone interested is encouraged to take a look at the guide or implementation. The patterns & practices team has been very welcoming to anyone who wants to collaborate on covering additional areas, alternative implementations or further extending what is currently in place.

—*Kelly Sommers, Developer*

Congratulations on getting to what looks to be nice guidance. I know that the announcement that p&p was going to embark on this project caused a twitter firestorm but you seem to have come through it well. I'm a fan of the p&p books and think you've done a great job in sharing good practices with the community.

—*Neil Mackenzie, Windows Azure MVP*

CQRS is as much about architecture community as it is about concrete patterns—thus the project is aptly named "CQRS Journey." The community involvement and engagement in this project is unprecedented for Microsoft and reflects the enthusiasm amongst the many (if may say: young) software architects from across the industry who are rediscovering proven architecture patterns and are recomposing them in new ways to solve today's challenges. For me, one takeaway from this project is that the recipes developed here need to be carefully weighed against their alternatives. As with any software architecture approaches that promise easy scalability or evolvability of solutions, the proof will be in concrete, larger production implementations and how they hold up to changing needs over time. Thus, the results of this Journey project mark a start and not a finish line.

—*Clemens Vasters, Principal Technical Lead, Microsoft Corporation*

The experiences and conclusions of the p&p team match up very well with our own real-world experiences. Their conclusions in Chapter 8 are spot on. One of the best aspects of this guidance is that the p&p team exposes more of their thought processes and learning throughout the Journey than most write-ups that you may read. From arguments between Developer 1 and Developer 2 on the team, to discussions with experts such as Greg Young and Udi Dahan, to an excellent post-project review in Chapter 8, the thought process is out there for you to learn from.
    Thanks for this great work, guys. I hope you keep this style with your upcoming guidance pieces.

—*Jon Wagner, SVP & Chief Architect, eMoney Advisor*

The CQRS journey release by patterns & practices provides real world insight into the increasingly popular CQRS pattern used in distributed systems that rely upon asynchronous, message based approaches to achieve very large scale. The exploration of the issues the team faced throughout the implementation of the pattern is extremely useful for organizations considering CQRS, both to determine where the pattern is appropriate for them, and to go into the design and implementation with a baseline understanding of the complexity it will introduce. I really enjoyed the candor around the approach taken, the issues encountered, and the early design choices that the team would change in hindsight. This is a must read for any organization embarking upon CQRS, regardless of what platform they are using.

—*Chris Keyser, VP Engineering, CaseNetwork*

It is a great resource on tactical and technical aspects of building a distributed system.

—*Rinat Abdullin, Technology Leader, Lokad*

I'd like to personally thank the team for putting together such a transparent journey throughout this project. I'm very pleased with the final release.

—*Truong Nguyen, CEO, Nepsoft*

It's a good read. Lots to learn from it.

—*Christian Horsdal Gammelgaard, Lead Software Architect, Mjølner Informatics*

Foreword by Greg Young

I started off the new year on January 3rd with a few hour long meeting showing the team at patterns & practices a bit about Command and Query Responsibility Segregation (CQRS) and Event Sourcing (ES). Most of the team had previously not been exposed to these ideas. Today is almost exactly six months later and they have produced a document of over 200 pages of discussions and guidance as well as a full end to end example hosted in Windows Azure. This is certainly not a small feat.

When the announcement of the project came out, the twitter stream near instantly went negative as many thought that Microsoft was building a CQRS framework; which was premature from the community. The process followed similar paths to other patterns & practices projects with a large advisor board being set up. I believe however that the most interesting part of the process was the decision to host the work on GitHub and allow pull requests which is an extremely open and transparent way of communicating during the project.

One of the main benefits for the community as a whole of going through such a process is that people were forced to refine their vocabularies. There are in the DDD/CQRS/ES communities many different voices and often times, especially in younger groups, vocabularies will go down divergent paths leading to fractured community. An example of nebulous terminologies can be seen in the terms "saga," "process manager," and "workflow"; the community as a whole I believe benefited from the discussions over defining what it actually is. One of the most interesting conversations brought up for me personally was defining the difference between an Event Store and a Transaction Log as legitimate arguments can be made that either is a higher level abstraction of the other. This has led not only to many interesting discussions in the community but to a far stricter future definition of what an Event Store is.

> "For the things we have to learn before we can do them, we learn by doing them. ~Aristotle"

The quote above was the team motto during the project. Many will be looking towards the guidance presented as being authoritative guidance of how things should be done. This is however not the optimal way to look at the guidance as presented (though it does contain many bits of good authoritative guidance). The main benefit of the guidance is the learning experience that it contains. It is important to remember that the team came into the ideas presented as non-experienced in CQRS and they learned in the process of doing. This gives a unique perspective throughout much of the text where things are learned along the way or are being seen through fresh eyes of someone recently having learned and attempted to apply the ideas. This perspective has also brought up many interesting conversations within the community. The patterns & practices team deserves credit for digging deep, facilitating these discussions, and bringing to light various incongruities, confusions and inconsistencies as they went along.

Keeping in mind the origination point of the team, the most valuable bits in the text that a reader should focus on aside from general explanations are places where tradeoffs are discussed. There is an unfortunate tendency to seek authoritative answers that "things should be done in this way" when they in fact do not exist. There are many ways to proverbially skin a cat and all have their pros and cons. The text is quite good at discussing alternative points of view that came up as possible answers, or that received heavy discussion within the advisor group, these can often be seen in the "developer 1/ developer 2 discussions." One such discussion I mentioned previously in defining the difference between event sourcing and a transaction log. Many of these types of discussions come at the end of the guidance.

How might things be approached differently? One of my favourite discussions towards the end of the guidance dealing with performance is the independent realization that messaging is not equivalent to distribution. This is a very hard lesson for many people to understand and the way that it comes up rather organically and much like it would on most teams as a performance problem is a great explanation. I can say 100 times to apply the first law of distributed computing, don't distribute; however seeing it from the eyes of a team dealing with a performance problem who has already made the mistake of equating the two is a very understandable path and a great teaching tool. This section also contains a *smörgåsbord* of information and insights in terms of how to build performant applications in Windows Azure.

Out in the wild, there are plenty of naïve samples of CQRS/ES implementations, which are great for describing the concepts. There are details and challenges that will not surface till you work on a complex, real-world production system. The value of the p&p's sample application is that it uses a fairly complex domain and the team went through multiple releases and focused on infrastructure hardening, performance optimizations, dealing with transient faults and versioning, etc. — many practical issues that you face when implementing CQRS and ES.

As with any project, people may disagree with implementation choices and decisions made. It is important to remember the scoping of the project. The guidance is not coming from an expert viewpoint throughout the process, but that of a group "learning by doing." The process was and remains open to contributions, and in fact this version has been reviewed, validated, and guided by experts in the community. In the spirit of OSS "send a pull request." This guide can serve as a valuable point to start discussions, clear up misconceptions, and refine how we explain things, as well as drive improvement both in the guidance itself and in getting consistent viewpoints throughout the community.

In conclusion I think patterns & practices has delivered to the community a valuable service in the presentation of this guidance. The view point the guidance is written from is both an uncommon and valuable one. It has also really been a good overall exercise for the community in terms of setting the bar for what is being discussed and refining of the vocabularies that people speak in. Combine this with the amount of previously difficult to find Windows Azure guidance and the guidance becomes quite valuable to someone getting into the ideas.

Greg Young

Preface

Why are we embarking on this journey?

"The best way to observe a fish is to become a fish."
Jacques Cousteau

Why we created this guidance now

The Command Query Responsibility Segregation (CQRS) pattern and event sourcing (ES) are currently generating a great deal of interest from developers and architects who are designing and building large-scale, distributed systems. There are conference sessions, blogs, articles, and frameworks all dedicated to the CQRS pattern and to event sourcing, and all explaining how they can help you to improve the maintainability, testability, scalability, and flexibility of your systems.

However, like anything new, it takes some time before a pattern, approach, or methodology is fully understood and consistently defined by the community and has useful, practical guidance to help you to apply or implement it.

This guidance is designed to help you get started with the CQRS pattern and event sourcing. It is not intended to be the guide to the CQRS pattern and event sourcing, but a guide that describes the experiences of a development team in implementing the CQRS pattern and event sourcing in a real-world application. The development team did not work in isolation; they actively sought input from industry experts and from a wider group of advisors to ensure that the guidance is both detailed and practical.

The CQRS pattern and event sourcing are not mere simplistic solutions to the problems associated with large-scale, distributed systems. By providing you with both a working application and written guidance, we expect you'll be well prepared to embark on your own CQRS journey.

How is this guidance structured?

There are two closely related parts to this guidance:
- A working reference implementation (RI) sample, which is intended to illustrate many of the concepts related to the CQRS pattern and event sourcing approaches to developing complex enterprise applications.
- This written guidance, which is intended to complement the RI by describing how it works, what decisions were made during its development, and what trade-offs were considered.

This written guidance is itself split into three distinct sections that you can read independently: a description of the journey we took as we learned about CQRS, a collection of CQRS reference materials, and a collection of case studies that describe the experiences other teams have had with the CQRS pattern. The map in Figure 1 illustrates the relationship between the first two sections: a journey with some defined stopping points that enables us to explore a space.

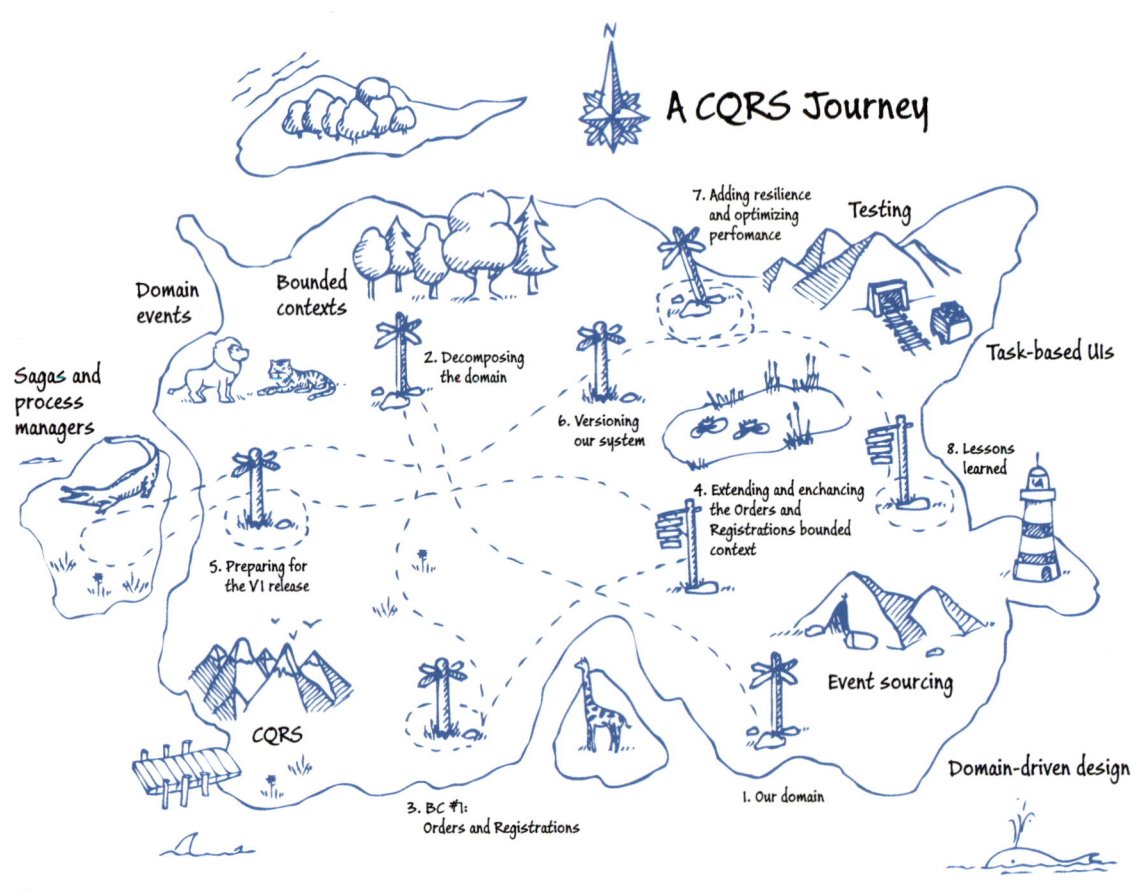

FIGURE 1
A CQRS journey

A CQRS journey

This section is closely related to the RI and the chapters follow the chronology of the project to develop the RI. Each chapter describes relevant features of the domain model, infrastructure elements, architecture, and user interface (UI) that the team was concerned with during that phase of the project. Some parts of the system are discussed in several chapters, and this reflects the fact that the team revisited certain areas during later stages. Each of these chapters discuss how and why particular CQRS patterns and concepts apply to the design and development of particular bounded contexts, describe the implementation, and highlight any implications for testing.

Other chapters look at the big picture. For example, there is a chapter that explains the rationale for splitting the RI into the bounded contexts we chose, another chapter analyzes the implications of our approach for versioning the system, and other chapters look at how the different bounded contexts in the RI communicate with each other.

This section describes our journey as we learned about CQRS, and how we applied that learning to the design and implementation of the RI. It is not prescriptive guidance and is not intended to illustrate the only way to apply the CQRS approach to our RI. We have tried wherever possible to capture alternative viewpoints through consultation with our advisors and to explain why we made particular decisions. You may disagree with some of those decisions; please let us know at cqrsjourney@microsoft.com.

This section of the written guidance makes frequent cross-references to the material in the second section for readers who wish to explore any of the concepts or patterns in more detail.

CQRS reference

The second section of the written guidance is a collection of reference material collated from many sources. It is not the definitive collection, but should contain enough material to help you to understand the core patterns, concepts, and language of CQRS.

Tales from the trenches

This section of the written guidance is a collection of case studies from other teams that describe their experiences of implementing the CQRS pattern and event sourcing in the real world. These case studies are not as detailed as the journey section of the guidance and are intended to give an overview of these projects and to summarize some of the key lessons learned.

The following is a list of the chapters that comprise both sections of the written guidance:

A CQRS journey

- Chapter 1, "The Contoso Conference Management System," introduces our sample application and our team of (fictional) experts.
- Chapter 2, "Decomposing the Domain," provides a high-level view of the sample application and describes the bounded contexts that make up the application.
- Chapter 3, "Orders and Registrations Bounded Context," introduces our first bounded context, explores some CQRS concepts, and describes some elements of our infrastructure.
- Chapter 4, "Extending and Enhancing the Orders and Registrations Bounded Context," describes adding new features to the bounded context and discusses our testing approach.
- Chapter 5, "Preparing for the V1 Release," describes adding two new bounded contexts and handling integration issues between them, and introduces our event-sourcing implementation. This is our first pseudo-production release.
- Chapter 6, "Versioning Our System," discusses how to version the system and handle upgrades with minimal down time.
- Chapter 7, "Adding Resilience and Optimizing Performance," describes what we did to make the system more resilient to failure scenarios and how we optimized the performance of the system. This was the last release of the system in our journey.
- Chapter 8, "Lessons Learned," collects the key lessons we learned from our journey and suggests how you might continue the journey.

CQRS reference

- Chapter 1, "CQRS in Context," provides some context for CQRS, especially in relation to the domain-driven design approach.
- Chapter 2, "Introducing the Command Query Responsibility Segregation Pattern," provides a conceptual overview of the CQRS pattern.
- Chapter 3, "Introducing Event Sourcing," provides a conceptual overview of event sourcing.
- Chapter 4, "A CQRS and ES Deep Dive," describes the CQRS pattern and event sourcing in more depth.
- Chapter 5, "Communicating between Bounded Contexts," describes some options for communicating between bounded contexts.
- Chapter 6, "A Saga on Sagas," explains our choice of terminology: process manager instead of saga. It also describes the role of process managers.
- Chapter 7, "Technologies Used in the Reference Implementation," provides a brief overview of some of the other technologies we used, such as the Windows Azure Service Bus.
- Appendix 1, "Release Notes," contains detailed instructions for downloading, building, and running the sample application and test suites.
- Appendix 2, "Migrations," contains instructions for performing the code and data migrations between the pseudo-production releases of the Contoso Conference Management System.

Tales from the trenches

- Chapter 1, "Twilio," describes a highly available, cloud-hosted, communications platform. Although the team who developed this product did not explicitly use CQRS, many of the architectural concepts they adopted are very closely related to the CQRS pattern.
- Chapter 2, "Lokad Hub," describes a project that made full use of domain-driven design, CQRS, and event sourcing in an application designed to run on multiple cloud platforms.
- Chapter 3, "DDD/CQRS for large financial company," describes a project that made full use of domain-driven design and CQRS to build a reference application for a large financial company. It used CQRS to specifically address the issues of performance, scalability, and reliability.
- Chapter 4, "Digital Marketing," describes how an existing application was refactored over time while delivering new features. This project adopted the CQRS pattern for one of its pieces as the project progressed.
- Chapter 5, "TOPAZ Technologies," describes a project that used the CQRS pattern and event sourcing to simplify the development of an off-the-shelf enterprise application.
- Chapter 6, "eMoney Nexus," describes migration project for an application that used legacy three-tier architecture to an architecture that used the CQRS pattern and event sourcing. Many of the conclusions drawn in this project are similar to our own experiences on our CQRS journey.

SELECTING THE DOMAIN FOR THE RI

Before embarking on our journey, we needed to have an outline of the route we planned to take and an idea of what the final destination should be. We needed to select an appropriate domain for the RI.

We engaged with the community and our advisory board to help us choose a domain that would enable us to highlight as many of the features and concepts of CQRS as possible. To help us select between our candidate domains, we used the criteria in the following list. The domain selected should be:

- **Non-trivial**. The domain must be complex enough to exhibit real problems, but at the same time simple enough for most people to understand without weeks of study. The problems should involve dealing with temporal data, stale data, receiving out-of-order events, and versioning. The domain should enable us to illustrate solutions using event sourcing, sagas, and event merging.
- **Collaborative**. The domain must contain collaborative elements where multiple actors can operate simultaneously on shared data.
- **End to end**. We wanted to be able illustrate the concepts and patterns in action from the back-end data store through to the user interface. This might include disconnected mobile and smart clients.
- **Cloud friendly**. We wanted to have the option of hosting parts of the RI on Windows Azure and be able to illustrate how you can use CQRS for cloud-hosted applications.
- **Large**. We wanted to be able to show how our domain can be broken down into multiple bounded contexts to highlight when to use and when not use CQRS. We also wanted to illustrate how multiple architectural approaches (CQRS, CQRS/ES, and CRUD) and legacy systems can co-exist within the same domain. We also wanted to show how multiple development teams could carry out work in parallel.
- **Easily deployable**. The RI needed to be easily deployable so that you can install it and experiment with it as you read this guidance.

As a result, we chose to implement the conference management system that Chapter 1, "*Our Domain: The Contoso Conference Management System,*" introduces.

ARROW LEGEND

Many illustrations in the guidance have arrows. Here is their associated meaning.

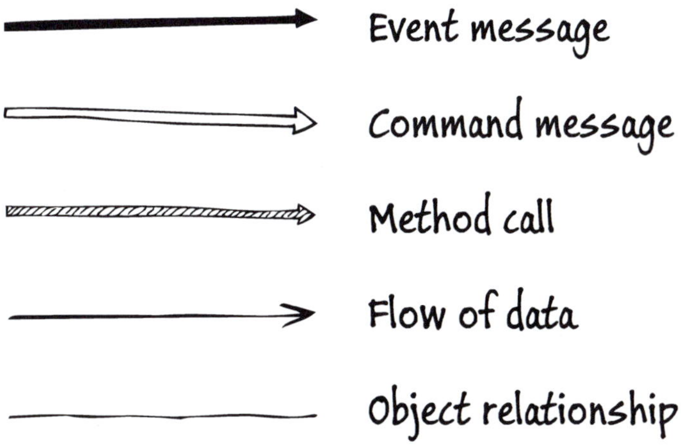

- Event message
- Command message
- Method call
- Flow of data
- Object relationship

FIGURE 2
Legend for arrows

Where to go for more information

There are a number of resources listed in text throughout the book. These resources will provide additional background, bring you up to speed on various technologies, and so forth. For your convenience, there is a bibliography online that contains all the links so that these resources are just a click away.

You can find the bibliography on MSDN at: *http://msdn.microsoft.com/en-us/library/jj619274*.

The Crew

Captain Ernest Shackleton's Antarctic expedition recruitment ad (1913) stated:

No fewer than 5000 people replied...

When we embarked on our journey half a year ago, it felt almost the same. With no fewer than 70 community members (both experts and enthusiastic novices) answering the call for advisory board and offering to volunteer their time to help us steer this project!

We have now reached the end of the journey. These are the members of the development team who endured the challenges of the journey and produced this guide:

Vision and Program Management *Grigori Melnik* (Microsoft Corporation)

Development *Julián Domínguez* (Microsoft Corporation), *Daniel Cazzulino* and *Fernando Simonazzi* (Clarius Consulting)

Testing *Mani Subramanian* (Microsoft Corporation), *Hernan de Lahitte* (Digit Factory), and *Rathi Velusamy* (Infosys Technologies Ltd.)

Documentation *Dominic Betts* (Content Master Ltd.), *Julián Domínguez, Grigori Melnik*, and Mani Subramanian (Microsoft Corporation), and *Fernando Simonazzi* (Clarius Consulting)

Graphic Design *Alexander Ustinov* and Anton Rusecki (JetStyle)

Editing and Production *RoAnn Corbisier* and *Nelly Delgado* (Microsoft Corporation), *Nancy Michell* (Content Master Ltd.), and *Chris Burns* (Linda Werner & Associates Inc)

The development team didn't embark on this journey by themselves and didn't work in isolation. We actively sought input from industry experts and from a wider group of advisors to ensure that the guidance is detailed, practical, and informed by real-world experience. We would like to thank our *advisory board members* and the DDD/CQRS community members in general who have accompanied us on this journey for their active participation, insights, critiques, challenges, and reviews. We have learned and unlearned many things, we've explored and experimented a lot. The journey wasn't easy but it was so worth it and we enjoyed it. Thank you for keeping us grounded in the real-world challenges. Thank you for your ongoing support of our effort. We hope the community will continue exploring the space, pushing the state of the practice further, and extending the reference implementation and the guidance.

Specifically, we'd like to acknowledge the following people who have contributed to the journey in many different ways:

- *Greg Young* for your pragmatism, patience with us, continuous mentoring and irreplaceable advice;
- *Udi Dahan* for challenging us and offering alternative views on many concepts;
- *Clemens Vasters* for pushing back on terminology and providing a very valuable perspective from the distributed database field;
- *Kelly Sommers* for believing in us and bringing sanity to the community as well as for deep technical insights;
- *Adam Dymitruk* for jumpstarting us on git and extending the RI;
- *Glenn Block* for encouraging us to go all the way with the OSS initiative and for introducing us to many community members;
- Our GM *Lori Brownell* and our director *Björn Rettig* for providing sponsorship of the initiative and believing in our vision;
- *Scott Guthrie* for supporting the project and helping amplify the message;
- *Josh Elster* for exploring and designing the MIL (Messaging Intermediate Language) and pushing us to make it easier to follow the workflow of messages in code;
- *Cesar De la Torre Llorente* for helping us spike on the alternatives and bringing up terminological incongruities between various schools and thought leaders;
- *Rinat Abdullin* for active participation at the beginning of the project and contributing a case study;
- *Bruno Terkaly* and *Ricardo Villalobos* for exploring the disconnected client scenario that would integrate with the RI;
- *Einar Otto Stangvik* for spiking on the Schedule Builder bounded context implementation in Node.js;
- *Mark Seemann* for sending the very first pull request focusing on code quality;
- *Christopher Bennage* for helping us overcome GitHub limitations by creating the pundit review system and the export-to-Excel script to manage iteration backlog more effectively;
- *Bob Brumfield, Eugenio Pace, Carlos Farre, Hanz Zhang*, and *Rohit Sharma* for many insights especially on the perf and hardening challenges;
- *Chris Tavares* for putting out the first CQRS experiment at p&p and suggesting valuable scenarios;
- *Tim Sharkinian* for your perspectives on CQRS and for getting us on the SpecFlow train;
- *Jane Sinyagina* for helping solicit and process feedback from the advisors;
- *Howard Wooten* and *Thomas Petchel* for feedback on the UI style and usability;
- *Kelly Leahy* for sharing your experience and making us aware of potential pitfalls;
- *Dylan Smith* for early conversations and support of this project in pre-flight times;
- *Evan Cooke, Tim Walton, Alex Dubinkov, Scott Brown, Jon Wagner*, and *Gabriel N. Schenker* for sharing your experiences and contributing mini-case studies.

We feel honored to be supported by such an incredible group of people.
Thank you!

Journey 1:

Our Domain: Conference Management System

The starting point: Where have we come from, what are we taking, and who is coming with us?

"I am prepared to go anywhere, provided it be forward."
David Livingstone

This chapter introduces a fictitious company named Contoso. It describes Contoso's plans to launch the Contoso Conference Management System, a new online service that will enable other companies or individuals to organize and manage their own conferences and events. This chapter describes, at a high-level, some of the functional and non-functional requirements of the new system, and why Contoso wants to implement parts of it using the Command Query Responsibility Segregation (CQRS) pattern and event sourcing (ES). As with any company considering this process, there are many issues to consider and challenges to be met, particularly because this is the first time Contoso has used both the CQRS pattern and event sourcing. The chapters that follow show, step by step, how Contoso designed and built its conference management application.

This chapter also introduces a panel of fictional experts to comment on the development efforts.

The Contoso Corporation

Contoso is a startup ISV company of approximately 20 employees that specializes in developing solutions using Microsoft technologies. The developers at Contoso are knowledgeable about various Microsoft products and technologies, including the .NET Framework, ASP.NET MVC, and Windows Azure. Some of the developers have previous experience using the domain-driven design (DDD) approach, but none of them have used the CQRS pattern previously.

The Conference Management System application is one of the first innovative online services that Contoso wants to take to market. As a startup, Contoso wants to develop and launch these services with a minimal investment in hardware and IT personnel. Contoso wants to be quick to market in order to start growing market share, and cannot afford the time to implement all of the planned functionality in the first releases. Therefore, it is important that the architecture it adopts can easily accommodate changes and enhancements with minimal impact on existing users of the system. Contoso has chosen to deploy the application on Windows Azure in order to take advantage of its ability to scale applications as demand grows.

Who is coming with us on the journey?

As mentioned earlier, this guide and the accompanying RI describe a CQRS journey. A panel of experts will comment on our development efforts as we go. This panel includes a CQRS expert, a software architect, a developer, a domain expert, an IT Pro, and a business manager. They will all comment from their own perspectives.

Gary is a CQRS expert. He ensures that a CQRS-based solution will work for a company and will provide tangible benefits. He is a cautious person, for good reason.

> "Defining the CQRS pattern is easy. Realizing the benefits that implementing the CQRS pattern can offer is not always so straightforward."

Jana is a software architect. She plans the overall structure of an application. Her perspective is both practical and strategic. In other words, she considers not only what technical approaches are needed today, but also what direction a company needs to consider for the future. Jana has worked on projects that used the domain-driven design approach.

> "It's not easy to balance the needs of the company, the users, the IT organization, the developers, and the technical platforms we rely on."

Markus is a software developer who is new to the CQRS pattern. He is analytical, detail-oriented, and methodical. He's focused on the task at hand, which is building a great application. He knows that he's the person who's ultimately responsible for the code.

> "I don't care what architecture you want to use for the application; I'll make it work."

Carlos is the domain expert. He understands all the ins and outs of conference management. He has worked in a number of organizations that help people run conferences. He has also worked in a number of different roles: sales and marketing, conference management, and consultant.

> "I want to make sure that the team understands how this business works so that we can deliver a world-class online conference management system."

Poe is an IT professional who's an expert in deploying and running applications in the cloud. Poe has a keen interest in practical solutions; after all, he's the one who gets paged at 3:00 AM when there's a problem.

> "Running complex applications in the cloud involves challenges that are different than the challenges in managing on-premises applications. I want to make sure our new conference management system meets our published service-level agreements (SLA)."

Beth is a business manager. She helps companies to plan how their business will develop. She understands the market that the company operates in, the resources that the company has available, and the goals of the company. She has both a strategic view and an interest in the day-to-day operations of the company.

> "Organizations face many conflicting demands on their resources. I want to make sure that our company balances those demands and adopts a business plan that will make us successful in the medium and long term." If you have a particular area of interest, look for notes provided by the specialists whose interests align with yours.

The Contoso Conference Management System

This section describes the Contoso Conference Management System as the team envisaged it at the start of the journey. The team has not used the CQRS pattern before; therefore, the system that is delivered at the end of our journey may not match this description exactly because:

- What we learn as we go may impact what we ultimately deliver.
- Because this is a learning journey, it is more difficult to estimate what we can achieve in the available time.

Overview of the system

Contoso plans to build an online conference management system that will enable its customers to plan and manage conferences that are held at a physical location. The system will enable Contoso's customers to:

- Manage the sale of different seat types for the conference.
- Create a conference and define characteristics of that conference.

The Contoso Conference Management System will be a multi-tenant, cloud-hosted application. Business customers will need to register with the system before they can create and manage their conferences.

Selling seats for a conference

The business customer defines the number of seats available for the conference. The business customer may also specify events at a conference such as workshops, receptions, and premium sessions for which attendees must have a separate ticket. The business customer also defines how many seats are available for these events.

The system manages the sale of seats to ensure that the conference and sub-events are not oversubscribed. This part of the system will also operate wait-lists so that if other attendees cancel, their seats can be reallocated.

The system will require that the names of the attendees be associated with the purchased seats so that an on-site system can print badges for the attendees when they arrive at the conference.

Creating a conference

A business customer can create new conferences and manage information about the conference such as its name, description, and dates. The business customer can also make a conference visible on the Contoso Conference Management System website by publishing it, or hide it by unpublishing it.

Additionally, the business customer defines the seat types and available quantity of each seat type for the conference.

Contoso also plans to enable the business customer to specify the following characteristics of a conference:

- Whether the paper submission process will require reviewers.
- What the fee structure for paying Contoso will be.
- Who key personnel, such as the program chair and the event planner, will be.

Nonfunctional requirements

Contoso has two major nonfunctional requirements for its conference management system—scalability and flexibility—and it hopes that the CQRS pattern will help it meet them.

Scalability

The conference management system will be hosted in the cloud; one of the reasons Contoso chose a cloud platform was its scalability and potential for elastic scalability.

Although cloud platforms such as Windows Azure enable you to scale applications by adding (or removing) role instances, you must still design your application to be scalable. By splitting responsibility for the application's read and write operations into separate objects, the CQRS pattern allows Contoso to split those operations into separate Windows Azure roles that can scale independently of each other. This recognizes the fact that for many applications, the number of read operations vastly exceeds the number of write operations. This gives Contoso the opportunity to scale the conference management system more efficiently, and make better use of the Windows Azure role instances it uses.

Flexibility

The market that the Contoso Conference Management System operates in is very competitive, and very fast moving. In order to compete, Contoso must be able to quickly and cost effectively adapt the conference management system to changes in the market. This requirement for flexibility breaks down into a number of related aspects:

- Contoso must be able to evolve the system to meet new requirements and to respond to changes in the market.
- The system must be able to run multiple versions of its software simultaneously in order to support customers who are in the middle of a conference and who do not wish to upgrade to a new version immediately. Other customers may wish to migrate their existing conference data to a new version of the software as it becomes available.
- Contoso intends the software to last for at least five years. It must be able to accommodate significant changes over that period.
- Contoso does not want the complexity of some parts of the system to become a barrier to change.
- Contoso would like to be able to use different developers for different elements of the system, using cheaper developers for simpler tasks and restricting its use of more expensive and experienced developers to the more critical aspects of the system.

> Contoso plans to compete by being quick to respond to changes in the market and to changing customer requirements. Contoso must be able to evolve the system quickly and painlessly.

Beginning the journey

The next chapter is the start of our CQRS journey. It provides more information about the Contoso Conference Management System and describes some of the high-level parts of the system. Subsequent chapters describe the stages of the journey as Contoso implements the conference management system.

> This is a big challenge: keeping the system running for all our customers while we perform upgrades with no down time.

More information

All links in this book are accessible from the book's online bibliography available at: *http://msdn.microsoft.com/en-us/library/jj619274*.

> There is some debate in the CQRS community about whether, in practice, you can use different development teams for different parts of the CQRS pattern implementation.

Journey 2:

Decomposing the Domain

Planning the stops.

"Without stones there is no arch."
Marco Polo

In this chapter, we provide a high-level overview of the Contoso Conference Management System. The discussion will help you understand the structure of the application, the integration points, and how the parts of the application relate to each other.

Here we describe this high-level structure in terms borrowed from the domain-driven design (DDD) approach that Eric Evans describes in his book, *Domain-Driven Design: Tackling Complexity in the Heart of Software* (Addison-Wesley Professional, 2003). Although there is no universal consensus that DDD is a prerequisite for implementing the Command Query Responsibility Segregation (CQRS) pattern successfully, our team decided to use many of the concepts from the DDD approach, such as *domain, bounded context*, and *aggregate*, in line with common practice within the CQRS community. Chapter 1, "CQRS in Context," in the Reference Guide discusses the relationship between the DDD approach and the CQRS pattern in more detail.

Definitions used in this chapter

Throughout this chapter we use a number of terms, which we'll define in a moment. For more detail, and possible alternative definitions, see Chapter 1, "CQRS in Context," in the Reference Guide.

Domain: The *domain* refers to the business domain for the Contoso Conference Management System (the reference implementation). Chapter 1, "Our Domain: The Contoso Conference Management System," provides an overview of this domain.

> When you use the CQRS pattern, you often use events to communicate between bounded contexts. There are alternative approaches to integration, such as sharing data at the database level.

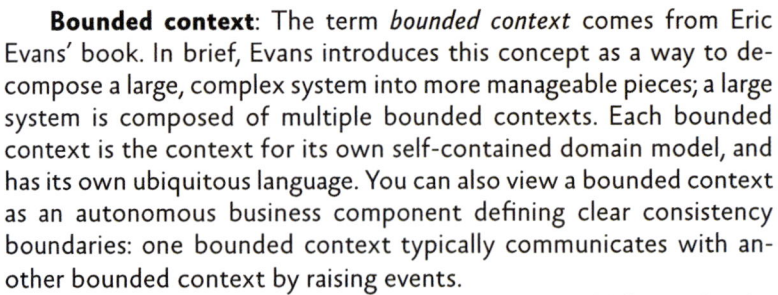

Bounded context: The term *bounded context* comes from Eric Evans' book. In brief, Evans introduces this concept as a way to decompose a large, complex system into more manageable pieces; a large system is composed of multiple bounded contexts. Each bounded context is the context for its own self-contained domain model, and has its own ubiquitous language. You can also view a bounded context as an autonomous business component defining clear consistency boundaries: one bounded context typically communicates with another bounded context by raising events.

Context map: According to Eric Evans, you should "Describe the points of contact between the models, outlining explicit translation for any communication and highlighting any sharing." This exercise results in what is called a *context map*, which serves several purposes that include providing an overview of the whole system and helping people to understand the details of how different bounded contexts interact with each other.

Bounded contexts in the conference management system

The Orders and Registrations bounded context: Within the *orders and registrations bounded context* are the reservations, payment, and registration items. When a registrant interacts with the system, the system creates an order to manage the reservations, payment, and registrations. An order contains one or more order items.

A *reservation* is a temporary reservation of one or more seats at a conference. When a registrant begins the ordering process to purchase a number of seats at a conference, the system creates reservations for that number of seats. Those seats are then unavailable for other registrants to reserve. The reservations are held for 15 minutes, during which time the registrant can complete the ordering process by making a payment for the seats. If the registrant does not pay for the tickets within 15 minutes, the system deletes the reservation and the seats become available for other registrants to reserve.

The Conference Management bounded context: Within this bounded context, a business customer can create new conferences and manage them. After a business customer creates a new conference, he can access the details of the conference by using his email address and conference locator access code. The system generates the access code when the business customer creates the conference.

> We discussed making the period of time that the system holds reservations a parameter that a business customer can adjust for each conference. This may be a feature that we add if we determine that there is a requirement for this level of control.

The business customer can specify the following information about a conference:
- The name, description, and slug (part of the URL used to access the conference).
- The start and end dates of the conference.
- The different types and quotas of seats available at the conference.

Additionally, the business customer can control the visibility of the conference on the public website by either publishing or unpublishing the conference.

The business customer can also use the conference management website to view a list of orders and attendees.

The Payments bounded context: The *payments bounded context* is responsible for managing the interactions between the conference management system and external payment systems. It forwards the necessary payment information to the external system and receives an acknowledgement that the payment was either accepted or rejected. It reports the success or failure of the payment back to the conference management system.

Initially, the payments bounded context will assume that the business customer has an account with the third-party payment system (although not necessarily a merchant account), or that the business customer will accept payment by invoice.

Bounded contexts not included

Although they didn't make it into the final release of the Contoso Conference Management System, some work was done on three additional bounded contexts. Members of the community are working on these and other features, and any out-of-band releases and updates will be announced on the Project *"a CQRS Journey"* website. If you would like to contribute to these bounded contexts or any other aspect of the system, visit the Project "a CQRS Journey" website or let us know at *cqrsjourney@ microsoft.com*.

The Discounts bounded context: This is a bounded context to handle the process of managing and applying discounts to the purchase of conference seats that would integrate with all three existing bounded contexts.

The Occasionally Disconnected Conference Management client: This is a bounded context to handle management of conferences on-site with functionality to handle label printing, recording attendee arrivals, and additional seat sales.

The Submissions And Schedule Management bounded context: This is a bounded context to handle paper submissions and conference event scheduling written using Node.js.

> **Note:** *Wait listing is not implemented in this release, but members of the community are working on this and other features. Any out-of-band releases and updates will be announced on the Project "a CQRS Journey" website.*

The context map for the Contoso Conference Management System

Figure 1 and the table that follows it represent a context map that shows the relationships between the different bounded contexts that make up the complete system, and as such it provides a high-level overview of how the system is put together. Even though this context map appears to be quite simple, the implementation of these bounded contexts, and more importantly the interactions between them, are relatively sophisticated; this enabled us to address a wide range of issues relating to the CQRS pattern and event sourcing (ES), and provided a rich source from which to capture many valuable lessons learned.

Figure 1 shows the three bounded contexts that make up the Contoso Conference Management System. The arrows in the diagram indicate the flow of data as events between them.

> A frequent comment about CQRS projects is that it can be difficult to understand how all of the pieces fit together, especially if there a great many commands and events in the system. Often, you can perform some static analysis on the code to determine where events and commands are handled, but it is more difficult to automatically determine where they originate. At a high level, a context map can help you understand the integration between the different bounded contexts and the events involved. Maintaining up-to-date documentation about the commands and events can provide more detailed insight. Additionally, if you have tests that use commands as inputs and then check for events, you can examine the tests to understand the expected consequences of particular commands (see the section on testing in Chapter 4, "Extending and Enhancing the Orders and Registrations Bounded Context" for an example of this style of test).

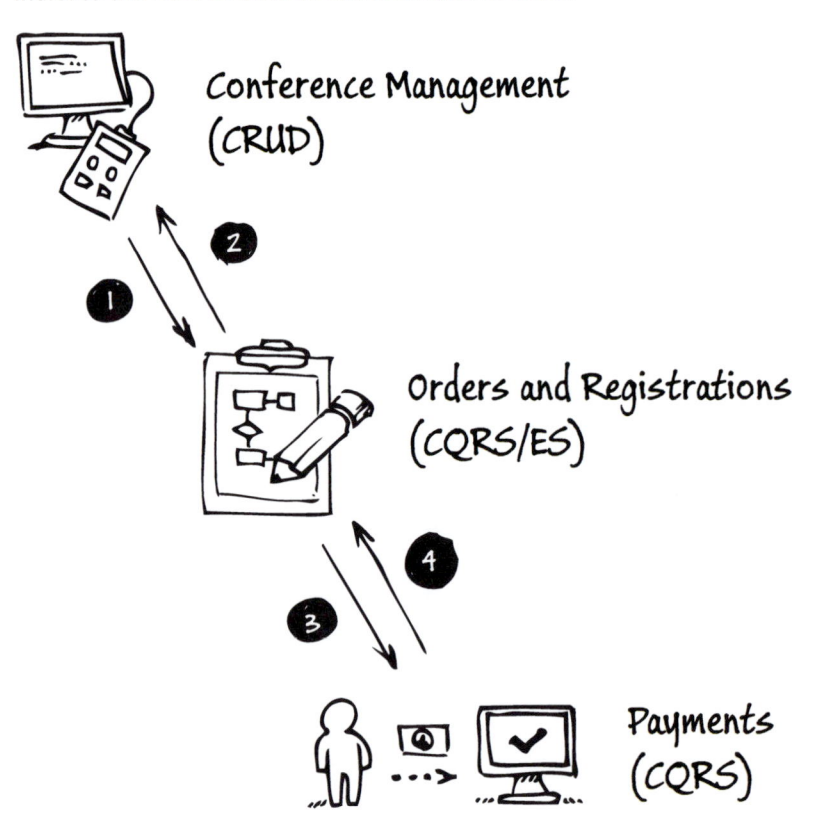

FIGURE 1
Bounded contexts in the Contoso Conference Management System

The following list provides more information about the arrows in Figure 1. You can find additional details in the chapters that discuss the individual bounded contexts.

1. Events that report when conferences have been created, updated, or published. Events that report when seat types have been created or updated.
2. Events that report when orders have been created or updated. Events that report when attendees have been assigned to seats.
3. Requests for a payment to be made.
4. Acknowledgement of the success or failure of the payment.

Why did we choose these bounded contexts?

During the planning stage of the journey, it became clear that these were the natural divisions in the domain that could each contain their own, independent domain models. Some of these divisions were easier to identify than others. For example, it was clear early on that the conference management bounded context is independent of the remainder of the domain. It has clearly defined responsibilities that relate to defining conferences and seat types and clearly defined points of integration with the rest of the application.

On the other hand, it took some time to realize that the orders and registrations bounded context is separate from the Payments bounded context. For example, it was not until the V2 release of the application that all concepts relating to payments disappeared from the orders and registrations bounded context when the **OrderPaymentConfirmed** event became the **OrderConfirmed** event.

More practically, from the perspective of the journey, we wanted a set of bounded contexts that would enable us to release a working application with some core functionality and that would enable us to explore a number of different implementation patterns: CQRS, CQRS/ES, as well as integration with a legacy, CRUD-style bounded context.

More information

All links in this book are accessible from the book's online bibliography available at: *http://msdn.microsoft.com/en-us/library/jj619274*.

> Some of the events that the Conference Management bounded context raises are coarse-grained and contain multiple fields. Remember that conference management is a create, read, update and delete (CRUD)-style bounded context and does not raise fine-grained domain-style events. For more information, see Chapter 5, "Preparing for the V1 Release."

> We continued to refine the domain models right through the journey as our understanding of the domain deepened.

> Contoso wants to release a usable application as soon as possible, but be able to add both planned features and customer-requested features as they are developed and with no down time for the upgrades.

Journey 3:

Orders and Registrations Bounded Context

The first stop on our CQRS journey.

"The Allegator is the same, as the Crocodile, and differs only in Name."
John Lawson

A description of the bounded context

The Orders and Registrations bounded context is partially responsible for the booking process for attendees planning to come to a conference. In the Orders and Registrations bounded context, a person (the registrant) purchases seats at a particular conference. The registrant also assigns names of attendees to the purchased seats (this is described in Chapter 5, "Preparing for the V1 Release").

This was the first stop on our CQRS journey, so the team decided to implement a core, but self-contained part of the system—orders and registrations. The registration process must be as painless as possible for attendees. The process must enable the business customer to ensure that the maximum possible number of seats can be booked, and give them the flexibility set the prices for the different seat types at a conference.

Because this was the first bounded context addressed by the team, we also implemented some infrastructure elements of the system to support the domain's functionality. These included command and event message buses and a persistence mechanism for aggregates.

> *The Contoso Conference Management System described in this chapter is not the final version of the system. This guidance describes a journey, so some of the design decisions and implementation details change later in the journey. These changes are described in subsequent chapters.*

Plans for enhancements to this bounded context in some future journey include support for wait listing, whereby requests for seats are placed on a wait list if there aren't sufficient seats available, and enabling the business customer to set various types of discounts for seat types.

> *Wait listing is not implemented in this release, but members of the community are working on this and other features. Any out-of-band releases and updates will be announced on the Project "a CQRS Journey" website.*

Working definitions for this chapter

This chapter uses a number of terms that we will define in a moment. For more detail, and possible alternative definitions, see "A CQRS and ES Deep Dive" in the Reference Guide.

Command. A *command* is a request for the system to perform an action that changes the state of the system. Commands are imperatives; **MakeSeatReservation** is one example. In this bounded context, commands originate either from the UI as a result of a user initiating a request, or from a process manager when the process manager is directing an aggregate to perform an action.

A single recipient processes a command. A command bus transports commands that command handlers then dispatch to aggregates. Sending a command is an asynchronous operation with no return value.

Event. An *event*, such as **OrderConfirmed**, describes something that has happened in the system, typically as a result of a command. Aggregates in the domain model raise events.

Multiple subscribers can handle a specific event. Aggregates publish events to an event bus; handlers register for specific types of events on the event bus and then deliver the event to the subscriber. In this bounded context, the only subscriber is a process manager.

Process manager. In this bounded context, a *process manager* is a class that coordinates the behavior of the aggregates in the domain. A process manager subscribes to the events that the aggregates raise, and then follow a simple set of rules to determine which command or commands to send. The process manager does not contain any business logic; it simply contains logic to determine the next command to send. The process manager is implemented as a state machine, so when it responds to an event, it can change its internal state in addition to sending a new command.

Our process manager is an implementation of the Process Manager pattern defined on pages 312 to 321 of the book by Gregor Hohpe and Bobby Woolf, entitled *Enterprise Integration Patterns: Designing, Building, and Deploying Messaging Solutions* (Addison-Wesley Professional, 2003).

> For a discussion of some possible optimizations that also involve a slightly different definition of a command, see Chapter 6, "Versioning our System."

> It can be difficult for someone new to the code to follow the flow of commands and events through the system. For a discussion of a technique that can help, see the section "Impact on testing" in Chapter 4, "Extending and Enhancing the Orders and Registrations Bounded Contexts."

The process manager in this bounded context can receive commands as well as subscribe to events.

The Reference Guide contains additional definitions and explanations of CQRS-related terms.

Domain definitions (ubiquitous language)

The following list defines the key domain-related terms that the team used during the development of this Orders and Registrations bounded context.

Attendee. An attendee is someone who is entitled to attend a conference. An Attendee can interact with the system to perform tasks such as manage his agenda, print his badge, and provide feedback after the conference. An attendee could also be a person who doesn't pay to attend a conference such as a volunteer, speaker, or someone with a 100% discount. An attendee may have multiple associated attendee types (speaker, student, volunteer, track chair, and so on.)

Registrant. A registrant is a person who interacts with the system to place orders and to make payments for those orders. A registrant also creates the registrations associated with an order. A registrant may also be an attendee.

User. A user is a person such as an attendee, registrant, speaker, or volunteer who is associated with a conference. Each user has a unique record locator code that the user can use to access user-specific information in the system. For example, a registrant can use a record locator code to access her orders, and an attendee can use a record locator code to access his personalized conference agenda.

Seat assignment. A seat assignment associates an attendee with a seat in a confirmed order. An order may have one or more seat assignments associated with it.

Order. When a registrant interacts with the system, the system creates an order to manage the reservations, payment, and registrations. An order is confirmed when the registrant has successfully paid for the order items. An order contains one or more order items.

Order item. An order item represents a seat type and quantity, and is associated with an order. An order item exists in one of three states: created, reserved, or rejected. An order item is initially in the created state. An order item is in the reserved state if the system has reserved the quantity of seats of the seat type requested by the registrant. An order item is in the rejected state if the system cannot reserve the quantity of seats of the seat type requested by the registrant.

> The team initially referred to the process manager class in the orders bounded context as a saga. To find out why we decided to change the terminology, see the section "Patterns and concepts" later in this chapter.

> We intentionally implemented a record locator mechanism to return to a previously submitted order via the mechanism. This eliminates an often annoying requirement for users to create an account in the system and sign in in order to evaluate its usefulness. Our customers were adamant about this.

Seat. A seat represents the right to be admitted to a conference or to access a specific session at the conference such as a cocktail party, a tutorial, or a workshop. The business customer may change the quota of seats for each conference. The business customer may also change the quota of seats for each session.

Reservation. A reservation is a temporary reservation of one or more seats. The ordering process creates reservations. When a registrant begins the ordering process, the system makes reservations for the number of seats requested by the registrant. These seats are then not available for other registrants to reserve. The reservations are held for n minutes during which the registrant can complete the ordering process by making a payment for those seats. If the registrant does not pay for the seats within n minutes, the system cancels the reservation and the seats become available to other registrants to reserve.

Seat availability. Every conference tracks seat availability for each type of seat. Initially, all of the seats are available to reserve and purchase. When a seat is reserved, the number of available seats of that type is decremented. If the system cancels the reservation, the number of available seats of that type is incremented. The business customer defines the initial number of each seat type to be made available; this is an attribute of a conference. A conference owner may adjust the numbers for the individual seat types.

Conference site. You can access every conference defined in the system by using a unique URL. Registrants can begin the ordering process from this site.

Each of the terms defined here was formulated through active discussions between the development team and the domain experts. The following is a sample conversation between developers and domain experts that illustrates how the team arrived at a definition of the term attendee.

Developer 1: Here's an initial stab at a definition for attendee. "An attendee is someone who has paid to attend a conference. An attendee can interact with the system to perform tasks such as manage his agenda, print his badge, and provide feedback after the conference."

Domain Expert 1: Not all attendees will pay to attend the conference. For example, some conferences will have volunteer helpers, also speakers typically don't pay. And, there may be some cases where an attendee gets a 100% discount.

Domain Expert 1: Don't forget that it's not the attendee who pays; that's done by the registrant.

Developer 1: So we need to say that Attendees are people who are authorized to attend a conference?

Developer 2: We need to be careful about the choice of words here. The term authorized will make some people think of security and authentication and authorization.

Developer 1: How about entitled?

Domain Expert 1: When the system performs tasks such as printing badges, it will need to know what type of attendee the badge is for. For example, speaker, volunteer, paid attendee, and so on.

Developer 1: Now we have this as a definition that captures everything we've discussed. An attendee is someone who is entitled to attend a conference. An attendee can interact with the system to perform tasks such as manage his agenda, print his badge, and provide feedback after the conference. An attendee could also be a person who doesn't pay to attend a conference such as a volunteer, speaker, or someone with a 100% discount. An attendee may have multiple associated attendee types (speaker, student, volunteer, track chair, and so on.)

Requirements for creating orders

A registrant is the person who reserves and pays for (orders) seats at a conference. Ordering is a two-stage process: first, the registrant reserves a number of seats and then pays for the seats to confirm the reservation. If registrant does not complete the payment, the seat reservations expire after a fixed period and the system makes the seats available for other registrants to reserve.

Figure 1 shows some of the early UI mockups that the team used to explore the seat-ordering story.

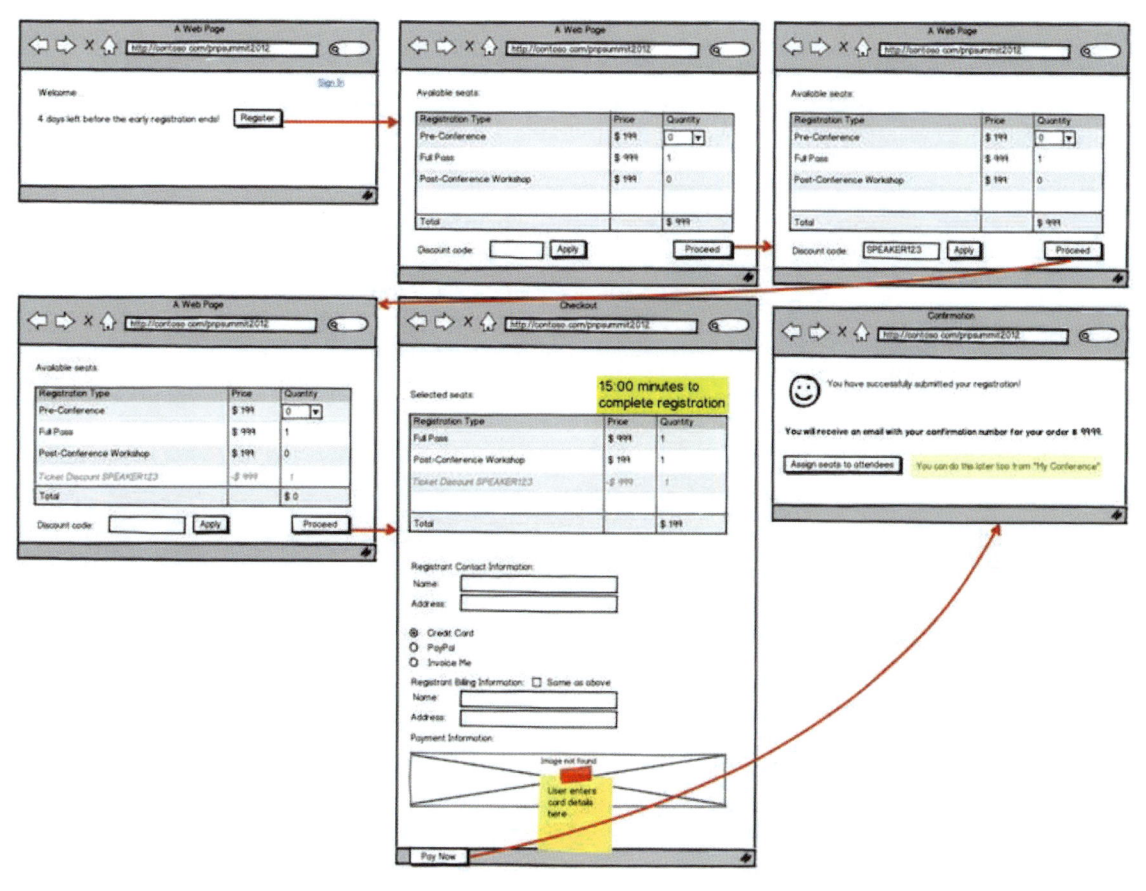

FIGURE 1
Ordering UI mockups

> A frequently cited advantage of the CQRS pattern is that it enables you to scale the read side and write side of the application independently to support the different usage patterns. In this bounded context, however, the number of read operations from the UI is not likely to hugely out-number the write operations: this bounded context focuses on registrants creating orders. Therefore, the read side and the write side are deployed to the same Windows Azure worker role rather than to two separate worker roles that could be scaled independently.

These UI mockups helped the team in several ways, allowing them to:
- Communicate the core team's vision for the system to the graphic designers who are on an independent team at a third-party company.
- Communicate the domain expert's knowledge to the developers.
- Refine the definition of terms in the ubiquitous language.
- Explore "what if" questions about alternative scenarios and approaches.
- Form the basis for the system's suite of acceptance tests.

Architecture

The application is designed to deploy to Windows Azure. At this stage in the journey, the application consists of a web role that contains the ASP.NET MVC web application and a worker role that contains the message handlers and domain objects. The application uses a Windows Azure SQL Database instance for data storage, both on the write side and the read side. The application uses the Windows Azure Service Bus to provide its messaging infrastructure.

While you are exploring and testing the solution, you can run it locally, either using the Windows Azure compute emulator or by running the MVC web application directly and running a console application that hosts the handlers and domain objects. When you run the application locally, you can use a local SQL Server Express database instead of SQL Database, and use a simple messaging infrastructure implemented in a SQL Server Express database.

For more information about the options for running the application, see Appendix 1, "Release Notes."

Patterns and concepts

The team decided to implement the first bounded context without using event sourcing in order to keep things simple. However, they did agree that if they later decided that event sourcing would bring specific benefits to this bounded context, then they would revisit this decision.

> For a description of how event sourcing relates to the CQRS pattern, see "Introducing Event Sourcing" in the Reference Guide.

One of the important discussions the team had concerned the choice of aggregates and entities that they would implement. The following images from the team's whiteboard illustrate some of their initial thoughts, and questions about the alternative approaches they could take with a simple conference seat reservation scenario to try and understand the pros and cons of alternative approaches.

"A value I think developers would benefit greatly from recognizing is the de-emphasis on the means and methods for persistence of objects in terms of relational storage. Teach them to avoid modeling the domain as if it was a relational store, and I think it will be easier to introduce and understand both domain-driven design (DDD) and CQRS."
—Josh Elster, CQRS Advisors Mail List

This scenario considers what happens when a registrant tries to book several seats at a conference. The system must:
- Check that sufficient seats are available.
- Record details of the registration.
- Update the total number of seats booked for the conference.

We deliberately kept the scenario simple to avoid distractions while the team examines the alternatives. These examples do not illustrate the final implementation of this bounded context.

The first approach considered by the team, shown in Figure 2, uses two separate aggregates.

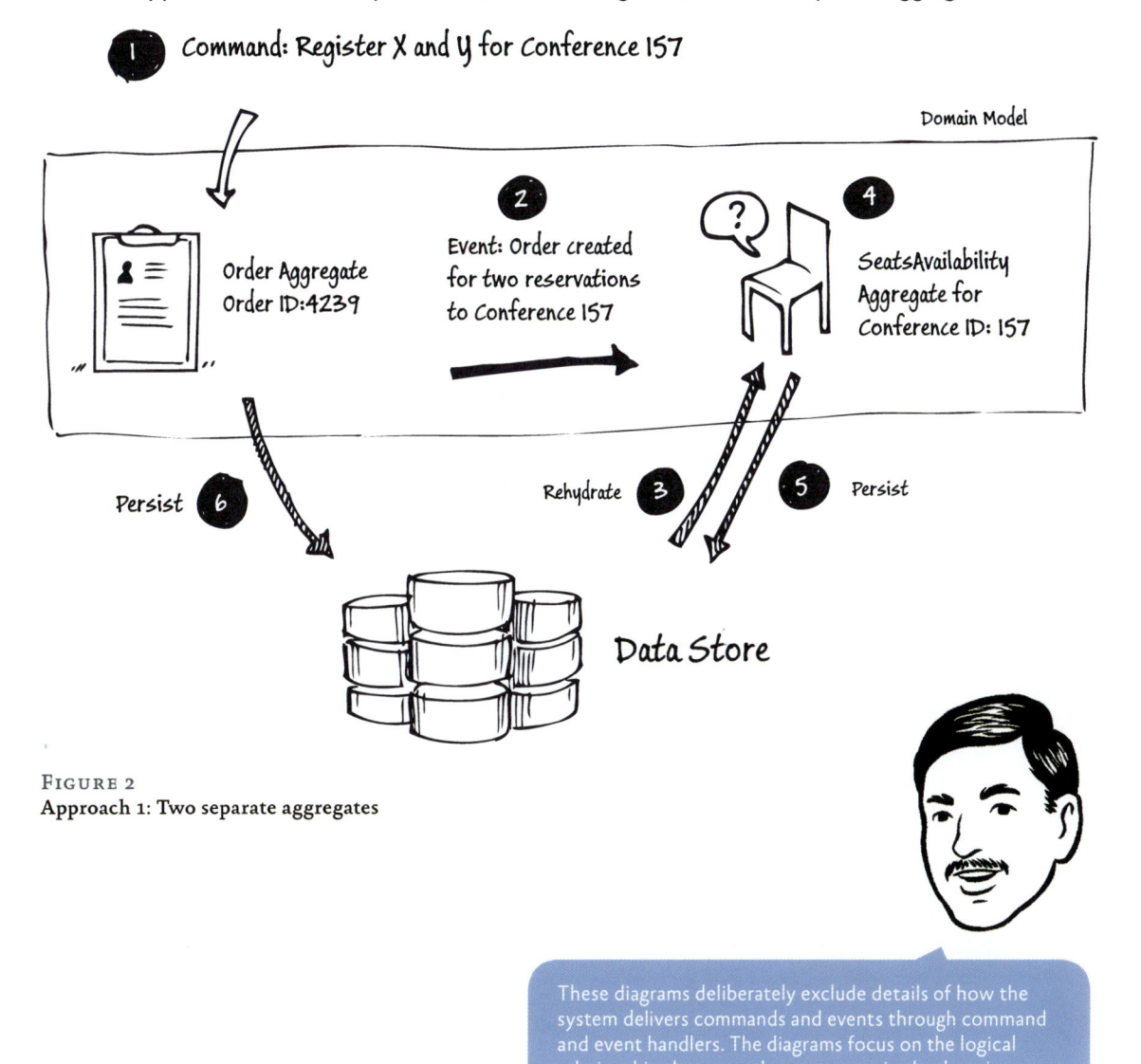

Figure 2
Approach 1: Two separate aggregates

> These diagrams deliberately exclude details of how the system delivers commands and events through command and event handlers. The diagrams focus on the logical relationships between the aggregates in the domain.

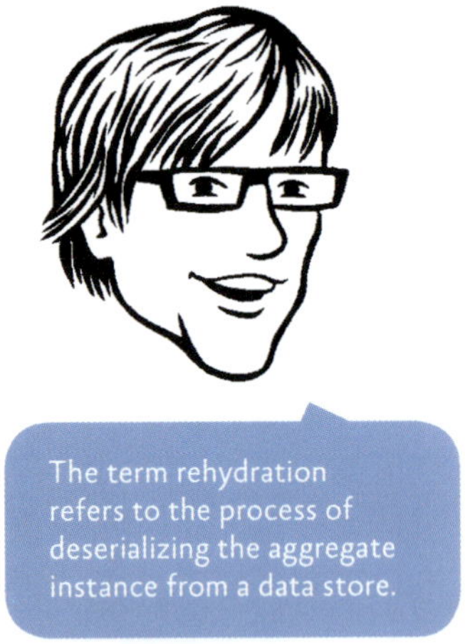

The numbers in the diagram correspond to the following steps:

1. The UI sends a command to register attendees X and Y for conference 157. The command is routed to a new **Order** aggregate.
2. The **Order** aggregate raises an event that reports that an order has been created. The event is routed to the **SeatsAvailability** aggregate.
3. The **SeatsAvailability** aggregate with an ID of 157 is rehydrated from the data store.
4. The **SeatsAvailability** aggregate updates its total number of seats booked.
5. The updated version of the **SeatsAvailability** aggregate is persisted to the data store.
6. The new **Order** aggregate, with an ID of 4239, is persisted to the data store.

> The term rehydration refers to the process of deserializing the aggregate instance from a data store.

> You could consider using the *Memento pattern* to handle the persistence and rehydration.

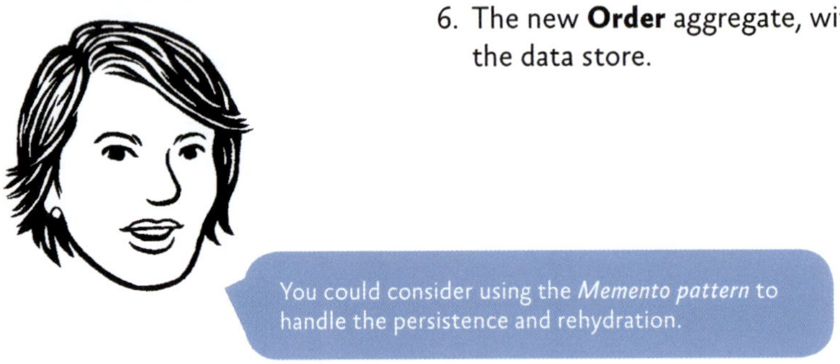

Orders and Registrations Bounded Context

The second approach considered by the team, shown in Figure 3, uses a single aggregate in place of two.

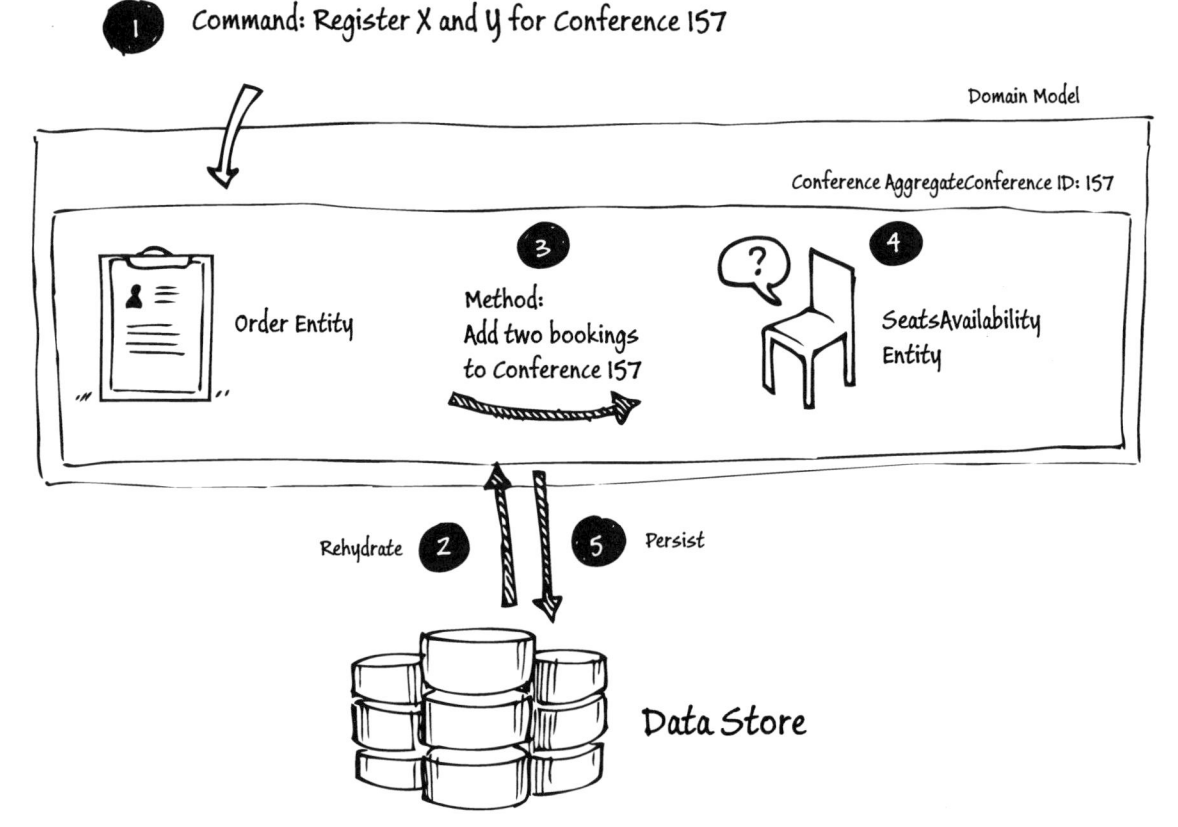

FIGURE 3
Approach 2: A single aggregate

The numbers in the diagram correspond to the following steps:
1. The UI sends a command to register Attendees X and Y for conference 157. The command is routed to the **Conference** aggregate with an ID of 157.
2. The **Conference** aggregate with an ID of 157 is rehydrated from the data store.
3. The **Order** entity validates the booking (it queries the **SeatsAvailability** entity to see if there are enough seats left), and then invokes the method to update the number of seats booked on the **Conference** entity.
4. The **SeatsAvailability** entity updates its total number of seats booked.
5. The updated version of the **Conference** aggregate is persisted to the data store.

Journey three

The third approach considered by the team, shown in Figure 4, uses a process manager to coordinate the interaction between two aggregates.

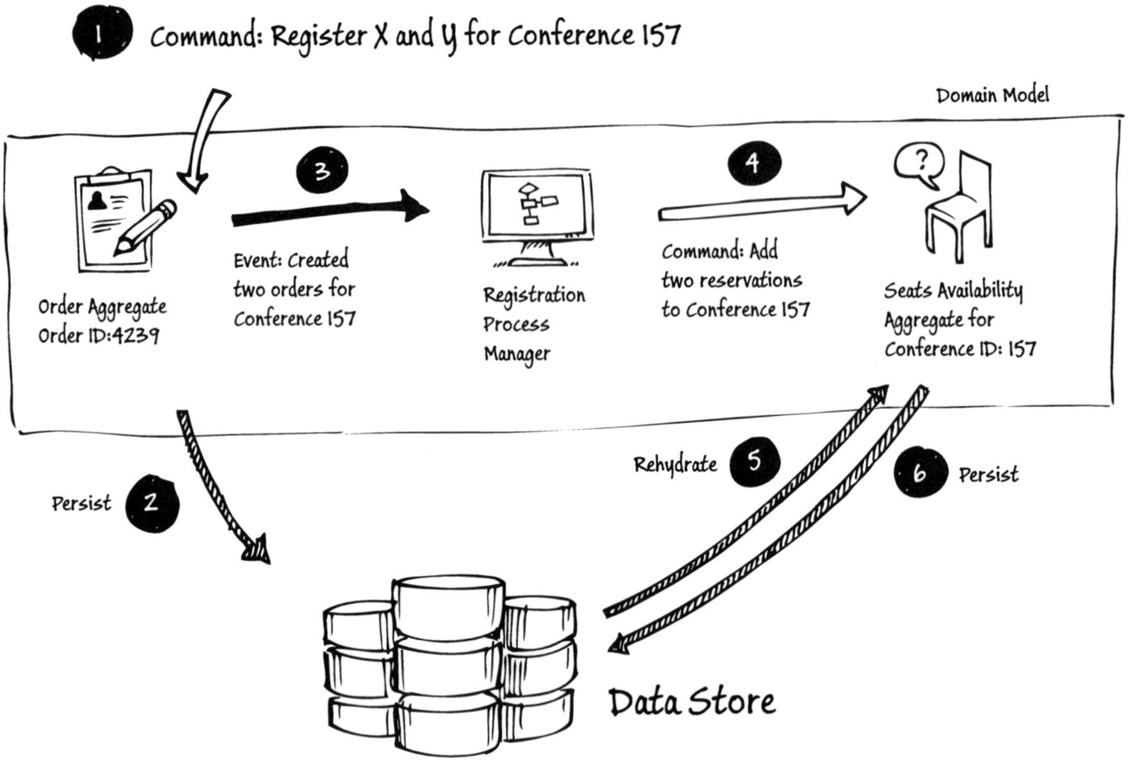

Figure 4
Approach 3: Using a process manager

The numbers in the diagram correspond to the following steps:
1. The UI sends a command to register Attendees X and Y for conference 157. The command is routed to a new **Order** aggregate.
2. The new **Order** aggregate, with an ID of 4239, is persisted to the data store.
3. The **Order** aggregate raises an event that is handled by the **RegistrationProcessManager** class.

4. The **RegistrationProcessManager** class determines that a command should be sent to the **SeatsAvailability** aggregate with an ID of 157.
5. The **SeatsAvailability** aggregate is rehydrated from the data store.
6. The total number of seats booked is updated in the **SeatsAvailability** aggregate and it is persisted to the data store.

For more information about process managers and sagas, see Chapter 6, "A Saga on Sagas" in the Reference Guide.

The team identified the following questions about these approaches:

- Where does the validation that there are sufficient seats for the registration take place: in the **Order** or **SeatsAvailability** aggregate?
- Where are the transaction boundaries?
- How does this model deal with concurrency issues when multiple registrants try to place orders simultaneously?
- What are the aggregate roots?

The following sections discuss these questions in relation to the three approaches considered by the team.

Validation

Before a registrant can reserve a seat, the system must check that there are enough seats available. Although logic in the UI can attempt to verify that there are sufficient seats available before it sends a command, the business logic in the domain must also perform the check; this is because the state may change between the time the UI performs the validation and the time that the system delivers the command to the aggregate in the domain.

> Process manager or saga? Initially the team referred to the **RegistrationProcessManager** class as a saga. However, after they reviewed the original definition of a saga from the paper *"Sagas"* by Hector Garcia-Molina and Kenneth Salem, they revised their decision. The key reasons for this are that the reservation process does not include explicit compensation steps, and does not need to be represented as a long-lived transaction.

> When we talk about UI validation here, we are talking about validation that the Model-View Controller (MVC) controller performs, not the browser.

> Undo is just one of many compensating actions that occur in real life. The compensating actions could even be outside of the system implementation and involve human actors: for example, a Contoso clerk or the business customer calls the registrant to tell them that an error was made and that they should ignore the last confirmation email they received from the Contoso system.

In the first model, the validation must take place in either the **Order** or **SeatsAvailability** aggregate. If it is the former, the **Order** aggregate must discover the current seat availability from the **SeatsAvailability** aggregate before the reservation is made and before it raises the event. If it is the latter, the **SeatsAvailability** aggregate must somehow notify the **Order** aggregate that it cannot reserve the seats, and that the **Order** aggregate must undo (or compensate for) any work that it has completed so far.

The second model behaves similarly, except that it is **Order** and **SeatsAvailability** entities cooperating within a **Conference** aggregate.

In the third model, with the process manager, the aggregates exchange messages through the process manager about whether the registrant can make the reservation at the current time.

All three models require entities to communicate about the validation process, but the third model with the process manager appears more complex than the other two.

Transaction boundaries

An aggregate, in the DDD approach, represents a consistency boundary. Therefore, the first model with two aggregates, and the third model with two aggregates and a process manager will involve two transactions: one when the system persists the new **Order** aggregate and one when the system persists the updated **SeatsAvailability** aggregate.

> *The term consistency boundary refers to a boundary within which you can assume that all the elements remain consistent with each other all the time.*

To ensure the consistency of the system when a registrant creates an order, both transactions must succeed. To guarantee this, we must take steps to ensure that the system is eventually consistent by ensuring that the infrastructure reliably delivers messages to aggregates.

In the second approach, which uses a single aggregate, we will only have a single transaction when a registrant makes an order. This appears to be the simplest approach of the three.

Concurrency

The registration process takes place in a multi-user environment where many registrants could attempt to purchase seats simultaneously. The team decided to use the *Reservation pattern* to address the concurrency issues in the registration process. In this scenario, this means that a registrant initially reserves seats (which are then unavailable to other registrants); if the registrant completes the payment within a timeout period, the system retains the reservation; otherwise the system cancels the reservation.

This reservation system introduces the need for additional message types; for example, an event to report that a registrant has made a payment, or report that a timeout has occurred.

This timeout also requires the system to incorporate a timer somewhere to track when reservations expire.

Modeling this complex behavior with sequences of messages and the requirement for a timer is best done using a process manager.

Aggregates and aggregate roots

In the two models that have the **Order** aggregate and the **SeatsAvailability** aggregate, the team easily identified the entities that make up the aggregate, and the aggregate root. The choice is not so clear in the model with a single aggregate: it does not seem natural to access orders through a **SeatsAvailability** entity, or to access the seat availability through an **Order** entity. Creating a new entity to act as an aggregate root seems unnecessary.

The team decided on the model that incorporated a process manager because this offers the best way to handle the concurrency requirements in this bounded context.

Implementation details

This section describes some of the significant features of the Orders and Registrations bounded context implementation. You may find it useful to have a copy of the code so you can follow along. You can download it from the *Download center*, or check the evolution of the code in the repository on github: *mspnp/cqrs-journey-code*.

> *Do not expect the code samples to match the code in the reference implementation exactly. This chapter describes a step in the CQRS journey, the implementation may well change as we learn more and refactor the code.*

High-level architecture

As we described in the previous section, the team initially decided to implement the reservations story in the conference management system using the CQRS pattern but without using event sourcing. Figure 5 shows the key elements of the implementation: an MVC web application, a data store implemented using a Windows Azure SQL Database instance, the read and write models, and some infrastructure components.

> *We'll describe what goes on inside the read and write models later in this section.*

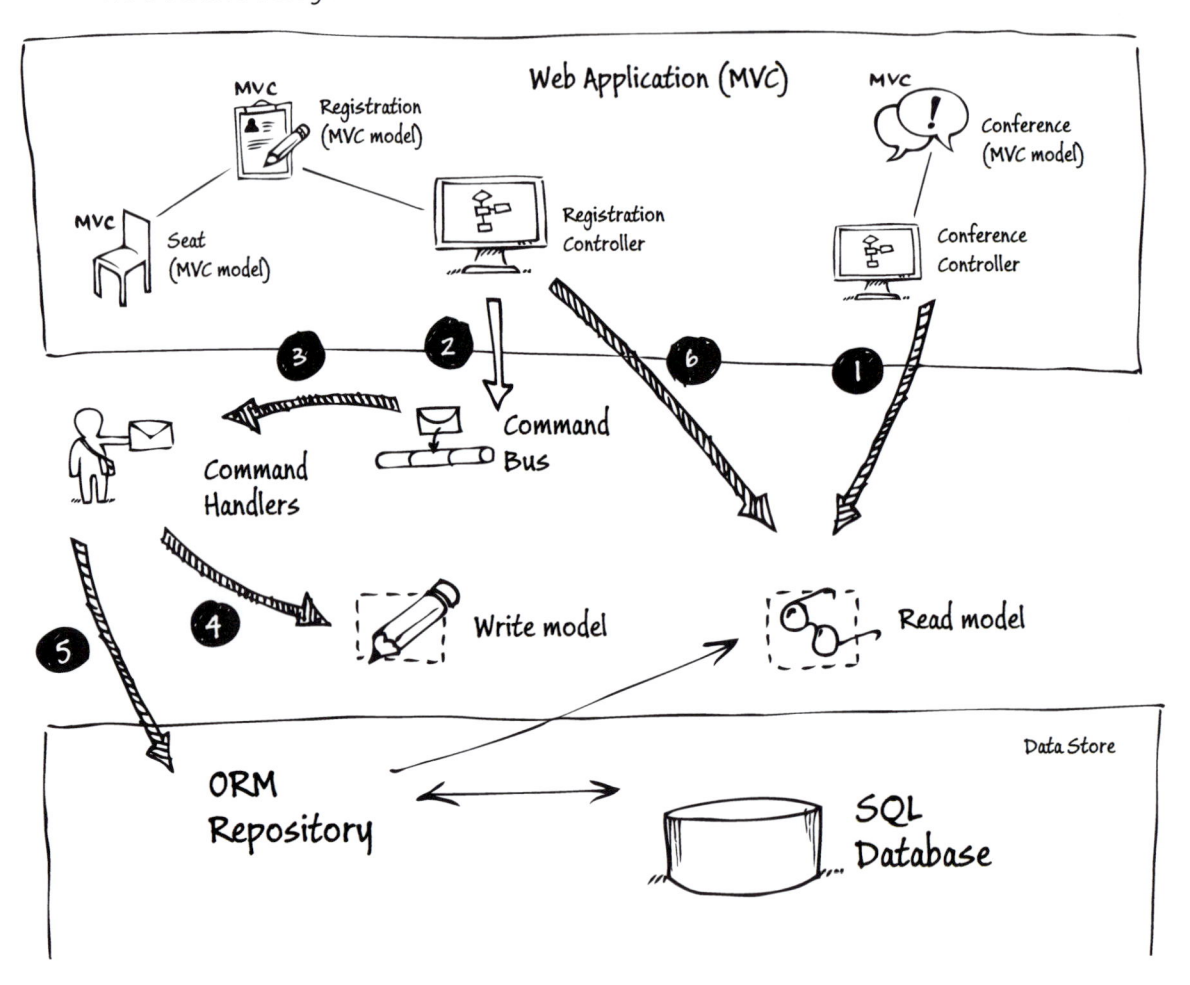

Figure 5
High-level architecture of the registrations bounded context

The following sections relate to the numbers in Figure 5 and provide more detail about these elements of the architecture.

1. Querying the read model

The **ConferenceController** class includes an action named **Display** that creates a view that contains information about a particular conference. This controller class queries the read model using the following code:

```
public ActionResult Display(string conferenceCode)
{
    var conference = this.GetConference(conferenceCode);
    return View(conference);
}
private Conference.Web.Public.Models.Conference GetConference(string conferenceCode)
{
    var repo = this.repositoryFactory();
    using (repo as IDisposable)
    {
        var conference = repo.Query<Conference>()
                            .First(c => c.Code == conferenceCode);

        var conference =
            new Conference.Web.Public.Models.Conference
                {
                    Code = conference.Code,
                    Name = conference.Name,
                    Description = conference.Description
                };

        return conference;
    }
}
```

The read model retrieves the information from the data store and returns it to the controller using a data transfer object (DTO) class.

2. Issuing commands

The web application sends commands to the write model through a command bus. This command bus is an infrastructure element that provides reliable messaging. In this scenario, the bus delivers messages asynchronously and once only to a single recipient.

The **RegistrationController** class can send a **RegisterToConference** command to the write model in response to user interaction. This command sends a request to register one or more seats at the conference. The **RegistrationController** class then polls the read model to discover whether the registration request succeeded. See the section "6. Polling the Read Model" below for more details.

The following code sample shows how the **RegistrationController** sends a **RegisterToConference** command:

```
var viewModel = this.UpdateViewModel(conferenceCode, contentModel);

var command =
    new RegisterToConference
    {
        OrderId = viewModel.Id,
        ConferenceId = viewModel.ConferenceId,
        Seats = viewModel.Items.Select(x =>
                    new RegisterToConference.Seat
                    {
                        SeatTypeId = x.SeatTypeId,
                        Quantity = x.Quantity
                    }).ToList()
    };

this.commandBus.Send(command);
```

All of the commands are sent asynchronously and do not expect return values.

3. Handling commands

Command handlers register with the command bus; the command bus can then forward commands to the correct handler.

The **OrderCommandHandler** class handles the **RegisterToConference** command sent from the UI. Typically, the handler is responsible for initiating any business logic in the domain and for persisting any state changes to the data store.

The following code sample shows how the **OrderCommandHandler** class handles the **RegisterToConference** command:

```
public void Handle(RegisterToConference command)
{
    var repository = this.repositoryFactory();

    using (repository as IDisposable)
    {
        var seats = command.Seats
                    .Select(t => new OrderItem(t.SeatTypeId, t.Quantity))
                    .ToList();

        var order = new Order(
                    command.OrderId,
                    Guid.NewGuid(),
                    command.ConferenceId,
                    seats);

        repository.Save(order);
    }
}
```

4. Initiating business logic in the domain
In the previous code sample, the **OrderCommandHandler** class creates a new **Order** instance. The **Order** entity is an aggregate root, and its constructor contains code to initiate the domain logic. See the section "Inside the Write Model" below for more details of what actions this aggregate root performs.

5. Persisting the changes
In the previous code sample, the handler persists the new **Order** aggregate by calling the **Save** method in the repository class. This **Save** method also publishes any events raised by the **Order** aggregate on the command bus.

6. Polling the read model
To provide feedback to the user, the UI must have a way to check whether the **RegisterToConference** command succeeded. Like all commands in the system, this command executes asynchronously and does not return a result. The UI queries the read model to check whether the command succeeded.

The following code sample shows the initial implementation where the **RegistrationController** class polls the read model until either the system creates the order or a timeout occurs. The **WaitUntilUpdated** method polls the read-model until it finds either that the order has been persisted or it times out.

```
[HttpPost]
public ActionResult StartRegistration(string conferenceCode,
                                      OrderViewModel contentModel)
{
    ...

    this.commandBus.Send(command);

    var draftOrder = this.WaitUntilUpdated(viewModel.Id);

    if (draftOrder != null)
    {
        if (draftOrder.State == "Booked")
        {
            return RedirectToAction(
                "SpecifyPaymentDetails",
                new { conferenceCode = conferenceCode, orderId = viewModel.Id });
        }
        else if (draftOrder.State == "Rejected")
        {
            return View("ReservationRejected", viewModel);
        }
    }

    return View("ReservationUnknown", viewModel);
}
```

The team later replaced this mechanism for checking whether the system saves the order with an implementation of the Post-Redirect-Get pattern. The following code sample shows the new version of the **StartRegistration** action method.

> *For more information about the Post-Redirect-Get pattern see the article Post/Redirect/Get on Wikipedia.*

```
[HttpPost]
public ActionResult StartRegistration(string conferenceCode,
                                      OrderViewModel contentModel)
{

    ...

    this.commandBus.Send(command);

    return RedirectToAction(
        "SpecifyRegistrantDetails",
        new { conferenceCode = conferenceCode, orderId = command.Id });
}
```

The action method now redirects to the **SpecifyRegistrantDetails** view immediately after it sends the command. The following code sample shows how the **SpecifyRegistrantDetails** action polls for the order in the repository before returning a view.

```
[HttpGet]
public ActionResult SpecifyRegistrantDetails(string conferenceCode, Guid orderId)
{
    var draftOrder = this.WaitUntilUpdated(orderId);

    ...
}
```

The advantages of this second approach, using the Post-Redirect-Get pattern instead of in the **StartRegistration** post action are that it works better with the browser's forward and back navigation buttons, and that it gives the infrastructure more time to process the command before the MVC controller starts polling.

Inside the write model

Aggregates
The following code sample shows the **Order** aggregate.

```
public class Order : IAggregateRoot, IEventPublisher
{
    public static class States
    {
        public const int Created = 0;
        public const int Booked = 1;
        public const int Rejected = 2;
        public const int Confirmed = 3;
    }
```

```csharp
    private List<IEvent> events = new List<IEvent>();

    ...

    public Guid Id { get; private set; }

    public Guid UserId { get; private set; }

    public Guid ConferenceId { get; private set; }

    public virtual ObservableCollection<TicketOrderLine> Lines { get; private set; }

    public int State { get; private set; }

    public IEnumerable<Ievent> Events
    {
        get { return this.events; }
    }

    public void MarkAsBooked()
    {
        if (this.State != States.Created)
            throw new InvalidOperationException();

        this.State = States.Booked;
    }

    public void Reject()
    {
        if (this.State != States.Created)
            throw new InvalidOperationException();

        this.State = States.Rejected;
    }
}
```

Notice how the properties of the class are not virtual. In the original version of this class, the properties **Id**, **UserId**, **ConferenceId**, and **State** were all marked as virtual. The following conversation between two developers explores this decision.

> **Developer 1:** I'm really convinced you should not make the property virtual, except if required by the object-relational mapping (ORM) layer. If this is just for testing purposes, entities and aggregate roots should never be tested using mocking. If you need mocking to test your entities, this is a clear smell that something is wrong in the design.
>
> **Developer 2:** I prefer to be open and extensible by default. You never know what needs may arise in the future, and making things virtual is hardly a cost. This is certainly controversial and a bit non-standard in .NET, but I think it's OK. We may only need virtuals on lazy-loaded collections.
>
> **Developer 1:** Since CQRS usually makes the need for lazy load vanish, you should not need it either. This leads to even simpler code.
>
> **Developer 2:** CQRS does not dictate usage of event sourcing (ES), so if you're using an aggregate root that contains an object graph, you'd need that anyway, right?
>
> **Developer 1:** This is not about ES, it's about DDD. When your aggregate boundaries are right, you don't need delay loading.
>
> **Developer 2:** To be clear, the aggregate boundary is here to group things that should change together for reasons of consistency. A lazy load would indicate that things that have been grouped together don't really need this grouping.
>
> **Developer 1:** I agree. I have found that lazy-loading in the command side means I have it modeled wrong. If I don't need the value in the command side, then it shouldn't be there. In addition, I dislike virtuals unless they have an intended purpose (or some artificial requirement from an object-relational mapping (ORM) tool). In my opinion, it violates the Open-Closed principle: you have opened yourself up for modification in a variety of ways that may or may not be intended and where the repercussions might not be immediately discoverable, if at all.
>
> **Developer 2:** Our **Order** aggregate in the model has a list of **Order Items**. Surely we don't need to load the lines to mark it as Booked? Do we have it modeled wrong there?
>
> **Developer 1:** Is the list of **Order Items** that long? If it is, the modeling may be wrong because you don't necessarily need transactionality at that level. Often, doing a late round trip to get and updated **Order Items** can be more costly that loading them up front: you should evaluate the usual size of the collection and do some performance measurement. Make it simple first, optimize if needed.
>
> —Thanks to Jérémie Chassaing and Craig Wilson

Aggregates and process managers

Figure 6 shows the entities that exist in the write-side model. There are two aggregates, **Order** and **SeatsAvailability**, each one containing multiple entity types. Also there is a **RegistrationProcessManager** class to manage the interaction between the aggregates.

The table in the Figure 6 shows how the process manager behaves given a current state and a particular type of incoming message.

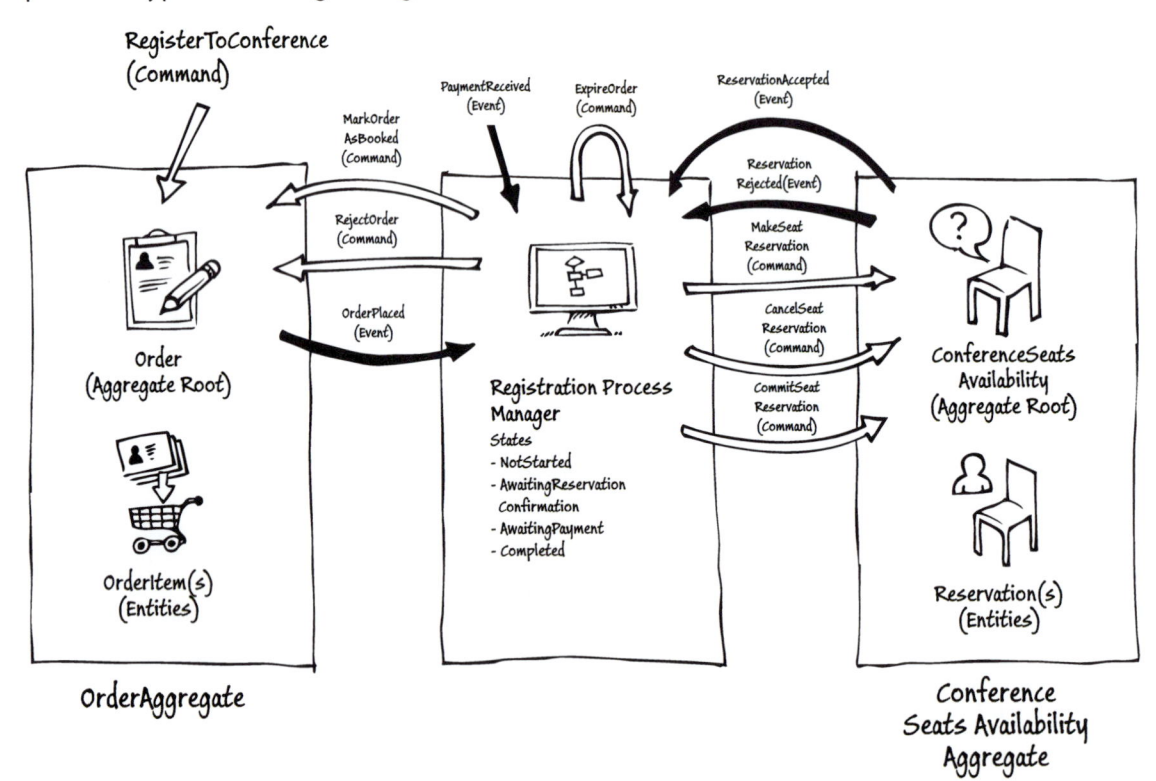

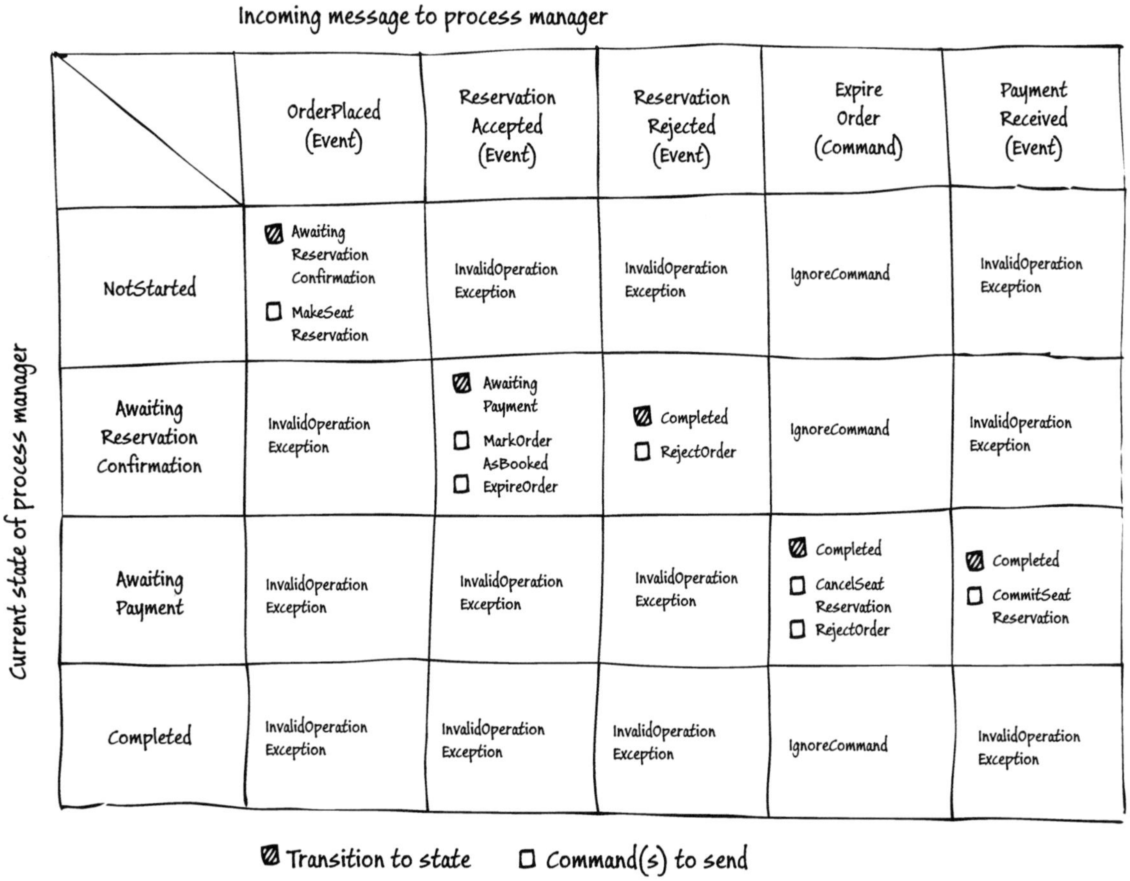

Incoming message to process manager

Current state of process manager	OrderPlaced (Event)	Reservation Accepted (Event)	Reservation Rejected (Event)	Expire Order (Command)	Payment Received (Event)
NotStarted	▨ Awaiting Reservation Confirmation ☐ MakeSeat Reservation	InvalidOperation Exception	InvalidOperation Exception	IgnoreCommand	InvalidOperation Exception
Awaiting Reservation Confirmation	InvalidOperation Exception	▨ Awaiting Payment ☐ MarkOrder AsBooked ☐ ExpireOrder	▨ Completed ☐ RejectOrder	IgnoreCommand	InvalidOperation Exception
Awaiting Payment	InvalidOperation Exception	InvalidOperation Exception	InvalidOperation Exception	▨ Completed ☐ CancelSeat Reservation ☐ RejectOrder	▨ Completed ☐ CommitSeat Reservation
Completed	InvalidOperation Exception	InvalidOperation Exception	InvalidOperation Exception	IgnoreCommand	InvalidOperation Exception

▨ Transition to state   ☐ Command(s) to send

FIGURE 6
Domain objects in the write model

The process of registering for a conference begins when the UI sends a **RegisterToConference** command. The infrastructure delivers this command to the **Order** aggregate. The result of this command is that the system creates a new **Order** instance, and that the new **Order** instance raises an **OrderPlaced** event. The following code sample from the constructor in the **Order** class shows this happening. Notice how the system uses GUIDs to identify the different entities.

```
public Order(Guid id, Guid userId, Guid conferenceId, IEnumerable<OrderItem> lines)
{
    this.Id = id;
    this.UserId = userId;
    this.ConferenceId = conferenceId;
    this.Lines = new ObservableCollection<OrderItem>(items);

    this.events.Add(
        new OrderPlaced
        {
            OrderId = this.Id,
            ConferenceId = this.ConferenceId,
            UserId = this.UserId,
            Seats = this.Lines.Select(x =>
                new OrderPlaced.Seat
                    {
                        SeatTypeId = x.SeatTypeId,
                        Quantity = x.Quantity
                    }).ToArray()
        });
}
```

To see how the infrastructure elements deliver commands and events, see Figure 7.

The system creates a new **RegistrationProcessManager** instance to manage the new order. The following code sample from the **RegistrationProcessManager** class shows how the process manager handles the event.

```
public void Handle(OrderPlaced message)
{
    if (this.State == ProcessState.NotStarted)
    {
        this.OrderId = message.OrderId;
        this.ReservationId = Guid.NewGuid();
        this.State = ProcessState.AwaitingReservationConfirmation;

        this.AddCommand(
            new MakeSeatReservation
            {
                ConferenceId = message.ConferenceId,
                ReservationId = this.ReservationId,
                NumberOfSeats = message.Items.Sum(x => x.Quantity)
            });
    }
    else
    {
        throw new InvalidOperationException();
    }
}
```

The code sample shows how the process manager changes its state and sends a new **MakeSeatReservation** command that the **SeatsAvailability** aggregate handles. The code sample also illustrates how the process manager is implemented as a state machine that receives messages, changes its state, and sends new messages.

When the **SeatsAvailability** aggregate receives a **MakeReservation** command, it makes a reservation if there are enough available seats. The following code sample shows how the **SeatsAvailability** class raises different events depending on whether or not there are sufficient seats.

> Notice how we generate a new globally unique identifier (GUID) to identify the new reservation. We use these GUIDs to correlate messages to the correct process manager and aggregate instances.

```
public void MakeReservation(Guid reservationId, int numberOfSeats)
{
    if (numberOfSeats > this.RemainingSeats)
    {
        this.events.Add(new ReservationRejected
            {
                ReservationId = reservationId,
                ConferenceId = this.Id
            });
    }
    else
    {
        this.PendingReservations.Add(new Reservation(reservationId, numberOfSeats));
        this.RemainingSeats -= numberOfSeats;
        this.events.Add(new ReservationAccepted
            {
                ReservationId = reservationId,
                ConferenceId = this.Id
            });
    }
}
```

The **RegistrationProcessManager** class handles the **ReservationAccepted** and **ReservationRejected** events. This reservation is a temporary reservation for seats to give the user the opportunity to make a payment. The process manager is responsible for releasing the reservation when either the purchase is complete, or the reservation timeout period expires. The following code sample shows how the process manager handles these two messages.

```
public void Handle(ReservationAccepted message)
{
    if (this.State == ProcessState.AwaitingReservationConfirmation)
    {
        this.State = ProcessState.AwaitingPayment;

        this.AddCommand(new MarkOrderAsBooked { OrderId = this.OrderId });
        this.commands.Add(
            new Envelope<ICommand>(
                new ExpireOrder
                {
                    OrderId = this.OrderId,
                    ConferenceId = message.ConferenceId
                })
```

```
            {
                Delay = TimeSpan.FromMinutes(15),
            });
        }
        else
        {
            throw new InvalidOperationException();
        }
    }

    public void Handle(ReservationRejected message)
    {
        if (this.State == ProcessState.AwaitingReservationConfirmation)
        {
            this.State = ProcessState.Completed;
            this.AddCommand(new RejectOrder { OrderId = this.OrderId });
        }
        else
        {
            throw new InvalidOperationException();
        }
    }
```

If the reservation is accepted, the process manager starts a timer running by sending an **ExpireOrder** command to itself, and sends a **MarkOrderAsBooked** command to the **Order** aggregate. Otherwise, it sends a **ReservationRejected** message back to the **Order** aggregate.

The previous code sample shows how the process manager sends the **ExpireOrder** command. The infrastructure is responsible for holding the message in a queue for the delay of fifteen minutes.

You can examine the code in the **Order**, **SeatsAvailability**, and **RegistrationProcessManager** classes to see how the other message handlers are implemented. They all follow the same pattern: receive a message, perform some logic, and send a message.

> The code samples shown in this chapter are from an early version of the conference management system. The next chapter shows how the design and implementation evolved as the team explored the domain and learned more about the CQRS pattern.

Infrastructure

The sequence diagram in Figure 7 shows how the infrastructure elements interact with the domain objects to deliver messages.

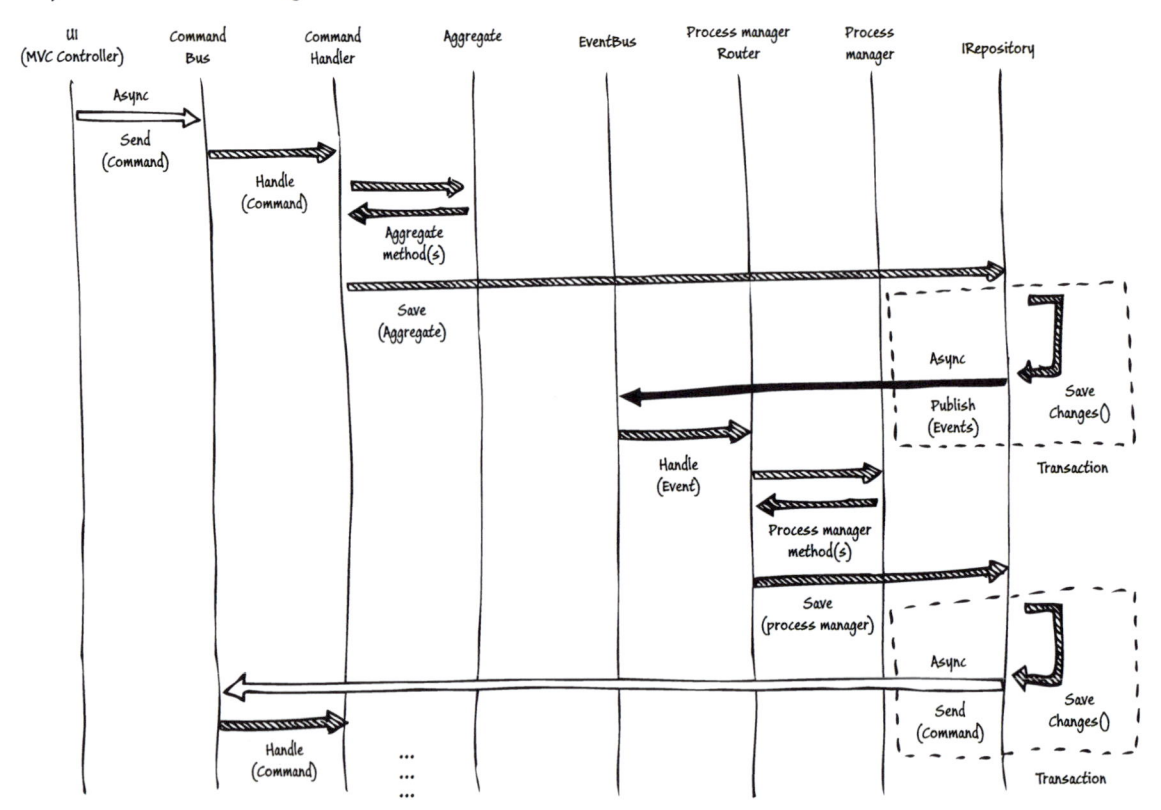

FIGURE 7
Infrastructure sequence diagram

A typical interaction begins when an MVC controller in the UI sends a message using the command bus. The message sender invokes the **Send** method on the command bus asynchronously. The command bus then stores the message until the message recipient retrieves the message and forwards it to the appropriate handler. The system includes a number of command handlers that register with the command bus to handle specific types of commands. For example, the **OrderCommandHandler** class defines handler methods for the **RegisterToConference**, **MarkOrderAsBooked**, and **RejectOrder** commands. The following code sample shows the handler method for the **MarkOrderAsBooked** command. Handler methods are responsible for locating the correct aggregate instance, calling methods on that instance, and then saving that instance.

```
public void Handle(MarkOrderAsBooked command)
{
    var repository = this.repositoryFactory();

    using (repository as IDisposable)
    {
        var order = repository.Find<Order>(command.OrderId);

        if (order != null)
        {
            order.MarkAsBooked();
            repository.Save(order);
        }
    }
}
```

The class that implements the **IRepository** interface is responsible for persisting the aggregate and publishing any events raised by the aggregate on the event bus, all as part of a transaction.

The only event subscriber in the reservations bounded context is the **RegistrationProcessManager** class. Its router subscribes to the event bus to handle specific events, as shown in the following code sample from the **RegistrationProcessManager** class.

> *We use the term handler to refer to the classes that handle commands and events and forward them to aggregate instances, and the term router to refer to the classes that handle events and commands and forward them to process manager instances.*

> The team later discovered an issue with this when they tried to use Windows Azure Service Bus as the messaging infrastructure. Windows Azure Service Bus does not support distributed transactions with databases. For a discussion of this issue, see Chapter 5, "Preparing for the V1 Release."

```
public void Handle(ReservationAccepted @event)
{
    var repo = this.repositoryFactory.Invoke();
    using (repo as IDisposable)
    {
        lock (lockObject)
        {
            var process = repo.Find<RegistrationProcessManager>(@event.ReservationId);
            process.Handle(@event);

            repo.Save(process);
        }
    }
}
```

Typically, an event handler method loads a process manager instance, passes the event to the process manager, and then persists the process manager instance. In this case, the **IRepository** instance is responsible for persisting the process manager instance and for sending any commands from the process manager instance to the command bus.

Using the Windows Azure Service Bus

To transport command and event messages, the team decided to use the Windows Azure Service Bus to provide the low-level messaging infrastructure. This section describes how the system uses the Windows Azure Service Bus and some of the alternatives and trade-offs the team considered during the design phase.

Figure 8 shows how both command and event messages flow through the system. MVC controllers in the UI and domain objects use **CommandBus** and **EventBus** instances to send **BrokeredMessage** messages to one of the two topics in the Windows Azure Service Bus. To receive messages, the handler classes register with the **CommandProcessor** and **EventProcessor** instances that retrieve messages from the topics by using the **SubscriptionReceiver** class. The **CommandProcessor** class determines which single handler should receive a command message; the **EventProcessor** class determines which handlers should receive an event message. The handler instances are responsible for invoking methods on the domain objects.

> *A Windows Azure Service Bus topic can have multiple subscribers. The Windows Azure Service Bus delivers messages sent to a topic to all its subscribers. Therefore, one message can have multiple recipients.*

> The team at Contoso decided to use the Windows Azure Service Bus because it offers out-of-the-box support for the messaging scenarios in the conference management system. This minimizes the amount of code that the team needs to write, and provides for a robust, scalable messaging infrastructure. The team plans to use features such as duplicate message detection and guaranteed message ordering. For a summary of the differences between Windows Azure Service Bus and Windows Azure Queues, see *"Windows Azure Queues and Windows Azure Service Bus Queues - Compared and Contrasted"* on MSDN.

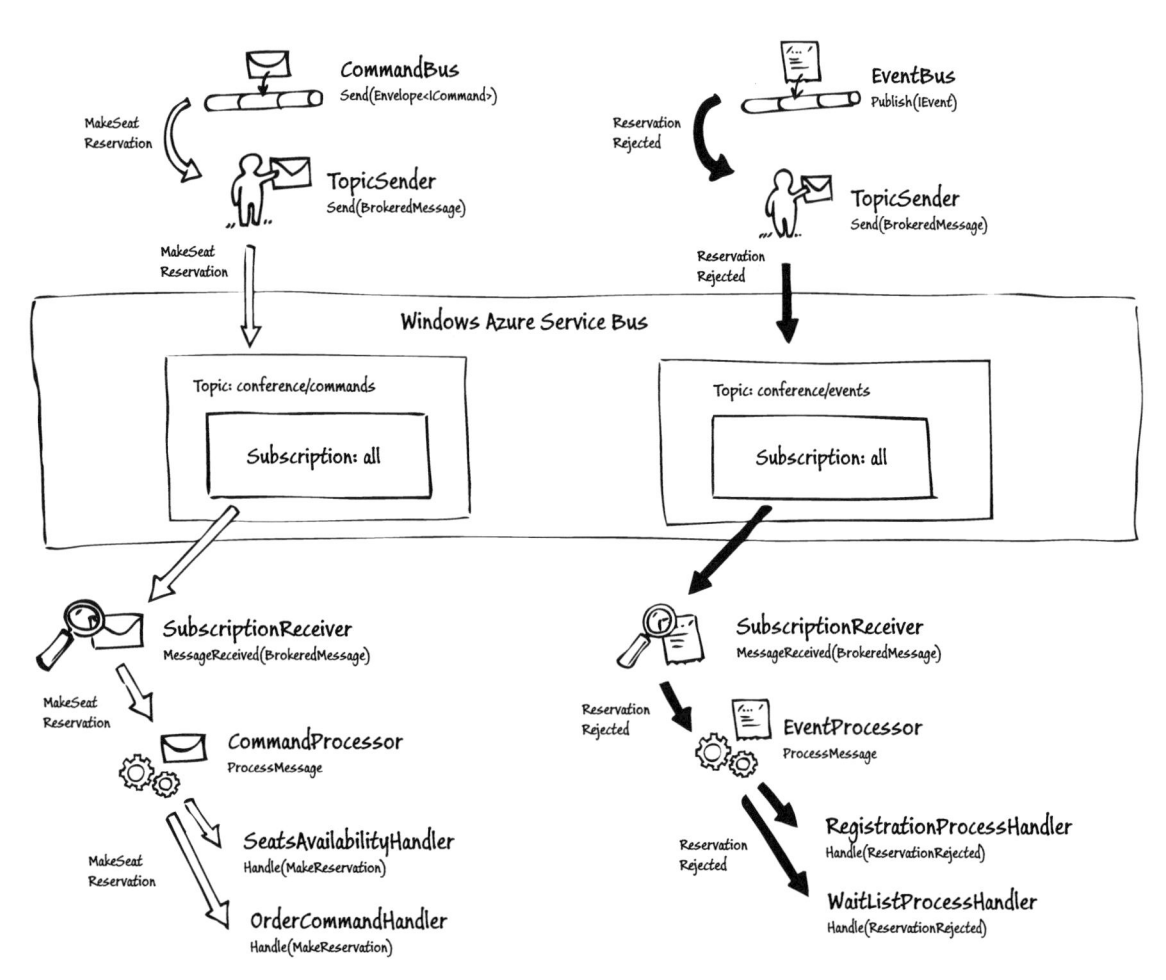

FIGURE 8
Message flows through a Windows Azure Service Bus topic

In the initial implementation, the **CommandBus** and **EventBus** classes are very similar. The only difference between the **Send** method and the **Publish** method is that the **Send** method expects the message to be wrapped in an **Envelope** class. The **Envelope** class enables the sender to specify a time delay for the message delivery.

Events can have multiple recipients. In the example shown in Figure 8, the **ReservationRejected** event is sent to the **RegistrationProcessManager**, the **WaitListProcessManager**, and one other destination. The **EventProcessor** class identifies the list of handlers to receive the event by examining its list of registered handlers.

A command has only one recipient. In Figure 8, the **MakeSeatReservation** is sent to the **SeatsAvailability** aggregate. There is just a single handler registered for this subscription. The **CommandProcessor** class identifies the handler to receive the command by examining its list of registered handlers.

This implementation gives rise to a number of questions:
- How do you limit delivery of a command to a single recipient?
- Why have separate **CommandBus** and **EventBus** classes if they are so similar?
- How scalable is this approach?
- How robust is this approach?
- What is the granularity of a topic and a subscription?
- How are commands and events serialized?

The following sections discuss these questions.

Delivering a command to a single recipient

This discussion assumes you that you have a basic understanding of the differences between Windows Azure Service Bus queues and topics. For an introduction to Windows Azure Service Bus, see "Technologies Used in the Reference Implementation" in the Reference Guide.

With the implementation shown in Figure 8, two things are necessary to ensure that a single handler handles a command message. First, there should only be a single subscription to the **conference/commands** topic in Windows Azure Service Bus; remember that a Windows Azure Service Bus topic may have multiple subscribers. Second, the **CommandProcessor** should invoke a single handler for each command message that it receives. There is no way in Windows Azure Service Bus to restrict a topic to a single subscription; therefore, the developers must be careful to create just a single subscription on a topic that is delivering commands.

> *It is possible to have multiple **SubscriptionReceiver** instances running, perhaps in multiple worker role instances. If multiple **SubscriptionReceiver** instances can receive messages from the same topic subscription, then the first one to call the **Receive** method on the **SubscriptionClient** object will get and handle the command.*

An alternative approach is to use a Windows Azure Service Bus queue in place of a topic for delivering command messages. Windows Azure Service Bus queues differ from topics in that they are designed to deliver messages to a single recipient instead of to multiple recipients through multiple subscriptions. The developers plan to evaluate this option in more detail with the intention of implementing this approach later in the project.

> A separate issue is to ensure that the handler retrieves commands from the topic and processes them only once. You must ensure either that the command is idempotent, or that the system guarantees to process the command only once. The team will address this issue in a later stage of the journey. See Chapter 7, "Adding Resilience and Optimizing Performance" for more information.

The following code sample from the **SubscriptionReceiver** class shows how it receives a message from the topic subscription.

```
private SubscriptionClient client;

...

private void ReceiveMessages(CancellationToken cancellationToken)
{
    while (!cancellationToken.IsCancellationRequested)
    {
        BrokeredMessage message = null;

        try
        {
            message = this.receiveRetryPolicy
                        .ExecuteAction(this.DoReceiveMessage);
        }
        catch (Exception e)
        {
            Trace.TraceError(
                "An unrecoverable error occurred while trying to receive" +
                "a new message:\r\n{0}",
                e);

            throw;
        }

        try
        {
            if (message == null)
            {
                Thread.Sleep(100);
                continue;
            }

            this.MessageReceived(this, new BrokeredMessageEventArgs(message));
        }
        finally
        {
            if (message != null)
            {
                message.Dispose();
            }
```

```
        }
    }
}

protected virtual BrokeredMessage DoReceiveMessage()
{
    return this.client.Receive(TimeSpan.FromSeconds(10));
}
```

> This code sample shows how the system uses the *Transient Fault Handling Application Block* to retrieve messages reliably from the topic.

The Windows Azure Service Bus **SubscriptionClient** class uses a peek/lock technique to retrieve a message from a subscription. In the code sample, the **Receive** method locks the message on the subscription. While the message is locked, other clients cannot see it. The **Receive** method then tries to process the message. If the client processes the message successfully, it calls the **Complete** method; this deletes the message from the subscription. Otherwise, if the client fails to process the message successfully, it calls the **Abandon** method; this releases the lock on the message and the same, or a different client can then receive it. If the client does not call either the **Complete** or **Abandon** methods within a fixed time, the lock on the message is released.

> *The **MessageReceived** event passes a reference to the **SubscriptionReceiver** instance so that the handler can call either the **Complete** or **Abandon** methods when it processes the message.*

The following code sample from the **MessageProcessor** class shows how to call the **Complete** and **Abandon** methods using the **BrokeredMessage** instance passed as a parameter to the **Message-Received** event.

```
private void OnMessageReceived(object sender, BrokeredMessageEventArgs args)
{
    var message = args.Message;

    object payload;
    using (var stream = message.GetBody<Stream>())
    using (var reader = new StreamReader(stream))
    {
```

```
        payload = this.serializer.Deserialize(reader);
    }

    try
    {
        ...

        ProcessMessage(payload);

        ...
    }
    catch (Exception e)
    {
        if (args.Message.DeliveryCount > MaxProcessingRetries)
        {
            Trace.TraceWarning(
                "An error occurred while processing a new message and" +
                "will be dead-lettered:\r\n{0}",
                e);
            message.SafeDeadLetter(e.Message, e.ToString());
        }
        else
        {
            Trace.TraceWarning(
                "An error occurred while processing a new message and" +
                "will be abandoned:\r\n{0}",
                e);
            message.SafeAbandon();
        }

        return;
    }

    Trace.TraceInformation("The message has been processed and will be completed.");
    message.SafeComplete();
}
```

*This example uses an extension method to invoke the **Complete** and **Abandon** methods of the **BrokeredMessage** reliably using the Transient Fault Handling Application Block.*

> There may be differences in how we invoke handlers and what context we capture for them: commands may want to capture additional runtime state, whereas events typically don't need to. Because of these potential future differences, I didn't want to unify the implementations. I've been there before and ended up splitting them when further requirements came in.

> There are no costs associated with having multiple topics, subscriptions, or queues. Windows Azure Service Bus usage is billed based on the number of messages sent and the amount of data transferred out of a Windows Azure sub-region.

Why have separate CommandBus and EventBus classes?

Although at this early stage in the development of the conference management system the implementations of the **CommandBus** and **EventBus** classes are very similar and you may wonder why we have both, the team anticipates that they will diverge in the future.

How scalable is this approach?

With this approach, you can run multiple instances of the **SubscriptionReceiver** class and the various handlers in different Windows Azure worker role instances, which enables you to scale out your solution. You can also have multiple instances of the **CommandBus**, **EventBus**, and **TopicSender** classes in different Windows Azure worker role instances.

For information about scaling the Windows Azure Service Bus infrastructure, see *Best Practices for Performance Improvements Using Service Bus Brokered Messaging* on MSDN.

How robust is this approach?

This approach uses the brokered messaging option of the Windows Azure Service Bus to provide asynchronous messaging. The Service Bus reliably stores messages until consumers connect and retrieve their messages.

Also, the peek/lock approach to retrieving messages from a queue or topic subscription adds reliability in the scenario in which a message consumer fails while it is processing the message. If a consumer fails before it calls the **Complete** method, the message is still available for processing when the consumer restarts.

What is the granularity of a topic and a subscription?

The current implementation uses a single topic (**conference/commands**) for all commands within the system, and a single topic (**conference/events**) for all events within the system. There is a single subscription for each topic, and each subscription receives all of the messages published to the topic. It is the responsibility of the **CommandProcessor** and **EventProcessor** classes to deliver the messages to the correct handlers.

In the future, the team will examine the options of using multiple topics—for example, using a separate command topic for each bounded context; and multiple subscriptions—such as one per event type. These alternatives may simplify the code and facilitate scaling of the application across multiple worker roles.

How are commands and events serialized?

The Contoso Conference Management System uses the *Json.NET* serializer. For details on how the application uses this serializer, see "Technologies Used in the Reference Implementation" in the Reference Guide.

Impact on testing

Because this was the first bounded context the team tackled, one of the key concerns was how to approach testing given that the team wanted to adopt a test-driven development approach. The following conversation between two developers about how to do TDD when they are implementing the CQRS pattern without event sourcing summarizes their thoughts:

> *"You should consider whether you always need to use the Windows Azure Service Bus for commands. Commands are typically used within a bounded context and you may not need to send them across a process boundary (on the write side you may not need additional tiers), in which case you could use an in memory queue to deliver your commands."*
> —Greg Young, conversation with the patterns & practices team

Developer 1: If we were using event sourcing, it would be easy to use a TDD approach when we were creating our domain objects. The input to the test would be a command (that perhaps originated in the UI), and we could then test that the domain object fires the expected events. However if we're not using event sourcing, we don't have any events: the behavior of the domain object is to persist its changes in data store through an ORM layer.

Developer 2: So why don't we raise events anyway? Just because we're not using event sourcing doesn't mean that our domain objects can't raise events. We can then design our tests in the usual way to check for the correct events firing in response to a command.

Developer 1: Isn't that just making things more complicated than they need to be? One of the motivations for using CQRS is to simplify things! We now have domain objects that need to persist their state using an ORM layer and raise events that report on what they have persisted just so we can run our unit tests.

Developer 2: I see what you mean.

Developer 1: Perhaps we're getting stuck on how we're doing the tests. Maybe instead of designing our tests based on the expected behavior of the domain objects, we should think about testing the state of the domain objects after they've processed a command.

Developer 2: That should be easy to do; after all, the domain objects will have all of the data we want to check stored in properties so that the ORM can persist the right information to the store.

Developer 1: So we really just need to think about a different style of testing in this scenario.

> **Developer 2**: There is another aspect of this we'll need to consider: we might have a set of tests that we can use to test our domain objects, and all of those tests might be passing. We might also have a set of tests to verify that our ORM layer can save and retrieve objects successfully. However, we will also have to test that our domain objects function correctly when we run them against the ORM layer. It's possible that a domain object performs the correct business logic, but can't properly persist its state, perhaps because of a problem related to how the ORM handles specific data types.

For more information about the two approaches to testing discussed here, see Martin Fowler's article *"Mocks Aren't Stubs"* and *"Point/Counterpoint"* by Steve Freeman, Nat Pryce, and Joshua Kerievsky.

The tests included in the solution are written using xUnit.net.

The following code sample shows two examples of tests written using the behavioral approach discussed above.

> These are the tests we started with, but we then replaced them with state-based tests.

```
public SeatsAvailability given_available_seats()
{
    var sut = new SeatsAvailability(SeatTypeId);
    sut.AddSeats(10);
    return sut;
}

[TestMethod]
public void when_reserving_less_seats_than_total_then_succeeds()
{
    var sut = this.given_available_seats();
    sut.MakeReservation(Guid.NewGuid(), 4);
}

[TestMethod]
[ExpectedException(typeof(ArgumentOutOfRangeException))]
public void when_reserving_more_seats_than_total_then_fails()
{
    var sut = this.given_available_seats();
    sut.MakeReservation(Guid.NewGuid(), 11);
}
```

These two tests work together to verify the behavior of the **SeatsAvailability** aggregate. In the first test, the expected behavior is that the **MakeReservation** method succeeds and does not throw an exception. In the second test, the expected behavior is for the **MakeReservation** method to throw an exception because there are not enough free seats available to complete the reservation.

It is difficult to test the behavior in any other way without the aggregate raising events. For example, if you tried to test the behavior by checking that the correct call is made to persist the aggregate to the data store, the test becomes coupled to the data store implementation (which is a smell); if you want to change the data store implementation, you will need to change the tests on the aggregates in the domain model.

The following code sample shows an example of a test written using the state of the objects under test. This style of test is the one used in the project.

```
public class given_available_seats
{
    private static readonly Guid SeatTypeId = Guid.NewGuid();

    private SeatsAvailability sut;
    private IPersistenceProvider sutProvider;

    protected given_available_seats(IPersistenceProvider sutProvider)
    {
        this.sutProvider = sutProvider;
        this.sut = new SeatsAvailability(SeatTypeId);
        this.sut.AddSeats(10);

        this.sut = this.sutProvider.PersistReload(this.sut);
    }

    public given_available_seats()
        : this(new NoPersistenceProvider())
    {
    }

    [Fact]
    public void when_reserving_less_seats_than_total_then_seats_become_unavailable()
    {
        this.sut.MakeReservation(Guid.NewGuid(), 4);
        this.sut = this.sutProvider.PersistReload(this.sut);

        Assert.Equal(6, this.sut.RemainingSeats);
    }
```

```
    [Fact]
    public void when_reserving_more_seats_than_total_then_rejects()
    {
        var id = Guid.NewGuid();
        sut.MakeReservation(id, 11);

        Assert.Equal(1, sut.Events.Count());
        Assert.Equal(id, ((ReservationRejected)sut.Events.Single()).ReservationId);
    }
}
```

The two tests shown here test the state of the **SeatsAvailability** aggregate after invoking the **MakeReservation** method. The first test tests the scenario in which there are enough seats available. The second test tests the scenario in which there are not enough seats available. This second test can make use of the behavior of the **SeatsAvailability** aggregate because the aggregate does raise an event if it rejects a reservation.

Summary

In the first stage in our journey, we explored some of the basics of implementing the CQRS pattern and made some preparations for the next stages.

The next chapter describes how we extended and enhanced the work already completed by adding more features and functionality to the Orders and Registrations bounded context. We will also look at some additional testing techniques to see how they might help us on our journey.

More information

All links in this book are accessible from the book's online bibliography available at:
http://msdn.microsoft.com/en-us/library/jj619274.

Journey 4:

Extending and Enhancing the Orders and Registrations Bounded Context

Further exploration of the Orders and Registrations bounded context.

"I see that it is by no means useless to travel, if a man wants to see something new."
Jules Verne, Around the World in Eighty Days

Changes to the bounded context

The previous chapter described the Orders and Registrations bounded context in some detail. This chapter describes some changes that the team made in this bounded context during the second stage of our CQRS journey.

The specific topics described in this chapter include:
- Improvements to the way message correlation works with the **RegistrationProcessManager** class. This illustrates how aggregate instances within the bounded context can interact in a complex manner.
- Implementing a record locator to enable a registrant to retrieve an order that she saved during a previous session. This illustrates adding some additional logic to the write side that enables you to locate an aggregate instance without knowing its unique ID.
- Adding a countdown timer to the UI to enable a registrant to track how much longer they have to complete an order. This illustrates enhancements to the write side to support the display of rich information in the UI.
- Supporting orders for multiple seat types simultaneously. For example, a registrant requests five seats for a preconference event and eight seats for the full conference. This requires more complex business logic on the write side.
- CQRS command validation. This illustrates how to make use of the model validation feature in MVC to validate your CQRS commands before you send them to the domain.

The Contoso Conference Management System described in this chapter is not the final version of the system. This guidance describes a journey, so some of the design decisions and implementation details change in later steps in the journey. These changes are described in subsequent chapters.

Working definitions for this chapter

This chapter uses a number of terms, which we will describe next. For more detail, and possible alternative definitions, see Chapter 4, "A CQRS and ES Deep Dive," in the Reference Guide.

Command. A *command* is a request for the system to perform an action that changes the state of the system. Commands are imperatives; for example, **MakeSeatReservation**. In this bounded context, commands originate from either the UI as a result of a user initiating a request, or from a process manager when the process manager is directing an aggregate to perform an action.

A single recipient processes a command. A command bus transports commands that command handlers then dispatch to aggregates. Sending a command is an asynchronous operation with no return value.

Event. An *event*, such as **OrderConfirmed**, describes something that has happened in the system, typically as a result of a command. Aggregates in the domain model raise events.

Multiple subscribers can handle a specific event. Aggregates publish events to an event bus; handlers register for specific types of events on the event bus and then deliver the events to the subscriber. In this bounded context, the only subscriber is a process manager.

Process manager. In this bounded context, a *process manager* is a class that coordinates the behavior of the aggregates in the domain. A process manager subscribes to the events that the aggregates raise, and then follows a simple set of rules to determine which command or commands to send. The process manager does not contain any business logic, only logic to determine the next command to send. The process manager is implemented as a state machine, so when the process manager responds to an event, it can change its internal state in addition to sending a new command.

The process manager in this bounded context can receive commands as well as subscribe to events.

Our process manager is an implementation of the Process Manager pattern defined on pages 312 to 321 in the book *Enterprise Integration Patterns: Designing, Building, and Deploying Messaging Solutions* by Gregor Hohpe and Bobby Woolf (Addison-Wesley Professional, 2003).

User stories

This chapter discusses the implementation of two user stories in addition to describing some changes and enhancements to the Orders and Registrations bounded context.

Implement a login using a record locator

When a registrant creates an order for seats at a conference, the system generates a five-character order access code and sends it to the registrant by email. The registrant can use her email address and the order access code on the conference web site as a record locator to retrieve the order from the system at a later date. The registrant may wish to retrieve the order to review it, or to complete the registration process by assigning attendees to seats.

> From the business perspective it was important for us to be as user-friendly as possible: we don't want to block or unnecessarily burden anyone who is trying to register for a conference. Therefore, we have no requirement for a user to create an account in the system prior to registration, especially since users must enter most of their information in a standard checkout process anyway.

Tell the registrant how much time remains to complete an order

When a registrant creates an order, the system reserves the seats requested by the registrant until the order is complete or the reservations expire. To complete an order, the registrant must submit her details, such as name and email address, and make a successful payment.

To help the registrant, the system displays a countdown timer to inform her how much time remains to complete the order before the seat reservations expire.

Enable a registrant to create an order that includes multiple seat types

When a registrant creates an order, she may request different numbers of different seat types. For example, a registrant may request five seats for the full conference and three seats for the preconference workshop.

Architecture

The application is designed to deploy to Windows Azure. At this stage in the journey, the application consists of a web role that contains the ASP.NET MVC web application and a worker role that contains the message handlers and domain objects. The application uses Windows Azure SQL Database (SQL Database) instances for data storage, both on the write side and the read side. The application uses the Windows Azure Service Bus to provide its messaging infrastructure. Figure 1 shows this high-level architecture.

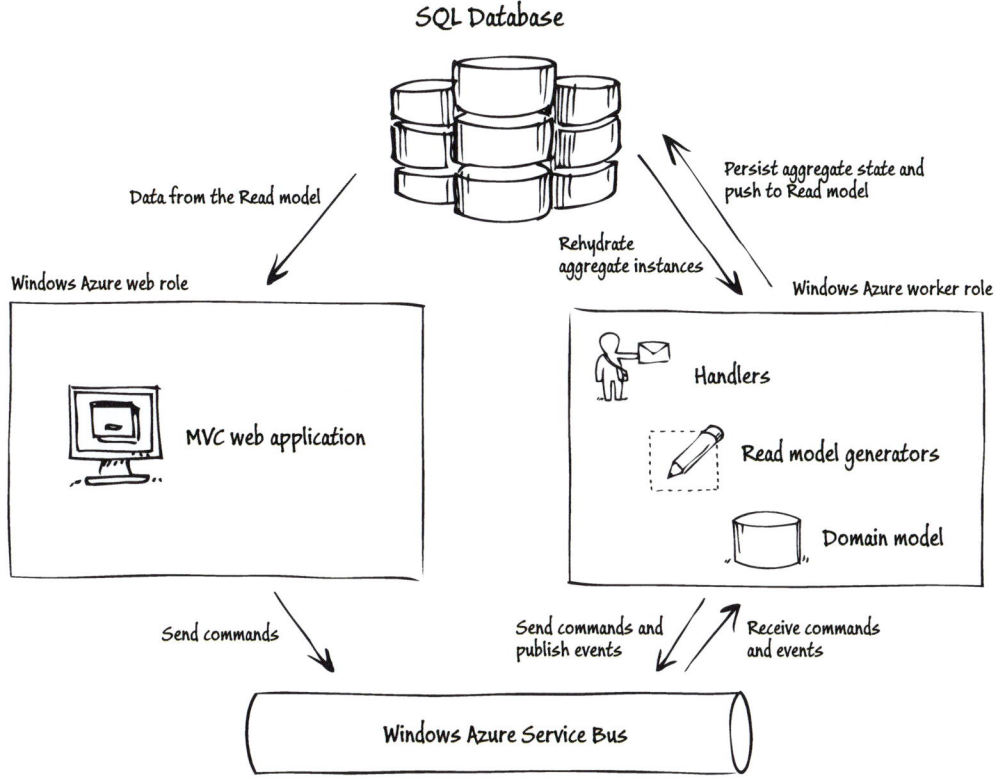

Figure 1
Contoso Conference Management System high-level architecture

While you are exploring and testing the solution, you can run it locally, either using the Windows Azure compute emulator or by running the MVC web application directly and running a console application that hosts the handlers and domain objects. When you run the application locally, you can use a local SQL Server Express database instead of SQL Database, and use a simple messaging infrastructure implemented in a SQL Server Express database.

For more information about the options for running the application, see Appendix 1, "Release Notes."

Patterns and concepts

This section describes some of the key areas of the application that the team visited during this stage of the journey and introduces some of the challenges met by the team when we addressed these areas.

Record locators

The system uses access codes instead of passwords so the registrant is not forced to set up an account with the system. Many registrants may use the system only once, so there is no need to create a permanent account with a user ID and a password.

The system needs to be able to retrieve order information quickly based on the registrant's email address and access code. To provide a minimum level of security, the access codes that the system generates should not be predictable, and the order information that registrants can retrieve should not contain any sensitive information.

Querying the read side

The previous chapter focused on the write-side model and implementation; in this chapter we'll explore the read-side implementation in more detail. In particular, we'll explain how we implemented the read model and the querying mechanism from the MVC controllers.

In this initial exploration of the CQRS pattern, the team decided to use SQL views in the database as the underlying source of the data queried by the MVC controllers on the read side. To minimize the work that the queries on the read side must perform, these SQL views provide a denormalized version of the data. These views currently exist in the same database as the normalized tables that the write model uses.

> The team will split the database into two and explore options for pushing changes from the normalized write side to the denormalized read side in a later stage of the journey. For an example of using Windows Azure blob storage instead of SQL tables for storing the read-side data, see the **SeatAssignmentsViewModelGenerator** class.

Storing denormalized views in a database

One common option for storing the read-side data is to use a set of relational database tables to hold the denormalized views. You should optimize the read side for fast reads, so there is typically no benefit in storing normalized data because this will require complex queries to construct the data for the client. This implies that goals for the read side should be to keep the queries as simple as possible, and to structure the tables in the database in such a way that they can be read quickly and efficiently.

An important area for consideration is the interface whereby a client such as an MVC controller action submits a query to the read-side model.

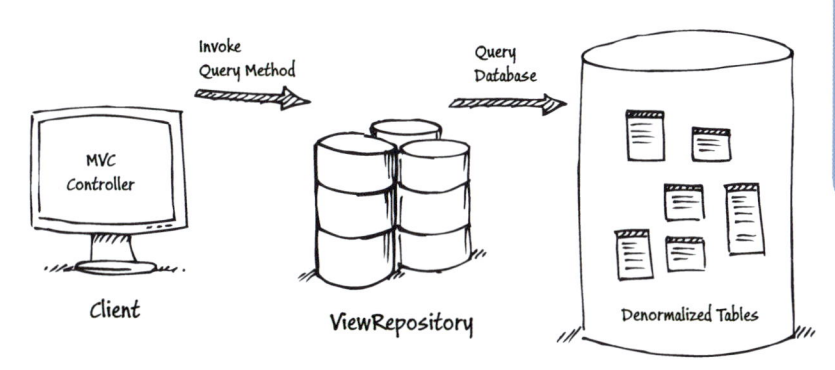

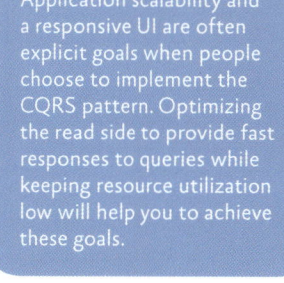

> Application scalability and a responsive UI are often explicit goals when people choose to implement the CQRS pattern. Optimizing the read side to provide fast responses to queries while keeping resource utilization low will help you to achieve these goals.

FIGURE 2
The read side storing data in a relational database

In Figure 2, a client, such as an MVC controller action, invokes a method on the **ViewRepository** class to request the data it needs. The **ViewRepository** class in turn runs a query against the denormalized data in the database.

The team at Contoso evaluated two approaches to implementing the **ViewRepository** class: using the **IQueryable** interface and using non-generic data access objects (DAOs).

Using the IQueryable interface

One approach to consider for the **ViewRepository** class is to have it return an **IQueryable** instance that enables the client to use language-integrated query (LINQ) to specify its query. It is very easy to return an **IQueryable** instance from many ORMs such as *Entity Framework* or *NHibernate*. The following code snippet illustrates how the client can submit such queries.

> A normalized database schema can fail to provide adequate response times because of the excessive table JOIN operations. Despite advances in relational database technology, a JOIN operation is still very expensive compared to a single-table read.

> The Repository pattern mediates between the domain and data mapping layers using a collection-like interface for accessing domain objects. For more info see Martin Fowler, Catalog of Patterns of Enterprise Application Architecture, *Repository*.

```
var ordersummary = repository
                    .Query<OrderSummary>()
                    .Where(LINQ query to retrieve order summary);
var orderdetails = repository
                    .Query<OrderDetails>()
                    .Where(LINQ query to retrieve order details);
```

This approach has a number of advantages:

Simplicity
- This approach uses a thin abstraction layer over the underlying database. Many ORMs support this approach and it minimizes the amount of code that you must write.
- You only need to define a single repository and a single **Query** method.
- You don't need a separate query object. On the read side, the queries should be simple because you have already denormalized the data from the write side to support the read-side clients.
- You can make use of Language-Integrated Query (LINQ) to provide support for features such as filtering, paging, and sorting on the client.

Testability
- You can use LINQ to Objects for mocking.

There are possible objections to this approach including that:
- It is not easy to replace the data store with a non-relational database that does not expose an **IQueryable** object. However, you can choose to implement the read model differently in each bounded context using an approach that is appropriate to that bounded context.
- The client might abuse the **IQueryable** interface by performing operations that can be done more efficiently as a part of the denormalization process. You should ensure that the denormalized data fully meets the requirements of the clients.
- Using the **IQueryable** interface hides the queries away. However, since you denormalize the data from the write side, the queries against the relational database tables are unlikely to be complex.
- It's hard to know if your integration tests cover all the different uses of the **Query** method.

> In the RI, using Entity Framework, we didn't need to write any code at all to expose the **IQueryable** instance. We also had just a single **ViewRepository** class.

Using non-generic DAOs

An alternative approach is to have the **ViewRepository** expose custom **Find** and **Get** methods, as shown in the following code snippets.

```
var ordersummary = dao.FindAllSummarizedOrders(userId);
var orderdetails = dao.GetOrderDetails(orderId);
```

You could also choose to use different DAO classes. This would make it easier to access different data sources.

```
var ordersummary = OrderSummaryDAO.FindAll(userId);
var orderdetails = OrderDetailsDAO.Get(orderId);
```

This approach has a number of advantages:

Simplicity
- Dependencies are clearer for the client. For example, the client references an explicit **IOrderSummaryDAO** instance rather than a generic **IViewRepository** instance.
- For the majority of queries, there are only one or two predefined ways to access the object. Different queries typically return different projections.

Flexibility
- The **Get** and **Find** methods hide details such as the partitioning of the data store and the data access methods such as an object relational mapping (ORM) or executing SQL code explicitly. This makes it easier to change these choices in the future.
- The **Get** and **Find** methods could use an ORM, LINQ, and the **IQueryable** interface behind the scenes to get the data from the data store. This is a choice that you could make on a method-by-method basis.

Performance
- You can easily optimize the queries that the **Find** and **Get** methods run.
- The data access layer executes all queries. There is no risk that the client MVC controller action tries to run complex and inefficient LINQ queries against the data source.

Testability
- It is easier to specify unit tests for the **Find** and **Get** methods than to create suitable unit tests for the range of possible LINQ queries that a client could specify.

Maintainability
- All of the queries are defined in the same location, the DAO classes, making it easier to modify the system consistently.

Possible objections to this approach include:
- Using the **IQueryable** interface makes it much easier to use grids that support features such as paging, filtering, and sorting in the UI. However, if the developers are aware of this downside and are committed to delivering a task-based UI, then this should not be an issue.

The team decided to adopt the second approach because of the clarity it brings to the code; in this context, we did not see any significant advantage in the simplicity of the first approach. For examples, see the **ConferenceDao** and **OrderDao** classes in the **Registration** project.

Making information about partially fulfilled orders available to the read side

The UI displays data about orders that it obtains by querying the model on the read side. Part of the data that the UI displays to the registrant is information about partially fulfilled orders: for each seat type in the order, the number of seats requested and the number of seats that are available. This is temporary data that the system only uses while the registrant is creating the order using the UI; the business only needs to store information about seats that were actually purchased, not the difference between what the registrant requested and what the registrant purchased.

The consequence of this is that the information about how many seats the registrant requested only needs to exist in the model on the read side.

A further consequence is that the underlying storage on the read side cannot be simple SQL views because it includes data that is not stored in the underlying table storage on the write side. Therefore, you must pass this information to the read side using events.

Figure 3 shows all the commands and events that the **Order** and **SeatsAvailability** aggregates use and how the **Order** aggregate pushes changes to the read side by raising events.

> You can't store this information in an HTTP session because the registrant may leave the site between requesting the seats and completing the order.

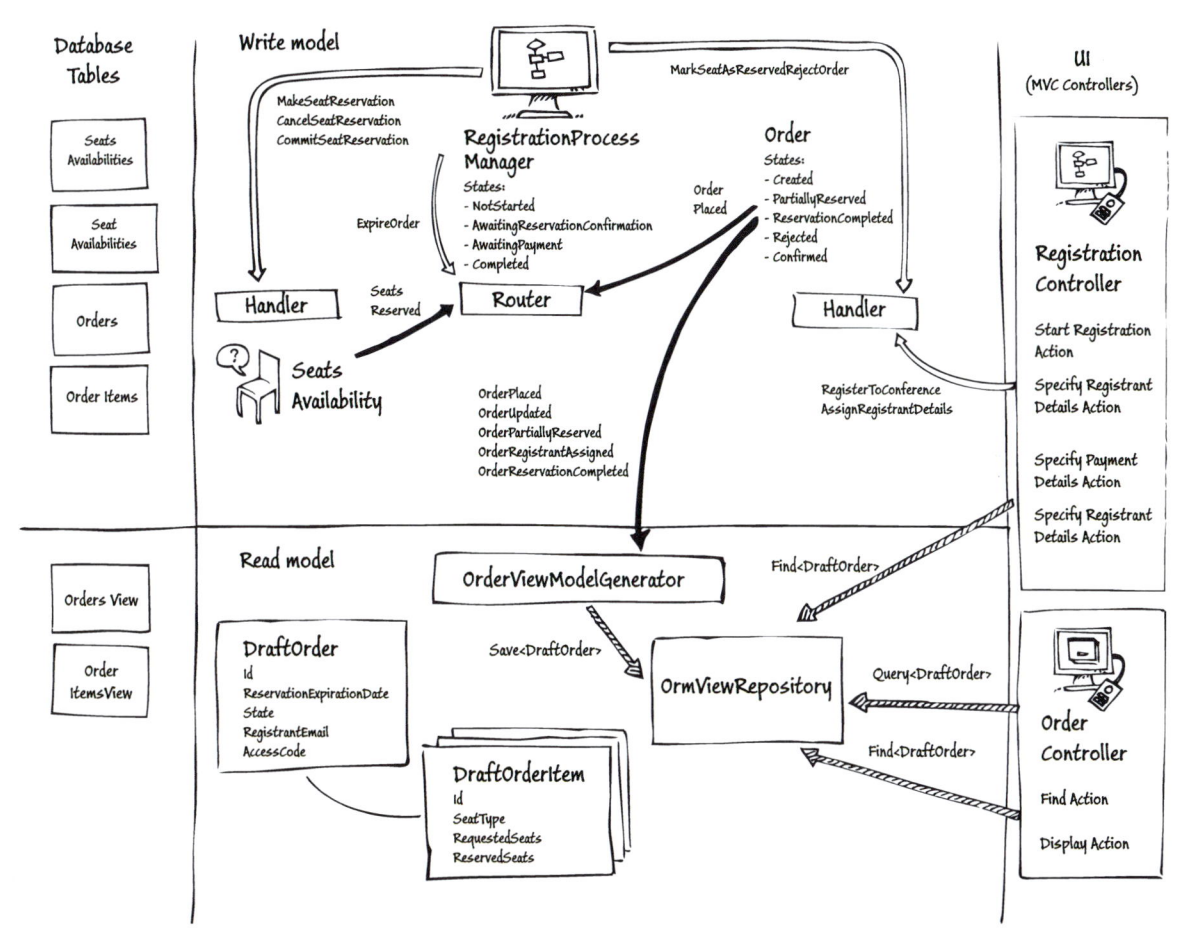

Extending and Enhancing the Orders and Registrations Bounded Context 61

Figure 3 — The new architecture of the reservation process

Figure 3
The new architecture of the reservation process

The **OrderViewModelGenerator** class handles the **OrderPlaced**, **OrderUpdated**, **OrderPartiallyReserved**, **OrderRegistrantAssigned**, and **OrderReservationCompleted** events and uses **DraftOrder** and **DraftOrderItem** instances to persist changes to the view tables.

CQRS command validation

When you implement the write model, you should try to ensure that commands very rarely fail. This gives the best user experience, and makes it much easier to implement the asynchronous behavior in your application.

One approach, adopted by the team, is to use the model validation features in ASP.NET MVC.

> If you look ahead to Chapter 5, "Preparing for the V1 Release," you'll see that the team extended the use of events and migrated the Orders and Registrations bounded context to use event sourcing.

You should be careful to distinguish between errors and business failures. Examples of errors include:
- A message is not delivered due to a failure in the messaging infrastructure.
- Data is not persisted due to a connectivity problem with the database.

In many cases, especially in the cloud, you can handle these errors by retrying the operation.

A business failure should have a predetermined business response. For example:
- If the system cannot reserve a seat because there are no seats left, then it should add the request to a wait list.
- If a credit card payment fails, the user should be given the chance to either try a different card, or set up payment by invoice.

> The Transient Fault Handling Application Block from Microsoft patterns & practices is designed to make it easier to implement consistent retry behavior for any transient faults. It comes with a set of built-in detection strategies for Windows Azure SQL Database, Windows Azure storage, Windows Azure Caching, and Windows Azure Service Bus, and it also allows you to define your own strategies. Similarly, it comes with a set of handy built-in retry policies and supports custom ones. For more information, see *The Transient Fault Handling Application Block*.

THE COUNTDOWN TIMER AND THE READ MODEL

The countdown timer that displays how much time remains to complete the order to the registrant is part of the business data in the system, and not just a part of the infrastructure. When a registrant creates an order and reserves seats, the countdown begins. The countdown continues, even if the registrant leaves the conference website. The UI must be able to display the correct countdown value if the registrant returns to the site; therefore, the reservation expiry time is a part of the data that is available from the read model.

Implementation details

This section describes some of the significant features of the implementation of the Orders and Registrations bounded context. You may find it useful to have a copy of the code so you can follow along. You can download a copy from the *Download center*, or check the evolution of the code in the repository on GitHub: *https://github.com/mspnp/cqrs-journey-code*.

> **Note:** *Do not expect the code samples to match exactly the code in the reference implementation. This chapter describes a step in the CQRS journey, but the implementation may well change as we learn more and refactor the code.*

> Your domain experts should help you to identify possible business failures and determine the way that you handle them: either using an automated process or manually.

The order access code record locator

A registrant may need to retrieve an order, either to view it, or to complete the assignment of attendees to seats. This may happen in a different web session, so the registrant must supply some information to locate the previously saved order.

The following code sample shows how the **Order** class generates a new five-character order access code that is persisted as part of the **Order** instance.

```
public string AccessCode { get; set; }

protected Order()
{
    ...
    this.AccessCode = HandleGenerator.Generate(5);
}
```

To retrieve an **Order** instance, a registrant must provide her email address and the order access code. The system will use these two items to locate the correct order. This logic is part of the read side.

The following code sample from the **OrderController** class in the web application shows how the MVC controller submits the query to the read side using the **LocateOrder** method to discover the unique **OrderId** value. This **Find** action passes the **OrderId** value to a **Display** action that displays the order information to the registrant.

```
[HttpPost]
public ActionResult Find(string email, string accessCode)
{
    var orderId = orderDao.LocateOrder(email, accessCode);

    if (!orderId.HasValue)
    {
        return RedirectToAction(
                "Find",
                new { conferenceCode = this.ConferenceCode });
    }

    return RedirectToAction(
                "Display",
                new
                    {
                        conferenceCode = this.ConferenceCode,
                        orderId = orderId.Value
                    });
}
```

The countdown timer

When a registrant creates an order and makes a seat reservation, those seats are reserved for a fixed period of time. The **RegistrationProcessManager** instance, which forwards the reservation from the **SeatsAvailability** aggregate, passes the time that the reservation expires to the **Order** aggregate. The following code sample shows how the **Order** aggregate receives and stores the reservation expiry time.

```
public DateTime? ReservationExpirationDate { get; private set; }

public void MarkAsReserved(DateTime expirationDate, IEnumerable<SeatQuantity> seats)
{
    ...

    this.ReservationExpirationDate = expirationDate;
    this.Items.Clear();
    this.Items.AddRange(
                seats.Select(
                    seat => new OrderItem(seat.SeatType, seat.Quantity)));
}
```

> The **ReservationExpirationDate** is initially set in the **Order** constructor to a time 15 minutes after the **Order** is instantiated. The **RegistrationProcessManager** class may revise this time based on when the reservations are actually made. It is this time that the process manager sends to the **Order** aggregate in the **MarkSeatsAsReserved** command.

When the **RegistrationProcessManager** sends the **MarkSeatsAsReserved** command to the **Order** aggregate with the expiry time that the UI will display, it also sends a command to itself to initiate the process of releasing the reserved seats. This **ExpireRegistrationProcess** command is held for the expiry duration plus a buffer of five minutes. This buffer ensures that time differences between the servers don't cause the **RegistrationProcessManager** class to release the reserved seats before the timer in the UI counts down to zero. In the following code sample from the **RegistrationProcessManager** class, the UI uses the **Expiration** property in the **MarkSeatsAsReserved** command to display the countdown timer, and the **Delay** property in the **ExpireRegistrationProcess** command determines when the reserved seats are released.

```
public void Handle(SeatsReserved message)
{
    if (this.State == ProcessState.AwaitingReservationConfirmation)
    {
        var expirationTime = this.ReservationAutoExpiration.Value;
        this.State = ProcessState.ReservationConfirmationReceived;

        if (this.ExpirationCommandId == Guid.Empty)
        {
            var bufferTime = TimeSpan.FromMinutes(5);

            var expirationCommand =
                new ExpireRegistrationProcess { ProcessId = this.Id };
            this.ExpirationCommandId = expirationCommand.Id;

            this.AddCommand(new Envelope<ICommand>(expirationCommand)
            {
                Delay = expirationTime.Subtract(DateTime.UtcNow).Add(bufferTime),
            });
        }


        this.AddCommand(new MarkSeatsAsReserved
        {
            OrderId = this.OrderId,
            Seats = message.ReservationDetails.ToList(),
            Expiration = expirationTime,
        });
    }

    ...
}
```

The MVC **RegistrationController** class retrieves the order information on the read side. The **DraftOrder** class includes the reservation expiry time that the controller passes to the view using the **ViewBag** class, as shown in the following code sample.

Journey four

```
[HttpGet]
public ActionResult SpecifyRegistrantDetails(string conferenceCode, Guid orderId)
{
    var repo = this.repositoryFactory();
    using (repo as IDisposable)
    {
        var draftOrder = repo.Find<DraftOrder>(orderId);
        var conference = repo.Query<Conference>()
            .Where(c => c.Code == conferenceCode)
            .FirstOrDefault();

        this.ViewBag.ConferenceName = conference.Name;
        this.ViewBag.ConferenceCode = conference.Code;
        this.ViewBag.ExpirationDateUTCMilliseconds =
          draftOrder.BookingExpirationDate.HasValue
          ? ((draftOrder.BookingExpirationDate.Value.Ticks - EpochTicks) / 10000L)
            : 0L;
        this.ViewBag.OrderId = orderId;

        return View(new AssignRegistrantDetails { OrderId = orderId });
    }
}
```

The MVC view then uses JavaScript to display an animated countdown timer.

Using ASP.NET MVC validation for commands

You should try to ensure that any commands that the MVC controllers in your application send to the write model will succeed. You can use the features in MVC to validate the commands on both the client side and server side before sending them to the write model.

The following code sample shows the **AssignRegistrantDetails** command class that uses **DataAnnotations** to specify the validation requirements; in this example, the requirement is that the **FirstName**, **LastName**, and **Email** fields are not empty.

> Client-side validation is primarily a convenience to the user in that it avoids the need for round trips to the server to help the user complete a form correctly. You still need to implement server-side validation to ensure that the data is validated before it is forwarded to the write model.

```csharp
using System;
using System.ComponentModel.DataAnnotations;
using Common;

public class AssignRegistrantDetails : ICommand
{
    public AssignRegistrantDetails()
    {
        this.Id = Guid.NewGuid();
    }

    public Guid Id { get; private set; }

    public Guid OrderId { get; set; }

    [Required(AllowEmptyStrings = false)]
    public string FirstName { get; set; }

    [Required(AllowEmptyStrings = false)]
    public string LastName { get; set; }

    [Required(AllowEmptyStrings = false)]
    public string Email { get; set; }
}
```

The MVC view uses this command class as its model class. The following code sample from the **SpecifyRegistrantDetails.cshtml** file shows how the model is populated.

```
@model Registration.Commands.AssignRegistrantDetails

...

<div class="editor-label">@Html.LabelFor(model => model.FirstName)</div>
<div class="editor-field">@Html.EditorFor(model => model.FirstName)</div>
<div class="editor-label">@Html.LabelFor(model => model.LastName)</div>
<div class="editor-field">@Html.EditorFor(model => model.LastName)</div>
<div class="editor-label">@Html.LabelFor(model => model.Email)</div>
<div class="editor-field">@Html.EditorFor(model => model.Email)</div>
```

The **Web.config** file configures the client-side validation based on the **DataAnnotations** attributes, as shown in the following snippet.

```
<appSettings>
    ...
    <add key="ClientValidationEnabled" value="true" />
    <add key="UnobtrusiveJavaScriptEnabled" value="true" />
</appSettings>
```

The server-side validation occurs in the controller before it sends the command. The following code sample from the **RegistrationController** class shows how the controller uses the **IsValid** property to validate the command. Remember that this example uses an instance of the command as the model.

```
[HttpPost]
public ActionResult SpecifyRegistrantDetails(
    string conferenceCode,
    Guid orderId,
    AssignRegistrantDetails command)
{
    if (!ModelState.IsValid)
    {
        return SpecifyRegistrantDetails(conferenceCode, orderId);
    }

    this.commandBus.Send(command);

    return RedirectToAction(
                "SpecifyPaymentDetails",
                new { conferenceCode = conferenceCode, orderId = orderId });
}
```

For an additional example, see the **RegisterToConference** command and the **StartRegistration** action in the **RegistrationController** class.

For more information, see *Models and Validation in ASP.NET MVC* on MSDN.

Pushing changes to the read side

Some information about orders only needs to exist on the read side. In particular, the information about partially fulfilled orders is only used in the UI and is not part of the business information persisted by the domain model on the write side.

This means that the system can't use SQL views as the underlying storage mechanism on the read side because views cannot contain data that does not exist in the tables that they are based on.

The system stores the denormalized order data in a SQL Database instance in two tables: the **OrdersView** and **OrderItemsView** tables. The **OrderItemsView** table includes the **RequestedSeats** column that contains data that only exists on the read side.

Column	Description
OrderId	A unique identifier for the Order
ReservationExpirationDate	The time when the seat reservations expire
StateValue	The state of the Order: Created, PartiallyReserved, ReservationCompleted, Rejected, Confirmed
RegistrantEmail	The email address of the Registrant
AccessCode	The Access Code that the Registrant can use to access the Order

OrdersView Table descriptions

Column	Description
OrderItemId	A unique identifier for the Order Item
SeatType	The type of seat requested
RequestedSeats	The number of seats requested
ReservedSeats	The number of seats reserved
OrderID	The OrderId in the parent OrdersView table

OrderItemsView Table descriptions

To populate these tables in the read model, the read side handles events raised by the write side and uses them to write to these tables. See Figure 3 above for more details.

The **OrderViewModelGenerator** class handles these events and updates the read-side repository.

```csharp
public class OrderViewModelGenerator :
    IEventHandler<OrderPlaced>, IEventHandler<OrderUpdated>,
    IEventHandler<OrderPartiallyReserved>, IEventHandler<OrderReservationCompleted>,
    IEventHandler<OrderRegistrantAssigned>
{
    private readonly Func<ConferenceRegistrationDbContext> contextFactory;

    public OrderViewModelGenerator(
        Func<ConferenceRegistrationDbContext> contextFactory)
    {
        this.contextFactory = contextFactory;
    }

    public void Handle(OrderPlaced @event)
    {
        using (var context = this.contextFactory.Invoke())
        {
            var dto = new DraftOrder(@event.SourceId, DraftOrder.States.Created)
            {
                AccessCode = @event.AccessCode,
            };
            dto.Lines.AddRange(
                @event.Seats.Select(
                    seat => new DraftOrderItem(seat.SeatType, seat.Quantity)));

            context.Save(dto);
        }
    }

    public void Handle(OrderRegistrantAssigned @event)
    {
        ...
    }

    public void Handle(OrderUpdated @event)
    {
        ...
    }

    public void Handle(OrderPartiallyReserved @event)
    {
        ...
    }
```

```
    public void Handle(OrderReservationCompleted @event)
    {
        ...
    }

    ...
}
```

The following code sample shows the **ConferenceRegistrationDbContext** class.

```
public class ConferenceRegistrationDbContext : DbContext
{
    ...

    public T Find<T>(Guid id) where T : class
    {
        return this.Set<T>().Find(id);
    }

    public IQueryable<T> Query<T>() where T : class
    {
        return this.Set<T>();
    }

    public void Save<T>(T entity) where T : class
    {
        var entry = this.Entry(entity);

        if (entry.State == System.Data.EntityState.Detached)
            this.Set<T>().Add(entity);

        this.SaveChanges();
    }
}
```

> Notice that this *ConferenceRegistrationDbContext* in the read side includes a *Save* method to persist the changes sent from the write side and handled by the *OrderViewModelGenerator* handler class.

Querying the read side

The following code sample shows a nongeneric DAO class that the MVC controllers use to query for conference information on the read side. It wraps the **ConferenceRegistrationDbContext** class shown previously.

```
public class ConferenceDao : IConferenceDao
{
    private readonly Func<ConferenceRegistrationDbContext> contextFactory;

    public ConferenceDao(Func<ConferenceRegistrationDbContext> contextFactory)
    {
        this.contextFactory = contextFactory;
    }

    public ConferenceDetails GetConferenceDetails(string conferenceCode)
    {
        using (var context = this.contextFactory.Invoke())
        {
            return context
                .Query<Conference>()
                .Where(dto => dto.Code == conferenceCode)
                .Select(x =>
                    new ConferenceDetails
                    {
                        Id = x.Id,
                        Code = x.Code,
                        Name = x.Name,
                        Description = x.Description,
                        StartDate = x.StartDate
                    })
                .FirstOrDefault();
        }
    }

    public ConferenceAlias GetConferenceAlias(string conferenceCode)
    {
        ...
    }

    public IList<SeatType> GetPublishedSeatTypes(Guid conferenceId)
    {
        ...
    }
}
```

Refactoring the SeatsAvailability aggregate

In the first stage of our CQRS journey, the domain included a **ConferenceSeatsAvailabilty** aggregate root class that modeled the number of seats remaining for a conference. In this stage of the journey, the team replaced the **ConferenceSeatsAvailabilty** aggregate with a **SeatsAvailability** aggregate to reflect the fact that there may be multiple seat types available at a particular conference; for example, full conference seats, pre-conference workshop seats, and cocktail party seats. Figure 4 shows the new **SeatsAvailability** aggregate and its constituent classes.

> Notice how this **ConferenceDao** class contains only methods that return data. It is used by the MVC controllers to retrieve data to display in the UI.

Commands

MakeSeatReservation
ConferenceId
ReservationId
Seats*

CancelSeatReservation
ConferenceId
ReservationId

CommitSeatReservation
ConferenceId
ReservationId

Events

SeatsReserved
ReservationId
Seats*

Seats Availability Aggregate

SeatsAvailability (Aggregate Root)
Id
AddSeats(seatType, quantity)
MakeReservation(reservationId, seats*)
CommitReservation(reservationId)
CancelReservation(reservationId)

*SeatQuantity
SeatType
Quantity

SeatAvailability
SeatType
RemainingSeats
AddSeats(quantity)
Reserve(reservationId, quantity)
CommitReservation(reservationId)
CancelReservation(reservationId)

Reservation
Id
Quantity

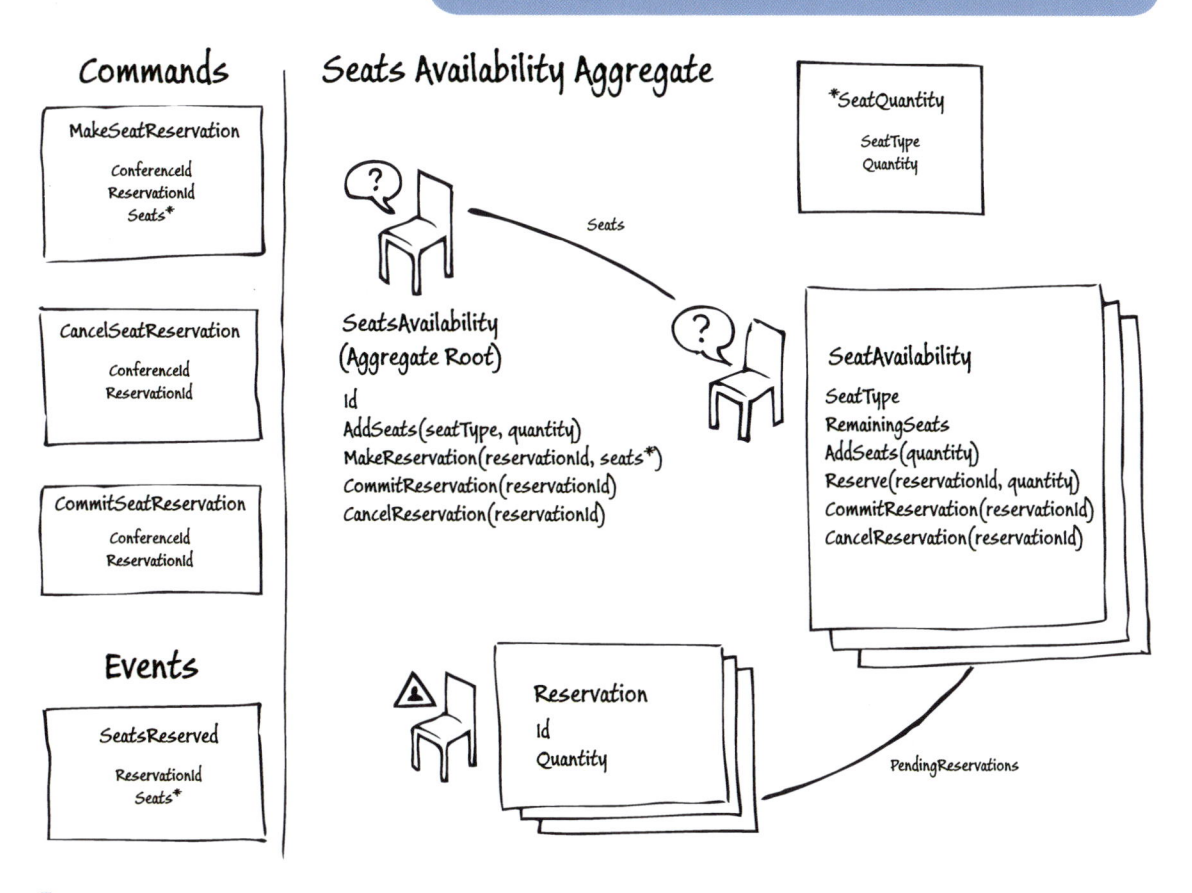

Seats — *PendingReservations*

Figure 4
The SeatsAvailability aggregate and its associated commands and events

This aggregate now models the following facts:
- There may be multiple seat types at a conference.
- There may be different numbers of seats available for each seat type.

The domain now includes a **SeatQuantity** value type that you can use to represent a quantity of a particular seat type.

Previously, the aggregate raised either a **ReservationAccepted** or a **ReservationRejected** event, depending on whether there were sufficient seats. Now the aggregate raises a **SeatsReserved** event that reports how many seats of a particular type it could reserve. This means that the number of seats reserved may not match the number of seats requested; this information is passed back to the UI for the registrant to make a decision on how to proceed with the registration.

The AddSeats method

You may have noticed in Figure 3 that the **SeatsAvailability** aggregate includes an **AddSeats** method with no corresponding command. The **AddSeats** method adjusts the total number of available seats of a given type. The business customer is responsible for making any such adjustments, and does this in the Conference Management bounded context. The Conference Management bounded context raises an event whenever the total number of available seats changes. The **SeatsAvailability** class then handles the event when its handler invokes the **AddSeats** method.

Impact on testing

This section discusses some of the testing issues addressed during this stage of the journey.

ACCEPTANCE TESTS AND THE DOMAIN EXPERT

In Chapter 3, "Orders and Registrations Bounded Context," you saw some of the UI mockups that the developers and the domain expert worked on together to refine some of the functional requirements for the system. One of the planned uses for these UI mockups was to form the basis of a set of acceptance tests for the system.

The team had the following goals for their acceptance testing approach:
- The acceptance tests should be expressed clearly and unambiguously in a format that the domain expert could understand.
- It should be possible to execute the acceptance tests automatically.

To achieve these goals, the domain expert paired with a member of the test team and used *SpecFlow* to specify the core acceptance tests.

Defining acceptance tests using SpecFlow features

The first step in defining acceptance tests using SpecFlow is to define the acceptance tests using the SpecFlow notation. These tests are saved as feature files in a Visual Studio project. The following code sample from the **ConferenceConfiguration.feature** file in the Features\UserInterface\Views\Management folder shows an acceptance test for the Conference Management bounded context. A typical SpecFlow test scenario consists of a collection of **Given**, **When**, and **Then** statements. Some of these statements include the data that the test uses.

> In fact, SpecFlow feature files use the Gherkin language—a domain specific language (DSL) created especially for behavior descriptions.

```
Feature: Conference configuration scenarios for creating and editing Conference settings
  In order to create or update a Conference configuration
  As a Business Customer
  I want to be able to create or update a Conference and set its properties

Background:
Given the Business Customer selected the Create Conference option

Scenario: An existing unpublished Conference is selected and published
Given this conference information
| Owner         | Email                | Name      | Description                         | Slug   | Start      | End        |
| William Flash | william@fabrikam.com | CQRS2012P | CQRS summit 2012 conference (Published) | random | 05/02/2012 | 05/12/2012 |
When the Business Customer proceeds to publish the Conference
Then the state of the Conference changes to Published

Scenario: An existing Conference is edited and updated
Given an existing published conference with this information
| Owner         | Email                | Name      | Description                         | Slug   | Start      | End        |
| William Flash | william@fabrikam.com | CQRS2012U | CQRS summit 2012 conference (Original) | random | 05/02/2012 | 05/12/2012 |
| Description                             |
| CQRS summit 2012 conference (Updated)   |
When the Business Customer proceeds to save the changes
Then this information appears in the Conference settings
| Description                             |
| CQRS summit 2012 conference (Updated)   |
...
```

> I found these acceptance tests were a great way for me to clarify my definitions of the expected behavior of the system to the developers.

For additional examples, see the **Conference.AcceptanceTests** Visual Studio solution file included with the downloadable source.

Making the tests executable

An acceptance test in a feature file is not directly executable; you must provide some plumbing code to bridge the gap between the SpecFlow feature file and your application.

For examples of implementations, see the classes in the **Steps** folder in the **Conference.Specflow** project in the **Conference.AcceptanceTests** solution.

These step implementations use two different approaches.

The first approach runs the test by simulating a user of the system. It does this by driving a web browser directly using the *WatiN* open source library. The advantages of this approach are that it exercises the system in exactly the same way that a real user would interact with the system and that it is simple to implement initially. However, these tests are fragile and will require a considerable maintenance effort to keep them up to date as the UI and system change. The following code sample shows an example of this approach, defining some of the **Given**, **When**, and **Then** steps from the feature file shown previously. SpecFlow uses the **Given**, **When**, and **Then** attributes to link the steps to the clauses in the feature file and to pass parameter values to step methods:

```
public class ConferenceConfigurationSteps : StepDefinition
{
    ...

    [Given(@"the Business Customer proceeds to edit the existing settings" +
        "with this information")]
    public void
      GivenTheBusinessCustomerProceedToEditTheExistingSettignsWithThisInformation(
        Table table)
    {
        Browser.Click(Constants.UI.EditConferenceId);
        PopulateConferenceInformation(table);
    }

    [Given(@"an existing published conference with this information")]
    public void GivenAnExistingPublishedConferenceWithThisInformation(Table table)
    {
        ExistingConferenceWithThisInformation(table, true);
    }
```

```csharp
private void ExistingConferenceWithThisInformation(Table table, bool publish)
{
    NavigateToCreateConferenceOption();
    PopulateConferenceInformation(table, true);
    CreateTheConference();
    if(publish) PublishTheConference();

    ScenarioContext.Current.Set(
        table.Rows[0]["Email"],
        Constants.EmailSessionKey);
    ScenarioContext.Current.Set(
        Browser.FindText(Slug.FindBy),
        Constants.AccessCodeSessionKey);
}

...

[When(@"the Business Customer proceeds to save the changes")]
public void WhenTheBusinessCustomerProceedToSaveTheChanges()
{
    Browser.Click(Constants.UI.UpdateConferenceId);
}

...

[Then(@"this information appears in the Conference settings")]
public void ThenThisInformationIsShowUpInTheConferenceSettings(Table table)
{
    Assert.True(
        Browser.SafeContainsText(table.Rows[0][0]),
        string.Format(
            "The following text was not found on the page: {0}",
            table.Rows[0][0]));
}

private void PublishTheConference()
{
    Browser.Click(Constants.UI.PublishConferenceId);
}

private void CreateTheConference()
{
    ScenarioContext.Current.Browser().Click(Constants.UI.CreateConferenceId);
}
```

```csharp
private void NavigateToCreateConferenceOption()
{
    // Navigate to Registration page
    Browser.GoTo(Constants.ConferenceManagementCreatePage);
}

private void PopulateConferenceInformation(Table table, bool create = false)
{
    var row = table.Rows[0];

    if (create)
    {
        Browser.SetInput("OwnerName", row["Owner"]);
        Browser.SetInput("OwnerEmail", row["Email"]);
        Browser.SetInput("name", row["Email"], "ConfirmEmail");
        Browser.SetInput("Slug", Slug.CreateNew().Value);
    }

    Browser.SetInput("Tagline", Constants.UI.TagLine);
    Browser.SetInput("Location", Constants.UI.Location);
    Browser.SetInput("TwitterSearch", Constants.UI.TwitterSearch);

    if (row.ContainsKey("Name")) Browser.SetInput("Name", row["Name"]);
    if (row.ContainsKey("Description"))
        Browser.SetInput("Description", row["Description"]);
    if (row.ContainsKey("Start")) Browser.SetInput("StartDate", row["Start"]);
    if (row.ContainsKey("End")) Browser.SetInput("EndDate", row["End"]);
}
```

You can see how this approach simulates clicking on, and entering text into, UI elements in the web browser.

The second approach is to implement the tests by interacting with the MVC controller classes. In the longer-term, this approach will be less fragile at the cost of an initially more complex implementation that requires some knowledge of the internal implementation of the system. The following code samples show an example of this approach.

First, an example scenario from the **SelfRegistrationEndToEndWithControllers.feature** file in the Features\UserInterface\Controllers\Registration project folder:

```
Scenario: End to end Registration implemented using controllers
    Given the Registrant proceeds to make the Reservation
    And these Order Items should be reserved
    | seat type               | quantity |
    | General admission       | 1        |
    | Additional cocktail party | 1      |
    And these Order Items should not be reserved
    | seat type     |
    | CQRS Workshop |
    And the Registrant enters these details
    | first name | last name | email address        |
    | William    | Flash     | william@fabrikam.com |
    And the Registrant proceeds to Checkout:Payment
    When the Registrant proceeds to confirm the payment
    Then the Order should be created with the following Order Items
    | seat type               | quantity |
    | General admission       | 1        |
    | Additional cocktail party | 1      |
    And the Registrant assigns these seats
    | seat type                 | first name | last name | email address        |
    | General admission         | William    | Flash     | William@fabrikam.com |
    | Additional cocktail party | Jim        | Corbin    | Jim@litwareinc.com   |
    And these seats are assigned
    | seat type               | quantity |
    | General admission       | 1        |
    | Additional cocktail party | 1      |
```

Second, some of the step implementations from the **SelfRegistrationEndToEndWithControllersSteps** class:

```
[Given(@"the Registrant proceeds to make the Reservation")]
public void GivenTheRegistrantProceedToMakeTheReservation()
{
    var redirect = registrationController.StartRegistration(
        registration,
        registrationController.ViewBag.OrderVersion) as RedirectToRouteResult;

    Assert.NotNull(redirect);

    // Perform external redirection
    var timeout = DateTime.Now.Add(Constants.UI.WaitTimeout);

    while (DateTime.Now < timeout && registrationViewModel == null)
```

```
        {
            //ReservationUnknown
            var result = registrationController.SpecifyRegistrantAndPaymentDetails(
                (Guid)redirect.RouteValues["orderId"],
                registrationController.ViewBag.OrderVersion);

            Assert.IsNotType<RedirectToRouteResult>(result);
            registrationViewModel =
                RegistrationHelper.GetModel<RegistrationViewModel>(result);
        }

        Assert.NotNull(
            registrationViewModel,
            "Could not make the reservation and get the RegistrationViewModel");
    }

...

    [When(@"the Registrant proceeds to confirm the payment")]
    public void WhenTheRegistrantProceedToConfirmThePayment()
    {
        using (var paymentController = RegistrationHelper.GetPaymentController())
        {
            paymentController.ThirdPartyProcessorPaymentAccepted(
                conferenceInfo.Slug, (Guid) routeValues["paymentId"], " ");
        }
    }
...

    [Then(@"the Order should be created with the following Order Items")]
    public void ThenTheOrderShouldBeCreatedWithTheFollowingOrderItems(Table table)
    {
        draftOrder =
            RegistrationHelper.GetModel<DraftOrder>(
                registrationController.ThankYou(registrationViewModel.Order.OrderId));
        Assert.NotNull(draftOrder);

        foreach (var row in table.Rows)
        {
            var orderItem = draftOrder
                                .Lines
                                .FirstOrDefault(l =>
                                    l.SeatType == conferenceInfo
                                        .Seats.First(s =>
                                            s.Description == row["seat type"]).Id);
```

```
        Assert.NotNull(orderItem);
        Assert.Equal(Int32.Parse(row["quantity"]), orderItem.ReservedSeats);
    }
}
```

You can see how this approach uses the **RegistrationController** MVC class directly.

> **Note:** *In these code samples, you can see how the values in the attributes link the step implementation to the statements in the related SpecFlow feature files.*

The team chose to implement these steps as *xUnit.net* tests. To run these tests within Visual Studio, you can use any of the test runners supported by xUnit.net such as ReSharper, CodeRush, or TestDriven.NET.

USING TESTS TO HELP DEVELOPERS UNDERSTAND MESSAGE FLOWS

A common comment about implementations that use the CQRS pattern or that use messaging extensively is the difficulty in understanding how all of the different pieces of the application fit together through sending and receiving commands and events. You can help someone to understand your code base through appropriately designed unit tests.

Consider this first example of a unit test for the **Order** aggregate:

> Remember that these acceptance tests are not the only tests performed on the system. The main solution includes comprehensive unit and integration tests, and the test team also performed exploratory and performance testing on the application.

```
public class given_placed_order
{
    ...

    private Order sut;

    public given_placed_order()
    {
        this.sut = new Order(
            OrderId, new[]
            {
                new OrderPlaced
                {
                    ConferenceId = ConferenceId,
                    Seats = new[] { new SeatQuantity(SeatTypeId, 5) },
                    ReservationAutoExpiration = DateTime.UtcNow
                }
            });
    }
```

```
[Fact]
public void when_updating_seats_then_updates_order_with_new_seats()
{
    this.sut.UpdateSeats(new[] { new OrderItem(SeatTypeId, 20) });

    var @event = (OrderUpdated)sut.Events.Single();
    Assert.Equal(OrderId, @event.SourceId);
    Assert.Equal(1, @event.Seats.Count());
    Assert.Equal(20, @event.Seats.ElementAt(0).Quantity);
}

...
}
```

This unit test creates an **Order** instance and directly invokes the **UpdateSeats** method. It does not provide any information to the person reading the test code about the command or event that causes this method to be invoked.

Now consider this second example that performs the same test, but in this case by sending a command:

```
public class given_placed_order
{
    ...

    private EventSourcingTestHelper<Order> sut;

    public given_placed_order()
    {
        this.sut = new EventSourcingTestHelper<Order>();
        this.sut.Setup(
            new OrderCommandHandler(sut.Repository, pricingService.Object));

        this.sut.Given(
            new OrderPlaced
            {
                SourceId = OrderId,
                ConferenceId = ConferenceId,
                Seats = new[] { new SeatQuantity(SeatTypeId, 5) },
                ReservationAutoExpiration = DateTime.UtcNow
            });
    }
```

```
    [Fact]
    public void when_updating_seats_then_updates_order_with_new_seats()
    {
        this.sut.When(
            new RegisterToConference
               {
                   ConferenceId = ConferenceId,
                   OrderId = OrderId,
                   Seats = new[] { new SeatQuantity(SeatTypeId, 20)
            }});

        var @event = sut.ThenHasSingle<OrderUpdated>();
        Assert.Equal(OrderId, @event.SourceId);
        Assert.Equal(1, @event.Seats.Count());
        Assert.Equal(20, @event.Seats.ElementAt(0).Quantity);
    }
    ...
}
```

This example uses a helper class that enables you to send a command to the **Order** instance. Now someone reading the test can see that when you send a **RegisterToConference** command, you expect to see an **OrderUpdated** event.

A journey into code comprehension: A tale of pain, relief, and learning

This section describes the journey taken by Josh Elster, a member of the CQRS Advisory Board, as he explored the source code of the Contoso Conference Management System.

Testing is important

I've once believed that well-factored applications are easy to comprehend, no matter how large or broad the codebase. Any time I had a problem understanding how some feature of an application behaved, the fault would lie with the code and not in me.

Never let your ego get in the way of common sense.

Truth was, up until a certain point in my career, I simply hadn't had exposure to a large, well-factored codebase. I wouldn't have known what one looked like if it walked up and hit me in the face. Thankfully, as I got more experienced reading code, I learned to recognize the difference.

> **Note:** *In any well-organized project, tests are a cornerstone of comprehension for developers seeking to understand the project. Topics ranging from naming conventions and coding styles to design approaches and usage patterns are baked into test suites, providing an excellent starting point for integrating into a codebase. It's also good practice in code literacy, and practice makes perfect!*

My first action after cloning the Conference code was to skim the tests. After a perusal of the integration and unit test suites in the Conference Visual Studio solution, I focused my attention on the Conference.AcceptanceTests Visual Studio solution that contains the *SpecFlow* acceptance tests. Other members of the project team had done some initial work on the .feature files, which worked out nicely for me since I wasn't familiar with the details of the business rules. Implementing step bindings for these features would be an excellent way to both contribute to the project and learn about how the system worked.

Domain tests

My goal then was to take a feature file looking something like this:

```
Feature: Self Registrant scenarios for making a Reservation for
a Conference site with all Order Items initially available
In order to reserve Seats for a conference
As an Attendee
I want to be able to select an Order Item from one or many of
the available Order Items and make a Reservation

Background:
Given the list of the available Order Items for the CQRS
Summit 2012 conference with the slug code SelfRegFull
| seat type                  | rate  | quota |
| General admission          | $199  | 100   |
| CQRS Workshop              | $500  | 100   |
| Additional cocktail party  | $50   | 100   |
And the selected Order Items
| seat type                  | quantity |
| General admission          | 1        |
| CQRS Workshop              | 1        |
| Additional cocktail party  | 1        |

Scenario: All the Order Items are available and all get reserved
When the Registrant proceeds to make the Reservation
Then the Reservation is confirmed for all the selected Order Items
And these Order Items should be reserved
| seat type                  |
| General admission          |
| CQRS Workshop              |
| Additional cocktail party  |
And the total should read $749
And the countdown started
```

And bind it to code that either performs an action, creates expectations, or makes assertions:

```
[Given(@"the '(.*)' site conference")]
public void GivenAConferenceNamed(string conference)
{
    ...
}
```

All at a level just below the UI, but above (and beyond) infrastructure concerns. Testing is tightly focused on the behavior of the overall solution domain, which is why I'll call these types of tests Domain Tests. Other terms such as behavior-driven development (BDD) can be used to describe this style of testing.

It may seem a little redundant to rewrite application logic already implemented on the website, but there are a number of reasons why it is worth the time:

- You aren't interested (for these purposes) in testing how the website or any other piece of infrastructure behaves; you're only interested in the domain. Unit and integration-level tests will validate the correct functioning of that code, so there's no need to duplicate those tests.
- When iterating stories with product owners, spending time on pure UI concerns can slow down the feedback cycle, reducing the quality and usefulness of feedback.
- Discussing a feature in more abstract terms can lead to a better understanding of the problem that the business is trying to solve, given the sometimes large mismatches between the vocabularies used by different people when they discuss technological issues.
- Obstacles encountered in implementing the testing logic can help improve the system's overall design quality. Difficulty in separating infrastructure code from application logic is generally regarded as a smell.

Note: *There are many more reasons not listed here why these types of tests are a good idea, but these are the important ones for this example.*

The architecture for the Contoso Conference Management System is loosely coupled, utilizing messages to transfer commands and events to interested parties. Commands are routed to a single handler via a command bus, while events are routed to their *0...N* handlers via an event bus. A bus isn't tied to any specific technology as far as consuming applications are concerned, allowing arbitrary implementations to be created and used throughout the system in a manner transparent to users.

> These "below the UI" tests are also known as *subcutaneous tests*, (see *Meszaros, G., Melnik, G., Acceptance Test Engineering Guide*).

Another bonus when it comes to behavioral testing of a loosely coupled message architecture is related to the fact that BDD (or similarly styled) tests do not involve themselves with the inner workings of application code. They only care about the observable *behavior* of the application under test. This means that for the SpecFlow tests, we need only concern ourselves with publishing some commands to the bus and examining the outward results by asserting expected message traffic and payloads against the actual traffic/data.

> **Note:** *It's OK to use mocks and stubs with these types of tests where appropriate. An appropriate example would be in using a mock **ICommandBus** object instead of the **AzureCommandBus** type. Mocking a complete domain service is an example where it is not appropriate. Use mocking minimally, limiting yourself to infrastructure concerns and you'll make your life—and your tests—a lot less stressful.*

The other side of the coin

With all of the pixels I just spent describing how awesome and easy things are, where's the pain? The pain is in comprehending what goes on in a system. The loose coupling of the architecture has a wicked flip side; techniques such as Inversion of Control and Dependency Injection hinder code readability by their very nature, since one can never be sure what concrete class is being injected at a particular point without examining the container's initialization closely. In the journey code, the **IProcess** interface marks classes representing long-running business processes (also known as sagas or process managers) responsible for coordinating business logic between different aggregates. In order to maintain the integrity, idempotency, and transactionality of the system's data and state, processes leave the actual publishing of their issued commands to the individual persistence repository's implementation. Since IoC and DI containers hide these types of details from consumers, it and other properties of the system create a bit of difficulty when it comes to answering seemingly trivial questions such as:

- Who issues or issued a particular command or event?
- What class handles a particular command or event?
- Where are processes or aggregates created or persisted?
- When is a command sent in relation to other commands or events?
- Why does the system behave the way it does?
- How does the application's state change as a result of a particular command?

Because the application's dependencies are so loose, many traditional tools and methods of code analysis become either less useful or completely useless.

Let's take an example of this and work out some heuristics involved in answering these questions. We'll use as an example the **RegistrationProcessManager**.

1. Open the RegistrationProcessManager.cs file, noting that, like many process managers it has a **ProcessState** enumeration. We take note of the beginning state for the process, **NotStarted**. Next, we want to find code that does one of the following:
   - A new instance of the process is created (where are processes created or persisted?)
   - The initial state is changed to a different state (how does state change?)

2. Locate the first place in the source code where either or both of the above occur. In this case, it's the **Handle** method in the **RegistrationProcessManagerRouter** class. **Important**: this does not necessarily mean that the process is a command handler! Process managers are responsible for creating and retrieving aggregate roots (AR) from storage for the purpose of routing messages to the AR, so while they have methods similar in name and signature to an **ICommandHandler** implementation, they do not implement a command's logic.
3. Take note of the message type that is received as a parameter to the method where the state change occurs, since we now need to figure out where that message originated.
   - We also note that a new command, **MakeSeatReservation**, is being issued by the **RegistrationProcessManager**.
   - As mentioned above, this command isn't actually published by the process issuing it; rather, publication occurs when the process is saved to disk.
   - These heuristics will need to be repeated to some degree or another on any commands issued as side-effects of a process handling a command.
4. Do a **find references** on the **OrderPlaced** symbol to locate the (or a) top-most (external facing) component that publishes a message of that type via the **Send** method on the **ICommandBus** interface.
   - Since internally issued commands are indirectly published (by a repository) on save, it may be safe to assume that any non-infrastructure logic that directly calls the **Send** method is an external point of entry.

While there is certainly more to these heuristics than noted here, what is there is likely sufficient to demonstrate the point that even discussing the interactions is a rather lengthy, cumbersome process. That makes it easily prone to misinterpretation. You can come to understand the various command/event messaging interactions in this manner, but it is not very efficient.

> **Note:** *As a rule, a person can really only maintain between four and eight distinct thoughts in their head at any given time. To illustrate this concept, let's take a conservative count of the number of simultaneous items you'll need to maintain in your short-term memory while following the above heuristics:*
> *Process type + Process state property + Initial State (NotStarted) + new() location + message type + intermediary routing class types + 2 *N^n Commands issued (location, type, steps) + discrimination rules (logic is data too!) > 8.*

When infrastructure requirements get mixed into the equation, the issue of information saturation becomes even more apparent. Being the competent, capable, developers that we all are (right?), we can start looking for ways to optimize these steps and improve the signal-to-noise ratio of relevant information.

To summarize, we have two problems:
- The number of items we are forced to keep in our heads is too great to allow efficient comprehension.
- Discussion and documentation for messaging interactions is verbose, error-prone, and complicated.

Fortunately, it is quite possible to kill two birds with a single stone, with MIL (messaging intermediate language).

MIL began as a series of LINQPad scripts and snippets that I created to help juggle all these facts while answering questions. Initially, all that these scripts accomplished was to reflect through one or more project assemblies and output the various types of messages and handlers. In discussions with members of the team it became apparent that others were experiencing the same types of problems I had. After a few chats and brainstorming sessions with members of the patterns & practices team, we came up with the idea of introducing a small *domain-specific language* (DSL) that would encapsulate the interactions being discussed. The tentatively named SawMIL toolbox, located at *http://jelster. github.com/CqrsMessagingTools/* provides utilities, scripts, and examples that enable you to use MIL as part of your development and analysis process managers.

In MIL, messaging components and interactions are represented in a specific manner: commands, since they are requests for the system to perform some action, are denoted by ?, as in DoSomething?. Events represent something definite that happened in the system, and hence gain a ! suffix, as in SomethingHappened!.

Another important element of MIL is message publication and reception. Messages received from a messaging source (such as Windows Azure Service Bus, nServiceBus, and so forth) are always preceded by the -> symbol, while messages that are being sent have the symbol following it. To keep the examples simple for now, the optional nil element, (a period, .) is used to indicate explicitly a no-op (in other words, nothing is receiving the message). The following snippet shows an example of the nil element syntax:

```
SendCustomerInvoice? -> .
CustomerInvoiceSent! -> .
```

Once a command or event has been published, something needs to do something with it. Commands have one and only one handler, while events can have multiple handlers. MIL represents this relationship between message and handler by placing the name of the handler on the other side of the messaging operation, as shown in the following snippet:

```
SendCustomerInvoice? -> CustomerInvoiceHandler
CustomerInvoiceSent! ->
    -> CustomerNotificationHandler
    -> AccountsAgeingViewModelGenerator
```

Notice how the command handler is on the same line as the command, while the event is separated from its handlers? That's because in CQRS, there is a 1:1 correlation between commands and command handlers. Putting them together helps reinforce that concept, while keeping events separate from event handlers helps reinforce the idea that a given event can have 0...*N* handlers.

Aggregate Roots are prefixed with the @ sign, a convention that should be familiar to anyone who has ever used twitter. Aggregate roots never handle commands, but occasionally may handle events. Aggregate roots are most frequently event sources, raising events in response to business operations invoked on the aggregate. Something that should be made clear about these events, however, is that in most systems there are other elements that decide upon and actually perform the publication of domain events. This is an interesting case where business and technical requirements blur boundaries, with the requirements being met by infrastructure logic rather than application or business logic. An example of this lies in the journey code: in order to ensure consistency between event sources and event subscribers, the implementation of the repository that persists the aggregate root is the element responsible for actually publishing the events to a bus. The following snippet shows an example of the **AggregateRoot** syntax:

```
SendCustomerInvoice? -> CustomerInvoiceHandler
@Invoice::CustomerInvoiceSent! -> .
```

In the above example, a new language element called the scope context operator appears alongside the @AggregateRoot. Denoted by double colons (::) the scope context element may or may not have whitespace between its two characters, and is used to identify relationships between two objects. Above, the AR '@Invoice' is generating the **CustomerSent!** event in response to logic invoked by the **CustomerInvoiceHandler** event handler. The next example demonstrates use of the scope element on an AR, which generates multiple events in response to a single command:

```
SendCustomerInvoice? -> CustomerInvoiceHandler
@Invoice:
    :CustomerInvoiceSent! -> .
    :InvoiceAged! -> .
```

Scope context is also used to signify intra-element routing that does not involve infrastructure messaging apparatus:

```
SendCustomerInvoice? -> CustomerInvoiceHandler
@Invoice::CustomerInvoiceSent! ->
    -> InvoiceAgeingProcessRouter::InvoiceAgeingProcess
```

The last element that I'll introduce is the **State Change** element. State changes are one of the best ways to track what is happening within a system, and thus MIL treats them as first-class citizens. These statements must appear on their own line of text, and are prefixed with the '*' character. It's the only time in MIL that there is any mention or appearance of assignment because it's just that important! The following snippet shows an example of the **State Change** element:

```
SendCustomerInvoice? -> CustomerInvoiceHandler
@Invoice::CustomerInvoiceSent! ->
    -> InvoiceAgeingProcessRouter::InvoiceAgeingProcess
        *InvoiceAgeingProcess.ProcessState = Unpaid
```

Summary

We've just walked through the basic steps used when describing messaging interactions in a loosely coupled application. Although the interactions described are only a subset of possible interactions, MIL is evolving into a way to compactly describe the interactions of a message-based system. Different nouns and verbs (elements and actions) are represented by distinct, mnemonically significant symbols. This provides a cross-substrate (squishy human brains < - > silicon CPU) means of communicating meaningful information about systems as a whole. Although the language describes some types of messaging interactions very well, it is very much a work in progress with many elements of the language and tooling in need of development or improvement. This presents some great opportunities for people looking to contribute to OSS, so if you've been on the fence about contributing or are wondering about OSS participation, there's no time like the present to head over to *http://jelster.github.com/CqrsMessagingTools/*, fork the repos, and get started!

More information

All links in this book are accessible from the book's online bibliography available at: *http://msdn.microsoft.com/en-us/library/jj619274*.

Journey 5:

Preparing for the V1 Release

Adding functionality and refactoring in preparation for the V1 release.

"Most people, after accomplishing something, use it over and over again like a gramophone record till it cracks, forgetting that the past is just the stuff with which to make more future."
Freya Stark

The Contoso Conference Management System V1 release

This chapter describes the changes made by the team to prepare for the first production release of the Contoso Conference Management System. This work includes some refactoring and additions to the Orders and Registrations bounded context that the previous two chapters introduced, as well as a new Conference Management bounded context and a new Payments bounded context.

One of the key refactorings undertaken by the team during this phase of the journey was to introduce event sourcing into the Orders and Registrations bounded context.

One of the anticipated benefits from implementing the CQRS pattern is that it will help us manage change in a complex system. Having a V1 release during the CQRS journey will help the team evaluate how the CQRS pattern and event sourcing deliver these benefits when we move forward from the V1 release to the next production release of the system. The remaining chapters will describe what happens after the V1 release.

This chapter describes the user interface (UI) that the team added to the public website during this phase and includes a discussion of task-based UIs.

Working definitions for this chapter

This chapter uses a number of terms that we will define next. For more detail, and possible alternative definitions, see Chapter 4, "A CQRS and ES Deep Dive" in the Reference Guide.

Access code. When a business customer creates a new conference, the system generates a five-character *access code* and sends it by email to the business customer. The business customer can use his email address and the access code on the conference management website to retrieve the conference details from the system at a later date. The system uses access codes instead of passwords so that the business customer need not set up an account just to make a purchase.

Event sourcing. *Event sourcing* is a way of persisting and reloading the state of aggregates within the system. Whenever the state of an aggregate changes, the aggregate raises an event detailing the state change. The system then saves this event in an event store. The system can recreate the state of an aggregate by replaying all of the previously saved events associated with that aggregate instance. The event store becomes the book of record for the data stored by the system.

In addition, you can use event sourcing as a source of audit data, as a way to query historic state, gain new business insights from past data, and replay events for debugging and problem analysis.

Eventual consistency. *Eventual consistency* is a consistency model that does not guarantee immediate access to updated values. After an update to a data object, the storage system does not guarantee that subsequent accesses to that object will return the updated value. However, the storage system does guarantee that if no new updates are made to the object during a sufficiently long period of time, then eventually all accesses can be expected to return the last updated value.

User stories

The team implemented the user stories described below during this stage of the journey.

Ubiquitous language definitions

Business customer. The *business customer* represents the organization that is using the conference management system to run its conference.

Seat. A *seat* represents a space at a conference or access to a specific session at the conference such as a welcome reception, tutorial, or workshop.

Registrant. A *registrant* is a person who interacts with the system to place orders and make payments for those orders. A registrant also creates the registrations associated with an order.

Conference Management bounded context user stories

A business customer can create new conferences and manage them. After a business customer creates a new conference, he can access the details of the conference by using his email address and conference locator access code. The system generates the access code when the business customer creates the conference.

The business customer can specify the following information about a conference:
- The name, description, and slug (part of the URL used to access the conference).
- The start and end dates of the conference.
- The different types and quotas of seats available at the conference.

Additionally, the business customer can control the visibility of the conference on the public website by either publishing or unpublishing the conference.

The business customer can use the conference management website to view a list of orders and attendees.

Ordering and Registration bounded context user stories

When a registrant creates an order, it may not be possible to fulfill the order completely. For example, a registrant may request five seats for the full conference, five seats for the welcome reception, and three seats for the preconference workshop. There may only be three seats available for the full conference and one seat for the welcome reception, but more than three seats available for the preconference workshop. The system displays this information to the registrant and gives her the opportunity to adjust the number of each type of seat in the order before continuing to the payment process.

After a registrant has selected the quantity of each seat type, the system calculates the total price for the order, and the registrant can then pay for those seats using an online payment service. Contoso does not handle payments on behalf of its customers; each business customer must have a mechanism for accepting payments through an online payment service. In a later stage of the project, Contoso will add support for business customers to integrate their invoicing systems with the conference management system. At some future time, Contoso may offer a service to collect payments on behalf of customers.

Preparing for the V1 Release

Note: *In this version of the system, the actual payment is simulated.*

After a registrant has purchased seats at a conference, she can assign attendees to those seats. The system stores the name and contact details for each attendee.

Architecture

Figure 1 illustrates the key architectural elements of the Contoso Conference Management System in the V1 release. The application consists of two websites and three bounded contexts. The infrastructure includes Windows Azure SQL Database (SQL Database) instances, an event store, and messaging infrastructure.

The table that follows Figure 1 lists all of the messages that the artifacts (aggregates, MVC controllers, read-model generators, and data access objects) shown in the diagram exchange with each other.

Note: *For reasons of clarity, the handlers (such as the **OrderCommandHandler** class) that deliver the messages to the domain objects are not shown.*

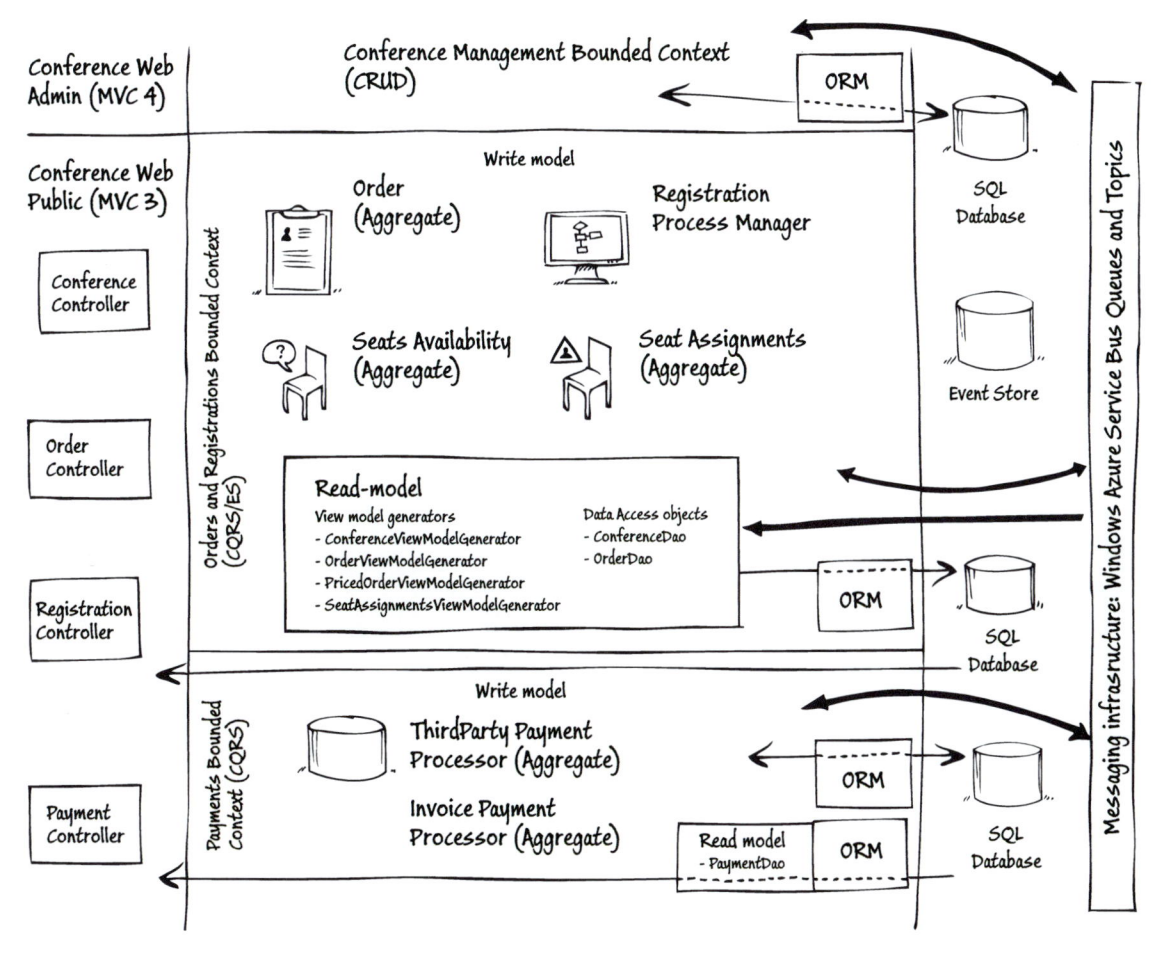

Figure 1
Architecture of the V1 release

Element	Type	Sends	Receives
ConferenceController	MVC Controller	N/A	ConferenceDetails
OrderController	MVC Controller	AssignSeat UnassignSeat	DraftOrder OrderSeats PricedOrder
RegistrationController	MVC Controller	RegisterToConference AssignRegistrantDetails InitiateThirdParty- ProcessorPayment	DraftOrder PricedOrder SeatType

PaymentController	MVC Controller	CompleteThirdParty-
		  ProcessorPayment
		CancelThirdParty-
		  ProcessorPayment
			ThirdPartyProcessor-
			  PaymentDetails

Conference Management	CRUD Bounded Context	ConferenceCreated ConferenceUpdated ConferencePublished ConferenceUnpublished SeatCreated SeatUpdated	OrderPlaced OrderRegistrantAssigned OrderTotalsCalculated OrderPaymentConfirmed SeatAssigned SeatAssignmentUpdated SeatUnassigned
Order	Aggregate	OrderPlaced *OrderExpired *OrderUpdated *OrderPartiallyReserved *OrderReservation- Completed *OrderPaymentConfirmed *OrderRegistrantAssigned	RegisterToConference MarkSeatsAsReserved RejectOrder AssignRegistrantDetails ConfirmOrderPayment
SeatsAvailability	Aggregate	SeatsReserved *AvailableSeatsChanged *SeatsReservation- Committed *SeatsReservationCancelled	MakeSeatReservation CancelSeatReservation CommitSeatReservation AddSeats RemoveSeats
SeatAssignments	Aggregate	*SeatAssignmentsCreated *SeatAssigned *SeatUnassigned *SeatAssignmentUpdated	AssignSeat UnassignSeat

Element	Type	Sends	Receives
RegistrationProcessManager	Process manager	MakeSeatReservation ExpireRegistrationProcess MarkSeatsAsReserved CancelSeatReservation RejectOrder CommitSeatReservation ConfirmOrderPayment	OrderPlaced PaymentCompleted SeatsReserved ExpireRegistrationProcess
RegistrationProcessManager	Process manager	MakeSeatReservation ExpireRegistrationProcess MarkSeatsAsReserved CancelSeatReservation RejectOrder CommitSeatReservation ConfirmOrderPayment	OrderPlaced PaymentCompleted SeatsReserved ExpireRegistrationProcess
OrderViewModelGenerator	Handler	DraftOrder	OrderPlaced OrderUpdated OrderPartiallyReserved OrderReservationCompleted OrderRegistrantAssigned
PricedOrderViewModelGenerator	Handler	N/A	SeatTypeName
ConferenceViewModelGenerator	Handler	Conference AddSeats RemoveSeats	ConferenceCreated ConferenceUpdated ConferencePublished ConferenceUnpublished **SeatCreated **SeatUpdated
ThirdPartyProcessorPayment	Aggregate	PaymentCompleted PaymentRejected PaymentInitiated	InitiateThirdParty- ProcessorPayment CompleteThirdParty- ProcessorPayment CancelThirdParty- ProcessorPayment

* These events are only used for persisting aggregate state using event sourcing.

** The **ConferenceViewModelGenerator** creates these commands from the **SeatCreated** and **SeatUpdated** events that it handles from the Conference Management bounded context.

The following list outlines the message naming conventions in the Contoso Conference Management System

- All events use the past tense in the naming convention.
- All commands use the imperative naming convention.
- All DTOs are nouns.

The application is designed to deploy to Windows Azure. At this stage in the journey, the application consists of two web roles that contain the ASP.NET MVC web applications and a worker role that contains the message handlers and domain objects. The application uses SQL Database instances for data storage, both on the write side and the read side. The Orders and Registrations bounded context now uses an event store to persist the state from the write side. This event store is implemented using Windows Azure table storage to store the events. The application uses the Windows Azure Service Bus to provide its messaging infrastructure.

While you are exploring and testing the solution, you can run it locally, either using the Windows Azure compute emulator or by running the ASP.NET MVC web application directly and running a console application that hosts the handlers and domain objects. When you run the application locally, you can use a local SQL Server Express database instead of SQL Database, use a simple messaging infrastructure implemented in a SQL Server Express database, and a simple event store also implemented using a SQL Server Express database.

> **Note:** *The SQL-based implementations of the event store and the messaging infrastructure are only intended to help you run the application locally for exploration and testing. They are not intended to illustrate a production-ready approach.*

For more information about the options for running the application, see Appendix 1, "Release Notes."

Conference Management bounded context

The Conference Management bounded context is a simple two-tier, create/read/update (CRUD)-style web application. It is implemented using ASP.NET MVC 4 and Entity Framework.

This bounded context must integrate with other bounded contexts that implement the CQRS pattern.

Patterns and concepts

This section describes some of the key areas of the application that the team visited during this stage of the journey and introduces some of the challenges met by the team when we addressed these areas.

EVENT SOURCING

The team at Contoso originally implemented the Orders and Registrations bounded context without using event sourcing. However, during the implementation it became clear that using event sourcing would help to simplify this bounded context.

In Chapter 4, "Extending and Enhancing the Orders and Registrations Bounded Contexts," the team found that we needed to use events to push changes from the write side to the read side. On the read side, the OrderViewModelGenerator class subscribed to the events published by the Order aggregate, and used those events to update the views in the database that were queried by the read model.

This was already half way to an event-sourcing implementation, so it made sense to use a single persistence mechanism based on events for the whole bounded context.

The event sourcing infrastructure is reusable in other bounded contexts, and the implementation of the Orders and Registrations becomes simpler.

The team implemented the basic event store using Windows Azure table storage. If you are hosting your application in Windows Azure, you could also consider using Windows Azure blobs or SQL Database to store your events.

> The team implemented this bounded context after it implemented the public conference management website that uses ASP.NET MVC 3. In a later stage of the journey, as part of the V3 release, the conference management site will be upgraded to ASP.NET MVC 4.

Evolution is key here; for example, one could show how implementing event sourcing allows you to get rid of those tedious data migrations, and even allows you to build reports from the past.
—Tom Janssens - CQRS Advisors Mail List

> As a practical problem, the team had limited time before the V1 release to implement a production-quality event store. They created a simple, basic event store based on Windows Azure tables as an interim solution. However, they will potentially face the problem in the future of migrating from one event store to another.

> When choosing the underlying technology for your event store, you should ensure that your choice can deliver the level of availability, consistency, reliability, scale, and performance your application requires.

> One of the issues to consider when choosing between storage mechanisms in Windows Azure is cost. If you use SQL Database you are billed based on the size of the database, if you use Windows Azure table or blob storage you are billed based on the amount of storage you use and the number of storage transactions. You need to carefully evaluate the usage patterns on the different aggregates in your system to determine which storage mechanism is the most cost effective. It may turn out that different storage mechanisms make sense for different aggregate types. You may be able to introduce optimizations that lower your costs, for example by using caching to reduce the number of storage transactions.

Identifying aggregates

In the Windows Azure table storage-based implementation of the event store that the team created for the V1 release, we used the aggregate ID as the partition key. This makes it efficient to locate the partition that holds the events for any particular aggregate.

In some cases, the system must locate related aggregates. For example, an order aggregate may have a related registrations aggregate that holds details of the attendees assigned to specific seats. In this scenario, the team decided to reuse the same aggregate ID for the related pair of aggregates (the **Order** and **Registration** aggregates) in order to facilitate look-ups.

My rule of thumb is that if you're doing green-field development, you need very good arguments in order to choose a SQL Database. Windows Azure Storage Services should be the default choice. However, if you already have an existing SQL Server database that you want to move to the cloud, it's a different case.
—Mark Seemann - CQRS Advisors Mail List

> You want to consider in this case whether you should have two aggregates. You could model the registrations as an entity inside the **Order** aggregate.

A more common scenario is to have a one-to-many relationship between aggregates instead of a one-to-one. In this case, it is not possible to share aggregate IDs; instead, the aggregate on the "one side" can store a list of the IDs of the aggregates on the "many side," and each aggregate on the "many side" can store the ID of the aggregate on the "one side."

Task-based UI

The design of UIs has improved greatly over the last decade. Applications are easier to use, more intuitive, and simpler to navigate than they were before. Some examples of UI design guidelines that can help you create such modern, user-friendly apps are the *Microsoft Inductive User Interface Guidelines* and the *Index of UX guidelines*.

An important factor that affects the design and usability of the UI is how the UI communicates with the rest of the application. If the application is based on a CRUD-style architecture, this can leak through to the UI. If the developers focus on CRUD-style operations, this can result in a UI that looks like the one shown in the first screen design in Figure 2 (on the left).

Sharing aggregate IDs is common when the aggregates exist in different bounded contexts. If you have aggregates in different bounded contexts that model different facets of the same real-world entity, it makes sense for them to share the same ID. This makes it easier to follow a real-world entity as different bounded contexts in your system process it.
—Greg Young - Conversation with the patterns & practices team

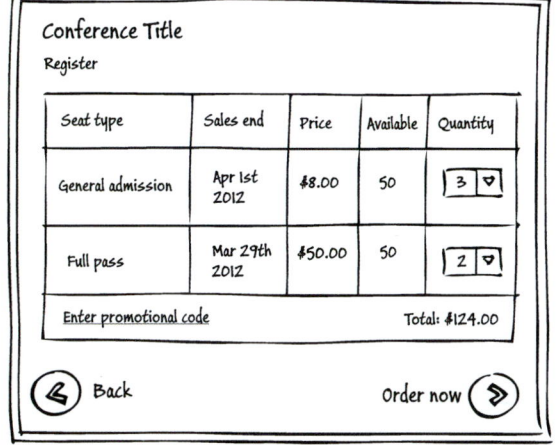

FIGURE 2
Example UIs for conference registration

On the first screen, the labels on the buttons reflect the underlying CRUD operations that the system will perform when the user clicks the **Submit** button, rather than displaying more user-focused action words. Unfortunately, the first screen also requires the user to apply some deductive knowledge about how the screen and the application function. For example, the function of the **Add** button is not immediately apparent.

A typical implementation behind the first screen will use a data transfer object (DTO) to exchange data between the back end and the UI. The UI will request data from the back end that will arrive encapsulated in a DTO, it will modify the data in the DTO, and then return the DTO to the back end. The back end will use the DTO to figure out what CRUD operations it must perform on the underlying data store.

The second screen is more explicit about what is happening in terms of the business process: the user is selecting quantities of seat types as a part of the conference registration task. Thinking about the UI in terms of the task that the user is performing makes it easier to relate the UI to the write model in your implementation of the CQRS pattern. The UI can send commands to the write side, and those commands are a part of the domain model on the write side. In a bounded context that implements the CQRS pattern, the UI typically queries the read side and receives a DTO, and sends commands to the write side.

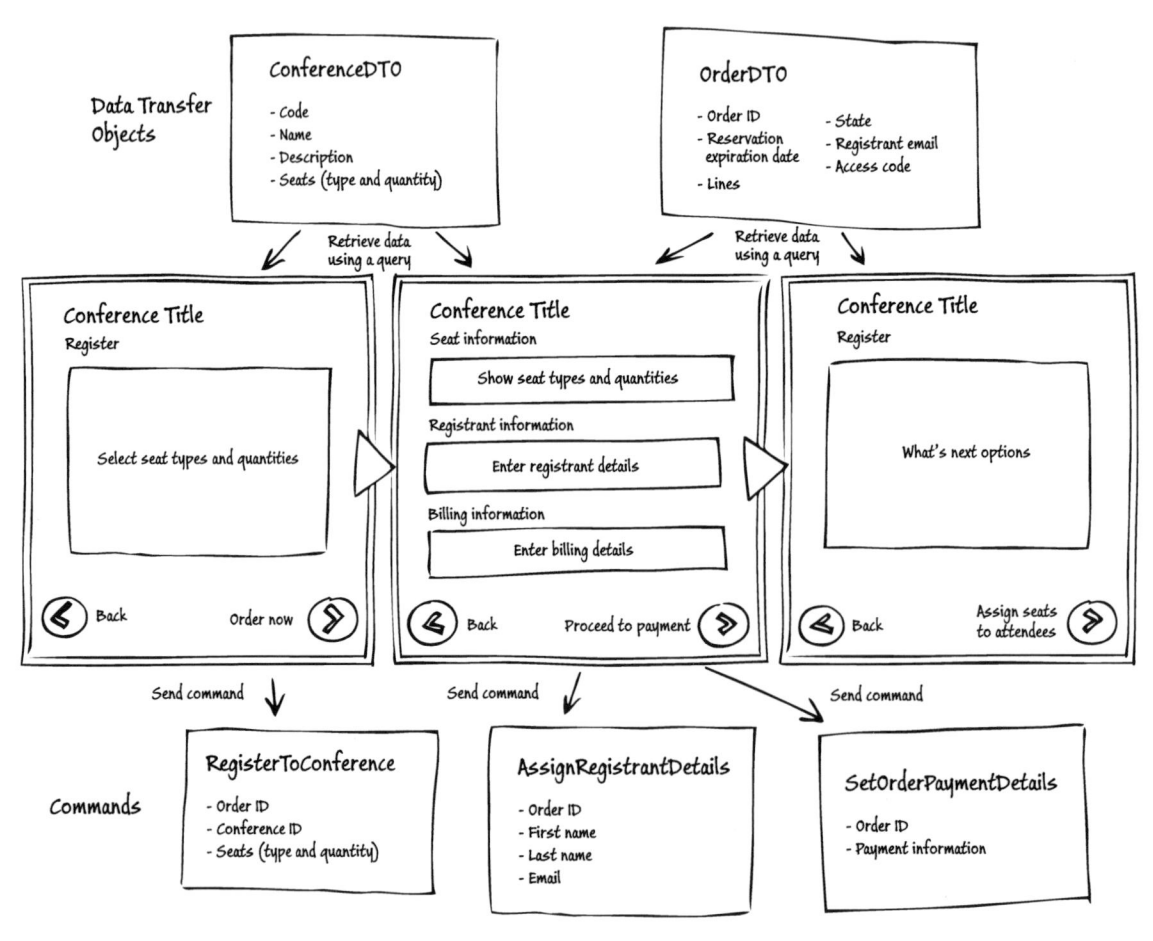

FIGURE 3
Task-based UI flow

Figure 3 shows a sequence of pages that enable the registrant to complete the "purchase seats at a conference" task. On the first page, the registrant selects the type and quantity of seats. On the second page, the registrant can review the seats she has reserved, enter her contact details, and complete the necessary payment information. The system then redirects the registrant to a payment provider, and if the payment completes successfully, the system displays the third page. The third page shows a summary of the order and provides a link to pages where the registrant can start additional tasks.

The sequence shown in Figure 3 is deliberately simplified in order to highlight the roles of the commands and queries in a task-based UI. For example, the real flow includes pages that the system will display based on the payment type selected by the registrant, and error pages that the system displays if the payment fails.

For more information, see Chapter 4, "A CQRS and ES Deep Dive" in the Reference Guide.

CRUD

You should not use the CQRS pattern as part of your top-level architecture; you should implement the pattern only in those bounded contexts where it brings clear benefits. In the Contoso Conference Management System, the Conference Management bounded context is a relatively simple, stable, and low-volume part of the overall system. Therefore, the team decided that we would implement this bounded context using a traditional two-tier, CRUD-style architecture.

For a discussion about when CRUD-style architecture is, or is not, appropriate see the blog post, *Why CRUD might be what they want, but may not be what they need*.

INTEGRATION BETWEEN BOUNDED CONTEXTS

The Conference Management bounded context needs to integrate with the Orders and Registrations bounded context. For example, if the business customer changes the quota for a seat type in the Conference Management bounded context, this change must be propagated to the Orders and Registrations bounded context. Also, if a registrant adds a new attendee to a conference, the Business Customer must be able to view details of the attendee in the list in the conference management website.

> You don't always need to use task-based UIs. In some scenarios, simple CRUD-style UIs work well. You must evaluate whether the benefits of task-based UIs outweigh the additional implementation effort required. Very often, the bounded contexts where you choose to implement the CQRS pattern are also the bounded contexts that benefit from task-based UIs because of the more complex business logic and more complex user interactions.

I would like to state once and for all that CQRS does not require a task-based UI. We could apply CQRS to a CRUD based interface (though things like creating separated data models would be much harder).
There is, however, one thing that does really require a task based UI. That is domain-driven design.
—Greg Young, CQRS, Task Based UIs, Event Sourcing agh!.

Pushing changes from the Conference Management bounded context

The following conversation between several developers and the domain expert highlights some of the key issues that the team needed to address in planning how to implement this integration.

Developer 1: I want to talk about how we should implement two pieces of the integration story associated with our CRUD-style, Conference Management bounded context. First of all, when a business customer creates a new conference or defines new seat types for an existing conference in this bounded context, other bounded contexts such as the Orders and Registrations bounded context will need to know about the change. Secondly, when a business customer changes the quota for a seat type, other bounded contexts will need to know about this change as well.

Developer 2: So in both cases you are pushing changes from the Conference Management bounded context. It's one way.

Developer 1: Correct.

Developer 2: What are the significant differences between the scenarios you outlined?

Developer 1: In the first scenario, these changes are relatively infrequent and typically happen when the business customer creates the conference. Also, these are append-only changes. We don't allow a business customer to delete a conference or a seat type after the conference has been published for the first time. In the second scenario, the changes might be more frequent and a business customer might increase or decrease a seat quota.

Developer 2: What implementation approaches are you considering for these integration scenarios?

Developer 1: Because we have a two-tier CRUD-style bounded context, for the first scenario I was planning to expose the conference and seat-type information directly from the database as a simple read-only service. For the second scenario, I was planning to publish events whenever the business customer updates the seat quotas.

Developer 2: Why use two different approaches here? It would be simpler to use a single approach. Using events is more flexible in the long run. If additional bounded contexts need this information, they can easily subscribe to the event. Using events provides for less coupling between the bounded contexts.

Developer 1: I can see that it would be easier to adapt to changing requirements in the future if we used events. For example, if a new bounded context required information about who changed the quota, we could add this information to the event. For existing bounded contexts, we could add an adapter that converted the new event format to the old.

Developer 2: You implied that the events that notify subscribers of quota changes would send the change that was made to the quota. For example, let's say the business customer increased a seat quota by 50. What happens if a subscriber wasn't there at the beginning and therefore doesn't receive the full history of updates?

> **Developer 1:** We may have to include some synchronization mechanism that uses snapshots of the current state. However, in this case the event could simply report the new value of the quota. If necessary, the event could report both the delta and the absolute value of the seat quota.
>
> **Developer 2**: How are you going to ensure consistency? You need to guarantee that your bounded context persists its data to storage and publishes the events on a message queue.
>
> **Developer 1**: We can wrap the database write and add-to-queue operations in a transaction.
>
> **Developer 2**: There are two reasons that's going to be problematic later when the size of the network increases, response times get longer, and the probability of failure increases. First, our infrastructure uses the Windows Azure Service Bus for messages. You can't use a single transaction to combine the sending of a message on the Service Bus and a write to a database. Second, we're trying to avoid two-phase commits because they always cause problems in the long run.
>
> **Domain Expert**: We have a similar scenario with another bounded context that we'll be looking at later. In this case, we can't make any changes to the bounded context; we no longer have an up-to-date copy of the source code.
>
> **Developer 1**: What can we do to avoid using a two-phase commit? And what can we do if we don't have access to the source code and thus can't make any changes?
>
> **Developer 2**: In both cases, we use the same technique to solve the problem. Instead of publishing the events from within the application code, we can use another process that monitors the database and sends the events when it detects a change in the database. This solution may introduce a small amount of latency, but it does avoid the need for a two-phase commit and you can implement it without making any changes to the application code.

Another issue concerns when and where to persist integration events. In the example discussed above, the Conference Management bounded context publishes the events and the Orders and Registrations bounded context handles them and uses them to populate its read model. If a failure occurs that causes the system to lose the read-model data, then without saving the events there is no way to recreate that read-model data.

Whether you need to persist these integration events will depend on the specific requirements and implementation of your application. For example:

- The write side may handle the integration instead of the read side, as in the current example. The events will then result in changes on the write side that are persisted as other events.
- Integration events may represent transient data that does not need to be persisted.
- Integration events from a CRUD-style bounded context may contain state data so that only the last event is needed. For example if the event from the Conference Management bounded context includes the current seat quota, you may not be interested in previous values.

Another approach to consider is to use an event store that many bounded contexts share. In this way, the originating bounded context (for example the CRUD-style Conference Management bounded context) could be responsible for persisting the integration events.
—Greg Young - Conversation with the patterns & practices team.

Some comments on Windows Azure Service Bus

The previous discussion suggested a way to avoid using a distributed two-phase commit in the Conference Management bounded context. However, there are alternative approaches.

Although the Windows Azure Service Bus does not support distributed transactions that combine an operation on the bus with an operation on a database, you can use the **RequiresDuplicateDetection** property when you send messages, and the **PeekLock** mode when you receive messages to create the desired level of robustness without using a distributed transaction.

As an alternative, you can use a distributed transaction to update the database and send a message using a local Microsoft message queuing (MSMQ) queue. You can then use a bridge to connect the MSMQ queue to a Windows Azure Service Bus queue.

For an example of implementing a bridge from MSMQ to Windows Azure Service Bus, see the sample in the *Windows Azure AppFabric SDK*.

For more information about the Windows Azure Service Bus, see Chapter 7, "Technologies Used in the Reference Implementation" in the Reference Guide.

Pushing changes to the Conference Management bounded context

Pushing information about completed orders and registrations from the Orders and Registrations bounded context to the Conference Management bounded context raised a different set of issues.

The Orders and Registrations bounded context typically raises many of the following events during the creation of an order: **OrderPlaced**, **OrderRegistrantAssigned**, **OrderTotalsCalculated**, **OrderPaymentConfirmed**, **SeatAssignmentsCreated**, **SeatAssignmentUpdated**, **SeatAssigned**, and **SeatUnassigned**. The bounded context uses these events to communicate between aggregates and for event sourcing.

For the Conference Management bounded context to capture the information it requires to display details about registrations and attendees, it must handle all of these events. It can use the information that these events contain to create a denormalized SQL table of the data, which the business customer can then view in the UI.

The issue with this approach is that the Conference Management bounded context needs to understand a complex set of events from another bounded context. It is a brittle solution because a change in the Orders and Registrations bounded context may break this feature in the Conference Management bounded context.

Contoso plans to keep this solution for the V1 release of the system, but will evaluate alternatives during the next stage of the journey. These alternative approaches will include:

- Modifying the Orders and Registrations bounded context to generate more useful events designed explicitly for integration.
- Generating the denormalized data in the Orders and Registrations bounded context and notifying the Conference Management bounded context when the data is ready. The Conference Management bounded context can then request the information through a service call.

> **Note:** *To see how the current approach works, look at the **OrderEventHandler** class in the **Conference** project.*

Choosing when to update the read-side data

In the Conference Management bounded context, the business customer can change the description of a seat type. This results in a **SeatUpdated** event that the **ConferenceViewModelGenerator** class in the Orders and Registrations bounded context handles; this class updates the read-model data to reflect the new information about the seat type. The UI displays the new seat description when a registrant is making an order.

However, if a registrant views a previously created order (for example to assign attendees to seats), the registrant sees the original seat description.

DISTRIBUTED TRANSACTIONS AND EVENT SOURCING

The previous section that discussed the integration options for the Conference Management bounded context raised the issue of using a distributed, two-phase commit transaction to ensure consistency between the database that stores the conference management data and the messaging infrastructure that publishes changes to other bounded contexts.

The same problem arises when you implement event sourcing: you must ensure consistency between the event store in the bounded context that stores all the events and the messaging infrastructure that publishes those events to other bounded contexts.

A key feature of an event store implementation should be that it offers a way to guarantee consistency between the events that it stores and the events that the bounded context publishes to other bounded contexts.

AUTONOMY VERSUS AUTHORITY

The Orders and Registrations bounded context is responsible for creating and managing orders on behalf of registrants. The **Payments** bounded context is responsible for managing the interaction with an external payments system so that registrants can pay for the seats that they have ordered.

When the team was examining the domain models for these two bounded contexts, it discovered that neither context knew anything about pricing. The Orders and Registrations bounded context created an order that listed the quantities of the different seat types that the registrant requested. The Payments bounded context simply passed a total to the external payments system. At some point, the system needed to calculate the total from the order before invoking the payment process.

> This is a deliberate business decision; we don't want to confuse registrants by changing the seat description after they create an order.

> If we did want to update the seat description on existing orders, we would need to modify the *PricedOrderViewModelGenerator* class to handle the *SeatUpdated* event and adjust its view model.

> This is a key challenge you should address if you decide to implement an event store yourself. If you are designing a scalable event store that you plan to deploy in a distributed environment such as Windows Azure, you must be very careful to ensure that you meet this requirement.

The team considered two different approaches to solve this problem: favoring autonomy and favoring authority.

Favoring autonomy

The autonomous approach assigns the responsibility for calculating the order total to the Orders and Registrations bounded context. The Orders and Registrations bounded context is not dependent on another bounded context when it needs to perform the calculation because it already has the necessary data. At some point in the past, it will have collected the pricing information it needs from other bounded contexts (such as the Conference Management bounded context) and cached it.

The advantage of this approach is that the Orders and Registrations bounded context is autonomous. It doesn't rely on the availability of another bounded context or service.

The disadvantage is that the pricing information could be out of date. The business customer might have changed the pricing information in the Conference Management bounded context, but that change might not yet have reached the Orders and Registrations bounded context.

Favoring authority

In this approach, the part of the system that calculates the order total obtains the pricing information from the bounded contexts (such as the Conference Management bounded context) at the point in time that it performs the calculation. The Orders and Registrations bounded context could still perform the calculation, or it could delegate the calculation to another bounded context or service within the system.

The advantage of this approach is that the system always uses the latest pricing information whenever it is calculating an order total.

The disadvantage is that the Orders and Registrations bounded context is dependent on another bounded context when it needs to determine the total for the order. It either needs to query the Conference Management bounded context for the up-to-date pricing information, or call another service that performs the calculation.

Choosing between autonomy and authority

The choice between the two alternatives is a business decision. The specific business requirements of your scenario should determine which approach to take. Autonomy is often the preference for large, online systems.

> This choice may change depending on the state of your system. Consider an overbooking scenario. The autonomy strategy may optimize for the normal case when lots of conference seats are still available, but as a particular conference fills up, the system may need to become more conservative and favor authority, using the latest information on seat availability.

The way that the conference management system calculates the total for an order represents an example of choosing autonomy over authority.

The section "Calculating totals" below describes how the system performs this calculation.

Approaches to implementing the read side

In the discussions of the read side in the previous chapters, you saw how the team used a SQL-based store for the denormalized projections of the data from the write side.

You can use other storage mechanisms for the read-model data; for example, you can use the file system or Windows Azure table or blob storage. In the Orders and Registrations bounded context, the system uses Windows Azure blobs to store information about the seat assignments.

> **Note:** *See the **SeatAssignmentsViewModelGenerator** class to understand how the data is persisted to blob storage and the **SeatAssignmentsDao** class to understand how the UI retrieves the data for display.*

Eventual consistency

During testing, the team discovered a scenario in which the registrant might see evidence of eventual consistency in action. If the registrant assigns attendees to seats on an order and then quickly navigates to view the assignments, then sometimes this view shows only some of the updates. However, refreshing the page displays the correct information. This happens because it takes time for the events that record the seat assignments to propagate to the read model, and sometimes the tester viewed the information queried from the read model too soon.

> For Contoso, the clear choice is autonomy. It's a serious problem if registrants can't purchase seats because some other bounded context is down. However, we don't really care if there's a short lag between the business customer modifying the pricing information, and that new pricing information being used to calculate order totals.

> When you are choosing the underlying storage mechanism for the read side, you should consider the costs associated with the storage (especially in the cloud) in addition to the requirement that the read-side data should be easy and efficient to access using the queries on the read side.

> So long as the registrant knows that the changes have been persisted, and that what the UI displays could be a few seconds out of date, they are not going to be concerned.

The team decided to add a note to the view page warning users about this possibility, although a production system is likely to update the read model faster than a debug version of the application running locally.

Implementation details

This section describes some of the significant features of the implementation of the Orders and Registrations bounded context. You may find it useful to have a copy of the code so you can follow along. You can download a copy from the *Download center*, or check the evolution of the code in the repository on GitHub: *https://github.com/mspnp/cqrs-journey-code*. You can download the code from the V1 release from the *Tags* page on GitHub.

> **Note:** *Do not expect the code samples to match exactly the code in the reference implementation. This chapter describes a step in the CQRS journey, the implementation may well change as we learn more and refactor the code.*

THE CONFERENCE MANAGEMENT BOUNDED CONTEXT

The Conference Management bounded context that enables a business customer to define and manage conferences is a simple two-tier, CRUD-style application that uses ASP.NET MVC 4.

In the Visual Studio solution, the **Conference** project contains the model code, and the **Conference.Web** project contains the MVC views and controllers.

Integration with the Orders and Registration bounded context

The Conference Management bounded context pushes notifications of changes to conferences by publishing the following events.

- **ConferenceCreated**. Published whenever a business customer creates a new conference.
- **ConferenceUpdated**. Published whenever a business customer updates an existing conference.
- **ConferencePublished**. Published whenever a business customer publishes a conference.
- **ConferenceUnpublished**. Published whenever a business customer unpublishes a new conference.
- **SeatCreated**. Published whenever a business customer defines a new seat type.
- **SeatsAdded**. Published whenever a business customer increases the quota of a seat type.

The **ConferenceService** class in the Conference project publishes these events to the event bus.

The Payments bounded context

The Payments bounded context is responsible for handling the interaction with the external systems that validate and process payments. In the V1 release, payments can be processed either by a fake, external, third-party payment processor (that mimics the behavior of systems such as PayPal) or by an invoicing system. The external systems can report either that a payment was successful or that it failed.

The sequence diagram in Figure 4 illustrates how the key elements that are involved in the payment process interact with each other. The diagram is shows a simplified view, ignoring the handler classes to better describe the process.

> At the moment, there is no distributed transaction to wrap the database update and the message publishing.

Figure 4
Overview of the payment process

Figure 4 shows how the Orders and Registrations bounded context, the Payments bounded context, and the external payments service all interact with each other. In the future, registrants will also be able to pay by invoice instead of using a third-party payment processing service.

The registrant makes a payment as a part of the overall flow in the UI, as shown in Figure 3. The **PaymentController** controller class does not display a view unless it has to wait for the system to create the **ThirdPartyProcessorPayment** aggregate instance. Its role is to forward payment information collected from the registrant to the third-party payment processor.

Typically, when you implement the CQRS pattern, you use events as the mechanism for communicating between bounded contexts. However, in this case, the **RegistrationController** and **PaymentController** controller classes send commands to the Payments bounded context. The Payments bounded context does use events to communicate with the **RegistrationProcessManager** instance in the Orders and Registrations bounded context.

The implementation of the Payments bounded context implements the CQRS pattern without event sourcing.

The write-side model contains an aggregate called **ThirdPartyProcessorPayment** that consists of two classes: **ThirdPartyProcessorPayment** and **ThirdPartyProcessorPaymentItem**. Instances of these classes are persisted to a SQL Database instance by using Entity Framework. The **PaymentsDbContext** class implements an Entity Framework context.

The **ThirdPartyProcessorPaymentCommandHandler** implements a command handler for the write side.

The read-side model is also implemented using Entity Framework. The **PaymentDao** class exposes the payment data on the read side. For an example, see the **GetThirdPartyProcessorPaymentDetails** method.

Figure 5 illustrates the different parts that make up the read side and the write side of the Payments bounded context.

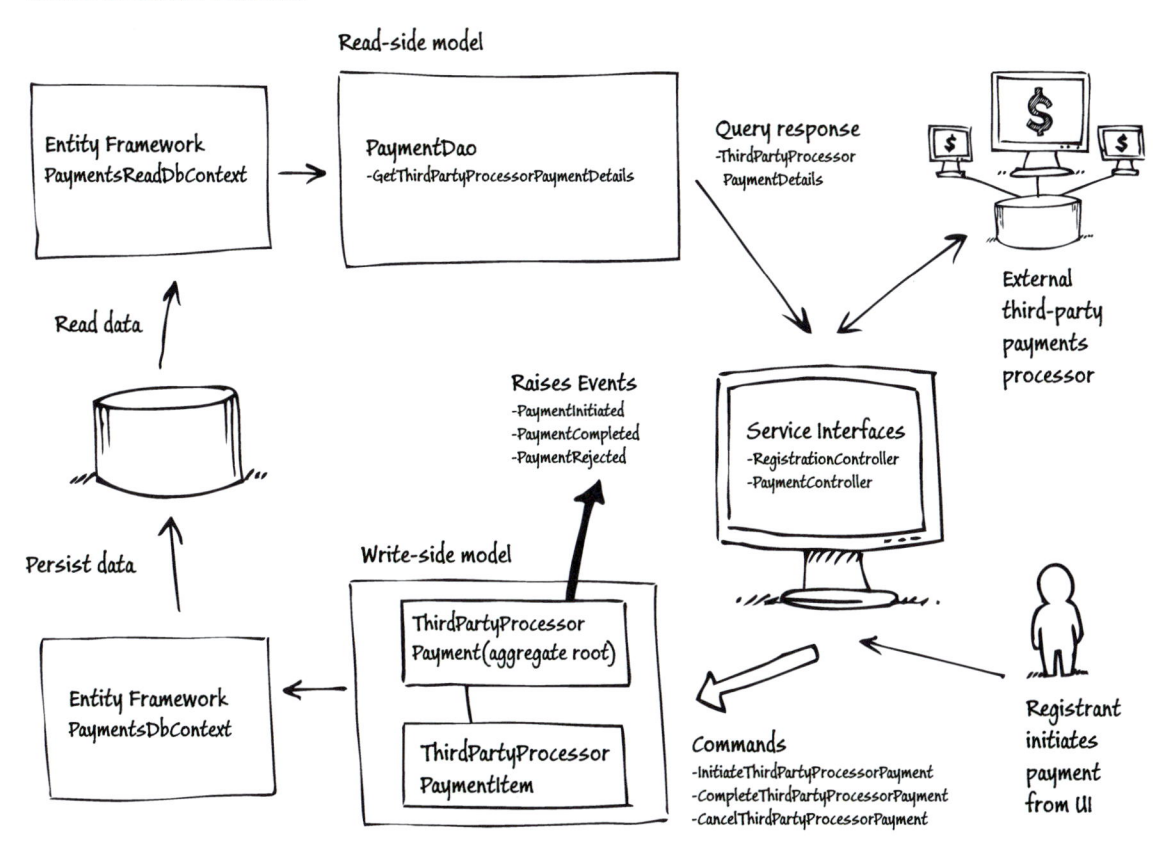

FIGURE 5
The read side and the write side in the Payments bounded context

Integration with online payment services, eventual consistency, and command validation

Typically, online payment services offer two levels of integration with your site:
- The simple approach, for which you don't need a merchant account with the payments provider, works through a simple redirect mechanism. You redirect your customer to the payment service. The payment service takes the payment, and then redirects the customer back to a page on your site along with an acknowledgement code.
- The more sophisticated approach, for which you do need a merchant account, is based on an API. It typically executes in two steps. First, the payment service verifies that your customer can pay the required amount, and sends you a token. Second, you can use the token within a fixed time to complete the payment by sending the token back to the payment service.

Contoso assumes that its business customers do not have a merchant account and must use the simple approach. One consequence of this is that a seat reservation could expire while the customer is completing the payment. If this happens, the system tries to re-acquire the seats after the customer makes the payment. In the event that the seats cannot be re-acquired, the system notifies the business customer of the problem and the business customer must resolve the situation manually.

> **Note:** *The system allows a little extra time over and above the time shown in the countdown clock to allow payment processing to complete.*

This specific scenario, in which the system cannot make itself fully consistent without a manual intervention by a user (in this case the business owner, who must initiate a refund or override the seat quota) illustrates the following more general point in relation to eventual consistency and command validation.

A key benefit of embracing eventual consistency is to remove the requirement for using distributed transactions, which have a significant, negative impact on the scalability and performance of large systems because of the number and duration of locks they must hold in the system. In this specific scenario, you could take steps to avoid the potential problem of accepting payment without seats being available in two ways:

- Change the system to re-check the seat availability just before completing the payment. This is not possible because of the way that the integration with the payments system works without a merchant account.
- Keep the seats reserved (locked) until the payment is complete. This is difficult because you do not know how long the payment process will take; you must reserve (lock) the seats for an indeterminate period while you wait for the registrant to complete the payment.

The team chose to allow for the possibility that a registrant could pay for seats only to find that they are no longer available; in addition to being very unlikely in practice because a timeout would have to occur while a registrant is paying for the very last seats, this approach has the smallest impact on the system because it doesn't require a long-term reservation (lock) on any seats.

In more general terms, you could restate the two options above as:

- Validate commands just before they execute to try to ensure that the command will succeed.
- Lock all the resources until the command completes.

> To minimize further the chance of this scenario occurring, the team decided to increase the buffer time for releasing reserved seats from five minutes to fourteen minutes. The original value of five minutes was chosen to account for any possible clock skew between the servers so that reservations were not released before the fifteen-minute countdown timer in the UI expired.

If the command only affects a single aggregate and does not need to reference anything outside of the consistency boundary defined by the aggregate, then there is no problem because all of the information required to validate the command is within the aggregate. This is not the case in the current scenario; if you could validate whether the seats were still available just before you made the payment, this check would involve checking information from outside the current aggregate.

If, in order to validate the command you need to look at data outside of the aggregate, for example, by querying a read model or by looking in a cache, the scalability of the system is going to be negatively impacted. Also, if you are querying a read model, remember that read models are eventually consistent. In the current scenario, you would need to query an eventually consistent read model to check on the seats availability.

If you decide to lock all of the relevant resources until the command completes, be aware of the impact this will have on the scalability of your system.

For a detailed discussion of this issue, see *Q/A Greg Young's Blog*.

It is far better to handle such a problem from a business perspective than to make large architectural constraints upon our system.
—Greg Young.

Event sourcing

The initial implementation of the event sourcing infrastructure is extremely basic: the team intends to replace it with a production-quality event store in the near future. This section describes the initial, basic implementation and lists the various ways to improve it.

The core elements of this basic event sourcing solution are that:

- Whenever the state of an aggregate instance changes, the instance raises an event that fully describes the state change.
- The system persists these events in an event store.
- An aggregate can rebuild its state by replaying its past stream of events.
- Other aggregates and process managers (possibly in different bounded contexts) can subscribe to these events.

Raising events when the state of an aggregate changes

The following two methods from the **Order** aggregate are examples of methods that the **OrderCommandHandler** class invokes when it receives a command for the order. Neither of these methods updates the state of the **Order** aggregate; instead, they raise an event that will be handled by the **Order** aggregate. In the **MarkAsReserved** method, there is some minimal logic to determine which of two events to raise.

```csharp
public void MarkAsReserved(
    DateTime expirationDate,
    IEnumerable<SeatQuantity> reservedSeats)
{
    if (this.isConfirmed)
        throw new InvalidOperationException("Cannot modify a confirmed order.");

    var reserved = reservedSeats.ToList();

    // Is there an order item which didn't get an exact reservation?
    if (this.seats.Any(item =>
        !reserved.Any(seat =>
            seat.SeatType == item.SeatType && seat.Quantity == item.Quantity)))
    {
        this.Update(
            new OrderPartiallyReserved
                {
                    ReservationExpiration = expirationDate,
                    Seats = reserved.ToArray()
                });
    }
    else
    {
        this.Update(
            new OrderReservationCompleted
                {
                    ReservationExpiration = expirationDate,
                    Seats = reserved.ToArray()
                });
    }
}

public void ConfirmPayment()
{
    this.Update(new OrderPaymentConfirmed());
}
```

The abstract base class of the **Order** class defines the **Update** method. The following code sample shows this method and the **Id** and **Version** properties in the **EventSourced** class.

```
private readonly Guid id;
private int version = -1;

protected EventSourced(Guid id)
{
    this.id = id;
}

public int Version { get { return this.version; } }

protected void Update(VersionedEvent e)
{
    e.SourceId = this.Id;
    e.Version = this.version + 1;
    this.handlers[e.GetType()].Invoke(e);
    this.version = e.Version;
    this.pendingEvents.Add(e);
}
```

The **Update** method sets the **Id** and increments the version of the aggregate. It also determines which of the event handlers in the aggregate it should invoke to handle the event type.

> Every time the system updates the state of an aggregate, it increments the version number of the aggregate.

The following code sample shows the event handler methods in the **Order** class that are invoked when the command methods shown above are called.

```
private void OnOrderPartiallyReserved(OrderPartiallyReserved e)
{
    this.seats = e.Seats.ToList();
}

private void OnOrderReservationCompleted(OrderReservationCompleted e)
{
    this.seats = e.Seats.ToList();
}

private void OnOrderExpired(OrderExpired e)
{
}

private void OnOrderPaymentConfirmed(OrderPaymentConfirmed e)
{
    this.isConfirmed = true;
}
```

These methods update the state of the aggregate.

An aggregate must be able to handle both events from other aggregates and events that it raises itself. The protected constructor in the **Order** class lists all the events that the **Order** aggregate can handle.

```
protected Order()
{
    base.Handles<OrderPlaced>(this.OnOrderPlaced);
    base.Handles<OrderUpdated>(this.OnOrderUpdated);
    base.Handles<OrderPartiallyReserved>(this.OnOrderPartiallyReserved);
    base.Handles<OrderReservationCompleted>(this.OnOrderReservationCompleted);
    base.Handles<OrderExpired>(this.OnOrderExpired);
    base.Handles<OrderPaymentConfirmed>(this.OnOrderPaymentConfirmed);
    base.Handles<OrderRegistrantAssigned>(this.OnOrderRegistrantAssigned);
}
```

Persisting events to the event store

When the aggregate processes an event in the **Update** method in the **EventSourcedAggregateRoot** class, it adds the event to a private list of pending events. This list is exposed as a public, **IEnumerable** property of the abstract **EventSourced** class called **Events**.

The following code sample from the **OrderCommandHandler** class shows how the handler invokes a method in the **Order** class to handle a command, and then uses a repository to persist the current state of the **Order** aggregate by appending all pending events to the store.

```
public void Handle(MarkSeatsAsReserved command)
{
    var order = repository.Find(command.OrderId);

    if (order != null)
    {
        order.MarkAsReserved(command.Expiration, command.Seats);
        repository.Save(order);
    }
}
```

The following code sample shows the initial simple implementation of the **Save** method in the **SqlEventSourcedRepository** class.

> **Note:** *These examples refer to a SQL Server-based event store. This was the initial approach that was later replaced with an implementation based on Windows Azure table storage. The SQL Server-based event store remains in the solution as a convenience; you can run the application locally and use this implementation to avoid any dependencies on Windows Azure.*

```
public void Save(T eventSourced)
{
    // TODO: guarantee that only incremental versions of the event are stored
    var events = eventSourced.Events.ToArray();
    using (var context = this.contextFactory.Invoke())
    {
        foreach (var e in events)
        {
            using (var stream = new MemoryStream())
            {
                this.serializer.Serialize(stream, e);
                var serialized = new Event
                                {
                                    AggregateId = e.SourceId,
                                    Version = e.Version,
                                    Payload = stream.ToArray()
                                };
                context.Set<Event>().Add(serialized);
            }
        }
    }
}
```

```
        context.SaveChanges();
    }

    // TODO: guarantee delivery or roll back,
    // or have a way to resume after a system crash
    this.eventBus.Publish(events);
}
```

Replaying events to rebuild state
When a handler class loads an aggregate instance from storage, it loads the state of the instance by replaying the stored event stream.

> We later found that using event sourcing and being able to replay events was invaluable as a technique for analyzing bugs in the production system running in the cloud. We could make a local copy of the event store, then replay the event stream locally and debug the application in Visual Studio to understand exactly what happened in the production system.

The following code sample from the **OrderCommandHandler** class shows how calling the **Find** method in the repository initiates this process.

```
public void Handle(MarkSeatsAsReserved command)
{
    var order = repository.Find(command.OrderId);

    ...
}
```

The following code sample shows how the **SqlEventSourcedRepository** class loads the event stream associated with the aggregate.

> The team later developed a simple event store using Windows Azure tables instead of the **SqlEventSourcedRepository**. The next section describes this Windows Azure table storage-based implementation.

```
public T Find(Guid id)
{
    using (var context = this.contextFactory.Invoke())
    {
        var deserialized = context.Set<Event>()
            .Where(x => x.AggregateId == id)
            .OrderBy(x => x.Version)
            .AsEnumerable()
            .Select(x => this.serializer.Deserialize(new MemoryStream(x.Payload)))
            .Cast<IVersionedEvent>()
            .AsCachedAnyEnumerable();

        if (deserialized.Any())
        {
            return entityFactory.Invoke(id, deserialized);
        }

        return null;
    }
}
```

The following code sample shows the constructor in the **Order** class that rebuilds the state of the order from its event stream when it is invoked by the **Invoke** method in the previous code sample.

```
public Order(Guid id, IEnumerable<IVersionedEvent> history) : this(id)
{
    this.LoadFrom(history);
}
```

The **LoadFrom** method is defined in the **EventSourced** class, as shown in the following code sample. For each stored event in the history, it determines the appropriate handler method to invoke in the **Order** class and updates the version number of the aggregate instance.

```
protected void LoadFrom(IEnumerable<IVersionedEvent> pastEvents)
{
    foreach (var e in pastEvents)
    {
        this.handlers[e.GetType()].Invoke(e);
        this.version = e.Version;
    }
}
```

Issues with the simple event store implementation

The simple implementation of event sourcing and an event store outlined in the previous sections has a number of shortcomings. The following list identifies some of these shortcomings that should be overcome in a production-quality implementation.

- There is no guarantee in the **Save** method in the **SqlEventRepository** class that the event is persisted to storage and published to the messaging infrastructure. A failure could result in an event being saved to storage but not being published.
- There is no check that when the system persists an event, that it is a later event than the previous one. Potentially, events could be stored out of sequence.
- There are no optimizations in place for aggregate instances that have a large number of events in their event stream. This could result in performance problems when replaying events.

WINDOWS AZURE TABLE STORAGE-BASED EVENT STORE

The Windows Azure table storage-based event store addresses some of the shortcomings of the simple SQL Server-based event store. However, at this point in time, it is still *not* a production-quality implementation.

The team designed this implementation to guarantee that events are both persisted to storage and published on the message bus. To achieve this, it uses the transactional capabilities of Windows Azure tables.

The **EventStore** class initially saves two copies of every event to be persisted. One copy is the permanent record of that event, and the other copy becomes part of a virtual queue of events that must be published on the Windows Azure Service Bus. The following code sample shows the **Save** method in the **EventStore** class. The prefix "Unpublished" identifies the copy of the event that is part of the virtual queue of unpublished events.

> Windows Azure table storage supports transactions across records that share the same partition key.

```csharp
public void Save(string partitionKey, IEnumerable<EventData> events)
{
    var context = this.tableClient.GetDataServiceContext();
    foreach (var eventData in events)
    {
        var formattedVersion = eventData.Version.ToString("D10");
        context.AddObject(
            this.tableName,
            new EventTableServiceEntity
                {
                    PartitionKey = partitionKey,
                    RowKey = formattedVersion,
                    SourceId = eventData.SourceId,
                    SourceType = eventData.SourceType,
                    EventType = eventData.EventType,
                    Payload = eventData.Payload
                });

        // Add a duplicate of this event to the Unpublished "queue"
        context.AddObject(
            this.tableName,
            new EventTableServiceEntity
            {
                PartitionKey = partitionKey,
                RowKey = UnpublishedRowKeyPrefix + formattedVersion,
                SourceId = eventData.SourceId,
                SourceType = eventData.SourceType,
                EventType = eventData.EventType,
                Payload = eventData.Payload
            });
    }
    try
    {
        this.eventStoreRetryPolicy.ExecuteAction(() =>
            context.SaveChanges(SaveChangesOptions.Batch));
    }
    catch (DataServiceRequestException ex)
    {
        var inner = ex.InnerException as DataServiceClientException;
        if (inner != null && inner.StatusCode == (int)HttpStatusCode.Conflict)
        {
            throw new ConcurrencyException();
        }
        throw;
    }
}
```

Note: *This code sample also illustrates how a duplicate key error is used to identify a concurrency error.*

The **Save** method in the repository class is shown below. This method is invoked by the event handler classes, invokes the **Save** method shown in the previous code sample, and invokes the **SendAsync** method of the **EventStoreBusPublisher** class.

```
public void Save(T eventSourced)
{
    var events = eventSourced.Events.ToArray();
    var serialized = events.Select(this.Serialize);

    var partitionKey = this.GetPartitionKey(eventSourced.Id);
    this.eventStore.Save(partitionKey, serialized);

    this.publisher.SendAsync(partitionKey);
}
```

The **EventStoreBusPublisher** class is responsible for reading the unpublished events for the aggregate from the virtual queue in the Windows Azure table store, publishing the event on the Windows Azure Service Bus, and then deleting the unpublished event from the virtual queue.

If the system fails between publishing the event on the Windows Azure Service Bus and deleting the event from the virtual queue then, when the application restarts, the event is published a second time. To avoid problems caused by duplicate events, the Windows Azure Service Bus is configured to detect duplicate messages and ignore them.

> In the case of a failure, the system must include a mechanism for scanning all of the partitions in table storage for aggregates with unpublished events and then publishing those events. This process will take some time to run, but will only need to run when the application restarts.

Calculating totals

To ensure its autonomy, the Orders and Registrations bounded context calculates order totals without accessing the Conference Management bounded context. The Conference Management bounded context is responsible for maintaining the prices of seats for conferences.

Whenever a business customer adds a new seat type or changes the price of a seat, the Conference Management bounded context raises an event. The Orders and Registrations bounded context handles these events and persists the information as part of its read model (see the **ConferenceViewModelGenerator** class in the reference implementation solution for details).

When the **Order** aggregate calculates the order total, it uses the data provided by the read model. See the **MarkAsReserved** method in the **Order** aggregate and the **PricingService** class for details.

Impact on testing

Timing issues

One of the acceptance tests verifies the behavior of the system when a business customer creates new seat types. The key steps in the test create a conference, create a new seat type for the conference, and then publish the conference. This raises the corresponding sequence of events: **ConferenceCreated**, **SeatCreated**, and **ConferencePublished**.

The Orders and Registrations bounded context handles these integration events. The test determined that the Orders and Registrations bounded context received these events in a different order from the order that the Conference Management bounded context sent them.

The Windows Azure Service Bus only offers best-effort first in first out (FIFO), therefore, it may not deliver events in the order in which they were sent. It is also possible in this scenario that the issue occurs because of the different times it takes for the steps in the test to create the messages and deliver them to the Windows Azure Service Bus. The introduction of an artificial delay between the steps in the test provided a temporary solution to this problem.

In the V2 release, the team plans to address the general issue of message ordering and either modify the infrastructure to guarantee proper ordering or make the system more robust if messages do arrive out of order.

Involving the domain expert

In Chapter 4, "Extending and Enhancing the Orders and Registrations Bounded Contexts," you saw how the domain expert was involved with designing the acceptance tests and how his involvement helped clarify domain knowledge.

> The UI also displays a dynamically calculated total as the registrant adds seats to an order. The application calculates this value using JavaScript. When the registrant makes a payment, the system uses the total that the **Order** aggregate calculates.

> Don't let your passing unit tests lull you into a false sense of security. There are lots of moving parts when you implement the CQRS pattern. You need to test that they all work correctly together.

> Don't forget to create unit tests for your read models. A unit test on the read-model generator uncovered a bug just prior to the V1 release whereby the system removed order items when it updated an order.

You should also ensure that the domain expert attends bug triage meetings. He or she can help clarify the expected behavior of the system, and during the discussion may uncover new user stories. For example, during the triage of a bug related to unpublishing a conference in the Conference Management bounded context, the domain expert identified a requirement to allow the business customer to add a redirect link for the unpublished conference to a new conference or alternate page.

Summary

During this stage of our journey, we completed our first pseudo-production release of the Contoso Conference Management System. It now comprises several integrated bounded contexts, a more polished UI, and uses event sourcing in the Orders and Registrations bounded context.

There is still more work for us to do, and the next chapter will describe the next stage in our CQRS journey as we head towards the V2 release and address the issues associated with versioning our system.

More information

All links in this book are accessible from the book's online bibliography available at: *http://msdn.microsoft.com/en-us/library/jj619274*.

Journey 6:

Versioning Our System

Preparing for the next stop: upgrading and migrating

"Variety is the very spice of life."
William Cowper

The top-level goal for this stage in the journey is to learn about how to upgrade a system that includes bounded contexts that implement the CQRS pattern and event sourcing. The user stories that the team implemented in this stage of the journey involve both changes to the code and changes to the data: some existing data schemas changed and new data schemas were added. In addition to upgrading the system and migrating the data, the team planned to do the upgrade and migration with no down time for the live system running in Windows Azure.

Working definitions for this chapter

This chapter uses a number of terms, which we will define next. For more detail, and possible alternative definitions, see Chapter 4, "A CQRS and ES Deep Dive" in the Reference Guide.

Command. A *command* is a request for the system to perform an action that changes the state of the system. Commands are imperatives; for example, **MakeSeatReservation**. In this bounded context, commands originate from either the user interface (UI) as a result of a user initiating a request, or from a process manager when the process manager is directing an aggregate to perform an action.

A single recipient processes a command. A command bus transports commands that command handlers then dispatch to aggregates. Sending a command is an asynchronous operation with no return value.

Event. An *event*, such as **OrderConfirmed**, describes something that has happened in the system, typically as a result of a command. Aggregates in the domain model raise events. Events can also come from other bounded contexts.

Multiple subscribers can handle a specific event. Aggregates publish events to an event bus; handlers register for specific types of events on the event bus and then deliver the events to the subscriber. In the orders and registrations bounded context, the subscribers are a process manager and the read model generators.

Idempotency. *Idempotency* is a characteristic of an operation that means the operation can be applied multiple times without changing the result. For example, the operation "set the value *x* to ten" is idempotent, while the operation "add one to the value of *x*" is not. In a messaging environment, a message is idempotent if it can be delivered multiple times without changing the result: either because of the nature of the message itself, or because of the way the system handles the message.

User stories

The team implemented the following user stories during this phase of the project.

No down time upgrade

The goal for the V2 release is to perform the upgrade, including any necessary data migration, without any down time for the system. If this is not feasible with the current implementation, then the down time should be minimized, and the system should be modified to support zero down-time upgrades in the future (starting with the V3 release).

Display remaining seat quantities

Currently, when a registrant creates an order, there is no indication of the number of seats remaining for each seat type. The UI should display this information when the registrant is selecting seats for purchase.

Handle zero-cost seats

Currently, when a registrant selects seats that have no cost, the UI flow still takes the registrant to the payments page even though there is nothing to pay. The system should detect when there is nothing to pay and adjust the flow to take the registrant directly to the confirmation page for the order.

Architecture

The application is designed to deploy to Windows Azure. At this stage in the journey, the application consists of web roles that contain the ASP.NET MVC web applications and a worker role that contains the message handlers and domain objects. The application uses Windows Azure SQL Database (SQL Database) instances for data storage, both on the write side and the read side. The application uses the Windows Azure Service Bus to provide its messaging infrastructure. Figure 1 shows this high-level architecture.

> Ensuring that we can perform upgrades with no down time is crucial to our credibility in the marketplace.

Versioning Our System

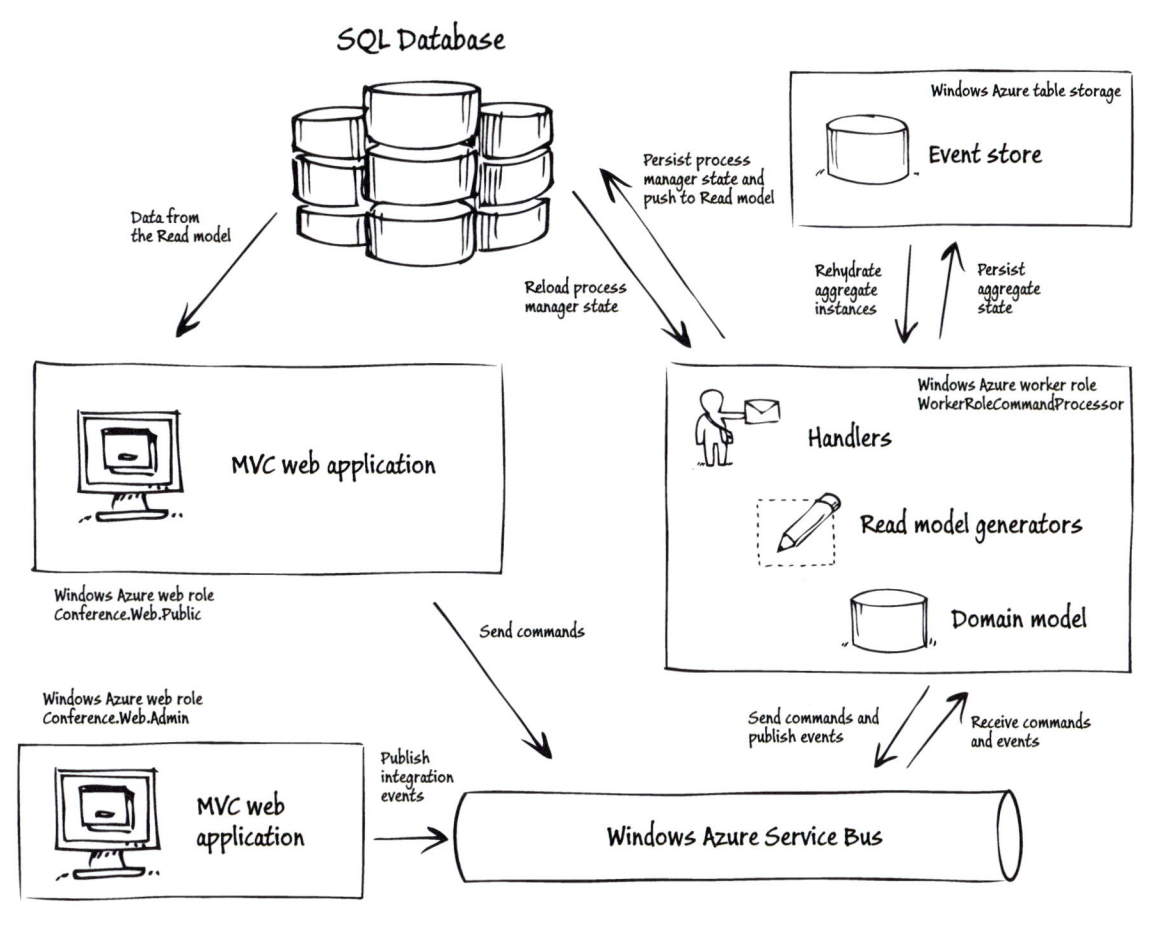

Figure 1
The top-level architecture in the V2 release

While you are exploring and testing the solution, you can run it locally, either using the Windows Azure compute emulator or by running the MVC web application directly and running a console application that hosts the handlers and domain objects. When you run the application locally, you can use a local SQL Server Express database instead of SQL Database, and use a simple messaging infrastructure implemented in a SQL Server Express database.

For more information about the options for running the application, see Appendix 1, "Release Notes."

Patterns and concepts

During this stage of the journey, most of the key challenges addressed by the team related to how best to perform the migration from V1 to V2. This section describes some of those challenges.

Handling changes to events definitions

When the team examined the requirements for the V2 release, it became clear that we would need to change some of the events used in the Orders and Registrations bounded context to accommodate some of the new features: the **RegistrationProcessManager** would change and the system would provide a better user experience when the order had a zero cost.

The Orders and Registrations bounded context uses event sourcing, so after the migration to V2, the event store will contain the old events but will start saving the new events. When the system events are replayed, the system must operate correctly when it processes both the old and new sets of events.

The team considered two approaches to handle this type of change in the system.

Mapping/filtering event messages in the infrastructure

Mapping and filtering event messages in the infrastructure is one approach. This option handles old event messages and message formats by dealing with them somewhere in the infrastructure before they reach the domain. You can filter out old messages that are no longer relevant and use mapping to transform old-format messages to a new format. This approach is initially the more complex approach because it requires changes in the infrastructure, but it has the advantage of keeping the domain pure because the domain only needs to understand the current set of events.

Handling multiple message versions in the aggregates

Handling multiple message versions in the aggregates is another alternative; in this approach all the message types (both old and new) are passed through to the domain where each aggregate must be able to handle both the old and new messages. This may be an appropriate strategy in the short term, but it will eventually cause the domain model to become polluted with legacy event handlers.

The team selected this option for the V2 release because it involved the minimum number of code changes.

Honoring message idempotency

One of the key issues to address in the V2 release is to make the system more robust. In the V1 release, in some scenarios it is possible that some messages might be processed more than once, resulting in incorrect or inconsistent data in the system.

> Dealing with both old and new events in the aggregates now does not prevent you from later employing the first option: using a mapping/filtering mechanism in the infrastructure.

In some scenarios, it would be possible to design idempotent messages; for example, by using a message that says "set the seat quota to 500" rather than a message that says "add 100 to the seat quota." You could safely process the first message multiple times, but not the second.

However, it is not always possible to use idempotent messages, so the team decided to use the de-duplication feature of the Windows Azure Service Bus to ensure that it delivers messages only once. The team made some changes to the infrastructure to ensure that Windows Azure Service Bus can detect duplicate messages, and configured Windows Azure Service Bus to perform duplicate message detection.

To understand how Contoso implemented this, see the section "De-duplicating command messages" below. Additionally, we needed to consider how the message handlers in the system retrieve messages from queues and topics. The current approach uses the Windows Azure Service Bus peek/lock mechanism. This is a three-stage process:

1. The handler retrieves a message from the queue or topic and leaves a locked copy of the message there. Other clients cannot see or access locked messages.

2. The handler processes the message.

3. The handler deletes the locked message from the queue. If a locked message is not unlocked or deleted after a fixed time, the message is unlocked and made available so that it can be retrieved again.

If step 3 fails for some reason, this means that the system can process the message more than once.

> Message idempotency is important in any system that uses messaging, not just in systems that implement the CQRS pattern or use event sourcing.

> The team plans to address this issue in the next stage of the journey. See Chapter 7, "Adding Resilience and Optimizing Performance" for more information.

Avoid processing events multiple times

In V1, in certain scenarios it was possible for the system to process an event multiple times if an error occurred while the event was being processed. To avoid this scenario, the team modified the architecture so that every event handler has its own subscription to a Windows Azure topic. Figure 2 shows the two different models.

V1 Model

Topic: conference/events

Subscription: all → Event Processor

- Handle → RegistrationProcessRouter
- Handle → OrderViewModelGenerator
- Handle → ConferenceViewModelGenerator
- Handle → SeatAssignmentsHandler

V2 Model

Topic: conference/events

- Subscription: RegistrationProcessRouter → EventProcessor — Handle → RegistrationProcessRouter
- Subscription: OrderViewModelGenerator → EventProcessor — Handle → OrderViewModelGenerator
- Subscription: ConferenceViewModelGenerator → EventProcessor — Handle → ConferenceViewModelGenerator
- Subscription: SeatAssignmentsHandler → EventProcessor — Handle → SeatAssignmentsHandler

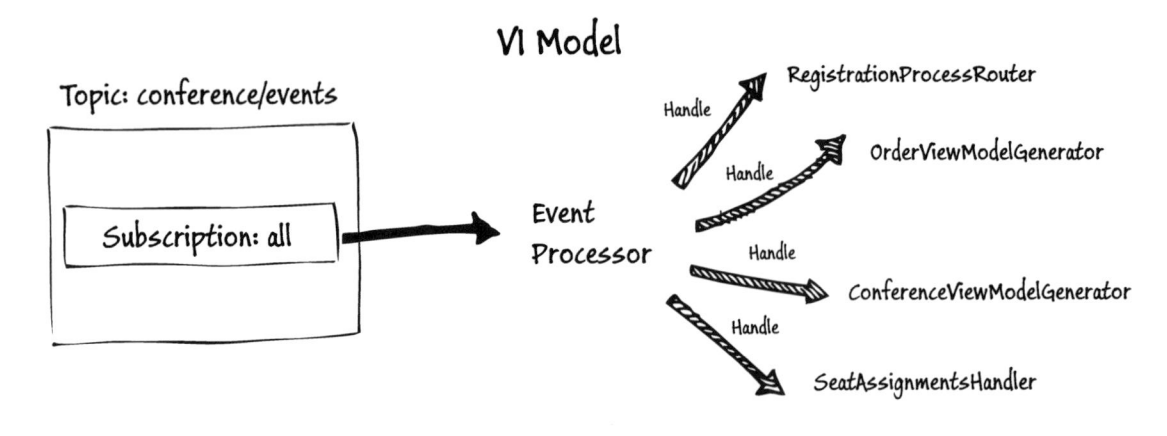

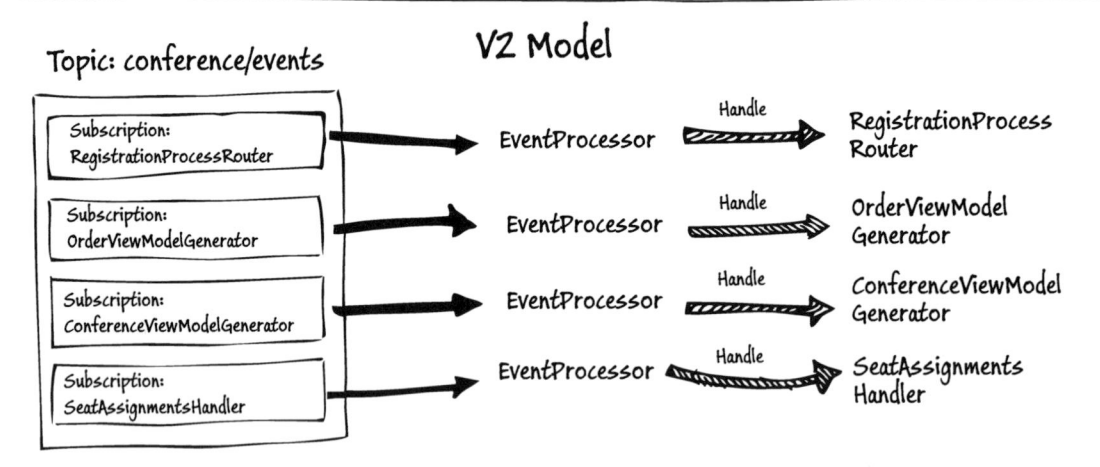

FIGURE 2
Using one subscription per event handler

In V1, the following behavior *could* occur:

1. The **EventProcessor** instance receives an **OrderPlaced** event from the **all** subscription in the service bus.
2. The **EventProcessor** instance has two registered handlers, the **RegistrationProcessManagerRouter** and **OrderViewModelGenerator** handler classes, so it invokes the **Handle** method on each of them.
3. The **Handle** method in the **OrderViewModelGenerator** class executes successfully.
4. The **Handle** method in the **RegistrationProcessManagerRouter** class throws an exception.

5. The **EventProcessor** instance catches the exception and abandons the event message. The message is automatically put back into the subscription.
6. The **EventProcessor** instance receives the **OrderPlaced** event from the **all** subscription for a second time.
7. It invokes the two Handle methods, causing the **RegistrationProcessManagerRouter** class to retry the message and the **OrderViewModelGenerator** class to process the message a second time.
8. Every time the **RegistrationProcessManagerRouter** class throws an exception, the **OrderViewModelGenerator** class processes the event.

In the V2 model, if a handler class throws an exception, the **EventProcessor** instance puts the event message back on the subscription associated with that handler class. The retry logic now only causes the **EventProcessor** instance to retry the handler that raised the exception, so no other handlers reprocess the message.

Persisting integration events

One of the concerns raised with the V1 release centered around the way the system persists the integration events that are sent from the Conference Management bounded context to the Orders and Registrations bounded context. These events include information about conference creation and publishing, and details of seat types and quota changes.

In the V1 release, the **ConferenceViewModelGenerator** class in the Orders and Registrations bounded context handles these events by updating its view model and sending commands to the **SeatsAvailability** aggregate to tell it to change its seat quota values.

This approach means that the Orders and Registrations bounded context is not storing any history, which could cause problems. For example, other views look up seat type descriptions from this projection, which contains only the latest value of the seat type description. As a result, replaying a set of events elsewhere may regenerate another read-model projection that contains incorrect seat type descriptions.

The team considered the following five options to rectify the situation:
- Save all of the events in the originating bounded context (the Conference Management bounded context) and use a shared event store that the Orders and Registrations bounded context can access to replay these events. The receiving bounded context could replay the event stream up to a point in time when it needed to see what the seat type description was previously.
- Save all of the events as soon as they arrive in the receiving bounded context (the Orders and Registrations bounded context).
- Let the command handler in the view-model generator save the events, selecting only those that it needs.
- Let the command handler in the view-model generator save different events, in effect using event sourcing for this view model.
- Store all command and event messages from all bounded contexts in a message log.

The first option is not always viable. In this particular case it would work because the same team is implementing both bounded contexts and the infrastructure, making it easy to use a shared event store.

A possible risk with the third option is that the set of events that are needed may change in the future. If we don't save events now, they are lost for good.

Although the fifth option stores all the commands and events, some of which you might never need to refer to again, it does provide a complete log of everything that happens in the system. This could be useful for troubleshooting, and also helps you to meet requirements that have not yet been identified. The team chose this option over option two because it offers a more general-purpose mechanism that may have future benefits.

> Although from a purist's perspective the first option breaks the strict isolation between bounded contexts, in some scenarios it may be an acceptable and pragmatic solution.

The purpose of persisting the events is to enable them to be played back when the Orders and Registrations bounded context needs the information about current seat quotas in order to calculate the number of remaining seats. To calculate these numbers consistently, you must always play the events back in the same order. There are several choices for this ordering:

- The order in which the events were sent by the Conference Management bounded context.
- The order in which the events were received by the Orders and Registrations bounded context.
- The order in which the events were processed by the Orders and Registrations bounded context.

Most of the time these orderings will be the same. There is no correct order; you just need to choose one to be consistent. Therefore, the choice is determined by simplicity. In this case, the simplest approach is to persist the events in the order that the handler in the Orders and Registrations bounded context receives them (the second option).

There is a similar issue with saving timestamps for these events. Timestamps may be useful in the future if there is a requirement to look at the number of remaining seats at a particular time. The choice here is whether you should create a timestamp when the event is created in the Conference Management bounded context or when it is received by the Orders and Registrations bounded context. It's possible that the Orders and Registrations bounded context is offline for some reason when the Conference Management bounded context creates an event; therefore, the team decided to create the timestamp when the Conference Management bounded context publishes the event.

> This choice does not typically arise with event sourcing. Each aggregate creates events in a fixed order, and that is the order that the system uses to persist the events. In this scenario, the integration events are not created by a single aggregate.

Message ordering

The acceptance tests that the team created and ran to verify the V1 release highlighted a potential issue with message ordering: the acceptance tests that exercised the Conference Management bounded context sent a sequence of commands to the Orders and Registrations bounded context that sometimes arrived out of order.

The team considered two alternatives for ensuring that messages arrive in the correct order.

- The first option is to use message sessions, a feature of the Windows Azure Service Bus. If you use message sessions, this guarantees that messages within a session are delivered in the same order that they were sent.
- The second alternative is to modify the handlers within the application to detect out-of-order messages through the use of sequence numbers or timestamps added to the messages when they are sent. If the receiving handler detects an out-of-order message, it rejects the message and puts it back onto the queue or topic to be processed later, after it has processed the messages that were sent before the rejected message.

The preferred solution in this case is to use Windows Azure Service Bus message sessions because this requires fewer changes to the existing code. Both approaches would introduce some additional latency into the message delivery, but the team does not anticipate that this will have a significant effect on the performance of the system.

> This effect was not noticed when a human user tested this part of the system because the time delay between the times that the commands were sent was much greater, making it less likely that the messages would arrive out of order.

Implementation details

This section describes some of the significant features of the implementation of the Orders and Registrations bounded context. You may find it useful to have a copy of the code so you can follow along. You can download a copy from the *Download center*, or check the evolution of the code in the repository on GitHub: *https://github.com/mspnp/cqrs-journey-code*. You can download the code from the V2 release from the *Tags* page on GitHub.

> **Note:** *Do not expect the code samples to exactly match the code in the reference implementation. This chapter describes a step in the CQRS journey; the implementation may well change as we learn more and refactor the code.*

Adding support for zero-cost orders

There were three specific goals in making this change, all of which are related. We wanted to:

- Modify the **RegistrationProcessManager** class and related aggregates to handle orders with a zero cost.
- Modify the navigation in the UI to skip the payment step when the total cost of the order is zero.
- Ensure that the system functions correctly after the upgrade to V2 with the old events as well as the new.

Changes to the RegistrationProcessManager class

Previously, the **RegistrationProcessManager** class sent a **ConfirmOrderPayment** command after it received notification from the UI that the registrant had completed the payment. Now, if there is a zero-cost order, the UI sends a **ConfirmOrder** command directly to the **Order** aggregate. If the order requires a payment, the **RegistrationProcessManager** class sends a **ConfirmOrder** command to the **Order** aggregate after it receives notification of a successful payment from the UI.

When the **Order** aggregate receives the **ConfirmOrder** command, it raises an **OrderConfirmed** event. In addition to being persisted, this event is also handled by the following objects:

- The **OrderViewModelGenerator** class, where it updates the state of the order in the read model.
- The **SeatAssignments** aggregate, where it initializes a new **SeatAssignments** instance.
- The **RegistrationProcessManager** class, where it triggers a command to commit the seat reservation.

> Notice that the name of the command has changed from **ConfirmOrderPayment** to **ConfirmOrder**. This reflects the fact that the order doesn't need to know anything about the payment; all it needs to know is that the order is confirmed. Similarly, there is a new **OrderConfirmed** event that is now used in place of the old **OrderPaymentConfirmed** event.

Changes to the UI

The main change in the UI is in the **RegistrationController** MVC controller class in the **SpecifyRegistrantAndPaymentDetails** action. Previously, this action method returned an **InitiateRegistrationWithThirdPartyProcessorPayment** action result; now, if the new **IsFreeOfCharge** property of the **Order** object is true, it returns a **CompleteRegistrationWithoutPayment** action result. Otherwise, it returns a **CompleteRegistrationWithThirdPartyProcessorPayment** action result.

```
[HttpPost]
public ActionResult SpecifyRegistrantAndPaymentDetails(
    AssignRegistrantDetails command,
    string paymentType,
    int orderVersion)
{
    ...

    var pricedOrder = this.orderDao.FindPricedOrder(orderId);
    if (pricedOrder.IsFreeOfCharge)
    {
        return CompleteRegistrationWithoutPayment(command, orderId);
    }

    switch (paymentType)
    {
        case ThirdPartyProcessorPayment:

            return CompleteRegistrationWithThirdPartyProcessorPayment(
                    command,
                    pricedOrder,
                    orderVersion);

        case InvoicePayment:
            break;

        default:
            break;
    }

    ...
}
```

The **CompleteRegistrationWithThirdPartyProcessorPayment** redirects the user to the **ThirdPartyProcessorPayment** action and the **CompleteRegistrationWithoutPayment** method redirects the user directly to the **ThankYou** action.

Data migration

The Conference Management bounded context stores order information from the Orders and Registrations bounded context in the **PricedOrders** table in its Windows Azure SQL Database instance. Previously, the Conference Management bounded context received the **OrderPaymentConfirmed** event; now it receives the **OrderConfirmed** event that contains an additional **IsFreeOfCharge** property. This becomes a new column in the database.

During the migration, any in-flight **ConfirmOrderPayment** commands could be lost because they are no longer handled by the **Order** aggregate. You should verify that none of these commands are currently on the command bus.

The system persists the state of **RegistrationProcessManager** class instances to a SQL Database table. There are no changes to the schema of this table. The only change you will see after the migration is an additional value in the **StateValue** column. This reflects the additional **PaymentConfirmationReceived** value in the **ProcessState** enumeration in the **RegistrationProcessManager** class, as shown in the following code sample:

```
public enum ProcessState
{
    NotStarted = 0,
    AwaitingReservationConfirmation = 1,
    ReservationConfirmationReceived = 2,
    PaymentConfirmationReceived = 3,
}
```

> We didn't need to modify the existing data in this table during the migration because the default value for a Boolean is **false**. All of the existing entries were created before the system supported zero-cost orders.

> We need to plan carefully how to deploy the V2 release so that we can be sure that all the existing, in-flight **ConfirmOrderPayment** commands are processed by a worker role instance running the V1 release.

In the V1 release, the events that the event sourcing system persisted for the **Order** aggregate included the **OrderPaymentConfirmed** event. Therefore, the event store contains instances of this event type. In the V2 release, the **OrderPaymentConfirmed** event is replaced with the **OrderConfirmed** event.

The team decided for the V2 release not to introduce mapping and filtering events at the infrastructure level when events are deserialized. This means that the handlers must understand both the old and new events when the system replays these events from the event store. The following code sample shows this in the **SeatAssignmentsHandler** class:

```
static SeatAssignmentsHandler()
{
    Mapper.CreateMap<OrderPaymentConfirmed, OrderConfirmed>();
}

public SeatAssignmentsHandler(
    IEventSourcedRepository<Order> ordersRepo,
    IEventSourcedRepository<SeatAssignments> assignmentsRepo)
{
    this.ordersRepo = ordersRepo;
    this.assignmentsRepo = assignmentsRepo;
}

public void Handle(OrderPaymentConfirmed @event)
{
    this.Handle(Mapper.Map<OrderConfirmed>(@event));
}

public void Handle(OrderConfirmed @event)
{
    var order = this.ordersRepo.Get(@event.SourceId);
    var assignments = order.CreateSeatAssignments();
    assignmentsRepo.Save(assignments);
}
```

You can also see the same technique in use in the **OrderViewModel-Generator** class.

The approach is slightly different in the **Order** class because this is one of the events that is persisted to the event store. The following code sample shows part of the **protected** constructor in the **Order** class:

```
protected Order(Guid id)
    : base(id)
{
    ...
    base.Handles<OrderPaymentConfirmed>(e =>
        this.OnOrderConfirmed(Mapper.Map<OrderConfirmed>(e)));
    base.Handles<OrderConfirmed>(this.OnOrderConfirmed);
    ...
}
```

> Handling the old events in this way was straightforward for this scenario because the only change needed was to the name of the event. It would be more complicated if the properties of the event changed as well. In the future, Contoso will consider doing the mapping in the infrastructure to avoid polluting the domain model with legacy events.

Displaying remaining seats in the UI

There were three specific goals in making this change, all of which are related. We wanted to
- Modify the system to include information about the number of remaining seats of each seat type in the conference read model.
- Modify the UI to display the number of remaining seats of each seat type.
- Ensure that the system functions correctly after the upgrade to V2.

Adding information about remaining seat quantities to the read model

The information that the system needs to be able to display the number of remaining seats comes from two places.
- The Conference Management bounded context raises the **SeatCreated** and **SeatUpdated** events whenever the business customer creates new seat types or modifies seat quotas.
- The **SeatsAvailability** aggregate in the Orders and Registrations bounded context raises the **SeatsReserved, SeatsReservationCancelled,** and **AvailableSeatsChanged** events while a registrant is creating an order.

> **Note:** *The **ConferenceViewModelGenerator** class does not use the **SeatCreated** and **SeatUpdated** events.*

The **ConferenceViewModelGenerator** class in the Orders and Registrations bounded context now handles these events and uses them to calculate and store the information about seat type quantities in the read model. The following code sample shows the relevant handlers in the **ConferenceViewModelGenerator** class:

```
public void Handle(AvailableSeatsChanged @event)
{
    this.UpdateAvailableQuantity(@event, @event.Seats);
}

public void Handle(SeatsReserved @event)
{
    this.UpdateAvailableQuantity(@event, @event.AvailableSeatsChanged);
}

public void Handle(SeatsReservationCancelled @event)
{
    this.UpdateAvailableQuantity(@event, @event.AvailableSeatsChanged);
}

private void UpdateAvailableQuantity(
    IVersionedEvent @event,
    IEnumerable<SeatQuantity> seats)
```

```
{
    using (var repository = this.contextFactory.Invoke())
    {
        var dto = repository.Set<Conference>()
                    .Include(x => x.Seats)
                    .FirstOrDefault(x => x.Id == @event.SourceId);
        if (dto != null)
        {
            if (@event.Version > dto.SeatsAvailabilityVersion)
            {
                foreach (var seat in seats)
                {
                    var seatDto = dto.Seats
                                    .FirstOrDefault(x => x.Id == seat.SeatType);
                    if (seatDto != null)
                    {
                        seatDto.AvailableQuantity += seat.Quantity;
                    }
                    else
                    {
                        Trace.TraceError(
            "Failed to locate Seat Type read model being updated with id {0}.",
            seat.SeatType);
                    }
                }

                dto.SeatsAvailabilityVersion = @event.Version;

                repository.Save(dto);
            }
            else
            {
                Trace.TraceWarning ...
            }
        }
        else
        {
            Trace.TraceError ...
        }
    }
}
```

The **UpdateAvailableQuantity** method compares the version on the event to current version of the read model to detect possible duplicate messages.

> This check only detects duplicate messages, not out-of-sequence messages.

Modifying the UI to display remaining seat quantities

Now, when the UI queries the conference read model for a list of seat types, the list includes the currently available number of seats. The following code sample shows how the **RegistrationController** MVC controller uses the **AvailableQuantity** of the **SeatType** class:

```
private OrderViewModel CreateViewModel()
{
    var seatTypes =
        this.ConferenceDao.GetPublishedSeatTypes(this.ConferenceAlias.Id);
    var viewModel =
        new OrderViewModel
        {
            ConferenceId = this.ConferenceAlias.Id,
            ConferenceCode = this.ConferenceAlias.Code,
            ConferenceName = this.ConferenceAlias.Name,
            Items =
                seatTypes.Select(s =>
                    new OrderItemViewModel
                    {
                        SeatType = s,
                        OrderItem = new DraftOrderItem(s.Id, 0),
                        AvailableQuantityForOrder = s.AvailableQuantity,
                        MaxSelectionQuantity = Math.Min(s.AvailableQuantity, 20)
                    }).ToList(),
        };

    return viewModel;
}
```

Data migration

The database table that holds the conference read-model data now has a new column to hold the version number that is used to check for duplicate events, and the table that holds the seat type read-model data now has a new column to hold the available quantity of seats.

As part of the data migration, it is necessary to replay all of the events in the event store for each of the **SeatsAvailability** aggregates in order to correctly calculate the available quantities.

DE-DUPLICATING COMMAND MESSAGES

The system currently uses the Windows Azure Service Bus to transport messages. When the system initializes the Windows Azure Service Bus from the start-up code in the **ConferenceProcessor** class, it configures the topics to detect duplicate messages, as shown in the following code sample from the **ServiceBusConfig** class:

```
private void CreateTopicIfNotExists()
{
    var topicDescription =
        new TopicDescription(this.topic)
        {
            RequiresDuplicateDetection = true,
            DuplicateDetectionHistoryTimeWindow = topic.DuplicateDetectionHistoryTimeWindow,
        };
    try
    {
        this.namespaceManager.CreateTopic(topicDescription);
    }
    catch (MessagingEntityAlreadyExistsException) { }
}
```

> **Note:** *You can configure the **DuplicateDetectionHistoryTimeWindow** in the Settings.xml file by adding an attribute to the **Topic** element. The default value is one hour.*

However, for the duplicate detection to work, you must ensure that every message has a unique ID. The following code sample shows the **MarkSeatsAsReserved** command:

```
public class MarkSeatsAsReserved : ICommand
{
    public MarkSeatsAsReserved()
    {
        this.Id = Guid.NewGuid();
        this.Seats = new List<SeatQuantity>();
    }

    public Guid Id { get; set; }

    public Guid OrderId { get; set; }

    public List<SeatQuantity> Seats { get; set; }

    public DateTime Expiration { get; set; }
}
```

The **BuildMessage** method in the **CommandBus** class uses the command Id to create a unique message Id that the Windows Azure Service Bus can use to detect duplicates:

```
private BrokeredMessage BuildMessage(Envelope command)
{
    var stream = new MemoryStream();
    ...

    var message = new BrokeredMessage(stream, true);
    if (!default(Guid).Equals(command.Body.Id))
    {
        message.MessageId = command.Body.Id.ToString();
    }

    ...

    return message;
}
```

Guaranteeing message ordering

The team decided to use Windows Azure Service Bus Message Sessions to guarantee message ordering in the system.

The system configures the Windows Azure Service Bus topics and subscriptions from the **OnStart** method in the **ConferenceProcessor** class. The configuration in the **Settings.xml** file specifies whether a particular subscription should use sessions. The following code sample from the **ServiceBusConfig** class shows how the system creates and configures subscriptions.

```
private void CreateSubscriptionIfNotExists(
    NamespaceManager namespaceManager,
    TopicSettings topic,
    SubscriptionSettings subscription)
{
    var subscriptionDescription =
        new SubscriptionDescription(topic.Path, subscription.Name)
        {
            RequiresSession = subscription.RequiresSession
        };

    try
    {
        namespaceManager.CreateSubscription(subscriptionDescription);
    }
    catch (MessagingEntityAlreadyExistsException) { }
}
```

The following code sample from the **SessionSubscriptionReceiver** class shows how to use sessions to receive messages:

```
private void ReceiveMessages(CancellationToken cancellationToken)
{
    while (!cancellationToken.IsCancellationRequested)
    {
        MessageSession session;
        try
        {
            session =
                this.receiveRetryPolicy.ExecuteAction(this.DoAcceptMessageSession);
        }
        catch (Exception e)
        {
            ...
        }

        if (session == null)
        {
            Thread.Sleep(100);
            continue;
        }


        while (!cancellationToken.IsCancellationRequested)
        {
            BrokeredMessage message = null;
            try
            {
                try
                {
                    message = this.receiveRetryPolicy.ExecuteAction(
                        () => session.Receive(TimeSpan.Zero));
                }
                catch (Exception e)
                {
                    ...
                }

                if (message == null)
                {
                    // If we have no more messages for this session,
                    // exit and try another.
                    break;
                }
```

Journey Six

```
                this.MessageReceived(this, new BrokeredMessageEventArgs(message));
            }
            finally
            {
                if (message != null)
                {
                    message.Dispose();
                }
            }
        }

        this.receiveRetryPolicy.ExecuteAction(() => session.Close());
    }
}

private MessageSession DoAcceptMessageSession()
{
    try
    {
        return this.client.AcceptMessageSession(TimeSpan.FromSeconds(45));
    }
    catch (TimeoutException)
    {
        return null;
    }
}
```

> You may find it useful to compare this version of the **ReceiveMessages** method that uses message sessions with the original version in the **SubscriptionReceiver** class.

To be able to use message sessions when you receive a message, you must ensure that when you send a message you include a session ID. The system uses the source ID from the event as the session ID, as shown in the following code sample from the **BuildMessage** method in the **EventBus** class.

```
var message = new BrokeredMessage(stream, true);
message.SessionId = @event.SourceId.ToString();
```

In this way, you can guarantee that all of the messages from an individual source will be received in the correct order.

However, sessions can only guarantee to deliver messages in order if the messages are placed on the bus in the correct order. If the system sends messages asynchronously, then you must take special care to ensure that messages are placed on the bus in the correct order. In our system, it is important that the events from each individual aggregate instance arrive in order, but we don't care about the ordering of events from different aggregate instances. Therefore, although the system sends events asynchronously, the **EventStoreBusPublisher** instance waits for an acknowledgement that the previous event was sent before sending the next one. The following sample from the **TopicSender** class illustrates this:

> In the V2 release, the team changed the way the system creates the Windows Azure Service Bus topics and subscriptions. Previously, the **SubscriptionReceiver** class created them if they didn't exist already. Now, the system creates them using configuration data when the application starts up. This happens early in the start-up process to avoid the risk of losing messages if one is sent to a topic before the system initializes the subscriptions.

```
public void Send(Func<BrokeredMessage> messageFactory)
{
    var resetEvent = new ManualResetEvent(false);
    Exception exception = null;
    this.retryPolicy.ExecuteAction(
        ac =>
        {
            this.DoBeginSendMessage(messageFactory(), ac);
        },
        ar =>
        {
            this.DoEndSendMessage(ar);
        },
        () => resetEvent.Set(),
        ex =>
        {
            Trace.TraceError(
            "An unrecoverable error occurred while trying to send a message:\n{0}"
            , ex);
            exception = ex;
            resetEvent.Set();
        });

    resetEvent.WaitOne();
    if (exception != null)
    {
        throw exception;
    }
}
```

For additional information about message ordering and Windows Azure Service Bus, see *Windows Azure Queues and Windows Azure Service Bus Queues - Compared and Contrasted*.

For information about sending messages asynchronously and ordering, see the blog post *Windows Azure Service Bus Splitter and Aggregator*.

Persisting events from the Conference Management bounded context

The team decided to create a message log of all the commands and events that are sent. This will enable the Orders and Registrations bounded context to query this log for the events from the Conference Management bounded context that it requires to build its read models. This is not event sourcing because we are not using these events to rebuild the state of our aggregates, although we are using similar techniques to capture and persist these integration events.

> This code sample shows how the system uses the *Transient Fault Handling Application Block* to make the asynchronous call reliably.

Adding additional metadata to the messages

The system now persists all messages to the message log. To make it easier to query the message log for specific commands or events, the system now adds more metadata to each message. Previously, the only metadata was the event type; now, the event metadata includes the event type, namespace, assembly, and path. The system adds the metadata to the events in the **EventBus** class and to the commands in the **CommandBus** class.

Capturing and persisting messages to the message log

The system uses an additional subscription to the **conference/commands** and **conference/events** topics in Windows Azure Service Bus to receive copies of every message in the system. It then appends the message to a Windows Azure table storage table. The following code sample shows the entity that the **AzureMessageLogWriter** class uses to save the message to the table:

> This message log ensures that no messages are lost, so that in the future it will be possible to meet additional requirements.

```
public class MessageLogEntity : TableServiceEntity
{
    public string Kind { get; set; }
    public string CorrelationId { get; set; }
    public string MessageId { get; set; }
    public string SourceId { get; set; }
    public string AssemblyName { get; set; }
    public string Namespace { get; set; }
    public string FullName { get; set; }
    public string TypeName { get; set; }
    public string SourceType { get; set; }
    public string CreationDate { get; set; }
    public string Payload { get; set; }
}
```

The **Kind** property specifies whether the message is either a command or an event. The **MessageId** and **CorrelationId** properties are set by the messaging infrastructure. The remaining properties are set from the message metadata.

The following code sample shows the definition of the partition and row keys for these messages:

```
PartitionKey = message.EnqueuedTimeUtc.ToString("yyyMM"),
RowKey = message.EnqueuedTimeUtc.Ticks.ToString("D20") + "_" + message.MessageId
```

Notice how the row key preserves the order in which the messages were originally sent and adds on the message ID to guarantee uniqueness just in case two messages were enqueued at exactly the same time.

> This is different from the event store where the partition key identifies the aggregate instance and the row key identifies the aggregate version number.

Data migration

When Contoso migrates the system from V1 to V2, it will use the message log to rebuild the conference and priced-order read models in the Orders and Registrations bounded context.

The conference read model holds information about conferences and contains information from the **ConferenceCreated**, **ConferenceUpdated**, **ConferencePublished**, **ConferenceUnpublished**, **SeatCreated**, and **SeatUpdated** events that come from the Conference Management bounded context.

The priced-order read model holds information from the **SeatCreated** and **SeatUpdated** events that come from the Conference Management bounded context.

However, in V1, these event messages were not persisted, so the read models cannot be repopulated in V2. To work around this problem, the team implemented a data migration utility that uses a best effort approach to generate events that contain the missing data to store in the message log. For example, after the migration to V2, the message log does not contain any **ConferenceCreated** events, so the migration utility finds this information in the database used by the Conference Management bounded context and creates the missing events. You can see how this is done in the **GeneratePastEventLogMessagesForConferenceManagement** method in the **Migrator** class in the **MigrationToV2** project.

The **RegenerateViewModels** method in the **Migrator** class shown below rebuilds the read models. It retrieves all the events from the message log by invoking the **Query** method, and then uses the **ConferenceViewModelGenerator** and **PricedOrderViewModelUpdater** classes to handle the messages.

> Contoso can use the message log whenever it needs to rebuild the read models that are built from events that are not associated with an aggregate, such as the integration events from the Conference Management bounded context.

> You can see in this class that Contoso also copies all of the existing event sourced events into the message log.

```
internal void RegenerateViewModels(
            AzureEventLogReader logReader,
            string dbConnectionString)
{
    var commandBus = new NullCommandBus();

    Database.SetInitializer<ConferenceRegistrationDbContext>(null);

    var handlers = new List<IEventHandler>();
    handlers.Add(new ConferenceViewModelGenerator(() =>
             new ConferenceRegistrationDbContext(dbConnectionString), commandBus));
    handlers.Add(new PricedOrderViewModelUpdater(() =>
             new ConferenceRegistrationDbContext(dbConnectionString)));

    using (var context =
             new ConferenceRegistrationMigrationDbContext(dbConnectionString))
    {
        context.UpdateTables();
    }

    try
    {
        var dispatcher = new MessageDispatcher(handlers);
        var events = logReader.Query(new QueryCriteria { });

        dispatcher.DispatchMessages(events);
    }
    catch
    {
        using (var context =
                 new ConferenceRegistrationMigrationDbContext(dbConnectionString))
        {
            context.RollbackTablesMigration();
        }

        throw;
    }
}
```

> The query may not be fast because it will retrieve entities from multiple partitions.

Notice how this method uses a **NullCommandBus** instance to swallow any commands from the **ConferenceViewModelGenerator** instance because we are only rebuilding the read model here.

Previously, the **PricedOrderViewModelGenerator** used the **ConferenceDao** class to obtain information about seats; now, it is autonomous and handles the **SeatCreated** and **SeatUpdated** events directly to maintain this information. As part of the migration, this information must be added to the read model. In the previous code sample, the **PricedOrderViewModelUpdater** class only handles the **SeatCreated** and **SeatUpdated** events and adds the missing information to the priced-order read model.

Migrating from V1 to V2

Migrating from V1 to V2 requires you to update the deployed application code and migrate the data. You should always rehearse the migration in a test environment before performing it in your production environment. These are the required steps:

1. Deploy the V2 release to your Windows Azure staging environment. The V2 release has a **MaintenanceMode** property that is initially set to **true**. In this mode, the application displays a message to the user stating that the site is currently undergoing maintenance and the worker role does not process messages.
2. When you are ready, swap the V2 release (still in maintenance mode) into your Windows Azure production environment.
3. Leave the V1 release (now running in the staging environment) to run for a few minutes to ensure that all in-flight messages complete their processing.
4. Run the migration program to migrate the data (see below).
5. After the data migration completes successfully, change the **MaintenanceMode** property of each role type to **false**.
6. The V2 release is now live in Windows Azure.

The following sections summarize the data migration from V1 to V2. Some of these steps were discussed previously in relation to a specific change or enhancement to the application.

One of the changes the team introduced for V2 is to keep a copy of all command and event messages in a message log in order to future-proof the application by capturing everything that might be used in the future. The migration process takes this new feature into account.

> The team considered using a separate application to display a message to users during the upgrade process telling them that the site is undergoing maintenance. However, using the **MaintenanceMode** property in the V2 release provides a simpler process, and adds a potentially useful new feature to the application.

> Because of the changes to the event store, it is not possible to perform a no down-time upgrade from V1 to V2. However, the changes that the team has made will ensure that the migration from V2 to V3 will be possible with no down time.

> The team applied various optimizations to the migration utility, such as batching the operations, in order to minimize the amount of down time.

Because the migration process copies large amounts of data around, you should run it in a Windows Azure worker role in order to minimize the cost. The migration utility is a console application, so you can use Windows Azure and Remote Desktop Services. For information about how to run an application inside a Windows Azure role instance, see *"Using Remote Desktop with Windows Azure Roles"* on MSDN.

Generating past log messages for the Conference Management bounded context

Part of the migration process is to recreate, where possible, the messages that the V1 release discarded after processing and then add them to the message log. In the V1 release, all of the integration events sent from the Conference Management bounded context to the Orders and Registrations bounded context were lost in this way. The system cannot recreate all of the lost events, but it can create events that represent the state of system at the time of the migration.

For more information, see the section "Persisting events from the Conference Management bounded context" earlier in this chapter.

> In some organizations, the security policy will not allow you to use Remote Desktop Services with Windows Azure in a production environment. However, you only need the worker role that hosts the Remote Desktop session for the duration of the migration; you can delete it after the migration is complete. You could also run your migration code as a worker role instead of as a console application and ensure that it logs the status of the migration for you to verify.

Migrating the event sourcing events

In the V2 release, the event store stores additional metadata for each event in order to facilitate querying for events. The migration process copies all of the events from the existing event store to a new event store with the new schema.

At the same time, the system adds a copy of all of these events to the message log that was introduced in the V2 release.

For more information, see the **MigrateEventSourcedAndGeneratePastEventLogs** in the **Migrator** class in the MigrationToV2 project.

Rebuilding the read models

The V2 release includes several changes to the definitions of the read models in the Orders and Registrations bounded context. The MigrationToV2 project rebuilds the Conference read model and Priced-order read model in the Orders and Registrations bounded context.

For more information, see the section "Persisting events from the Conference Management bounded context" earlier in this chapter.

Impact on testing

During this stage of the journey, the test team continued to expand the set of acceptance tests. They also created a set of tests to verify the data migration process.

> The original events are not updated in any way and are treated as being immutable.

SpecFlow revisited

Previously, the set of SpecFlow tests were implemented in two ways: either simulating user interaction by automating a web browser, or by operating directly on the MVC controllers. Both approaches had their advantages and disadvantages, which are discussed in Chapter 4, "Extending and Enhancing the Orders and Registrations Bounded Contexts."

After discussing these tests with another expert, the team also implemented a third approach. From the perspective of the domain-driven design (DDD) approach, the UI is not part of the domain model, and the focus of the core team should be on understanding the domain with the help of the domain expert and implementing the business logic in the domain. The UI is just the mechanical part added to enable users to interact with the domain. Therefore acceptance testing should include verifying that the domain model functions in the way that the domain expert expects. Therefore the team created a set of acceptance tests using SpecFlow that are designed to exercise the domain without the distraction of the UI parts of the system.

The following code sample shows the SelfRegistrationEndToEnd-WithDomain.feature file in the Features\Domain\Registration folder in the Conference.AcceptanceTests Visual Studio solution. Notice how the **When** and **Then** clauses use commands and events.

> Typically, you would expect the **When** clauses to send commands and the **Then** clauses to see events or exceptions if your domain model uses just aggregates. However, in this example, the domain-model includes a process manager that responds to events by sending commands. The test is checking that all of the expected commands are sent and all of the expected events are raised.

```
Feature: Self Registrant end to end scenario for making a Registration for
        a Conference site with Domain Commands and Events
    In order to register for a conference
    As an Attendee
    I want to be able to register for the conference, pay for the
    Registration Order and associate myself with the paid Order automatically


Scenario: Make a reservation with the selected Order Items
Given the list of the available Order Items for the CQRS summit 2012 conference
    | seat type                | rate  | quota |
    | General admission        | $199  | 100   |
    | CQRS Workshop            | $500  | 100   |
    | Additional cocktail party| $50   | 100   |
And the selected Order Items
    | seat type                | quantity |
    | General admission        | 1        |
    | Additional cocktail party| 1        |
When the Registrant proceeds to make the Reservation
    # command:RegisterToConference
Then the command to register the selected Order Items is received
    # event: OrderPlaced
And the event for Order placed is emitted
    # command: MakeSeatReservation
And the command for reserving the selected Seats is received
    # event: SeatsReserved
And the event for reserving the selected Seats is emitted
    # command: MarkSeatsAsReserved
And the command for marking the selected Seats as reserved is received
    # event: OrderReservationCompleted
And the event for completing the Order reservation is emitted
    # event: OrderTotalsCalculated
And the event for calculating the total of $249 is emitted
```

The following code sample shows some of the step implementations for the feature file. The steps use the command bus to send the commands.

```
[When(@"the Registrant proceed to make the Reservation")]
public void WhenTheRegistrantProceedToMakeTheReservation()
{
    registerToConference = ScenarioContext.Current.Get<RegisterToConference>();
    var conferenceAlias = ScenarioContext.Current.Get<ConferenceAlias>();

    registerToConference.ConferenceId = conferenceAlias.Id;
    orderId = registerToConference.OrderId;
    this.commandBus.Send(registerToConference);

    // Wait for event processing
    Thread.Sleep(Constants.WaitTimeout);
}

[Then(@"the command to register the selected Order Items is received")]
public void ThenTheCommandToRegisterTheSelectedOrderItemsIsReceived()
{
    var orderRepo = EventSourceHelper.GetRepository<Registration.Order>();
    Registration.Order order = orderRepo.Find(orderId);

    Assert.NotNull(order);
    Assert.Equal(orderId, order.Id);
}

[Then(@"the event for Order placed is emitted")]
public void ThenTheEventForOrderPlacedIsEmitted()
{
    var orderPlaced =
            MessageLogHelper.GetEvents<OrderPlaced>(orderId).SingleOrDefault();

    Assert.NotNull(orderPlaced);
    Assert.True(orderPlaced.Seats.All(os =>
       registerToConference.Seats.Count(cs =>
          cs.SeatType == os.SeatType && cs.Quantity == os.Quantity) == 1));
}
```

Discovering a bug during the migration

When the test team ran the tests on the system after the migration, we discovered that the number of seat types in the Orders and Registrations bounded context was different from the number prior to the migration. The investigation revealed the following cause.

The Conference Management bounded context allows a business customer to delete a seat type if the conference has never been published, but does not raise an integration event to report this fact to the Orders and Registrations bounded context. Therefore, the Orders and Registrations bounded context receives an event from the Conference Management bounded context when a business customer creates a new seat type, but not when a business customer deletes a seat type.

Part of the migration process creates a set of integration events to replace those that the V1 release discarded after processing. It creates these events by reading the database used by the Conference Management bounded context. This process did not create integration events for the deleted seat types.

In summary, in the V1 release, deleted seat types incorrectly appeared in the read models in the Orders and Registrations bounded context. After the migration to the V2 release, these deleted seat types did not appear in the read models in the Orders and Registrations bounded context.

Summary

During this stage of our journey, we versioned our system and completed the V2 pseudo-production release. This new release included some additional functionality and features, such as support for zero-cost orders and more information displayed in the UI.

We also made some changes in the infrastructure. For example, we made more messages idempotent and now persist integration events. The next chapter describes the final stage of our journey as we continue to enhance the infrastructure and harden the system in preparation for our V3 release.

> Testing the migration process not only verifies that the migration runs as expected, but potentially reveals bugs in the application itself.

More information

All links in this book are accessible from the book's online bibliography available at: *http://msdn.microsoft.com/en-us/library/jj619274*.

Journey 7:

Adding Resilience and Optimizing Performance

Reaching the end of our journey: the final tasks.

> *"You cannot fly like an eagle with the wings of a wren."*
> *Henry Hudson*

The three primary goals for this last stage in our journey are to make the system more resilient to failures, to improve the responsiveness of the UI, and to ensure that our design is scalable. The effort to harden the system focuses on the **RegistrationProcessManager** class in the Orders and Registrations bounded context. Performance improvement efforts are focused on the way the UI interacts with the domain model during the order creation process.

Working definitions for this chapter

The following terms are used in this chapter. For more detail, and possible alternative definitions, see Chapter 4, "A CQRS and ES Deep Dive" in the Reference Guide.

Command. A *command* is a request for the system to perform an action that changes the state of the system. Commands are imperatives; an example is **MakeSeatReservation**. In this bounded context, commands originate either from the user interface (UI) as a result of a user initiating a request, or from a process manager when the process manager is directing an aggregate to perform an action.

Commands are processed once by a single recipient. Commands are either transported to their recipients by a command bus, or delivered directly in-process. If a command is delivered through a command bus, then the command is sent asynchronously. If the command can be delivered directly in-process, then the command is sent synchronously.

Event. An *event*, such as **OrderConfirmed**, describes something that has happened in the system, typically as a result of a command. Aggregates in the domain model raise events. Events can also come from other bounded contexts.

Multiple subscribers can handle a specific event. Aggregates publish events to an event bus; handlers register for specific types of events on the event bus and then deliver the events to the subscriber. In the Orders and Registrations bounded context, the subscribers are a process manager and the read-model generators.

Snapshots. *Snapshots* are an optimization that you can apply to event sourcing; instead of replaying all of the persisted events associated with an aggregate when it is rehydrated, you load a recent copy of the state of the aggregate and then replay only the events that were persisted after saving the snapshot. In this way you can reduce the amount of data that you must load from the event store.

Idempotency. *Idempotency* is a characteristic of an operation that means the operation can be applied multiple times without changing the result. For example, the operation "set the value *x* to ten" is idempotent, while the operation "add one to the value of *x*" is not. In a messaging environment, a message is idempotent if it can be delivered multiple times without changing the result: either because of the nature of the message itself, or because of the way the system handles the message.

Eventual consistency. *Eventual consistency* is a consistency model that does not guarantee immediate access to updated values. After an update to a data object, the storage system does not guarantee that subsequent accesses to that object will return the updated value. However, the storage system does guarantee that if no new updates are made to the object during a sufficiently long period of time, then eventually all accesses can be expected to return the last updated value.

Architecture

The application is designed to deploy to Windows Azure. At this stage in the journey, the application consists of web roles that contain the ASP.NET MVC web applications and a worker role that contains the message handlers and domain objects. The application uses Windows Azure SQL Database (SQL Database) instances for data storage, both on the write side and the read side. The application also uses Windows Azure table storage on the write side and blob storage on the read side in some places. The application uses the Windows Azure Service Bus to provide its messaging infrastructure. Figure 1 shows this high-level architecture.

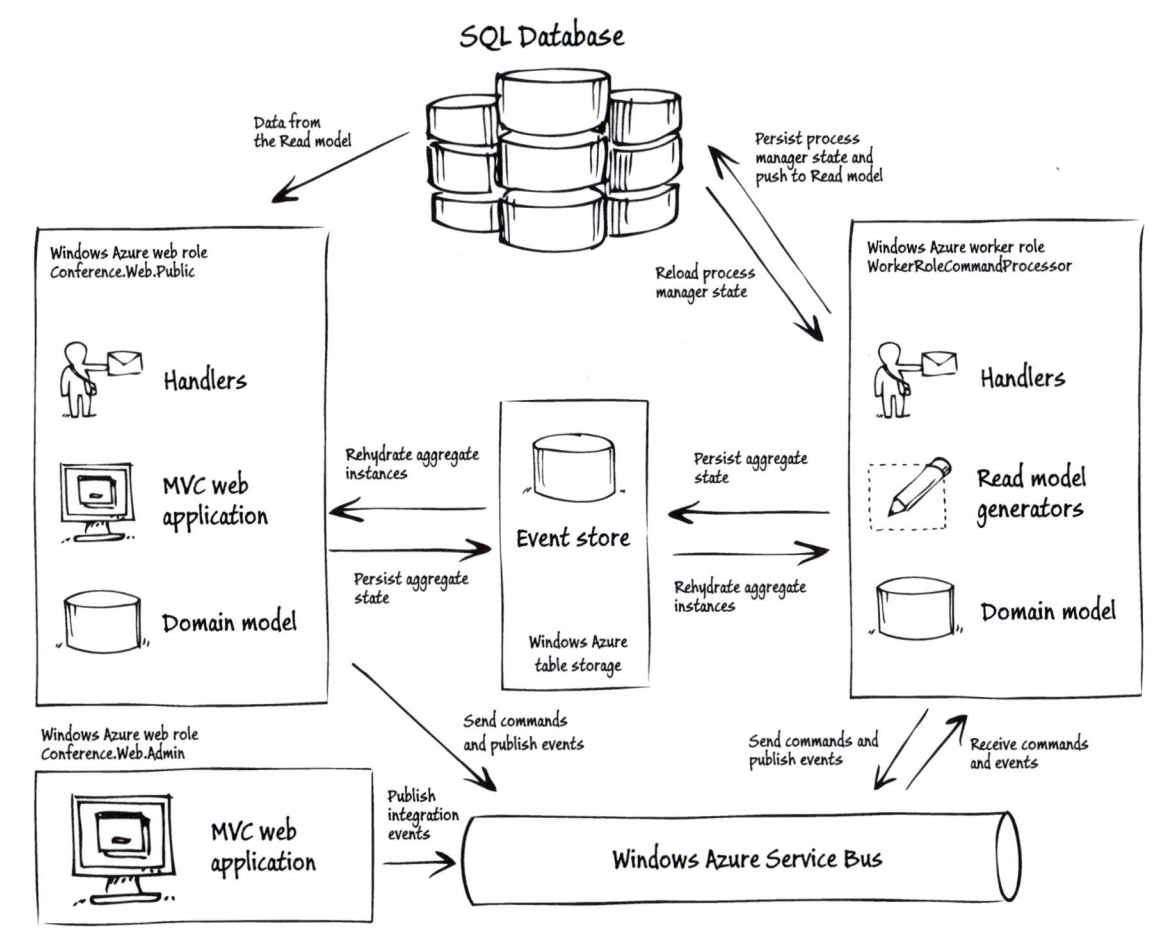

FIGURE 1
The top-level architecture in the V3 release

While you are exploring and testing the solution, you can run it locally, either using the Windows Azure compute emulator or by running the MVC web application directly and running a console application that hosts the handlers and domain objects. When you run the application locally, you can use a local SQL Server Express database instead of SQL Database, and use a simple messaging infrastructure implemented in a SQL Server Express database.

For more information about the options for running the application, see Appendix 1, "Release Notes."

Adding resilience

During this stage of the journey the team looked at options for hardening the **RegistrationProcessManager** class. This class is responsible for managing the interactions between the aggregates in the Orders and Registrations bounded context and for ensuring that they are all consistent with each other. It is important that this process manager is resilient to a wide range of failure conditions if the bounded context as a whole is to maintain its consistent state.

> An aggregate determines the consistency boundaries within the write model with respect to the consistency of the data that the system persists to storage. The process manager manages the relationship between different aggregates, possibly in different bounded contexts, and ensures that the aggregates are eventually consistent with each other.

Typically, a process manager receives incoming events and then, based on the state of the process manager, sends out one or more commands to aggregates within the bounded context. When a process manager sends out commands, it typically changes its own state.

The Orders and Registrations bounded context contains the **RegistrationProcessManager** class. This process manager is responsible for coordinating the activities of the aggregates in both this bounded context and the Payments bounded context by routing events and commands between them. The process manager is therefore responsible for ensuring that the aggregates in these bounded contexts are correctly synchronized with each other.

A failure in the registration process could have adverse consequences for the system; the aggregates could get out of synchronization with each other, which may cause unpredictable behavior in the system, or some processes might end up as zombie processes continuing to run and use resources while never completing. The team identified the following specific failure scenarios related to the **RegistrationProcessManager** process manager. The process manager could:

- Crash or be unable to persist its state after it receives an event but before it sends any commands. The message processor may not be able to mark the event as complete, so after a timeout, the event is placed back in the topic subscription and reprocessed.
- Crash after it persists its state but before it sends any commands. This puts the system into an inconsistent state because the process manager saves its new state without sending out the expected commands. The original event is put back in the topic subscription and reprocessed.
- Fail to mark that an event has been processed. The process manager will process the event a second time because after a timeout, the system will put the event back onto the Service Bus topic subscription.
- Timeout while it waits for a specific event that it is expecting. The process manager cannot continue processing and reach an expected end state.
- Receive an event that it does not expect to receive while the process manager is in a particular state. This may indicate a problem elsewhere that implies that it is unsafe for the process manager to continue.

These scenarios can be summarized to identify two specific issues to address:
- The **RegistrationProcessManager** handles an event successfully but fails to mark the message as complete. The **RegistrationProcessManager** will then process the event again after it is automatically returned to the Windows Azure Service Bus topic subscription.
- The **RegistrationProcessManager** handles an event successfully, marks it as complete, but then fails to send out the commands.

Making the system resilient when an event is reprocessed

If the behavior of the process manager itself is idempotent, then if it receives and processes an event a second time, no inconsistencies within the system will result. Making the behavior of the process manager idempotent would prevent the problems inherent in the first three failure conditions. After a crash, you could simply restart the process manager and reprocess the incoming event a second time.

Instead of making the process manager idempotent, you could ensure that all the commands that the process manager sends are idempotent. Restarting the process manager may result in sending commands a second time, but if those commands are idempotent, there will be no adverse effect on the process or the system. For this approach to work, you still need to modify the process manager to guarantee that it sends all commands at least once. If the commands are idempotent, it doesn't matter if they are sent multiple times, but it does matter if a command is never sent at all.

In the V1 release, most message handling is already either idempotent, or the system detects duplicate messages and sends them to a dead-letter queue. The exceptions are the **OrderPlaced** event and the **SeatsReserved** event, so the team modified the way that the V3 release of the system processes these two events in order to address this issue.

Ensuring that commands are always sent

Transactional behavior is required to ensure that the system always sends commands when the **RegistrationProcessManager** class saves its state. This requires the team to implement a pseudo-transaction because it is neither advisable nor possible to enlist the Windows Azure Service Bus and a SQL Database table together in a distributed transaction.

The solution adopted by the team for the V3 release ensures that the system persists all commands that the **RegistrationProcessManager** generates at the same time that it persists the state of the **RegistrationProcessManager** instance. Then the system tries to send the commands, removing them from storage after they have been sent successfully. The system also checks for undispatched messages whenever it loads a **RegistrationProcessManager** instance from storage.

Optimizing performance

During this stage of the journey we ran performance and stress tests using *Visual Studio 2010* to analyze response times and identify bottlenecks. The team used Visual Studio Load Test to simulate different numbers of users accessing the application, and added additional tracing into the code to record timing information for detailed analysis. The team created the performance test environment in Windows Azure, running the test controller and test agents in Windows Azure VM role instances. This enabled us to test how the Contoso Conference Management System performed under different loads by using the test agents to simulate different numbers of virtual users.

As a result of this exercise, the team made a number of changes to the system to optimize its performance.

UI FLOW BEFORE OPTIMIZATION

When a registrant creates an order, she visits the following sequence of screens in the UI.

1. The register screen. This screen displays the ticket types for the conference and the number of seats currently available according to the eventually consistent read model. The registrant selects the quantities of each seat type that she would like to purchase.

2. The checkout screen. This screen displays a summary of the order that includes a total price and a countdown timer that tells the registrant how long the seats will remain reserved. The registrant enters her details and preferred payment method.

3. The payment screen. This simulates a third-party payment processor.

4. The registration success screen. This displays if the payment succeeded. It displays to the registrant an order locator code and link to a screen that enables the registrant to assign attendees to seats.

See the section "Task-based UI" in Chapter 5, "Preparing for the V1 Release" for more information about the screens and flow in the UI.

In the V2 release, the system must process the following commands and events between the register screen and the checkout screen:

- **RegisterToConference**
- **OrderPlaced**
- **MakeSeatReservation**
- **SeatsReserved**
- **MarkSeatsAsReserved**
- **OrderReservationCompleted**
- **OrderTotalsCalculated**

> Although in this journey the team did their performance testing and optimization work at the end of the project, it typically makes sense to do this work as you go, addressing scalability issues and hardening the code as soon as possible. This is especially true if you are building your own infrastructure and need to be able to handle high volumes of throughput.

> Because implementing the CQRS pattern leads to a very clear separation of responsibilities for the many different parts that make up the system, we found it relatively easy to add optimizations and hardening because many of the necessary changes were very localized within the system.

In addition, the MVC controller is also validating that there are sufficient seats available by querying the read model to fulfill the order before it sends the initial **RegisterToConference** command.

When the team load tested the application using Visual Studio Load Test with different user load patterns, we noticed that with higher loads, the UI often has to wait for the domain to complete its processing and for the read models to receive data from the write model, before it can display the next screen to the registrant. In particular, with the V2 release deployed to medium-sized web and worker role instances we found that:

- With a constant load pattern of less than five orders per second, all orders are processed within a five-second window.
- With a constant load pattern of between eight and ten orders per second, many orders are not processed within the five-second window.
- With a constant load pattern of between eight and ten orders per second, the role instances are used sub-optimally (for example CPU usage is low).

> **Note:** *The five-second window is the maximum duration that we want to see between the time that the UI sends the initial command on the Service Bus and the time when the priced order becomes visible in the read model, enabling the UI to display the next screen to the user.*

To address this issue, the team identified two targets for optimization: the interaction between the UI and the domain, and the infrastructure. We decided to address the interaction between the UI and the domain first; when this did not improve performance sufficiently, we made infrastructure optimizations as well.

Optimizing the UI

The team discussed with the domain expert whether or not is always necessary to validate the seats availability before the UI sends the **RegisterToConference** command to the domain.

> This scenario illustrates some practical issues in relation to eventual consistency. The read side—in this case the priced order view model—is eventually consistent with the write side. Typically, when you implement the CQRS pattern you should be able to embrace eventual consistency and not need to wait in the UI for changes to propagate to the read side. However, in this case, the UI must wait for the write model to propagate to the read side information that relates to a specific order. This may indicate a problem with the original analysis and design of this part of the system.

The domain expert was clear that the system should confirm that seats are available before taking payment. Contoso does not want to sell seats and then have to explain to a registrant that those seats are not available. Therefore, the team looked for ways to streamline the process up to the point where the registrant sees the payment screen.

The team identified the following two optimizations to the UI flow.

UI optimization 1

Most of the time, there are plenty of seats available for a conference and registrants do not have to compete with each other to reserve seats. It is only for a brief time, as the conference comes close to selling out, that registrants do end up competing for the last few available seats.

If there are plenty of available seats for the conference, then there is minimal risk that a registrant will get as far as the payment screen only to find that the system could not reserve the seats. In this case, some of the processing that the V2 release performs before getting to the checkout screen can be allowed to happen asynchronously while the registrant is entering information on the checkout screen. This reduces the chance that the registrant experiences a delay before seeing the checkout screen.

However, if the controller checks and finds that there are not enough seats available to fulfill the order *before* it sends the **RegisterToConference** command, it can re-display the register screen to enable the registrant to update her order based on current availability.

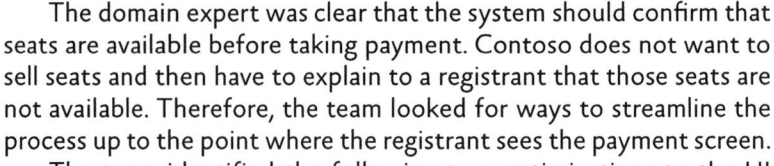

> This cautious strategy is not appropriate in all scenarios. In some cases, the business may prefer to take the money even if it cannot immediately fulfill the order. The business may know that the stock will be replenished soon, or that the customer will be happy to wait. In our scenario, although Contoso could refund the money to a registrant if tickets turned out not to be available, a registrant may decide to purchase flight tickets that are not refundable in the belief that the conference registration is confirmed. This type of decision is clearly one for the business and the domain expert.

> Essentially, we are relying on the fact that a reservation is likely to succeed, avoiding a time-consuming check. We still perform the check to ensure the seats are available before the registrant makes a payment.

UI optimization 2

In the V2 release, the MVC controller cannot display the checkout screen until the domain publishes the **OrderTotalsCalculated** event and the system updates the priced-order view model. This event is the last event that occurs before the controller can display the screen.

If the system calculates the total and updates the priced-order view model earlier, the controller can display the checkout screen sooner. The team determined that the **Order** aggregate could calculate the total when the order is placed instead of when the reservation is complete. This will enable the UI flow to move more quickly to the checkout screen than in the V2 release.

Optimizing the infrastructure

> *"Every day some new fact comes to light—some new obstacle which threatens the gravest obstruction. I suppose this is the reason which makes the game so well worth playing."*
> Robert Falcon Scott

The second set of optimizations that the team added in this stage of the journey related to the infrastructure of the system. These changes addressed both the performance and the scalability of the system. The following sections describe the most significant changes we made here.

Sending and receiving commands and events asynchronously

As part of the optimization process, the team updated the system to ensure that all messages sent on the Service Bus are sent asynchronously. This optimization is intended to improve the overall responsiveness of the application and improve the throughput of messages. As part of this change, the team also used the *Transient Fault Handling Application Block* to handle any transient errors encountered when using the Service Bus.

> This optimization resulted in major changes to the infrastructure code. Combining asynchronous calls with the Transient Fault Handling Application Block is complex; we would benefit from some of the new simplifying syntax in C# 4.5!

> For other proven practices to help you optimize performance when using the Windows Azure Service Bus, see this guide: *Best Practices for Performance Improvements Using Service Bus Brokered Messaging*.

An asynchronous command doesn't exist; it's actually another event. If I must accept what you send me and raise an event if I disagree, it's no longer you telling me to do something, it's you telling me something has been done. This seems like a slight difference at first, but it has many implications.
— Greg Young - Why do lots of developers use one-way command messaging (async handling) when it's not needed?, DDD/CQRS Group

> Once the team identified this bottleneck, it was easy to implement and test this solution. One of the advantages of the approach we followed when implementing the CQRS pattern is that we can make small localized changes in the system. Updates don't require us to make complex changes across multiple parts of the system.

Optimizing command processing

The V2 release used the same messaging infrastructure, the Windows Azure Service Bus, for both commands and events. The team evaluated whether the Contoso Conference Management System needs to send all its command messages using the same infrastructure.

There are a number of factors that we considered when we determined whether to continue using the Windows Azure Service Bus for transporting all command messages.

- Which commands, if any, can be handled in-process?
- Will the system become less resilient if it handles some commands in-process?
- Will there be any significant performance gains if it handles some commands in-process?

We identified a set of commands that the system can send synchronously and in-process from the public conference web application. To implement this optimization we had to add some infrastructure elements (the event store repositories, the event bus, and the event publishers) to the public conference web application; previously, these infrastructure elements were only in the system's worker role.

Using snapshots with event sourcing

The performance tests also uncovered a bottleneck in the use of the **SeatsAvailability** aggregate that we addressed by using a form of snapshot.

When the system rehydrates an aggregate instance from the event store, it must load and replay all of the events associated with that aggregate instance. A possible optimization here is to store a rolling snapshot of the state of the aggregate at some recent point in time so that the system only needs to load the snapshot and the subsequent events, thereby reducing the number of events that it must reload and replay. The only aggregate in the Contoso Conference Management System that is likely to accumulate a significant number of events over time is the **SeatsAvailability** aggregate. We decided to use the *Memento* pattern as the basis for the snapshot solution to use with the **SeatAvailability** aggregate. The solution we implemented uses a memento to capture the state of the **SeatAvailability** aggregate, and then keeps a copy of the memento in a cache. The system then tries to work with the cached data instead of always reloading the aggregate from the event store.

> Often, in the context of event sourcing, snapshots are persistent, not transient local caches as we have implemented in our project.

Publishing events in parallel

Publishing events in parallel proved to be one of the most significant optimizations in terms of improving the throughput of event messages in the system. The team went through several iterations to obtain the best results:

- Iteration 1: This approach used the *Parallel.ForEach* method with a custom partitioning scheme to assign messages to partitions and to set an upper bound on the degree of parallelism. It also used synchronous Windows Azure Service Bus API calls to publish the messages.
- Iteration 2: This approach used some asynchronous API calls. It required the use of custom semaphore-based throttling to handle the asynchronous callbacks correctly.
- Iteration 3: This approach uses dynamic throttling that takes into account the transient failures that indicate that too many messages are being sent to a specific topic. This approach uses more asynchronous Windows Azure Service Bus API calls.

> We adopted the same dynamic throttling approach in the **SubscriptionReceiver** and **SessionSubscriptionReceiver** classes when the system retrieves messages from the service bus.

Filtering messages in subscriptions

Another optimization adds filters to the Windows Azure Service Bus topic subscriptions to avoid reading messages that would later be ignored by the handlers associated with the subscription.

Creating a dedicated receiver for the SeatsAvailability aggregate

This enables the receiver for the **SeatsAvailability** aggregate to use a subscription that supports sessions. This is to guarantee that we have a single writer per aggregate instance because the **SeatsAvailability** aggregate is a high-contention aggregate. This prevents us from receiving a large number of concurrency exceptions when we scale out.

> Here we are taking advantage of a feature provided by Windows Azure Service Bus.

Caching conference information

This optimization caches several read models that the public conference web site uses extensively. It includes logic to determine how to keep the data in the cache based on the number of available seats for a particular conference: if there are plenty of seats available, the system can cache the data for a long period of time, but if there are very few seats available the data is not cached.

> Elsewhere, we use subscriptions with sessions to guarantee the ordering of events. In this case we are using sessions for a different reason—to guarantee that we have a single writer for each aggregate instance.

Partitioning the Service Bus

The team also partitioned the Service Bus to make the application more scalable and to avoid throttling when the volume of messages that the system sends approaches the maximum throughput that the Service Bus can handle. Each Service Bus topic may be handled by a different node in Windows Azure, so by using multiple topics we can increase our potential throughput. We considered the following partitioning schemes:

- Use separate topics for different message types.
- Use multiple, similar topics and listen to them all on a round-robin to spread the load.

For a detailed discussion of these partitioning schemes, see Chapter 11, "Asynchronous Communication and Message Buses" in "Scalability Rules: 50 Principles for Scaling Web Sites" by Martin L. Abbott and Michael T. Fisher (Addison-Wesley, 2011).

We decided to use separate topics for the events published by the **Order** aggregates and the **SeatAvailability** aggregates because these aggregates are responsible for the majority of events flowing through the service bus.

> Not all messages have the same importance. You could also use separate, prioritized message buses to handle different message types or even consider not using a message bus for some messages.

Other optimizations

The team performed some additional optimizations that are listed in the "Implementation details" section below. The primary goal of the team during this stage of the journey was to optimize the system to ensure that the UI appears sufficiently responsive to the user. There are additional optimizations that we could perform that would help to further improve performance and to optimize the way that the system uses resources. For example, a further optimization that the team considered was to scale out the view model generators that populate the various read models in the system. Every web role that hosts a view-model generator instance must handle the events published by the write side by creating a subscription to the Windows Azure Service Bus topics.

> Treat the Service Bus just like any other critical component of your system. This means you should ensure that your service bus can be scaled. Also, remember that not all data has the same value to your business. Just because you have a Service Bus, doesn't mean everything has to go through it. It's prudent to eliminate low-value, high-cost traffic.

Further changes that would improve performance

In addition to the changes we made during this last stage of the journey to improve the performance of the application, the team identified a number of other changes that would result in further improvements. However, the available time for this journey was limited so it was not possible to make these changes in the V3 release.

- We added asynchronous behavior to many areas of the application, especially in the calls the application makes to the Windows Azure Service Bus. However, there are other areas where the application still makes blocking, synchronous calls that we could make asynchronous: for example, when the system accesses the data stores. In addition, we would make use of new language features such as **async** and **await** in Visual Studio 2012 RC (the application is currently implemented using .NET 4.0 and Visual Studio 2010).

- There are opportunities to process messages in batches and to reduce the number of round-trips to the data store by adopting a *store-and-forward* design. For example, taking advantage of Windows Azure Service Bus sessions would enable us to accept a session from the Service Bus, read multiple items from the data store, process multiple messages, save once to the data store, and then complete all the messages.

- The website already caches some frequently accessed read-model data, but we could extend the use of caching to other areas of the system. The CQRS pattern means that we can regard a cache as part of the eventually consistent read model and, if necessary, provide access to read-model data from different parts of the system using different caches or no caching at all.

- We could improve the cached snapshot implementation that we have for the **SeatsAvailability** aggregate. The current implementation is described in detail later in this chapter, and is designed to always check the event store for events that arrived after the system created the latest cached snapshot. When we receive a new command to process, if we could check that we are still using the same Service Bus session as we were using when the system created the latest cached snapshot, then we would know if there could be other events in the event store. If the session hasn't changed, then we know we are the only writer, so there is no need to check the event store. If the session has changed, then someone else might have written events associated with the aggregate to the store, and we need to check.

> By accepting a Service Bus session you have a single writer and listener for that session for as long as you keep the lock; this reduces the chances of an optimistic concurrency exception. This design would fit particularly well in the **SeatsAvailability** read and write models. For the read models associated with the **Order** aggregates, which have very small partitions, you could acquire multiple small sessions from the Service Bus and use the store-and-forward approach on each session. Although both the read and write models in the system could benefit from this approach, it's easier to implement in the read models where we expect the data to be eventually consistent, not fully consistent.

> We could also use autoscaling to scale out the application when the load increases (for example by using the *Autoscaling Application Block*), but adding new instances takes time. By prioritizing certain message types, we can continue to deliver performance in key areas of the application while the autoscaler adds resources.

> The part of the system that is responsible for sending the messages can do so asynchronously. It could also implement dynamic throttling for sending the messages and dynamically control how many parallel senders to use.

- The application currently listens for all messages on all Service Bus subscriptions using the same priority. In practice, some messages are more important than others; therefore, when the application is under stress we should prioritize some message processing to minimize the impact on core application functionality. For example, we could identify certain read models where we are willing to accept more latency.

- The current implementation uses randomly generated GUIDs as keys for all of the entities stored in our SQL Database instance. When the system is under heavy load, it may perform better if we use sequential GUIDs, especially in relation to clustered indexes. For a discussion of sequential GUIDs, see *The Cost of GUIDs as Primary Keys*.

- As part of our optimizations to the system, we now process some commands in-process instead of sending them through the Service Bus. We could extend this to other commands and potentially the process manager.

- In the current implementation, the process manager processes incoming messages and then the repository tries to send the outgoing messages synchronously (it uses the *Transient Fault Handling Application Block* to retry sending commands if the Service Bus throws any exceptions due to throttling behavior). We could instead use a mechanism similar to that used by the **EventStoreBusPublisher** class so that the process manager saves a list of messages that must be sent along with its state in a single transaction, and then notifies a separate part of the system, which is responsible for sending the messages, that there are some new messages ready to send.

- Our current event store implementation publishes a single, small message on the Service Bus for every event that's saved in the event store. We could group some of these messages together to reduce the total number of I/O operations on the Service Bus. For example, a **SeatsAvailability** aggregate instance for a large conference publishes a large number of events, and the **Order** aggregate publishes events in bursts (when an **Order** aggregate is created it publishes both an **OrderPlaced** event and an **OrderTotalsCalculated** event). This will also help to reduce the latency in the system because currently, in those scenarios in which ordering is important, we must wait for a confirmation that one event has been sent before sending the next one. Grouping sequences of events in a single message would mean that we don't need to wait for the confirmation between publishing individual events.

Further changes that would enhance scalability

The Contoso Conference Management System is designed to allow you to deploy multiple instances of the web and worker roles to scale out the application to handle larger loads. However, the design is not fully scalable because some of the other elements of the system, such as the message buses and data stores place constraints on the maximum achievable throughput. This section outlines some changes that we could make to the system to remove some of these constraints and significantly enhance the scalability of the system. The available time for this journey was limited so it was not possible to make these changes in the V3 release.

- **Partition the data:** The system stores different types of data in different partitions. You can see in the bootstrapping code how the different bounded contexts use different connection strings to connect to the SQL Database instance. However, each bounded context currently uses a single SQL Database instance and we could change this to use multiple different instances, each holding a specific set of data that the system uses. For example the Orders and Registrations bounded context could use different SQL Database instances for the different read models. We could also consider using the federations feature to use sharding to scale out some of the SQL Database instances.

- **Further partition the Service Bus:** We already partition the Service Bus, by using different topics for different event publishers, to avoid throttling when the volume of messages that the system is sending approaches the maximum throughput that the Service Bus can handle. We could further partition the topics by using multiple, similar topics and listening to them all on a round-robin to spread the load. For a detailed description of this approach, see Chapter 11, "Asynchronous Communication and Message Buses" in *Scalability Rules: 50 Principles for Scaling Web Sites*, by Abbott and Fisher (Addison-Wesley, 2011).

- **Store and forward:** We introduced the store-and-forward design in the earlier section on performance improvement. By batching multiple operations, you not only reduce the number of round-trips to the data store and reduce the latency in the system, you also enhance the scalability of the system because issuing fewer requests reduces the stress on the data store.

"Data persistence is the hardest technical problem most scalable SaaS businesses face."
—Evan Cooke, CTO, Twilio, *Scaling High-Availability Infrastructure in the Cloud*

> Where the system stores data in Windows Azure table storage, we chose keys to partition the data for scalability. As an alternative to using SQL Database federations to shard the data, we could move some of the read-model data currently in the SQL Database instance to either Windows Azure table storage or blob storage.

- **Listen for and react to throttling indicators:** Currently, the system uses the *Transient Fault Handling Application Block* to detect transient error conditions such as throttling indicators from the Windows Azure Service Bus, the SQL Database instance, and Windows Azure table storage. The system uses the block to implement retries in these scenarios, typically by using an exponential back-off strategy. At present, we use dynamic throttling at the level of an individual subscription; however, we'd like to modify this to perform the dynamic throttling for all of the subscriptions to a specific topic. Similarly, we'd like to implement dynamic throttling at the level of the SQL Database instance, and at the level of the Windows Azure storage account.

For some additional information relating to scalability, see:
- *Windows Azure Storage Abstractions and their Scalability Targets*
- *Best Practices for Performance Improvements Using Service Bus Brokered Messaging*

It's important not to get a false sense of optimism when it comes to scalability and high availability. While with many of the suggested practices the applications tend to scale more efficiently and become more resilient to failure, they are still prone to high-demand bottlenecks. Make sure to allocate sufficient time for performance testing and for meeting your performance goals.

No down-time migration

> *"Preparation, I have often said, is rightly two-thirds of any venture."*
>
> — Amelia Earhart

The team planned to have a no-downtime migration from the V2 to the V3 release in Windows Azure. To achieve this, the migration process uses an ad-hoc processor running in a Windows Azure worker role to perform some of the migration steps.

The migration process still requires you to complete a configuration step to switch off the V2 processor and switch on the V3 processor. In retrospect, we would have used a different mechanism to streamline the transition from the V2 to the V3 processor based on feedback from the handlers themselves to indicate when they have finished their processing.

For details of these steps, see Appendix 1, "Release Notes."

> For an example of implementing dynamic throttling within the application to avoid throttling from the service, see how the **EventStoreBusPublisher**, **SubscriptionReceiver**, and **SessionSubscriptionReceiver** classes use the **DynamicThrottling** class to manage the degree of parallelism they use to send or receive messages.

> Each service (Windows Azure Service Bus, SQL Database, Windows Azure storage) has its own particular way of implementing throttling behavior and notifying you when it is placed under heavy load. For example, see *SQL Azure Throttling*. It's important to be aware of all the throttling that your application may be subjected to by different services your application uses.

> The team also considered using the Windows Azure SQL Database Business edition instead of the Windows Azure SQL Database Web edition but, upon investigation, we determined that at present the only difference between the editions is the maximum database size. The different editions are not tuned to support different types of workload, and both editions implement the same throttling behavior.

Rebuilding the read models

During the migration from V2 to V3, one of the steps we must perform is to rebuild the **DraftOrder** and **PricedOrder** view models by replaying events from the event log to populate the new V3 read-model tables. We can do this asynchronously. However, at some point in time, we need to start sending events from the live application to these read models. Furthermore, we need to keep both the V2 and V3 versions of these read models up to date until the migration process is complete because the V2 front-end web role will need the V2 read-model data to be available until we switch to the V3 front-end web role. At the point at which we switch to the V3 front end, we must ensure that the V3 read models are completely up to date.

To keep these read models up to date, we created an ad-hoc processor as a Windows Azure worker role that runs just while the migration is taking place. See the MigrationToV3 project in the Conference solution for more details. The steps that this processor performs are to:

- Create a new set of topic subscriptions that will receive the live events that will be used to populate the new V3 read models. These subscriptions will start accumulating the events that will be handled when the V3 application is deployed.

- Replay the events from the event log to populate the new V3 read models with historical data.

- Handle the live events and keep the V2 read models up to date until the V3 front end is live, at which point we no longer need the V2 read models.

The migration process first replays the events from the event store to populate the new V3 read models. When this is complete, we stop the V2 processor that contains the event handlers, and start the new handlers in their V3 processor. While these are running and catching up on the events that were accumulated in the new topic subscriptions, the ad-hoc processor is also keeping the V2 read models up to date because at this point we still have the V2 front end. When the V3 worker roles are ready, we can perform a VIP switch to bring the new V3 front end into use. After the V3 front end is running, we no longer have any need for the V2 read models.

> You should always rehearse the migration in a test environment before performing it in your production environment.

One of the issues to address with this approach is how to determine when the new V3 processor should switch from processing archived events in the event log to the live stream of events. There is some latency in the process that writes events to the event log, so an instantaneous switch could result in the loss of some events. The team decided to allow the V3 processor to temporarily handle both archived events and the live stream, which means there is a possibility that there will be duplicate events; the same event exists in the event store and in the list of events accumulated by the new subscription. However, we can detect these duplicates and handle them accordingly.

An alternative approach that we considered was to include both V2 and V3 handling in the V3 processor. With this approach, there is no need for an ad-hoc worker role to process the V2 events during the migration. However, we decided to keep the migration-specific code in a separate project to avoid bloating the V3 release with functionality that is only needed during the migration.

> Typically, we rely on the infrastructure to detect duplicate messages. In this particular scenario where duplicate events may come from different sources, we cannot rely on the infrastructure and must add the duplicate detection logic into our code explicitly.

> *The intervals between each step of the migration take some time to complete, so the migration achieves no downtime, but the user does experience delays. We would have benefited from some faster mechanisms to deal with the toggle switches, such as stopping the V2 processor and starting the V3 processor.*

Implementation details

This section describes some of the significant features of the implementation of the Orders and Registrations bounded context. You may find it useful to have a copy of the code so you can follow along. You can download a copy of the code from the *Download center,* or check the evolution of the code in the repository on GitHub: *https://github.com/mspnp/cqrs-journey-code*. You can download the code from the V3 release from the *Tags* page on GitHub.

> **Note:** *Do not expect the code samples to exactly match the code in the reference implementation. This chapter describes a step in the CQRS journey; the implementation may well change as we learn more and refactor the code.*

Hardening the RegistrationProcessManager class

This section describes how the team hardened the **RegistrationProcessManager** process manager by checking for duplicate instances of the **SeatsReserved** and **OrderPlaced** messages.

> The migration process would be slightly easier if we included both V2 and V3 handling in the V3 processor. We decided that the benefit of such an approach was outweighed by the benefit of not having to maintain duplicate functionality in the V3 processor.

Detecting out-of-order SeatsReserved events

Typically, the **RegistrationProcessManager** class sends a **MakeSeatReservation** command to the **SeatAvailability** aggregate, the **SeatAvailability** aggregate publishes a **SeatsReserved** event when it has made the reservation, and the **RegistrationProcessManager** receives this notification. The **RegistrationProcessManager** sends a **MakeSeatReservation** command both when the order is created and when it is updated. It is possible that the **SeatsReserved** events could arrive out of order; however, the system should honor the event related to the last command that was sent. The solution described in this section enables the **RegistrationProcessManager** to identify the most recent **SeatsReserved** message and then ignore any earlier messages instead of reprocessing them.

Before the **RegistrationProcessManager** class sends the **MakeSeatReservation** command, it saves the **Id** of the command in the **SeatReservationCommandId** variable, as shown in the following code sample:

```
public void Handle(OrderPlaced message)
{
    if (this.State == ProcessState.NotStarted)
    {
        this.ConferenceId = message.ConferenceId;
        this.OrderId = message.SourceId;
        // Use the order id as an opaque reservation id for the seat reservation.
        // It could be anything else, as long as it is deterministic from the
        // OrderPlaced event.
        this.ReservationId = message.SourceId;
        this.ReservationAutoExpiration = message.ReservationAutoExpiration;
        var expirationWindow =
            message.ReservationAutoExpiration.Subtract(DateTime.UtcNow);

        if (expirationWindow > TimeSpan.Zero)
        {
            this.State = ProcessState.AwaitingReservationConfirmation;
            var seatReservationCommand =
                new MakeSeatReservation
                {
                    ConferenceId = this.ConferenceId,
                    ReservationId = this.ReservationId,
                    Seats = message.Seats.ToList()
                };
            this.SeatReservationCommandId = seatReservationCommand.Id;

            this.AddCommand(new Envelope<ICommand>(seatReservationCommand)
            {
                TimeToLive = expirationWindow.Add(TimeSpan.FromMinutes(1)),
            });

            ...
}
```

Then, when it handles the **SeatsReserved** event, it checks that the **CorrelationId** property of the event matches the most recent value of the **SeatReservationCommandId** variable, as shown in the following code sample:

```
public void Handle(Envelope<SeatsReserved> envelope)
{
    if (this.State == ProcessState.AwaitingReservationConfirmation)
    {
        if (envelope.CorrelationId != null)
        {
            if (string.CompareOrdinal(
                this.SeatReservationCommandId.ToString(),
                envelope.CorrelationId)
                != 0)
            {
                // Skip this event.
                Trace.TraceWarning(
                    "Seat reservation response for reservation id {0}" +
                    "does not match the expected correlation id.",
                    envelope.Body.ReservationId);
                return;
            }
        }
        ...
}
```

Notice how this **Handle** method handles an **Envelope** instance instead of a **SeatsReserved** instance. As a part of the V3 release, events are wrapped in an **Envelope** instance that includes the **CorrelationId** property. The **DoDispatchMessage** method in the **EventDispatcher** assigns the value of the correlation Id.

During performance testing, the team identified a further issue with this specific **SeatsReserved** event. Because of a delay elsewhere in the system when it was under load, a second copy of the **SeatsReserved** event was being published. This **Handle** method was then throwing an exception that caused the system to retry processing the message several times before sending it to a dead-letter queue. To address this specific issue, the team modified this method by adding the **else if** clause, as shown in the following code sample:

> As a side-effect of adding this feature, the **EventProcessor** class can no longer use the **dynamic** keyword when it forwards events to handlers. Now in V3 it uses the new **EventDispatcher** class; this class uses reflection to identify the correct handlers for a given message type.

```
public void Handle(Envelope<SeatsReserved> envelope)
{
    if (this.State == ProcessState.AwaitingReservationConfirmation)
    {
        ...
    }
    else if (string.CompareOrdinal(
            this.SeatReservationCommandId.ToString(),
            envelope.CorrelationId) == 0)
    {
        Trace.TraceInformation(
            "Seat reservation response for request {1} for reservation" +
            "id {0} was already handled. Skipping event.",
            envelope.Body.ReservationId,
            envelope.CorrelationId);
    }
    else
    {
        throw new InvalidOperationException("Cannot handle seat reservation at this stage.");
    }
}
```

> This optimization was only applied for this specific message. Notice that it makes use of the value of the **SeatReservationCommandId** property that was previously saved in the instance. If you want to perform this kind of check on other messages you'll need to store more information in the process manager.

Detecting duplicate OrderPlaced events

To detect duplicate **OrderPlaced** events, the **RegistrationProcessManagerRouter** class now performs a check to see if the event has already been processed. The new V3 version of the code is shown in the following code sample:

```
public void Handle(OrderPlaced @event)
{
    using (var context = this.contextFactory.Invoke())
    {
        var pm = context.Find(x => x.OrderId == @event.SourceId);
        if (pm == null)
        {
            pm = new RegistrationProcessManager();
        }

        pm.Handle(@event);
        context.Save(pm);
    }
}
```

Creating a pseudo transaction when the Registration-Process-Manager class saves its state and sends a command

It is not possible to have a transaction in Windows Azure that includes persisting the **RegistrationProcessManager** to storage and sending the command. Therefore, the team decided to save all the commands that the process manager generates so that if the process crashes, the commands are not lost and can be sent later. We use another process to handle sending the commands reliably.

> The migration utility for moving to the V3 release updates the database schema to accommodate the new storage requirement.

The following code sample from the **SqlProcessDataContext** class shows how the system persists all the commands along with the state of the process manager:

```
public void Save(T process)
{
    var entry = this.context.Entry(process);

    if (entry.State == System.Data.EntityState.Detached)
        this.context.Set<T>().Add(process);

    var commands = process.Commands.ToList();
    UndispatchedMessages undispatched = null;
    if (commands.Count > 0)
    {
        // If there are pending commands to send, we store them as undispatched.
        undispatched = new UndispatchedMessages(process.Id)
                        {
                            Commands = this.serializer.Serialize(commands)
                        };
        this.context.Set<UndispatchedMessages>().Add(undispatched);
    }

    try
    {
        this.context.SaveChanges();
    }
    catch (DbUpdateConcurrencyException e)
    {
        throw new ConcurrencyException(e.Message, e);
    }

    this.DispatchMessages(undispatched, commands);
}
```

The following code sample from the **SqlProcessDataContext** class shows how the system tries to send the command messages:

```
private void DispatchMessages(UndispatchedMessages undispatched,
                  List<Envelope<ICommand>> deserializedCommands = null)
{
    if (undispatched != null)
    {
        if (deserializedCommands == null)
        {
            deserializedCommands = this.serializer
                .Deserialize<IEnumerable<Envelope<ICommand>>>(
                    undispatched.Commands).ToList();
        }

        var originalCommandsCount = deserializedCommands.Count;
        try
        {
            while (deserializedCommands.Count > 0)
            {
                this.commandBus.Send(deserializedCommands.First());
                deserializedCommands.RemoveAt(0);
            }
        }
        catch (Exception)
        {
            // We catch a generic exception as we don't know
            // what implementation of ICommandBus we might be using.
            if (originalCommandsCount != deserializedCommands.Count)
            {
                // If we were able to send some commands,
                // then update the undispatched messages.
                undispatched.Commands =
                this.serializer.Serialize(deserializedCommands);
                try
                {
                    this.context.SaveChanges();
                }
                catch (DbUpdateConcurrencyException)
                {
                    // If another thread already dispatched the messages,
                    // ignore and surface original exception instead.
                }
            }

            throw;
        }
```

```
                // We remove all the undispatched messages for this process manager.
                this.context.Set<UndispatchedMessages>().Remove(undispatched);
                this.retryPolicy.ExecuteAction(() => this.context.SaveChanges());
        }
}
```

The **DispatchMessages** method is also invoked from the **Find** method in the **SqlProcessDataContext** class so that it tries to send any un-dispatched messages whenever the system rehydrates a **RegistrationProcessManager** instance.

Optimizing the UI flow

The first optimization is to allow the UI to navigate directly to the registrant screen provided that there are plenty of seats still available for the conference. This change is introduced in the **StartRegistration** method in the **RegistrationController** class that now performs an additional check to verify that there are enough remaining seats to stand a good chance of making the reservation before it sends the **RegisterToConference** command, as shown in the following code sample:

```
[HttpPost]
public ActionResult StartRegistration(
    RegisterToConference command,
    int orderVersion)
{
    var existingOrder = orderVersion != 0
                          ? this.orderDao.FindDraftOrder(command.OrderId)
                          : null;
    var viewModel = existingOrder == null
                          ? this.CreateViewModel()
                          : this.CreateViewModel(existingOrder);
    viewModel.OrderId = command.OrderId;

    if (!ModelState.IsValid)
    {
        return View(viewModel);
    }

    // Checks that there are still enough available seats,
    //  and the seat type IDs submitted are valid.
    ModelState.Clear();
    bool needsExtraValidation = false;
    foreach (var seat in command.Seats)
    {
        var modelItem = viewModel.Items
                        .FirstOrDefault(x => x.SeatType.Id == seat.SeatType);
        if (modelItem != null)
        {
```

```
                    if (seat.Quantity > modelItem.MaxSelectionQuantity)
                    {
                        modelItem.PartiallyFulfilled = needsExtraValidation = true;
                        modelItem.OrderItem.ReservedSeats =
                            modelItem.MaxSelectionQuantity;
                    }
                }
                else
                {
                    // Seat type no longer exists for conference.
                    needsExtraValidation = true;
                }
            }

            if (needsExtraValidation)
            {
                return View(viewModel);
            }

            command.ConferenceId = this.ConferenceAlias.Id;
            this.commandBus.Send(command);

            return RedirectToAction(
                "SpecifyRegistrantAndPaymentDetails",
                new
                {
                    conferenceCode = this.ConferenceCode,
                    orderId = command.OrderId,
                    orderVersion = orderVersion
                });
        }
```

If there are not enough available seats, the controller redisplays the current screen, displaying the currently available seat quantities to enable the registrant to revise her order.

This remaining part of the change is in the **SpecifyRegistrantAndPaymentDetails** method in the **RegistrationController** class. The following code sample from the V2 release shows that before the optimization, the controller calls the **WaitUntilSeatsAreConfirmed** method before continuing to the registrant screen:

```
[HttpGet]
[OutputCache(Duration = 0, NoStore = true)]
public ActionResult SpecifyRegistrantAndPaymentDetails(
    Guid orderId,
    int orderVersion)
{
    var order = this.WaitUntilSeatsAreConfirmed(orderId, orderVersion);
    if (order == null)
    {
        return View("ReservationUnknown");
    }

    if (order.State == DraftOrder.States.PartiallyReserved)
    {
        return this.RedirectToAction(
            "StartRegistration",
            new
            {
                conferenceCode = this.ConferenceCode,
                orderId, orderVersion = order.OrderVersion
            });
    }

    if (order.State == DraftOrder.States.Confirmed)
    {
        return View("ShowCompletedOrder");
    }

    if (order.ReservationExpirationDate.HasValue
        && order.ReservationExpirationDate < DateTime.UtcNow)
    {
        return RedirectToAction(
            "ShowExpiredOrder",
            new { conferenceCode = this.ConferenceAlias.Code, orderId = orderId });
    }

    var pricedOrder = this.WaitUntilOrderIsPriced(orderId, orderVersion);
    if (pricedOrder == null)
    {
        return View("ReservationUnknown");
    }

    this.ViewBag.ExpirationDateUTC = order.ReservationExpirationDate;

    return View(
        new RegistrationViewModel
```

```
        {
            RegistrantDetails = new AssignRegistrantDetails { OrderId = orderId },
            Order = pricedOrder
        });
}
```

The following code sample shows the V3 version of this method, which no longer waits for the reservation to be confirmed:

```
[HttpGet]
[OutputCache(Duration = 0, NoStore = true)]
public ActionResult SpecifyRegistrantAndPaymentDetails(
    Guid orderId,
    int orderVersion)
{
    var pricedOrder = this.WaitUntilOrderIsPriced(orderId, orderVersion);
    if (pricedOrder == null)
    {
        return View("PricedOrderUnknown");
    }

    if (!pricedOrder.ReservationExpirationDate.HasValue)
    {
        return View("ShowCompletedOrder");
    }

    if (pricedOrder.ReservationExpirationDate < DateTime.UtcNow)
    {
        return RedirectToAction(
            "ShowExpiredOrder",
            new { conferenceCode = this.ConferenceAlias.Code, orderId = orderId });
    }

    return View(
        new RegistrationViewModel
        {
            RegistrantDetails = new AssignRegistrantDetails { OrderId = orderId },
            Order = pricedOrder
        });
}
```

Note: *We made this method asynchronous later on during this stage of the journey.*

The second optimization in the UI flow is to perform the calculation of the order total earlier in the process. In the previous code sample, the **SpecifyRegistrantAndPaymentDetails** method still calls the **WaitUntilOrderIsPriced** method, which pauses the UI flow until the system calculates an order total and makes it available to the controller by saving it in the priced-order view model on the read side.

The key change to implement this is in the **Order** aggregate. The constructor in the **Order** class now invokes the **CalculateTotal** method and raises an **OrderTotalsCalculated** event, as shown in the following code sample:

```
public Order(
    Guid id,
    Guid conferenceId,
    IEnumerable<OrderItem> items,
    IPricingService pricingService)
    : this(id)
{
    var all = ConvertItems(items);
    var totals = pricingService.CalculateTotal(conferenceId, all.AsReadOnly());

    this.Update(new OrderPlaced
    {
        ConferenceId = conferenceId,
        Seats = all,
        ReservationAutoExpiration = DateTime.UtcNow.Add(ReservationAutoExpiration),
        AccessCode = HandleGenerator.Generate(6)
    });
    this.Update(
        new OrderTotalsCalculated
        {
            Total = totals.Total,
            Lines = totals.Lines != null ? totals.Lines.ToArray() : null,
            IsFreeOfCharge = totals.Total == 0m
        });
}
```

Previously, in the V2 release the **Order** aggregate waited until it received a **MarkAsReserved** command before it called the **CalculateTotal** method.

Receiving, completing, and sending messages asynchronously

This section outlines how the system now performs all I/O on the Windows Azure Service Bus asynchronously.

Receiving messages asynchronously

The **SubscriptionReceiver** and **SessionSubscriptionReceiver** classes now receive messages asynchronously instead of synchronously in the loop in the **ReceiveMessages** method.

For details see either the **ReceiveMessages** method in the **SubscriptionReceiver** class or the **ReceiveMessagesAndCloseSession** method in the **SessionSubscriptionReceiver** class.

Completing messages asynchronously

The system uses the peek/lock mechanism to retrieve messages from the Service Bus topic subscriptions. To learn how the system performs these operations asynchronously, see the **ReceiveMessages** methods in the **SubscriptionReceiver** and **SessionSubscriptionReceiver** classes. This provides one example of how the system uses asynchronous APIs.

Sending messages asynchronously

The application now sends all messages on the Service Bus asynchronously. For more details, see the **TopicSender** class.

Handling commands synchronously and in-process

In the V2 release, the system used the Windows Azure Service Bus to deliver all commands to their recipients. This meant that the system delivered the commands asynchronously. In the V3 release, the MVC controllers now send their commands synchronously and in-process in order to improve the response times in the UI by bypassing the command bus and delivering commands directly to their handlers. In addition, in the **ConferenceProcessor** worker role, commands sent to **Order** aggregates are sent synchronously in-process using the same mechanism.

> This code sample also shows how to use the *Transient Fault Handling Application Block* to reliably receive messages asynchronously from the Service Bus topic. The asynchronous loops make the code much harder to read, but much more efficient. This is a recommended best practice. This code would benefit from the new **async** keywords in C# 4.

> We still continue to send commands to the **SeatsAvailability** aggregate asynchronously because with multiple instances of the **RegistrationProcessManager** running in parallel, there will be contention as multiple threads all try to access the same instance of the **SeatsAvailability** aggregate.

The team implemented this behavior by adding the **SynchronousCommandBusDecorator** and **CommandDispatcher** classes to the infrastructure and registering them during the start-up of the web role, as shown in the following code sample from the **OnCreateContainer** method in the Global.asax.Azure.cs file:

```
var commandBus = new CommandBus(
                    new TopicSender(settings.ServiceBus, "conference/commands"),
                    metadata,
                    serializer);
var synchronousCommandBus = new SynchronousCommandBusDecorator(commandBus);

container.RegisterInstance<ICommandBus>(synchronousCommandBus);
container.RegisterInstance<ICommandHandlerRegistry>(synchronousCommandBus);


container.RegisterType<ICommandHandler, OrderCommandHandler>(
    "OrderCommandHandler");
container.RegisterType<ICommandHandler, ThirdPartyProcessorPaymentCommandHandler>(
     "ThirdPartyProcessorPaymentCommandHandler");
container.RegisterType<ICommandHandler, SeatAssignmentsHandler>(
    "SeatAssignmentsHandler");
```

Note: *There is similar code in the Conference.Azure.cs file to configure the worker role to send some commands in-process.*

The following code sample shows how the **SynchronousCommandBusDecorator** class implements the sending of a command message:

```
public class SynchronousCommandBusDecorator : ICommandBus, ICommandHandlerRegistry
{
    private readonly ICommandBus commandBus;
    private readonly CommandDispatcher commandDispatcher;

    public SynchronousCommandBusDecorator(ICommandBus commandBus)
    {
        this.commandBus = commandBus;
        this.commandDispatcher = new CommandDispatcher();
    }

    ...

    public void Send(Envelope<ICommand> command)
    {
        if (!this.DoSend(command))
        {
```

```csharp
            Trace.TraceInformation(
        "Command with id {0} was not handled locally. Sending it through the bus.",
        command.Body.Id);
            this.commandBus.Send(command);
        }
    }

    ...

    private bool DoSend(Envelope<ICommand> command)
    {
        bool handled = false;

        try
        {
            var traceIdentifier =
                string.Format(
                    CultureInfo.CurrentCulture,
                    " (local handling of command with id {0})",
                    command.Body.Id);
            handled = this.commandDispatcher.ProcessMessage(traceIdentifier,
            command.Body, command.MessageId, command.CorrelationId);

        }
        catch (Exception e)
        {
            Trace.TraceWarning(
                "Exception handling command with id {0} synchronously: {1}",
                command.Body.Id,
                e.Message);
        }

        return handled;
    }
}
```

Notice how this class tries to send the command synchronously without using the Service Bus, but if it cannot find a handler for the command, it reverts to using the Service Bus. The following code sample shows how the **CommandDispatcher** class tries to locate a handler and deliver a command message:

Adding Resilience and Optimizing Performance

```
public bool ProcessMessage(
    string traceIdentifier,
    ICommand payload,
    string messageId,
    string correlationId)
{
    var commandType = payload.GetType();
    ICommandHandler handler = null;

    if (this.handlers.TryGetValue(commandType, out handler))
    {
        Trace.WriteLine(
            "-- Handled by " + handler.GetType().FullName + traceIdentifier);
        ((dynamic)handler).Handle((dynamic)payload);
        return true;
    }
    else
    {
        return false;
    }
}
```

Implementing snapshots with the memento pattern

In the Contoso Conference Management System, the only event sourced aggregate that is likely to have a significant number of events per instance and benefit from snapshots is the **SeatAvailability** aggregate.

The following code sample from the **Save** method in the **AzureEventSourcedRepository** class shows how the system creates a cached memento object if there is a cache and the aggregate implements the **IMementoOriginator** interface.

```
public void Save(T eventSourced, string correlationId)
{
    ...

    this.cacheMementoIfApplicable.Invoke(eventSourced);
}
```

> Because we chose to use the memento pattern, the snapshot of the aggregate state is stored in the memento.

Then, when the system loads an aggregate by invoking the **Find** method in the **AzureEventSourcedRepository** class, it checks to see if there is a cached memento containing a snapshot of the state of the object to use:

```
private readonly Func<Guid, Tuple<IMemento, DateTime?>> getMementoFromCache;

...

public T Find(Guid id)
{
        var cachedMemento = this.getMementoFromCache(id);
        if (cachedMemento != null && cachedMemento.Item1 != null)
        {
                IEnumerable<IVersionedEvent> deserialized;
                if (!cachedMemento.Item2.HasValue
                || cachedMemento.Item2.Value < DateTime.UtcNow.AddSeconds(-1))
                {
                        deserialized = this.eventStore
                        .Load(GetPartitionKey(id), cachedMemento.Item1.Version + 1)
                        .Select(this.Deserialize);
                }
                else
                {
                        deserialized = Enumerable.Empty<IVersionedEvent>();
                }

                return this.originatorEntityFactory

                        .Invoke(id, cachedMemento.Item1, deserialized);
        }
        else
        {
                var deserialized = this.eventStore.Load(GetPartitionKey(id), 0)
                        .Select(this.Deserialize)
                        .AsCachedAnyEnumerable();

                if (deserialized.Any())
                {
                        return this.entityFactory.Invoke(id, deserialized);
                }
        }

        return null;
}
```

If the cache entry was updated in the last few seconds, there is a high probability that it is not stale because we have a single writer for high-contention aggregates. Therefore, we optimistically avoid checking for new events in the event store since the memento was created. Otherwise, we check in the event store for events that arrived after the memento was created.

The following code sample shows how the **SeatsAvailability** class adds a snapshot of its state data to the memento object to be cached:

```
public IMemento SaveToMemento()
{
    return new Memento
    {
        Version = this.Version,
        RemainingSeats = this.remainingSeats.ToArray(),
        PendingReservations = this.pendingReservations.ToArray(),
    };
}
```

Publishing events in parallel

In Chapter 5, "Preparing for the V1 Release," you saw how the system publishes events whenever it saves them to the event store. This optimization enables the system to publish some of these events in parallel instead of publishing them sequentially. It is important that the events associated with a specific aggregate instance are sent in the correct order, so the system only creates new tasks for different partition keys. The following code sample from the **Start** method in the **EventStoreBus-Publisher** class shows how the parallel tasks are defined:

```
Task.Factory.StartNew(
    () =>
    {
        try
        {
            foreach (var key in GetThrottlingEnumerable(
                this.enqueuedKeys.GetConsumingEnumerable(cancellationToken),
                this.throttlingSemaphore,
                cancellationToken))
            {
                if (!cancellationToken.IsCancellationRequested)
                {
                    ProcessPartition(key);
                }
                else
                {
                    this.enqueuedKeys.Add(key);
                    return;
                }
            }
        }
        catch (OperationCanceledException)
        {
            return;
        }
    },
    TaskCreationOptions.LongRunning);
```

The **SubscriptionReceiver** and **SessionSubscriptionReceiver** classes use the same **Dynamic-Throttling** class to dynamically throttle the retrieval of messages from the service bus.

Filtering messages in subscriptions

The team added filters to the Windows Azure Service Bus subscriptions to restrict the messages that each subscription receives to those messages that the subscription is intended to handle. You can see the definitions of these filters in the Settings.Template.xml file, as shown in the following snippet:

```xml
<Topic Path="conference/events" IsEventBus="true">
  <Subscription Name="log" RequiresSession="false"/>
  <Subscription Name="Registration.RegistrationPMOrderPlaced"
                RequiresSession="false"
                SqlFilter="TypeName IN ('OrderPlaced')"/>
  <Subscription Name="Registration.RegistrationPMNextSteps"
                RequiresSession="false"
                SqlFilter="TypeName IN ('OrderUpdated','SeatsReserved',
                          'PaymentCompleted','OrderConfirmed')"/>
  <Subscription Name="Registration.OrderViewModelGenerator"
                RequiresSession="true"
                SqlFilter="TypeName IN ('OrderPlaced','OrderUpdated',
                          'OrderPartiallyReserved','OrderReservationCompleted',
                          'OrderRegistrantAssigned','OrderConfirmed',
                          'OrderPaymentConfirmed')"/>
  <Subscription Name="Registration.PricedOrderViewModelGenerator"
                RequiresSession="true" SqlFilter="TypeName IN ('OrderPlaced',
                                'OrderTotalsCalculated', 'OrderConfirmed','OrderExpired',
                                'SeatAssignmentsCreated','SeatCreated','SeatUpdated')"/>
  <Subscription Name="Registration.ConferenceViewModelGenerator"
                RequiresSession="true"
                SqlFilter="TypeName IN ('ConferenceCreated','ConferenceUpdated',
                          'ConferencePublished','ConferenceUnpublished',
                          'SeatCreated', 'SeatUpdated','AvailableSeatsChanged',
                          'SeatsReserved','SeatsReservationCancelled')"/>
  <Subscription Name="Registration.SeatAssignmentsViewModelGenerator"
                RequiresSession="true"
                SqlFilter="TypeName IN ('SeatAssignmentsCreated','SeatAssigned',
                          'SeatUnassigned','SeatAssignmentUpdated')"/>
  <Subscription Name="Registration.SeatAssignmentsHandler"
                RequiresSession="true"
                SqlFilter="TypeName IN ('OrderConfirmed','OrderPaymentConfirmed')"/>
  <Subscription Name="Conference.OrderEventHandler"
                RequiresSession="true"
                SqlFilter="TypeName IN ('OrderPlaced','OrderRegistrantAssigned',
                          'OrderTotalsCalculated','OrderConfirmed','OrderExpired',
                          'SeatAssignmentsCreated','SeatAssigned',
                          'SeatAssignmentUpdated','SeatUnassigned')"/>
  ...
</Topic>
```

Creating a dedicated SessionSubscriptionReceiver instance for the SeatsAvailability aggregate

In the V2 release, the system did not use sessions for commands because we do not require ordering guarantees for commands. However, we now want to use sessions for commands to guarantee a single listener for each **SeatsAvailability** aggregate instance, which will help us to scale out without getting a large number of concurrency exceptions from this high-contention aggregate.

The following code sample from the Conference.Processor.Azure.cs file shows how the system creates a dedicated **SessionSubscriptionReceiver** instance to receive messages destined for the **Seats-Availability** aggregate:

```
var seatsAvailabilityCommandProcessor =
    new CommandProcessor(
        new SessionSubscriptionReceiver(
            azureSettings.ServiceBus,
            Topics.Commands.Path,
            Topics.Commands.Subscriptions.SeatsAvailability,
            false),
        serializer);

...

container.RegisterInstance<IProcessor>(
    "SeatsAvailabilityCommandProcessor",
    seatsAvailabilityCommandProcessor);
```

The following code sample shows the new abstract **SeatsAvailabilityCommand** class that includes a session ID based on the conference that the command is associated with:

```
public abstract class SeatsAvailabilityCommand : ICommand, IMessageSessionProvider
{
    public SeatsAvailabilityCommand()
    {
        this.Id = Guid.NewGuid();
    }

    public Guid Id { get; set; }
    public Guid ConferenceId { get; set; }

    string IMessageSessionProvider.SessionId
    {
        get { return "SeatsAvailability_" + this.ConferenceId.ToString(); }
    }
}
```

The command bus now uses a separate subscription for commands destined for the **SeatsAvailability** aggregate.

Caching read-model data

As part of the performance optimizations in the V3 release, the team added caching behavior for the conference information stored in the Orders and Registrations bounded context read model. This reduces the time taken to read this commonly used data.

The following code sample from the **GetPublishedSeatTypes** method in the **CachingConferenceDao** class shows how the system determines whether to cache the data for a conference based on the number of available seats:

> The team applied a similar technique to the **RegistrationProcess-Manager** process manager by creating a separate subscription for **OrderPlaced** events to handle new orders. A separate subscription receives all the other events destined for the process manager.

```
TimeSpan timeToCache;
if (seatTypes.All(x => x.AvailableQuantity > 200 || x.AvailableQuantity <= 0))
{
    timeToCache = TimeSpan.FromMinutes(5);
}
else if (seatTypes.Any(x => x.AvailableQuantity < 30 && x.AvailableQuantity > 0))
{
    // There are just a few seats remaining. Do not cache.
    timeToCache = TimeSpan.Zero;
}
else if (seatTypes.Any(x => x.AvailableQuantity < 100 && x.AvailableQuantity > 0))
{
    timeToCache = TimeSpan.FromSeconds(20);
}
else
{
    timeToCache = TimeSpan.FromMinutes(1);
}

if (timeToCache > TimeSpan.Zero)
{
    this.cache.Set(
        key,
        seatTypes,
        new CacheItemPolicy
        {
            AbsoluteExpiration = DateTimeOffset.UtcNow.Add(timeToCache)
        });
}
```

Adding Resilience and Optimizing Performance

The system now also uses a cache to hold seat type descriptions in the **PricedOrderViewModelGenerator** class.

Using multiple topics to partition the service bus

To reduce the number of messages flowing through the service bus topics, we partitioned the service bus by creating two additional topics to transport events published by the **Order** and **SeatAvailability** aggregates. This helps us to avoid being throttled by the service bus when the application is experiencing very high loads. The following snippet from the Settings.xml file shows the definitions of these new topics:

> You can see how we manage the risks associated with displaying stale data by adjusting the caching duration, or even deciding not to cache the data at all.

```xml
<Topic Path="conference/orderevents" IsEventBus="true">
  <Subscription Name="logOrders" RequiresSession="false"/>
  <Subscription Name="Registration.RegistrationPMOrderPlacedOrders"
      RequiresSession="false" SqlFilter="TypeName IN ('OrderPlaced')"/>
  <Subscription Name="Registration.RegistrationPMNextStepsOrders"
      RequiresSession="false" SqlFilter="TypeName IN ('OrderUpdated',
                  'SeatsReserved','PaymentCompleted','OrderConfirmed')"/>
  <Subscription Name="Registration.OrderViewModelGeneratorOrders"
      RequiresSession="true" SqlFilter="TypeName IN ('OrderPlaced',
          'OrderUpdated','OrderPartiallyReserved','OrderReservationCompleted',
          'OrderRegistrantAssigned','OrderConfirmed','OrderPaymentConfirmed')"/>
  <Subscription Name="Registration.PricedOrderViewModelOrders"
      RequiresSession="true" SqlFilter="TypeName IN ('OrderPlaced',
          'OrderTotalsCalculated','OrderConfirmed', 'OrderExpired',
          'SeatAssignmentsCreated','SeatCreated','SeatUpdated')"/>
  <Subscription Name="Registration.SeatAssignmentsViewModelOrders"
      RequiresSession="true" SqlFilter="TypeName IN ('SeatAssignmentsCreated',
          'SeatAssigned','SeatUnassigned','SeatAssignmentUpdated')"/>
  <Subscription Name="Registration.SeatAssignmentsHandlerOrders"
      RequiresSession="true"
      SqlFilter="TypeName IN ('OrderConfirmed','OrderPaymentConfirmed')"/>
  <Subscription Name="Conference.OrderEventHandlerOrders" RequiresSession="true"
      SqlFilter="TypeName IN ('OrderPlaced','OrderRegistrantAssigned',
          'OrderTotalsCalculated', 'OrderConfirmed','OrderExpired',
          'SeatAssignmentsCreated','SeatAssigned','SeatAssignmentUpdated',
          'SeatUnassigned')"/>
</Topic>
```

```xml
<Topic Path="conference/availabilityevents" IsEventBus="true">
  <Subscription Name="logAvail" RequiresSession="false"/>
  <Subscription Name="Registration.RegistrationPMNextStepsAvail"
        RequiresSession="false" SqlFilter="TypeName IN ('OrderUpdated',
            'SeatsReserved','PaymentCompleted','OrderConfirmed')"/>
  <Subscription Name="Registration.PricedOrderViewModelAvail"
        RequiresSession="true" SqlFilter="TypeName IN ('OrderPlaced',
            'OrderTotalsCalculated','OrderConfirmed', 'OrderExpired',
            'SeatAssignmentsCreated','SeatCreated','SeatUpdated')"/>
  <Subscription Name="Registration.ConferenceViewModelAvail"
        RequiresSession="true" SqlFilter="TypeName IN ('ConferenceCreated',
            'ConferenceUpdated','ConferencePublished', 'ConferenceUnpublished',
            'SeatCreated','SeatUpdated','AvailableSeatsChanged',
            'SeatsReserved','SeatsReservationCancelled')"/>
</Topic>
```

Other optimizing and hardening changes

This section outlines some of the additional ways that the team optimized the performance of the application and improved its resilience:

- Using sequential GUIDs
- Using asynchronous ASP.NET MVC controllers.
- Using prefetch to retrieve multiple messages from the Service Bus.
- Accepting multiple Windows Azure Service Bus sessions in parallel.
- Expiring seat reservation commands.

Sequential GUIDs

Previously, the system generated the GUIDs that it used for the IDs of aggregates such as orders and reservations using the **Guid.NewGuid** method, which generates random GUIDs. If these GUIDs are used as primary key values in a SQL Database instance, this causes frequent page splits in the indexes, which has a negative impact on the performance of the database. In the V3 release, the team added a utility class that generates sequential GUIDs. This ensures that new entries in the SQL Database tables are always appends; this improves the overall performance of the database. The following code sample shows the new **GuidUtil** class:

```csharp
public static class GuidUtil
{
    private static readonly long EpochMilliseconds =
      new DateTime(1970, 1, 1, 0, 0, 0, DateTimeKind.Utc).Ticks / 10000L;


    /// <summary>
    /// Creates a sequential GUID according to SQL Server's ordering rules.
    /// </summary>
    public static Guid NewSequentialId()
    {
        // This code was not reviewed to guarantee uniqueness under most
        // conditions, nor completely optimize for avoiding page splits in SQL
        // Server when doing inserts from multiple hosts, so do not re-use in
        // production systems.
        var guidBytes = Guid.NewGuid().ToByteArray();

        // Get the milliseconds since Jan 1 1970.
        byte[] sequential = BitConverter.GetBytes(
          (DateTime.Now.Ticks / 10000L) - EpochMilliseconds);

        // Discard the 2 most significant bytes, as we only care about the
        // milliseconds increasing, but the highest ones should be 0 for several
        // thousand years to come.
        if (BitConverter.IsLittleEndian)
        {
            guidBytes[10] = sequential[5];
            guidBytes[11] = sequential[4];
            guidBytes[12] = sequential[3];
            guidBytes[13] = sequential[2];
            guidBytes[14] = sequential[1];
            guidBytes[15] = sequential[0];
        }
        else
        {
            Buffer.BlockCopy(sequential, 2, guidBytes, 10, 6);
        }

        return new Guid(guidBytes);
    }
}
```

For further information, see *The Cost of GUIDs as Primary Keys* and *Good Page Splits and Sequential GUID Key Generation*.

Asynchronous ASP.NET MVC controllers.
The team converted some of the MVC controllers in the public conference web application to be asynchronous controllers. This avoids blocking some ASP.NET threads and enabled us to use the support for the **Task** class in ASP.NET MVC 4.

For example, the team modified the way that the controller polls for updates in the read models to use timers.

Using prefetch with Windows Azure Service Bus
The team enabled the prefetch option when the system retrieves messages from the Windows Azure Service Bus. This option enables the system to retrieve multiple messages in a single round-trip to the server and helps to reduce the latency in retrieving existing messages from the Service Bus topics.

The following code sample from the **SubscriptionReceiver** class shows how to enable this option.

```
protected SubscriptionReceiver(
    ServiceBusSettings settings,
    string topic,
    string subscription,
    bool processInParallel,
    ISubscriptionReceiverInstrumentation instrumentation,
    RetryStrategy backgroundRetryStrategy)
{
    this.settings = settings;
    this.topic = topic;
    this.subscription = subscription;
    this.processInParallel = processInParallel;

    this.tokenProvider = TokenProvider.CreateSharedSecretTokenProvider(

        settings.TokenIssuer,

        settings.TokenAccessKey);
    this.serviceUri = ServiceBusEnvironment.CreateServiceUri(
        settings.ServiceUriScheme,
        settings.ServiceNamespace,
        settings.ServicePath);

    var messagingFactory = MessagingFactory.Create(this.serviceUri, tokenProvider);
    this.client = messagingFactory.CreateSubscriptionClient(topic, subscription);
    if (this.processInParallel)
    {
        this.client.PrefetchCount = 18;
    }
```

```
    else
    {
        this.client.PrefetchCount = 14;
    }
    ...
}
```

Accepting multiple sessions in parallel

In the V2 release, the **SessionSubscriptionReceiver** creates sessions to receive messages from the Windows Azure Service Bus in sequence. However if you are using a session, you can only handle messages from that session; other messages are ignored until you switch to a different session. In the V3 release, the **SessionSubscriptionReceiver** creates multiple sessions in parallel, enabling the system to receive messages from multiple sessions simultaneously.

For details, see the **AcceptSession** method in the **SessionSubscriptionReceiver** class.

> The **AcceptSession** method uses the Transient Fault Handling Application Block to reliably accept sessions.

Adding an optimistic concurrency check

The team also added an optimistic concurrency check when the system saves the **RegistrationProcessManager** class by adding a timestamp property to the **RegistrationProcessManager** class, as shown in the following code sample:

```
[ConcurrencyCheck]
[Timestamp]
public byte[] TimeStamp { get; private set; }
```

For more information, see *Code First Data Annotations* on the MSDN website.

With the optimistic concurrency check in place, we also removed the C# lock in the **Session-SubscriptionReceiver** class that was a potential bottleneck in the system.

Adding a time-to-live value to the MakeSeatReservation command

Windows Azure Service Bus brokered messages can have a value assigned to the **TimeToLive** property; when the time-to-live expires, the message is automatically sent to a dead-letter queue. The application uses this feature of the service bus to avoid processing **MakeSeatReservation** commands if the order they are associated with has already expired.

Reducing the number of round-trips to the database

We identified a number of locations in the **PricedOrderViewModelGenerator** class where we could optimize the code. Previously, the system made two calls to the SQL Database instance when this class handled an order being placed or expired; now the system only makes a single call.

Impact on testing

During this stage of the journey the team reorganized the **Conference.Specflow** project in the **Conference.AcceptanceTests** Visual Studio solution to better reflect the purpose of the tests.

INTEGRATION TESTS

The tests in the **Features\Integration** folder in the **Conference.Specflow** project are designed to test the behavior of the domain directly, verifying the behavior of the domain by looking at the commands and events that are sent and received. These tests are designed to be understood by programmers rather than domain experts and are formulated using a more technical vocabulary than the ubiquitous language. In addition to verifying the behavior of the domain and helping developers to understand the flow of commands and events in the system, these tests proved to be useful in testing the behavior of the domain in scenarios in which events are lost or are received out of order.

The **Conference** folder contains integration tests for the Conference Management bounded context, and the **Registration** folder contains tests for the Orders and Registrations bounded context.

USER INTERFACE TESTS

The **UserInterface** folder contains the acceptance tests. These tests are described in more detail in Chapter 4, "Extending and Enhancing the Orders and Registrations Bounded Context." The **Controllers** folder contains the tests that use the MVC controllers as the point of entry, and the **Views** folder contains the tests that use *WatiN* to drive the system through its UI.

> These integration tests make the assumption that the command handlers trust the sender of the commands to send valid command messages. This may not be appropriate for other systems you may be designing tests for.

Summary

The focus of the final stage in our CQRS journey and the V3 pseudo-production release was on resilience and performance. The next chapter summarizes the lessons we have learned during the entire journey and also suggest some things that we might have done differently if we had the chance to start over with the knowledge we've gained.

More information

All links in this book are accessible from the book's online bibliography available at: *http://msdn.microsoft.com/en-us/library/jj619274*.

Journey 8:

Epilogue: Lessons Learned

How good was our map? How far did we get?
What did we learn? Did we get lost?

"This land may be profitable to those that will adventure it."
Henry Hudson

This chapter summarizes the findings from our journey. It highlights what we feel were the most significant lessons we learned along the way, suggests some things we would do differently if we were embarking on the journey with our newfound knowledge, and points out some future paths for the Contoso Conference Management System.

You should bear in mind that this summary reflects our specific journey; not all of these findings will necessarily apply to your own CQRS journeys. For example, one of our goals was to explore how to implement the CQRS pattern in an application that is deployed to Windows Azure and that makes use of the scalability and reliability of the cloud. For our project, this meant using messaging to enable multiple role types and instances to communicate with each other. It may be that your project does not require multiple role instances or is not deployed to the cloud and therefore may not need to use messaging so extensively (or at all).

We hope these findings do prove useful, especially if you are just starting out with CQRS and event sourcing.

What did we learn?

This section describes the key lessons we learned. They are not presented in any particular order.

Performance matters

At the start of our journey, one of our notions about the CQRS pattern was that by separating the read and write sides of the application we could optimize each for performance. This perspective is shared by many in the CQRS community, for example:

"CQRS taught me that I can optimize reads and writes separately and I don't have to manually denormalize into flat tables all the time."
— *Kelly Sommers – CQRS Advisor*

This was borne out in practice during our journey and we benefited significantly from this separation when we did need to solve a performance issue.

During the last stage of our journey, testing revealed a set of performance issues in our application. When we investigated them, it turned out they had less to do with the way we had implemented the CQRS pattern and more to do with the way we were using our infrastructure. Discovering the root cause of these problems was the hard part; with so many moving parts in the application, getting the right tracing and the right data for analysis was the challenge. Once we identified the bottlenecks, fixing them turned out to be relatively easy, largely because of the way the CQRS pattern enables you to clearly separate different elements of the system, such as reads and writes. Although the separation of concerns that results from implementing the CQRS pattern can make it harder to identify an issue, once you have identified one, it is not only easier to fix, but also easier to prevent its return. The decoupled architecture makes it simpler to write unit tests that reproduce issues.

The challenges we encountered in tackling the performance issues in the system had more to do with the fact that our system is a distributed, message-based system than the fact that it implements the CQRS pattern.

Chapter 7, "Adding Resilience and Optimizing Performance" provides more information about the ways we addressed the performance issues in the system and makes some suggestions about additional changes that we would like to make, but didn't have time to implement.

Implementing a message-driven system is far from simple

Our approach to infrastructure on this project was to develop it as needed during the journey. We didn't anticipate (and had no forewarning of) how much time and effort we would need to create the robust infrastructure that our application required. We spent at least twice as much time as we originally planned on many development tasks because we continued to uncover additional infrastructure-related requirements. In particular, we learned that having a robust event store from the beginning is essential. Another key idea we took away from the experience is that all I/O on the message bus should be asynchronous.

Although our application is not large, it illustrated clearly to us the importance of having end-to-end tracing available, and the value of tools that help us understand all of the message flows in the system. Chapter 4, "Extending and Enhancing the Orders and Registrations Bounded Context," describes the value of tests in helping us understand the system, and discusses the messaging intermediate language (MIL) created by Josh Elster, one of our advisors.

> Although our event store is not production-ready, the current implementation gives a good indication of the type of issues you should address if you decide to implement your own event store.

> It would also help if we had a standard notation for messaging that would help us communicate some of the issues with the domain experts and people outside of the core team.

Epilogue: Lessons Learned

In summary, many of the issues we met along the way were not related specifically to the CQRS pattern, but were more related to the distributed, message-driven nature of our solution.

The cloud has challenges

Although the cloud provides many benefits, such as reliable, scalable, off-the-shelf services that you can provision with just a few mouse clicks, cloud environments also introduce some challenges:

- You may not be able to use transactions everywhere you want them because the distributed nature of the cloud makes ACID (atomicity, consistency, isolation, durability) transactions impractical in many scenarios. Therefore, you need to understand how to work with eventual consistency. For examples, see Chapter 5, "Preparing for the V1 Release," and the section *Options to reduce the delay in the UI* in Chapter 7, "Adding Resilience and Optimizing Performance."

- You may want to re-examine your assumptions about how to organize your application into different tiers. For example, see the discussion around in-process, synchronous commands in Chapter 7, "Adding Resilience and Optimizing Performance."

- You must take into account not only the latency between the browser or on-premises environment and the cloud, but also the latency between the different parts of your system that are running in the cloud.

- You must take into account transient errors and be aware of how different cloud services might implement throttling. If your application uses several cloud services that might be throttled, you must coordinate how your application handles being throttled by different services at different times.

A complex cloud environment can make it harder to run quick tests during development. A local test environment may not mimic the behavior of the cloud exactly, especially with respect to performance and throttling.

> **Note:** *The multiple build configurations in our Visual Studio solution were partially designed to address this, but also to help people downloading and playing with the code to get started quickly.*

> We found that partitioning our service bus by using different topics to transport events published by different aggregates helped us to achieve scalability. For more information, see Chapter 7, "Adding Resilience and Optimizing Performance." Also, see these blog posts: *"Windows Azure Storage Abstractions and their Scalability Targets"* and *"Best Practices for Performance Improvements Using Service Bus Brokered Messaging."*

> We found that having a single bus abstraction in our code obscured the fact that some messages are handled locally in-process and some are handled in a different role instance. To see how this is implemented, look at the **ICommandBus** interface and the **CommandBus** and **SynchronousCommandBusDecorator** classes. Chapter 7, "Adding Resilience and Optimizing Performance" includes a discussion of the **SynchronousCommandBusDecorator** class.

CQRS is different

At the start of our journey we were warned that although the CQRS pattern appears to be simple, in practice it requires a significant shift in the way you think about many aspects of the project. Again, this was borne out by our experiences during the journey. You must be prepared to throw away many assumptions and preconceived ideas, and you will probably need to implement the CQRS pattern in several bounded contexts before you begin to fully understand the benefits you can derive from the pattern.

An example of this is the concept of eventual consistency. If you come from a relational database background and are accustomed to the ACID properties of transactions, then embracing eventual consistency and understanding its implications at all levels in the system is a big step to take. Chapter 5, "Preparing for the V1 Release" and Chapter 7, "Adding Resilience and Optimizing Performance" both discuss eventual consistency in different areas of the system.

In addition to being different from what you might be familiar with, there is also no single correct way to implement the CQRS pattern. We made more false starts on pieces of functionality and estimated poorly how long things would take due to our unfamiliarity with the pattern and approach. As we become more comfortable with the approach, we hope to become faster at identifying how to implement the pattern in specific circumstances and improve the accuracy of our estimates.

Another situation in which we took some time to understand the CQRS approach and its implications was during the integration between our bounded contexts. Chapter 5, "Preparing for the V1 Release," includes a detailed discussion of how the team approached the integration issue between the Conference Management and the Orders and Registrations bounded contexts. This part of the journey uncovered some additional complexity that relates to the level of coupling between bounded contexts when you use events as the integration mechanism. Our assumption that events should only contain information about the change in the aggregate or the bounded context proved to be unhelpful; events can contain additional information that is useful to one or more subscribers and helps to reduce the amount of work that a subscriber must perform.

> The CQRS pattern is conceptually simple; the devil is in the details.

The CQRS pattern introduces additional considerations for how to partition your system. Not only do you need to consider how to partition your system into tiers, but also how to partition your system into bounded contexts, some of which will contain implementations of the CQRS pattern. We revised some of our assumptions about tiers in the last stage of our journey, bringing some processing into our web roles from the worker role where it was originally done. This is described in Chapter 7, "Adding Resilience and Optimizing Performance" in the section that discusses moving some command processing in-process. Partitioning the system into bounded contexts should be done based on your domain model: each bounded context has its own domain model and ubiquitous language. Once you have identified your bounded contexts, you can then identify in which bounded contexts to implement the CQRS pattern. This affects how and where you need to implement integration between these isolated bounded contexts. Chapter 2, "Decomposing the Domain," introduces our decisions for the Contoso Conference Management System.

> A single process (role instance in our deployment) can host multiple bounded contexts. In this scenario, you don't necessarily need to use a service bus for the bounded contexts to communicate with each other.

Implementing the CQRS pattern is more complex than implementing a traditional (create, read, update, delete) CRUD-style system. For this project, there was also the overhead of learning about CQRS for the first time, and creating a distributed, asynchronous messaging infrastructure. Our experiences during the journey have clearly confirmed to us why the CQRS pattern is not a top-level architecture. You must be sure that the costs associated with implementing a CQRS-based bounded context with this level of complexity are worth it; in general, it is in high-contention, collaborative domains that you will see the benefits of the CQRS pattern.

> Analyzing the business requirements, building a useful model, maintaining the model, expressing it in code, and implementing it using the CQRS pattern all take time and cost money. If this is the first time you have implemented the CQRS pattern, you'll also have the overhead of investing in your infrastructure elements such as message buses and event stores.

Event sourcing and transaction logging

We had some debate about whether or not event sourcing and transaction logging amount to the same thing: they both create a record of what happened, and they both enable you to recreate the state of your system by replaying the historical data. The conclusion was that the distinguishing feature is that events capture intent in addition to recording the facts of what happened. For more detail on what we mean by intent, see Chapter 4, "A CQRS and ES Deep Dive," in the Reference Guide.

Involving the domain expert

Implementing the CQRS pattern encourages involvement of the domain expert. The pattern enables you to separate out the domain on the write side and the reporting requirements on the read side and to separate these from infrastructure concerns. This separation makes it easier to involve the domain expert in those aspects of the system where his expertise is most valuable. The use of domain-driven design concepts such as bounded contexts and the ubiquitous language also help to focus the team and to foster clear communication with the domain expert.

Our acceptance tests proved to be an effective way to involve the domain expert and capture his knowledge. Chapter 4, "Extending and Enhancing the Orders and Registrations Bounded Context," describes this testing approach in detail.

> As a side-effect, these acceptance tests also contributed to our ability to handle our pseudo-production releases quickly because they enabled us to run a full set of tests at the UI level to verify the behavior of the system in addition to the unit and integration tests.

In addition to helping the team define the functional requirements of the system, the domain expert should also be involved in evaluating the trade-offs between consistency, availability, durability, and costs. For example, the domain expert should help to identify when a manual process is acceptable and what level of consistency is required in different areas of the system.

When to use CQRS

Now that we are at the end of our journey, we can suggest some of the criteria you should evaluate to determine whether or not you should consider implementing the CQRS pattern in one or more bounded contexts in your application. The more of these questions you can answer positively, the more likely it is that applying the CQRS pattern to a given bounded context will benefit your solution:

- Does the bounded context implement an area of business functionality that is a key differentiator in your market?
- Is the bounded context collaborative in nature with elements that are likely to have high levels of contention at run time? In other words, do multiple users compete for access to the same resources?
- Is the bounded context likely to experience ever-changing business rules?
- Do you have a robust, scalable messaging and persistence infrastructure already in place?
- Is scalability one of the challenges facing this bounded context?
- Is the business logic in the bounded context complex?
- Are you clear about the benefits that the CQRS pattern will bring to this bounded context?

> Developers have a tendency to try to lock everything down to transactions to guarantee full consistency, but sometimes it's just not worth the effort.

> These are rules of thumb, not hard and fast rules.

What would we do differently if we started over?

This section is a result of our reflection on our journey and identifies some things we'd do differently and some other opportunities we'd like to pursue if we were starting over with the knowledge of the CQRS pattern and event sourcing that we now have.

Start with a solid infrastructure for messaging and persistence

We'd start with a solid messaging and persistence infrastructure. The approach we took, starting simple and building up the infrastructure as required meant that we built up technical debt during the journey. We also found that taking this approach meant that in some cases, the choices we made about the infrastructure affected the way we implemented the domain.

Starting with a solid infrastructure would also enable us to start performance testing earlier. We would also do some more research into how other people do their performance testing on CQRS-based systems, and seek out performance benchmarks on other systems such as Jonathan Oliver's *EventStore*.

One of the reasons we took the approach that we did was the advice we received from our advisors: "Don't worry about the infrastructure."

> From the perspective of the journey, if we had started with a solid infrastructure, we would have had time to tackle some of the more complex parts of the domain such as wait-listing.

Leverage the capabilities of the infrastructure more

Starting with a solid infrastructure would also allow us to make more use of the capabilities of the infrastructure. For example, we use the identity of the message originator as the value of the session ID in Windows Azure Service Bus when we publish an event, but this is not always the best use of the session ID from the perspective of the parts of the system that process the event.

As part of this, we'd also investigate how the infrastructure could support other special cases of eventual consistency such as timing consistency, monotonic consistency, "read my writes," and self-consistency.

Another idea we'd like to explore is the use of the infrastructure to support migration between versions. Instead of treating migration in an ad-hoc manner for each version, we could consider using a message-based or real-time communication process to coordinate bringing the new version online.

Adopt a more systematic approach to implementing process managers

We began to implement our process manager very early in the journey and were still hardening it and ensuring that its behavior was idempotent in the last stage of the journey. Again, starting with some solid infrastructure support for process managers to make them more resilient would have helped us. However, if we were starting over, we'd also wait to implement a process manager until a later stage in the journey rather than diving straight in.

We began implementing the **RegistrationProcessManager** class during the first stage in our journey. The initial implementation is described in Chapter 3, "Orders and Registrations Bounded Context." We made changes to this process manager during every subsequent stage of our journey.

Partition the application differently

We would think more carefully at the start of the project about the tiering of the system. We found that the way we partitioned the application into web roles and worker roles as described in Chapter 4, "Extending and Enhancing the Orders and Registrations Bounded Context," was not optimal, and in the last stage of the journey, in Chapter 7, "Adding Resilience and Optimizing Performance," we made some major changes to this architecture as part of the performance optimization effort.

For example, as a part of this reorganization in the last stage of the journey, we introduced synchronous command processing in the web application alongside the pre-existing asynchronous command processing.

Organize the development team differently

The approach we took to learning about the CQRS pattern was to iterate—develop, go back, discuss, and then refactor. However, we may have learned more by having several developers work independently on the same feature and then compare the result; that might have uncovered a broader set of solutions and approaches.

Evaluate how appropriate the domain and the bounded contexts are for the CQRS pattern

We would like to start with a clearer set of heuristics, such as those outlined earlier in this chapter, to determine whether or not a particular bounded context will benefit from the CQRS pattern. We might have learned more if we had focused on a more complex area of the domain such as wait-listing instead of on the Orders and Registrations and Payments bounded contexts.

Plan for performance

We would address performance issues much earlier in the journey. In particular, we would:
- Set clear performance goals ahead of time.
- Run performance tests much earlier in the journey.
- Use larger and more realistic loads.

We didn't do any performance testing until the last stage of our journey. For a detailed discussion of the issues we found and how we addressed them, see Chapter 7, "Adding Resilience and Optimizing Performance."

During the last stage of our journey, we introduced some partitioning on the Service Bus to improve the throughput of events. This partitioning is done based on the publisher of the event, so events published by one aggregate type go to one topic. We'd like to extend this to use multiple topics where we currently have one, perhaps partitioning based on a hash of the order ID in the message (this approach is often referred to as sharding). This would enable greater scale-out for the application.

Think about the UI differently

We felt that the way our UI interacts with the write and read models, and how it handles eventual consistency worked well and met the business requirements. In particular, the way that the UI checks whether a reservation is likely to succeed and modifies its behavior accordingly and the way that the UI allows the user to continue entering data while it waits for the read model to be updated. For more details about how the current solution works, see the section "Optimizing the UI" in Chapter 7, "Adding Resilience and Optimizing Performance."

We'd like to investigate other ways to avoid waiting in the UI unless it's absolutely necessary, perhaps by using browser push techniques. The UI in the current system still needs to wait, in some places, for asynchronous updates to take place against the read model.

Explore some additional benefits of event sourcing

We found during the third stage of our journey, described in Chapter 5, "Preparing for the V1 Release," that modifying the Orders and Registrations bounded context to use event sourcing helped to simplify the implementation of this bounded context, in part because it was already using a large number of events.

In the current journey, we didn't get a chance to explore the further promises of flexibility and the ability to mine past events for new business insights from event sourcing. However, we did ensure that the system persists copies of all events (not just those that are needed to rebuild the state of the aggregates) and commands to enable these types of scenarios in the future.

> It would also be interesting to investigate whether the ability to mine past event streams for new business insights is easier to achieve with event sourcing or other technologies such as database transaction logs or the *StreamInsight* feature of SQL Server.

Explore the issues associated with integrating bounded contexts

In our V3 release, all of the bounded contexts are implemented by same core development team. We would like to investigate how easy it is, in practice, to integrate a bounded context implemented by a different development team with the existing system.

This is a great opportunity for you to contribute to the learning experience: go ahead and implement another bounded context (see the outstanding stories in the *product backlog*), integrate it into the Contoso Conference Management System, and write another chapter of the journey describing your experiences.

More information

All links in this book are accessible from the book's online bibliography available at: *http://msdn.microsoft.com/en-us/library/jj619274*.

Reference 1:

CQRS in Context

This chapter is intended to provide some context for the main subject of this guide: a discussion of the Command Query Responsibility Segregation (CQRS) pattern. It is useful to understand some of the origins of the CQRS pattern and some of the terminology you will encounter in this guide and in other material that discusses the CQRS pattern. It is particularly important to understand that the CQRS pattern is not intended for use as the top-level architecture of your system; rather, it should be applied to those subsystems that will gain specific benefits from the application of the pattern.

Before we look at the issues surrounding the use of different architectures within a complex application, we need to introduce some of the terminology that we will use in this chapter and subsequent chapters of this reference guide. Much of this terminology comes from an approach to developing software systems known as domain-driven design (DDD). There are a few important points to note about our use of this terminology:

- We are using the DDD terminology because many CQRS practitioners also use this terminology, and it is used in much of the existing CQRS literature.
- There are other approaches that tackle the same problems that DDD tackles, with similar concepts, but with their own specific terminologies.
- Using a DDD approach can lead naturally to an adoption of the CQRS pattern. However, the DDD approach does not always lead to the use of the CQRS pattern, nor is the DDD approach a prerequisite for using the CQRS pattern.
- You may question our interpretation of some of the concepts of DDD. The intention of this guide is to take what is useful from DDD to help us explain the CQRS pattern and related concepts, not to provide guidance on how to use the DDD approach.

To learn more about the foundational principles of DDD, you should read the book *Domain-Driven Design: Tackling Complexity in the Heart of Software* by Eric Evans (Addison-Wesley Professional, 2003). To see how these principles apply to a concrete development project on the .NET platform, along with insights and experimentation, you should read the book *Applying Domain-Driven Design and Patterns* by Jimmy Nilsson (Addison-Wesley Professional, 2006).

In addition, to see how Eric Evans describes what works and what doesn't in DDD, and for his view on how much has changed over the previous five years, we recommend his talk at *QCon London 2009*.

For a summary of the key points in Eric Evans' book, you should read the free book, *Domain-Driven Design Quickly* by Abel Avram and Floyd Marinescu (C4Media, 2007).

What is domain-driven design?

As previously stated, DDD is an approach to developing software systems, and in particular systems that are complex, that have ever-changing business rules, and that you expect to last for the long term within the enterprise.

The core of the DDD approach uses a set of techniques to analyze your domain and to construct a conceptual model that captures the results of that analysis. You can then use that model as the basis of your solution. The analysis and model in the DDD approach are especially well suited to designing solutions for large and complex domains. DDD also extends its influence to other aspects of the software development process as a part of the attempt to help you manage complexity:

- In focusing on the domain, DDD concentrates on the area where the business and the development team must be able to communicate with each other clearly, but where in practice they often misunderstand each other. The domain models that DDD uses should capture detailed, rich business knowledge, but should also be very close to the code that is actually written.
- Domain models are also useful in the longer term if they are kept up to date. By capturing valuable domain knowledge, they facilitate future maintenance and enhancement of the system.
- DDD offers guidance on how large problem domains can be effectively divided up, enabling multiple teams to work in parallel, and enabling you to direct appropriate resources to critical parts of the system with the greatest business value.

The DDD approach is appropriate for large, complex systems that are expected to have a long lifespan. You are unlikely to see a return on your investment in DDD if you use it on small, simple, or short-term projects.

Domain-driven design: concepts and terminology

This guide is not intended to provide guidance on using the DDD approach. However, it is useful to understand some of the concepts and terminology from DDD because they are useful when we describe some aspects of CQRS pattern implementations. These are not official or rigorous definitions; they are intended to be useful, working definitions for the purposes of this guide.

"Every effective DDD person is a Hands-on Modeler, including me."
—Eric Evans, What I've learned about DDD since the book

"Focus relentlessly on the core domain! Find the differentiator in software—something significant!"
—Eric Evans, What I've learned about DDD since the book

Domain model

At the heart of DDD lies the concept of the *domain model*. This model is built by the team responsible for developing the system in question, and that team consists of both domain experts from the business and software developers. The domain model serves several functions:

- It captures all of the relevant domain knowledge from the domain experts.
- It enables the team to determine the scope and verify the consistency of that knowledge.
- The model is expressed in code by the developers.
- It is constantly maintained to reflect evolutionary changes in the domain.

DDD focuses on the domain because that's where the business value is. An enterprise derives its competitive advantage and generates business value from its core domains. The role of the domain model is to capture what is valuable or unique to the business.

Much of the DDD approach focuses on how to create, maintain, and use these domain models. Domain models are typically composed of elements such as *entities, value objects, aggregates,* and described using terms from a *ubiquitous language*.

Ubiquitous language

The concept of a ubiquitous language is very closely related to that of the domain model. One of the functions of the domain model is to foster a common understanding of the domain between the domain experts and the developers. If both the domain experts and the developers use the same terms for objects and actions within the domain (for example, conference, chair, attendee, reserve, waitlist), the risk of confusion or misunderstanding is reduced. More specifically, if everyone uses the same language, there are less likely to be misunderstandings resulting from translations between languages. For example, if a developer has to think, "if the domain expert talks about a delegate, he is really talking about an attendee in the software," then eventually something will go wrong as a result of this lack of clarity.

> In our journey, we used SpecFlow to express business rules as acceptance tests. They helped us to communicate information about our domain with clarity and brevity, and formulate a ubiquitous language in the process. For more information, see Chapter 4, *"Extending and Enhancing the Orders and Registrations Bounded Context"* in *Exploring CQRS and Event Sourcing.*

Entities, value objects, and services

DDD uses the following terms to identify some of the internal artifacts (or building blocks, as Eric Evans calls them) that will make up the domain model.

Entities. *Entities* are objects that are defined by their identity, and that identity continues through time. For example, a conference in a conference management system will be an entity; many of its attributes could change over time (such as its status, size, and even name), but within the system each particular conference will have its own unique identity. The object that represents the conference may not always exist within the system's memory; at times it may be persisted to a database, only to be re-instantiated at some point in the future.

Value objects. Not all objects are defined by their identity. For some objects—*value objects*—what is important are the values of their attributes. For example, within our conference management system we do not need to assign an identity to every attendee's address (one reason is that all of the attendees from a particular organization may share the same address). All we are concerned with are the values of the attributes of an address: street, city, state, and so on. Value objects are usually immutable.

Services. You cannot always model everything as an object. For example, in the conference management system it may make sense to model a third-party payment processing system as a service. The system can pass the parameters required by the payment processing service and then receive a result back from the service. Notice that a common characteristic of a service is that it is stateless (unlike entities and value objects).

> **Note:** *Services are usually implemented as regular class libraries that expose a collection of stateless methods. A service in a DDD domain model is not a web service; these are two different concepts.*

The following video is a good refresher on using value objects properly, especially if you are confusing them with DTOs: *Power Use of Value Objects in DDD*.

Aggregates and aggregate roots

Whereas entities, value objects, and services are terms for the elements that DDD uses to describe things in the domain model, the terms aggregate and aggregate root relate specifically to the lifecycle and grouping of those elements.

When you design a system that allows multiple users to work on shared data, you will have to evaluate the trade-off between consistency and usability. At one extreme, when a user needs to make a change to some data, you could lock the entire database to ensure that the change is consistent. However, the system would be unusable for all other users for the duration of the update. At the other extreme, you could decide not to enforce any locks at all, allowing any user to edit any piece of data at any time, but you would soon end up with inconsistent or corrupt data within the system. Choosing the correct granularity for locking to balance the demands of consistency and usability requires detailed knowledge of the domain:

- You need to know which set of entities and value objects each transaction can potentially affect. For example, are there transactions in the system that can update attendee, conference, and room objects?
- You need to know how far the relationships from one object extend through other entities and value objects within the domain, and where you must define the consistency boundaries. For example, if you delete a room object, should you also delete a projector object, or a set of attendee objects?

DDD uses the term aggregate to define a cluster of related entities and value objects that form a consistency boundary within the system. That consistency boundary is usually based on transactional consistency.

An aggregate root (also known as a root entity) is the gatekeeper object for the aggregate. All access to the objects within the aggregate must occur through the aggregate root; external entities are only permitted to hold a reference to the aggregate root, and all invariants should be checked by the aggregate root.

In summary, aggregates are the mechanism that DDD uses to manage the complex set of relationships that typically exist between the many entities and value objects in a typical domain model.

Bounded contexts

So far, the DDD concepts and terminology that we have briefly introduced are related to creating, maintaining, and using a domain model. For a large system, it may not be practical to maintain a single domain model; the size and complexity make it difficult to keep it coherent and consistent. To manage this scenario, DDD introduces the concepts of bounded contexts and multiple models. Within a system, you might choose to use multiple smaller models rather than a single large model, each one focusing on some aspect or grouping of functionality within the overall system. A bounded context is the context for one particular domain model. Similarly, each bounded context (if implemented following the DDD approach) has its own ubiquitous language, or at least its own dialect of the domain's ubiquitous language.

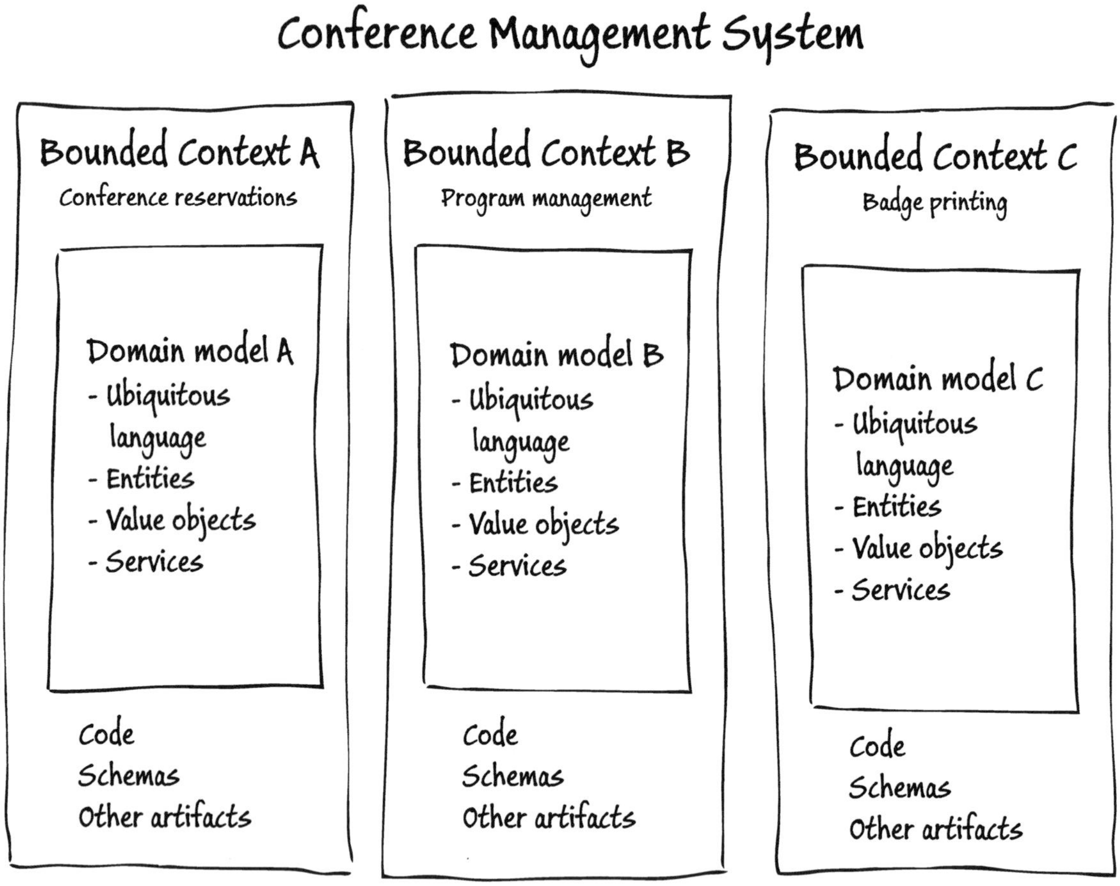

Conference Management System

Bounded Context A Conference reservations	Bounded Context B Program management	Bounded Context C Badge printing
Domain model A - Ubiquitous language - Entities - Value objects - Services	Domain model B - Ubiquitous language - Entities - Value objects - Services	Domain model C - Ubiquitous language - Entities - Value objects - Services
Code Schemas Other artifacts	Code Schemas Other artifacts	Code Schemas Other artifacts

FIGURE 1
Bounded contexts within a large, complex system

"A given bounded context should be divided into business components, where these business components have full UI through DB code, and are put together in composite UI's and other physical pipelines to fulfill the system's functionality. A business component can exist in only one bounded context."
—Udi Dahan, Udi & Greg Reach CQRS Agreement

Figure 1 shows an example of a system that is divided into multiple bounded contexts. In practice, there are likely to be more bounded contexts than the three shown in the diagram.

There are no hard and fast rules that specify how big a bounded context should be. Ultimately it's a pragmatic issue that is determined by your requirements and the constraints on your project.

Eric Evans makes the case for larger bounded contexts:
*"Favoring larger bounded contexts:
• Flow between user tasks is smoother when more is handled with a unified model.
• It is easier to understand one coherent model than two distinct ones plus mappings.
• Translation between two models can be difficult (sometimes impossible).
• Shared language fosters clear team communication.
Favoring smaller bounded contexts:
• Communication overhead between developers is reduced.
• Continuous Integration is easier with smaller teams and code bases.
• Larger contexts may call for more versatile abstract models, requiring skills that are in short supply.
• Different models can cater to special needs or encompass the jargon of specialized groups of users, along with specialized dialects of the Ubiquitous Language."*
—Eric Evans, **Domain-Driven Design: Tackling Complexity in the Heart of Software**, page 383.

"For me, a bounded context is an abstract concept (and it's still an important one!) but when it comes to technical details, the business component is far more important than the bounded context."
—Greg Young, Conversation with the patterns & practices team

You decide which patterns and approaches to apply (for example, whether to use the CQRS pattern or not) within a bounded context, not for the system.

ANTI-CORRUPTION LAYERS

Different bounded contexts have different domain models. When your bounded contexts communicate with each other, you need to ensure that concepts specific to one domain model do not leak into another domain model. An *anti-corruption layer* functions as a gatekeeper between bounded contexts and helps you keep your domain models clean.

> BC is often used as an acronym for bounded contexts (in DDD) and business components (in service-oriented architecture (SOA)). Do not confuse them. In our guidance, BC means "bounded context."

> *"I think context mapping is perhaps one thing in there that should be done on every project. The context map helps you keep track of all the models you are using."*
> —Eric Evans, What I've learned about DDD since the book

> *"Sometimes the process of gathering information to draw the context map is more important than the map itself."*
> —Alberto Brandolini, Context Mapping in action

Context maps

A large complex system can have multiple bounded contexts that interact with one another in various ways. A *context map* is the documentation that describes the relationships between these bounded contexts. It might be in the form of diagrams, tables, or text.

A context map helps you visualize the system at a high level, showing how some of the key parts relate to each other. It also helps to clarify the boundaries between the bounded contexts. It shows where and how the bounded contexts exchange and share data, and where you must translate data as it moves from one domain model to another.

A business entity, such as a customer, might exist in several bounded contexts. However, it may need to expose different facets or properties that are relevant to a particular bounded context. As a customer entity moves from one bounded context to another you may need to translate it so that it exposes the relevant facets or properties for its current context.

Bounded contexts and multiple architectures

A bounded context typically represents a slice of the overall system with clearly defined boundaries separating it from other bounded contexts within the system. If a bounded context is implemented by following the DDD approach, the bounded context will have its own domain model and its own ubiquitous language. Bounded contexts are also typically vertical slices through the system, so the implementation of a bounded context will include everything from the data store, right up to the UI.

The same domain concept can exist in multiple bounded contexts. For example, the concept of an attendee in a conference management system might exist in the bounded context that deals with bookings, in the bounded context that deals with badge printing, and in the bounded context that deals with hotel reservations. From the perspective of the domain expert, these different versions of the attendee may require different behaviors and attributes. For example, in the bookings bounded context the attendee is associated with a registrant who makes the bookings and payments. Information about the registrant is not relevant in the hotel reservations bounded context, where information such as dietary requirements or smoking preferences is important.

One important consequence of this split is that you can use different implementation architectures in different bounded contexts. For example, one bounded context might be implemented using a DDD layered architecture, another might use a two-tier CRUD architecture, and another might use an architecture derived from the CQRS pattern. Figure 2 illustrates a system with multiple bounded contexts, each using a different architectural style. It also highlights that each bounded context is typically end-to-end, from the persistence store through to the UI.

Scope of a Complex Domain

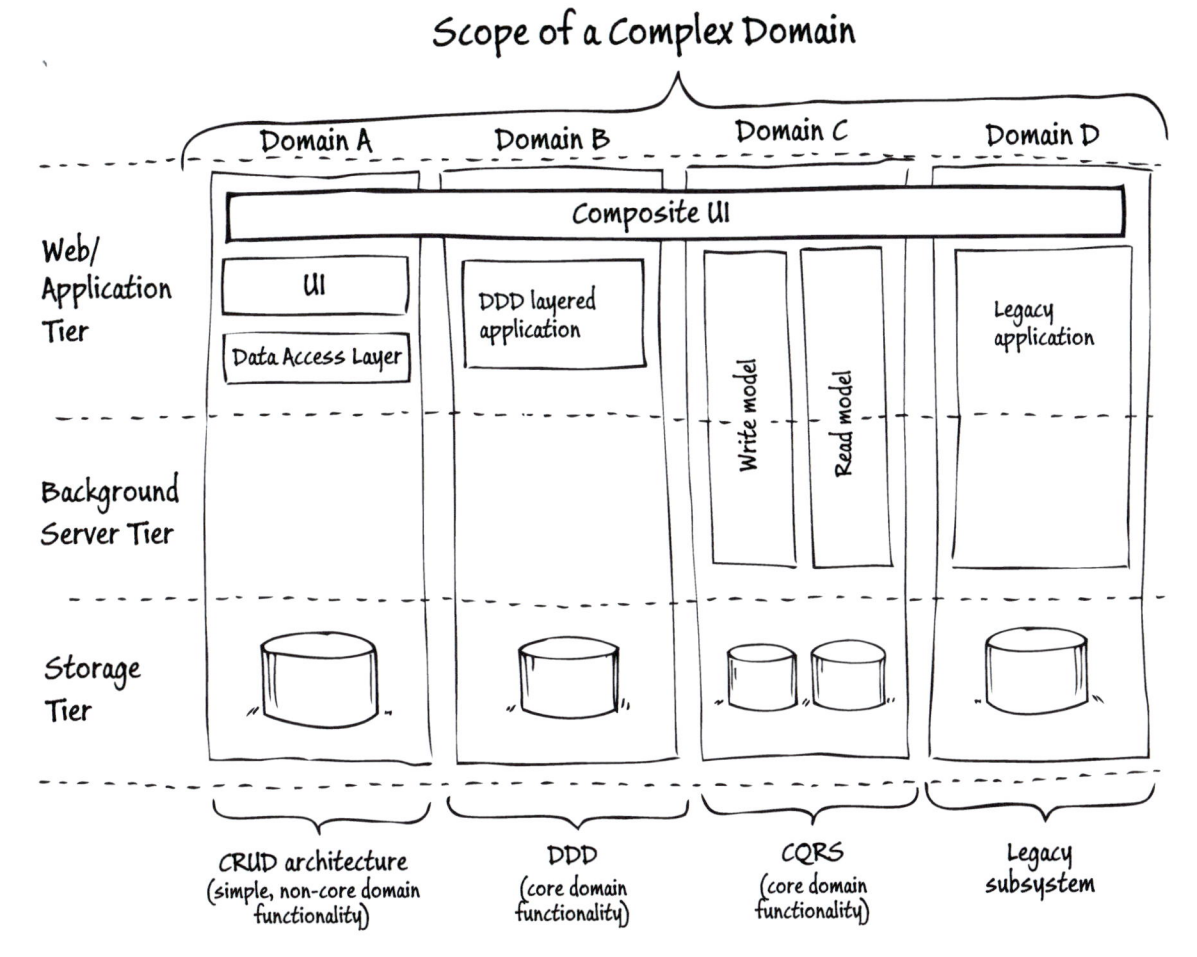

FIGURE 2
Multiple architectural styles within a large, complex application

In addition to managing complexity, there is another benefit of dividing the system into bounded contexts. You can use an appropriate technical architecture for different parts of the system to address the specific characteristics of each part. For example, you can address such questions as whether it is a complex part of the system, whether it contains core domain functionality, and what is its expected lifetime.

Bounded contexts and multiple development teams

Clearly separating out the different bounded contexts, and working with separate domain models and ubiquitous languages also makes it possible to parallelize the development work by using separate teams for each bounded context. This relates to the idea of using different technical architectures for different bounded contexts because the different development teams might have different skill sets and skill levels.

Maintaining multiple bounded contexts

Although bounded contexts help to manage the complexity of large systems because they're divided into more manageable pieces, it is unlikely that each bounded context will exist in isolation. Bounded contexts will need to exchange data with each other, and this exchange of data will be complicated if you need to translate between the different definitions of the same elements in the different domain models. In our conference management system, we may need to move information about attendees between the bounded contexts that deal with conference bookings, badge printing, and hotel reservations. The DDD approach offers a number of approaches for handling the interactions between multiple models in multiple bounded contexts such as using anti-corruption layers, or using shared kernels.

> **Note:** *At the technical implementation level, communication between bounded contexts is often handled asynchronously using events and a messaging infrastructure.*

For more information about how DDD deals with large systems and complex models, you should read "Part IV: Strategic Design" in Eric Evans' book, *Domain-Driven Design: Tackling Complexity in the Heart of Software*.

CQRS and DDD

As stated in the introduction to this chapter, it is useful to understand a little of the terminology and concepts from DDD when you are learning about the CQRS pattern.

Many of the ideas that informed the CQRS pattern arose from issues that DDD practitioners faced when applying the DDD approach to real-world problems. As such, if you decide to use the DDD approach, you may find that the CQRS pattern is a very natural fit for some of the bounded contexts that you identify within your system, and that it's relatively straightforward to move from your domain model to the physical implementation of the CQRS pattern.

Some experts consider the DDD approach to be an essential prerequisite for implementing the CQRS pattern.

> *"It is essential to write the whole domain model, ubiquitous language, use cases, domain and user intention specifications, and to identify both context boundaries and autonomous components. In my experience, those are absolutely mandatory."*
> —*José Miguel Torres (Customer Advisory Council)*

However, many people can point to projects where they have seen real benefits from implementing the CQRS pattern while not using the DDD approach for the domain analysis and model design.

In summary, the DDD approach is not a prerequisite for implementing the CQRS pattern, but in practice they do often go together.

More information

All links in this book are accessible from the book's online bibliography available at: *http://msdn.microsoft.com/en-us/library/jj619274*.

"It is something of a tradition to connect both paradigms because using DDD can lead naturally into CQRS, and also the available literature about CQRS tends to use DDD terminology. However, DDD is mostly appropriate for very large and complex projects. On the other hand, there is no reason why a small and simple project cannot benefit from CQRS. For example, a relatively small project that would otherwise use distributed transactions could be split into a write side and a read side with CQRS to avoid the distributed transaction, but it may be simple enough that applying DDD would be overkill."
—Alberto Población (Customer Advisory Council)

Reference 2:

Introducing the Command Query Responsibility Segregation Pattern

In this chapter, we describe the Command Query Responsibility Segregation (CQRS) pattern, which is at the heart of almost everything discussed in this guidance. Here we will show you how applying this pattern affects the architecture of your enterprise application. It is important to understand that CQRS is not a silver bullet for all the problems you encounter when you design and build enterprise applications, and that it is not a top-level architectural approach. You will see the full benefits of applying the CQRS pattern when you apply it selectively to key portions of your system. Chapter 2, "Decomposing the Domain" in Exploring CQRS and Event Sourcing describes how Contoso divided up the Contoso Conference Management System into bounded contexts and identified which bounded contexts would benefit from using the CQRS pattern.

Subsequent chapters in *Exploring CQRS and Event Sourcing* provide more in-depth guidance on how to apply the CQRS pattern and other related patterns when building your implementation.

What is CQRS?

In his book *"Object Oriented Software Construction,"* Betrand Meyer introduced the term *"Command Query Separation"* to describe the principle that an object's methods should be either commands or queries. A query returns data and does not alter the state of the object; a command changes the state of an object but does not return any data. The benefit is that you have a better understanding what does, and what does not, change the state in your system.

CQRS takes this principle a step further to define a simple pattern.

"CQRS is simply the creation of two objects where there was previously only one. The separation occurs based upon whether the methods are a command or a query (the same definition that is used by Meyer in Command and Query Separation: a command is any method that mutates state and a query is any method that returns a value)."
—Greg Young, CQRS, Task Based UIs, Event Sourcing agh!

"CQRS is a simple pattern that strictly segregates the responsibility of handling command input into an autonomous system from the responsibility of handling side-effect-free query/read access on the same system. Consequently, the decoupling allows for any number of homogeneous or heterogeneous query/read modules to be paired with a command processor. This principle presents a very suitable foundation for event sourcing, eventual-consistency state replication/fan-out and, thus, high-scale read access. In simple terms, you don't service queries via the same module of a service that you process commands through. In REST terminology, GET requests wire up to a different thing from what PUT, POST, and DELETE requests wire up to."
—*Clemens Vasters (CQRS Advisors Mail List)*

What is important and interesting about this simple pattern is how, where, and why you use it when you build enterprise systems. Using this simple pattern enables you to meet a wide range of architectural challenges, such as achieving scalability, managing complexity, and managing changing business rules in some portions of your system.

> The following conversation between Greg Young and Udi Dahan highlights some of the important aspects of the CQRS pattern:
>
> **Udi Dahan:** If you are going to be looking at applying CQRS, it should be done within a specific bounded context, rather than at the whole system level, unless you are in a special case, when your entire system is just one single bounded context.
>
> **Greg Young:** I would absolutely agree with that statement. CQRS is not a top-level architecture. CQRS is something that happens at a much lower level, where your top level architecture is probably going to look more like SOA and EDA [service-oriented or event-driven architectures].
>
> **Udi Dahan:** That's an important distinction. And that's something that a lot of people who are looking to apply CQRS don't give enough attention to: just how important on the one hand, and how difficult on the other, it is to identify the correct bounded contexts or services, or whatever you call that top-level decomposition and the event-based synchronization between them. A lot of times, when discussing CQRS with clients, when I tell them "You don't need CQRS for that," their interpretation of that statement is that, in essence, they think I'm telling them that they need to go back to an N-tier type of architecture, when primarily I mean that a two-tier style of architecture is sufficient. And even when I say two-tier, I don't necessarily mean that the second tier needs to be a relational database. To a large extent, for a lot of systems, a NoSQL, document-style database would probably be sufficient with a single data management-type tier operated on the client side. As an alternative to CQRS, it's important to lay out a bunch of other design styles or approaches, rather than thinking either you are doing N-tier object relational mapping or CQRS.

When asked whether he considers CQRS to be an approach or a pattern, and if it's a pattern, what problem it specifically solves, Greg Young answered:

"If we were to go by the definition that we set up for CQRS a number of years ago, it's going to be a very simple low-level pattern. It's not even that interesting as a pattern; it's more just pretty conceptual stuff; you just separate. What's more interesting about it is what it enables. It's the enabling that the pattern provides that's interesting. Everybody gets really caught up in systems and they talk about how complicated CQRS is with Service Bus and all the other stuff they are doing, and in actuality, none of that is necessary. If you go with the simplest possible definition, it would be a pattern. But it's more what happens once you apply that pattern—the opportunities that you get."

READ AND WRITE SIDES

Figure 1 shows a typical application of the CQRS pattern to a portion of an enterprise system. This approach shows how, when you apply the CQRS pattern, you can separate the read and write sides in this portion of the system.

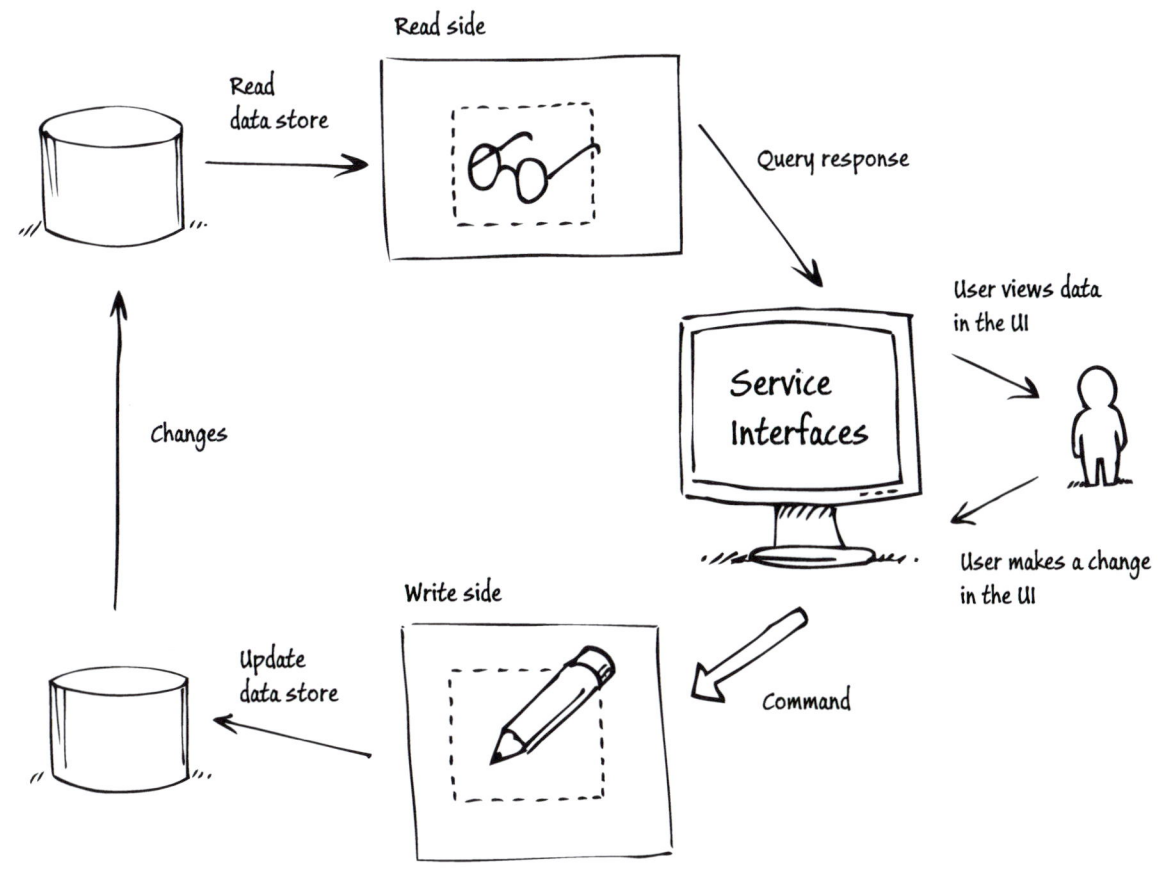

FIGURE 1
A possible architectural implementation of the CQRS pattern

In Figure 1, you can see how this portion of the system is split into a read side and a write side. The object or objects or the read side contain only query methods, and the objects on the write side contain only command methods.

There are several motivations for this segregation including:
- In many business systems, there is a large imbalance between the number of reads and the number of writes. A system may process thousands of reads for every write. Segregating the two sides enables you to optimize them independently. For example, you can scale out the read side to support the larger number of read operations independently of the write side.
- Typically, commands involve complex business logic to ensure that the system writes correct and consistent data to the data store. Read operations are often much simpler than write operations. A single conceptual model that tries to encapsulate both read and write operations may do neither well. Segregating the two sides ultimately results in simpler, more maintainable, and more flexible models.
- Segregation can also occur at the data store level. The write side may use a database schema that is close to third normal form (3NF) and optimized for data modifications, while the read side uses a denormalized database that is optimized for fast query operations.

Note: *Although Figure 1 shows two data stores, applying the CQRS pattern does not mandate that you split the data store, or that you use any particular persistence technology such as a relational database, NoSQL store, or event store (which in turn could be implemented on top of a relational database, NoSQL store, file storage, blob storage and so forth.). You should view CQRS as a pattern that facilitates splitting the data store and enabling you to select from a range of storage mechanisms.*

Figure 1 might also suggest a one-to-one relationship between the write side and the read side. However, this is not necessarily the case. It can be useful to consolidate the data from multiple write models into a single read model if your user interface (UI) needs to display consolidated data. The point of the read-side model is to simplify what happens on the read side, and you may be able to simplify the implementation of your UI if the data you need to display has already been combined.

There are some questions that might occur to you about the practicalities of adopting architecture such as the one shown in Figure 1.
- Although the individual models on the read side and write side might be simpler than a single compound model, the overall architecture is more complex than a traditional approach with a single model and a single data store. So, haven't we just shifted the complexity?
- How should we manage the propagation of changes in the data store on the write side to the read side?
- What if there is a delay while the updates on the write side are propagated to the read side?
- What exactly do we mean when we talk about models?

The remainder of this chapter will begin to address these questions and to explore the motivations for using the CQRS pattern. Later chapters will explore these issues in more depth.

CQRS and domain-driven design

The previous chapter, "CQRS in Context," introduced some of the concepts and terminology from the domain-driven design (DDD) approach that are relevant to the implementation of the CQRS pattern. Two areas are particularly significant.

The first is the concept of the model:

Eric Evans in his book *"Domain-Driven Design: Tackling Complexity in the Heart of Software,"* (Addison-Wesley Professional, 2003) provides the following list of ingredients for effective modeling. This list helps to capture the idea of a model, but is no substitute for reading the book to gain a deeper understanding of the concept:

- Models should be bound to the implementation.
- You should cultivate a language based on the model.
- Models should be knowledge rich.
- You should brainstorm and experiment to develop the model.

In Figure 1, the implementation of the model exists on the write side; it encapsulates the complex business logic in this portion of the system. The read side is a simpler, read-only view of the system state accessed through queries.

The second important concept is the way that DDD divides large, complex systems into more manageable units known as bounded contexts. A bounded context defines the context for a model:

> **Note:** *Other design approaches may use different terminology; for example, in event-driven service-oriented architecture (SOA), the service concept is similar to the bounded context concept in DDD.*

When we say that you should apply the CQRS pattern to a portion of a system, we mean that you should implement the CQRS pattern within a bounded context.

"CQRS is an architectural style that is often enabling of DDD."
—*Eric Evans, tweet February 2012.*

"The model is a set of concepts built up in the heads of people on the project, with terms and relationships that reflect domain insight. These terms and interrelationships provide the semantics of a language that is tailored to the domain while being precise enough for technical development."
—*Eric Evans, "Domain-Driven Design: Tackling Complexity in the Heart of Software," p23.*

"Explicitly define the context within which a model applies. Explicitly set boundaries in terms of team organization, usage within specific parts of the application, and physical manifestations such as code bases and database schemas. Keep the model strictly consistent within these bounds, but don't be distracted or confused by issues outside."
—*Eric Evans, "Domain-Driven Design: Tackling Complexity in the Heart of Software," p335.*

> *"A given bounded context should be divided into business components, where these business components have full UI through DB code, and are ultimately put together in composite UIs and other physical pipelines to fulfill the system's functionality.*
>
> *A business component can exist in only one bounded context.*
>
> *CQRS, if it is to be used at all, should be used within a business component."*
> —Udi Dahan, Udi & Greg Reach CQRS Agreement.

The reasons for identifying context boundaries for your domain models are not necessarily the same reasons for choosing the portions of the system that should use the CQRS pattern. In DDD, a bounded context defines the context for a model and the scope of a ubiquitous language. You should implement the CQRS pattern to gain certain benefits for your application such as scalability, simplicity, and maintainability. Because of these differences, it may make sense to think about applying the CQRS pattern to business components rather than bounded contexts.

It is quite possible that your bounded contexts map exactly onto your business components.

> **Note:** *Throughout this guide, we use the term **bounded context** in preference to the term **business component** to refer to the context within which we are implementing the CQRS pattern.*

In summary, you should **not** apply the CQRS pattern to the top level of your system. You should clearly identify the different portions of your system that you can design and implement largely independently of each other, and then only apply the CQRS pattern to those portions where there are clear business benefits in doing so.

Introducing commands, events, and messages

DDD is an analysis and design approach that encourages you to use models and a ubiquitous language to bridge the gap between the business and the development team by fostering a common understanding of the domain. Of necessity, the DDD approach is oriented towards analyzing behavior rather than just data in the business domain, and this leads to a focus on modeling and implementing behavior in the software. A natural way to implement the domain model in code is to use commands and events. This is particularly true of applications that use a task-oriented UI.

> **Note:** *DDD is not the only approach in which it is common to see tasks and behaviors specified in the domain model implemented using commands and events. However, many advocates of the CQRS pattern are also strongly influenced by the DDD approach so it is common to see DDD terminology in use whenever there is a discussion of the CQRS pattern.*

Commands are imperatives; they are requests for the system to perform a task or action. For example, "book two places for conference X" or "allocate speaker Y to room Z." Commands are usually processed just once, by a single recipient.

Events are notifications; they report something that has already happened to other interested parties. For example, "the customer's credit card has been billed $200" or "ten seats have been booked for conference X." Events can be processed multiple times, by multiple consumers.

Both commands and events are types of message that are used to exchange data between objects. In DDD terms, these messages represent business behaviors and therefore help the system capture the business intent behind the message.

A possible implementation of the CQRS pattern uses separate data stores for the read side and the write side; each data store is optimized for the use cases it supports. Events provide the basis of a mechanism for synchronizing the changes on the write side (that result from processing commands) with the read side. If the write side raises an event whenever the state of the application changes, the read side should respond to that event and update the data that is used by its queries and views. Figure 2 shows how commands and events can be used if you implement the CQRS pattern.

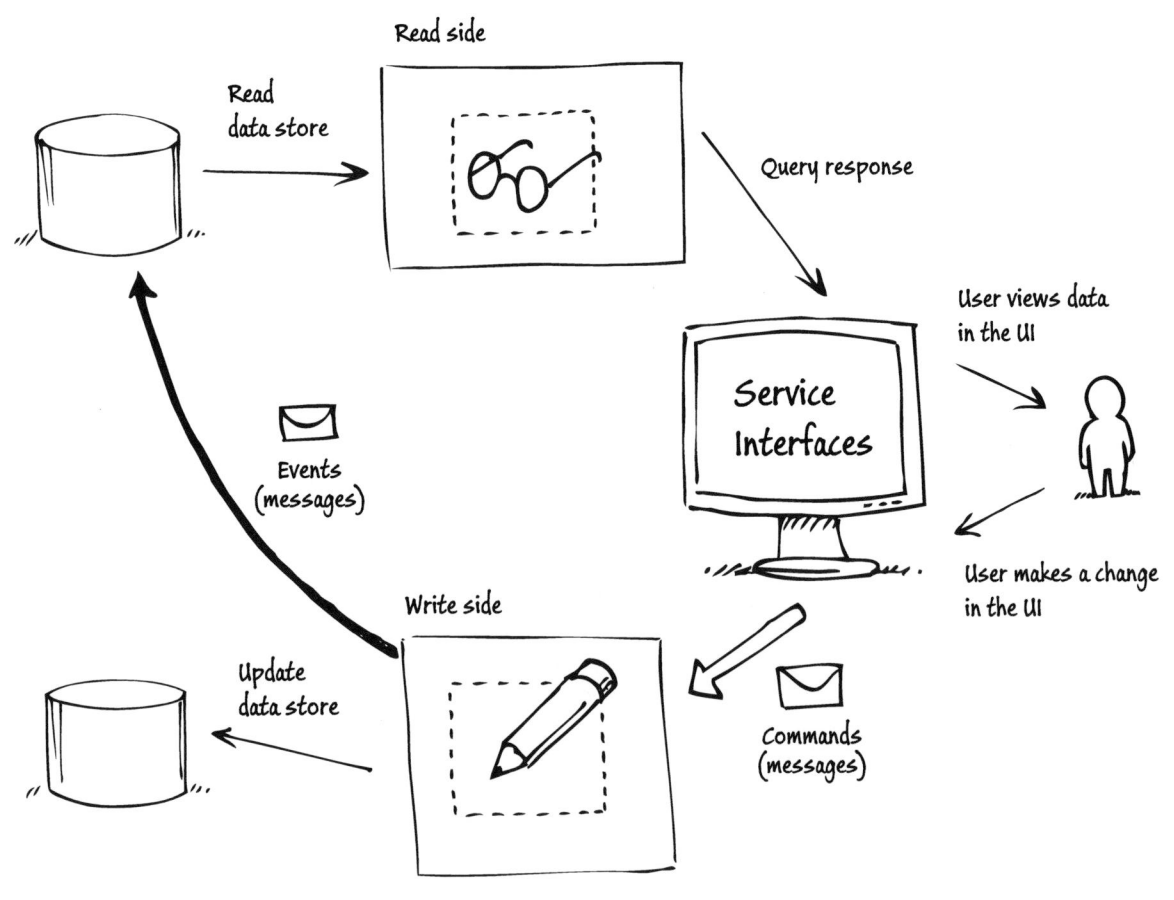

FIGURE 2
Commands and events in the CQRS pattern

We also require some infrastructure to handle commands and events, and we will explore this in more detail in later chapters.

Note: *Events are not the only way to manage the push synchronization of updates from the write side to the read side.*

Why should I use CQRS?

Stepping back from CQRS for a moment, one of the benefits of dividing the domain into bounded contexts in DDD is to enable you to identify and focus on those portions (bounded contexts) of the system that are more complex, subject to ever-changing business rules, or deliver functionality that is a key business differentiator.

You should consider applying the CQRS pattern within a specific bounded context only if it provides identifiable business benefits, not because it is the default pattern that you consider.

The most common business benefits that you might gain from applying the CQRS pattern are enhanced scalability, the simplification of a complex aspect of your domain, increased flexibility of your solution, and greater adaptability to changing business requirements.

Scalability

Scalability should not be the only reason why you choose to implement the CQRS pattern in a specific bounded context:
"In a non-collaborative domain, where you can horizontally add more database servers to support more users, requests, and data at the same time you're adding web servers, there is no real scalability problem (until you're the size of Amazon, Google, or Facebook). Database servers can be cheap if you're using MySQL, SQL Server Express, or others."
—Udi Dahan, When to avoid CQRS.

In many enterprise systems, the number of reads vastly exceeds the number of writes, so your scalability requirements will be different for each side. By separating the read side and the write side into separate models within the bounded context, you now have the ability to scale each one of them independently. For example, if you are hosting applications in Windows Azure, you can use a different role for each side and then scale them independently by adding a different number of role instances to each.

REDUCED COMPLEXITY

In complex areas of your domain, designing and implementing objects that are responsible for both reading and writing data can exacerbate the complexity. In many cases, the complex business logic is only applied when the system is handling updates and transactional operations; in comparison, read logic is often much simpler. When the business logic and read logic are mixed together in the same model, it becomes much harder to deal with difficult issues such as multiple users, shared data, performance, transactions, consistency, and stale data. Separating the read logic and business logic into separate models makes it easier to separate out and address these complex issues. However, in many cases it may require some effort to disentangle and understand the existing model in the domain.

Like many patterns, you can view the CQRS pattern as a mechanism for shifting some of the complexity inherent in your domain into something that is well known, well understood, and that offers a standard approach to solving certain categories of problems.

Another potential benefit of simplifying the bounded context by separating out the read logic and the business logic is that it can make testing easier.

Separation of concerns is the key motivation behind Bertrand Meyer's Command Query Separation Principle: "The really valuable idea in this principle is that it's extremely handy if you can clearly separate methods that change state from those that don't. This is because you can use queries in many situations with much more confidence, introducing them anywhere, changing their order. You have to be more careful with modifiers."
—Martin Fowler, CommandQuerySeparation

FLEXIBILITY

The flexibility of a solution that uses the CQRS pattern largely derives from the separation into the read-side and the write-side models. It becomes much easier to make changes on the read side, such as adding a new query to support a new report screen in the UI, when you can be confident that you won't have any impact on the behavior of the business logic. On the write side, having a model that concerns itself solely with the core business logic in the domain means that you have a simpler model to deal with than a model that includes read logic as well.

In the longer term, a good, useful model that accurately describes your core domain business logic will become a valuable asset. It will enable you to be more agile in the face of a changing business environment and competitive pressures on your organization.

This flexibility and agility relates to the concept of continuous integration in DDD:

In some cases, it may be possible to have different development teams working on the write side and the read side, although in practice this will probably depend on how large the particular bounded context is.

"Continuous integration means that all work within the context is being merged and made consistent frequently enough that when splinters happen they are caught and corrected quickly."
—Eric Evans, "Domain-Driven Design," p342.

Focus on the business

If you use an approach like CRUD, then the technology tends to shape the solution. Adopting the CQRS pattern helps you to focus on the business and build task-oriented UIs. A consequence of separating the different concerns into the read side and the write side is a solution that is more adaptable in the face of changing business requirements. This results in lower development and maintenance costs in the longer term.

Facilitates building task-based UIs

When you implement the CQRS pattern, you use commands (often from the UI), to initiate operations in the domain. These commands are typically closely tied to the domain operations and the ubiquitous language. For example, "book two seats for conference X." You can design your UI to send these commands to the domain instead of initiating CRUD-style operations. This makes it easier to design intuitive, task-based UIs.

Barriers to adopting the CQRS pattern

Although you can list a number of clear benefits to adopting the CQRS pattern in specific scenarios, you may find it difficult in practice to convince your stakeholders that these benefits warrant the additional complexity of the solution.

When should I use CQRS?

Although we have outlined some of the reasons why you might decide to apply the CQRS pattern to some of the bounded contexts in your system, it is helpful to have some rules of thumb to help identify the bounded contexts that might benefit from applying the CQRS pattern.

In general, applying the CQRS pattern may provide the most value in those bounded contexts that are collaborative, complex, include ever-changing business rules, and deliver a significant competitive advantage to the business. Analyzing the business requirements, building a useful model, expressing it in code, and implementing it using the CQRS pattern for such a bounded context all take time and cost money. You should expect this investment to pay dividends in the medium to long term. It is probably not worth making this investment if you don't expect to see returns such as increased adaptability and flexibility in the system, or reduced maintenance costs.

"In my experience, the most important disadvantage of using CQRS/event sourcing and DDD is the fear of change. This model is different from the well-known three-tier layered architecture that many of our stakeholders are accustomed to."
—Paweł Wilkosz (Customer Advisory Council)

"The learning curve of developer teams is steep. Developers usually think in terms of relational database development. From my experience, the lack of business, and therefore domain rules and specifications, became the biggest hurdle."
—José Miguel Torres (Customer Advisory Council)

Collaborative domains

Both Udi Dahan and Greg Young identify collaboration as the characteristic of a bounded context that provides the best indicator that you may see benefits from applying the CQRS pattern.

The CQRS pattern is particularly useful where the collaboration involves complex decisions about what the outcome should be when you have multiple actors operating on the same, shared data. For example, does the rule "last one wins" capture the expected business outcome for your scenario, or do you need something more sophisticated? It's important to note that actors are not necessarily people; they could be other parts of the system that can operate independently on the same data.

> **Note:** *Collaborative behavior is a good indicator that there will be benefits from applying the CQRS pattern; however, this is not a hard and fast rule!*

Such collaborative portions of the system are often the most complex, fluid, and significant bounded contexts. However, this characteristic is only a guide: not all collaborative domains benefit from the CQRS pattern, and some non-collaborative domains do benefit from the CQRS pattern.

Stale data

In a collaborative environment where multiple users can operate on the same data simultaneously, you will also encounter the issue of stale data; if one user is viewing a piece of data while another user changes it, then the first user's view of the data is stale.

Whatever architecture you choose, you must address this problem. For example, you can use a particular locking scheme in your database, or define the refresh policy for the cache from which your users read data.

The two previous examples show two different areas in a system where you might encounter and need to deal with stale data; in most collaborative enterprise systems there will be many more. The CQRS pattern helps you address the issue of stale data explicitly at the architecture level. Changes to data happen on the write side, users view data by querying the read side. Whatever mechanism you chose to use to push the changes from the write side to the read side is also the mechanism that controls when the data on the read side becomes stale, and how long it remains so. This differs from other architectures, where management of stale data is more of an implementation detail that is not always addressed in a standard or consistent manner.

In the chapter "A CQRS and ES Deep Dive," we will look at how the synchronization mechanism between write side and the read side determines how you manage the issue of stale data in your application.

> *"In a collaborative domain, an inherent property of the domain is that multiple actors operate in parallel on the same set of data. A reservation system for concerts would be a good example of a collaborative domain; everyone wants the good seats."*
> —Udi Dahan, Why you should be using CQRS almost everywhere...

> *"Standard layered architectures don't explicitly deal with either of these issues. While putting everything in the same database may be one step in the direction of handling collaboration, staleness is usually exacerbated in those architectures by the use of caches as a performance-improving afterthought."*
> —Udi Dahan talking about collaboration and staleness, Clarified CQRS.

Moving to the cloud

Moving an application to the cloud or developing an application for the cloud is not a sufficient reason for choosing to implement the CQRS pattern. However, many of the drivers for using the cloud such as requirements for scalability, elasticity, and agility are also drivers for adopting the CQRS pattern. Furthermore, many of the services typically offered as part of a platform as a service (PaaS) cloud-computing platform are well suited for building the infrastructure for a CQRS implementation: for example, highly scalable data stores, messaging services, and caching services.

When should I avoid CQRS?

> "Most people using CQRS (and event sourcing too) shouldn't have done so."
> —Udi Dahan, When to avoid CQRS.

Simple, static, non-core bounded contexts are less likely to warrant the up-front investment in detailed analysis, modeling, and complex implementation. Again, non-collaborative bounded contexts are less likely to see benefits from applying the CQRS pattern.

In most systems, the majority of bounded contexts will probably not benefit from using the CQRS pattern. You should only use the pattern when you can identify clear business benefits from doing so.

> "It's important to note though, that these are things you can do, not necessarily things you should do. Separating the read and write models can be quite costly."
> —Greg Young, CQRS and CAP Theorem.

Summary

The CQRS pattern is an enabler for building individual portions (bounded contexts) in your system. Identifying where to use the CQRS pattern requires you to analyze the trade-offs between the initial cost and overhead of implementing the pattern and the future business benefits. Useful heuristics for identifying where you might apply the CQRS pattern are to look for components that are complex, involve fluid business rules, deliver competitive advantage to the business, and are collaborative.

The next chapters will discuss how to implement the CQRS pattern in more detail. For example, we'll explain specific class-pattern implementations, explore how to synchronize the data between the write side and read side, and describe different options for storing data.

More information

All links in this book are accessible from the book's online bibliography available at: *http://msdn.microsoft.com/en-us/library/jj619274*.

Reference 3:

Introducing Event Sourcing

Event sourcing (ES) and Command Query Responsibility Segregation (CQRS) are frequently mentioned together. Although neither one necessarily implies the other, you will see that they do complement each other. This chapter introduces the key concepts that underlie event sourcing, and provides some pointers on the potential relationship with the CQRS pattern. This chapter is an introduction; Chapter 4, "A CQRS and ES Deep Dive," explores event sourcing and its relationship with CQRS in more depth.

To help understand event sourcing, it's important to have a basic definition of events that captures their essential characteristics:

- Events happen in the past. For example, "the speaker was booked," "the seat was reserved," "the cash was dispensed." Notice how we describe these events using the past tense.
- Events are immutable. Because events happen in the past, they cannot be changed or undone. However, subsequent events may alter or negate the effects of earlier events. For example, "the reservation was cancelled" is an event that changes the result of an earlier reservation event.
- Events are one-way messages. Events have a single source (publisher) that publishes the event. One or more recipients (subscribers) may receive events.
- Typically, events include parameters that provide additional information about the event. For example, "Seat E23 was booked by Alice."
- In the context of event sourcing, events should describe business intent. For example, "Seat E23 was booked by Alice" describes in business terms what has happened and is more descriptive than, "In the bookings table, the row with key E23 had the name field updated with the value Alice."

We will also assume that the events discussed in this chapter are associated with aggregates; see the chapter "CQRS in Context" for a description of the DDD terms: aggregates, aggregate roots, and entities. There are two features of aggregates that are relevant to events and event sourcing:

- Aggregates define consistency boundaries for groups of related entities; therefore, you can use an event raised by an aggregate to notify interested parties that a transaction (consistent set of updates) has taken place on that group of entities.
- Every aggregate has a unique ID; therefore, you can use that ID to record which aggregate in the system was the source of a particular event.

For the remainder of this chapter, we will use the term aggregate to refer to a cluster of associated objects that are treated as a unit for the purposes of data changes. This does not mean that event sourcing is directly related to the DDD approach; we are simply using the terminology from DDD to try to maintain some consistency in our language in this guide.

What is event sourcing?

Event sourcing is a way of persisting your application's state by storing the history that determines the current state of your application. For example, a conference management system needs to track the number of completed bookings for a conference so it can check whether there are still seats available when someone tries to make a new booking. The system could store the total number of bookings for a conference in two ways:

- It could store the total number of bookings for a particular conference and adjust this number whenever someone makes or cancels a booking. You can think of the number of bookings as being an integer value stored in a specific column of a table that has a row for each conference in the system.
- It could store all the booking and cancellation events for each conference and then calculate the current number of bookings by replaying the events associated with the conference for which you wanted to check the current total number of bookings.

Comparing using an ORM layer with event sourcing

Figure 1 illustrates the first approach to storing the total number of reservations. The following steps correspond to the numbers in the diagram:

1. A process manager or a UI issues a command to reserve seats for two attendees to the conference with an ID of 157. The command is handled by the command handler for the **SeatsAvailability** aggregate type.
2. If necessary, the object-relational mapping (ORM) layer populates an aggregate instance with data. The ORM layer retrieves the data by issuing a query against the table (or tables) in the data store. This data includes the existing number of reservations for the conference.
3. The command handler invokes the business method on the aggregate instance to make the reservations.
4. The **SeatsAvailability** aggregate performs its domain logic. In this example, this includes calculating the new number of reservations for the conference.
5. The ORM persists the information in the aggregate instance to the data store. The ORM layer constructs the necessary update (or updates) that must be executed.

Note: *For a definition of process manager, see Chapter 6, "A Saga on Sagas."*

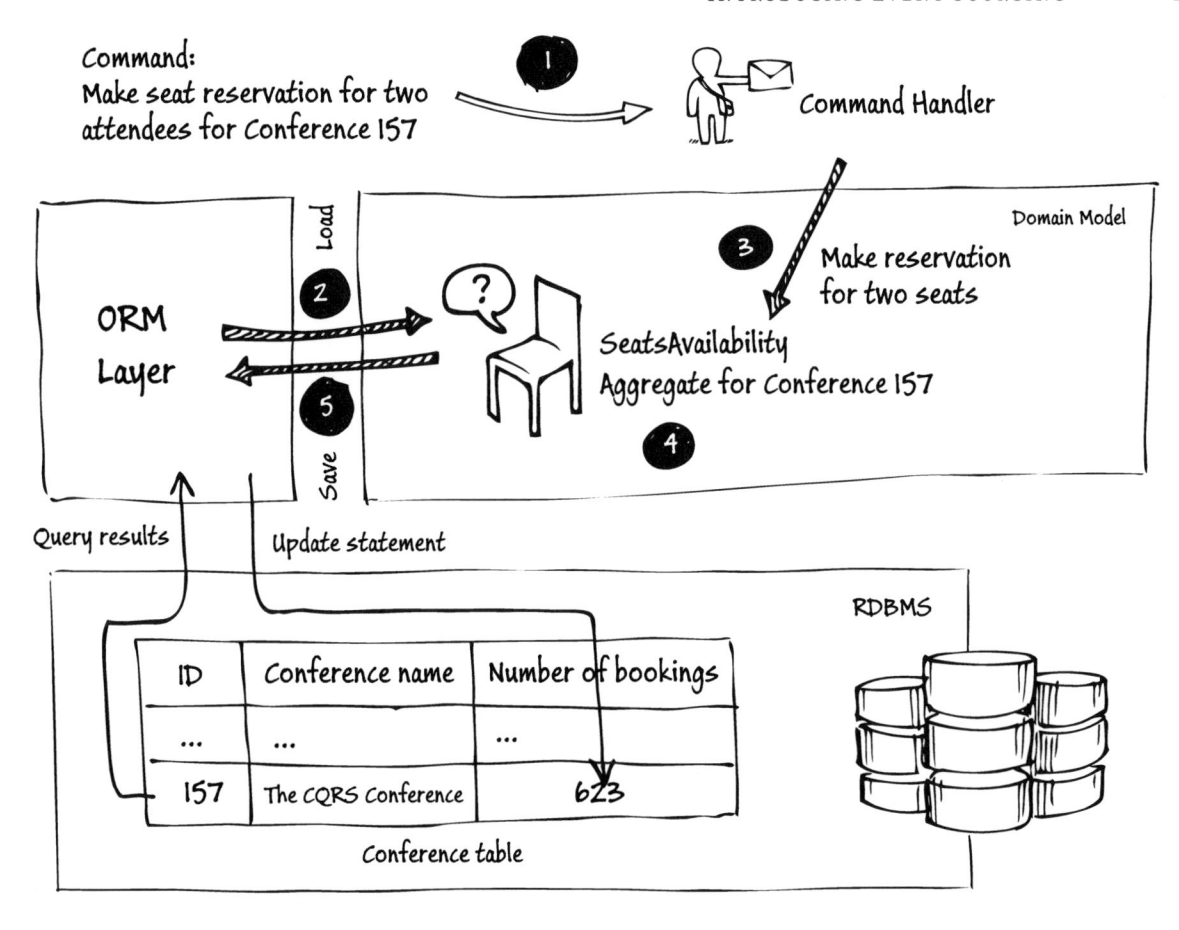

FIGURE 1
Using an object-relational mapping layer

Figure 1 provides a deliberately simplified view of the process. In practice, the mapping performed by the ORM layer will be significantly more complex. You will also need to consider exactly when the load and save operations must happen to balance the demands of consistency, reliability, scalability, and performance.

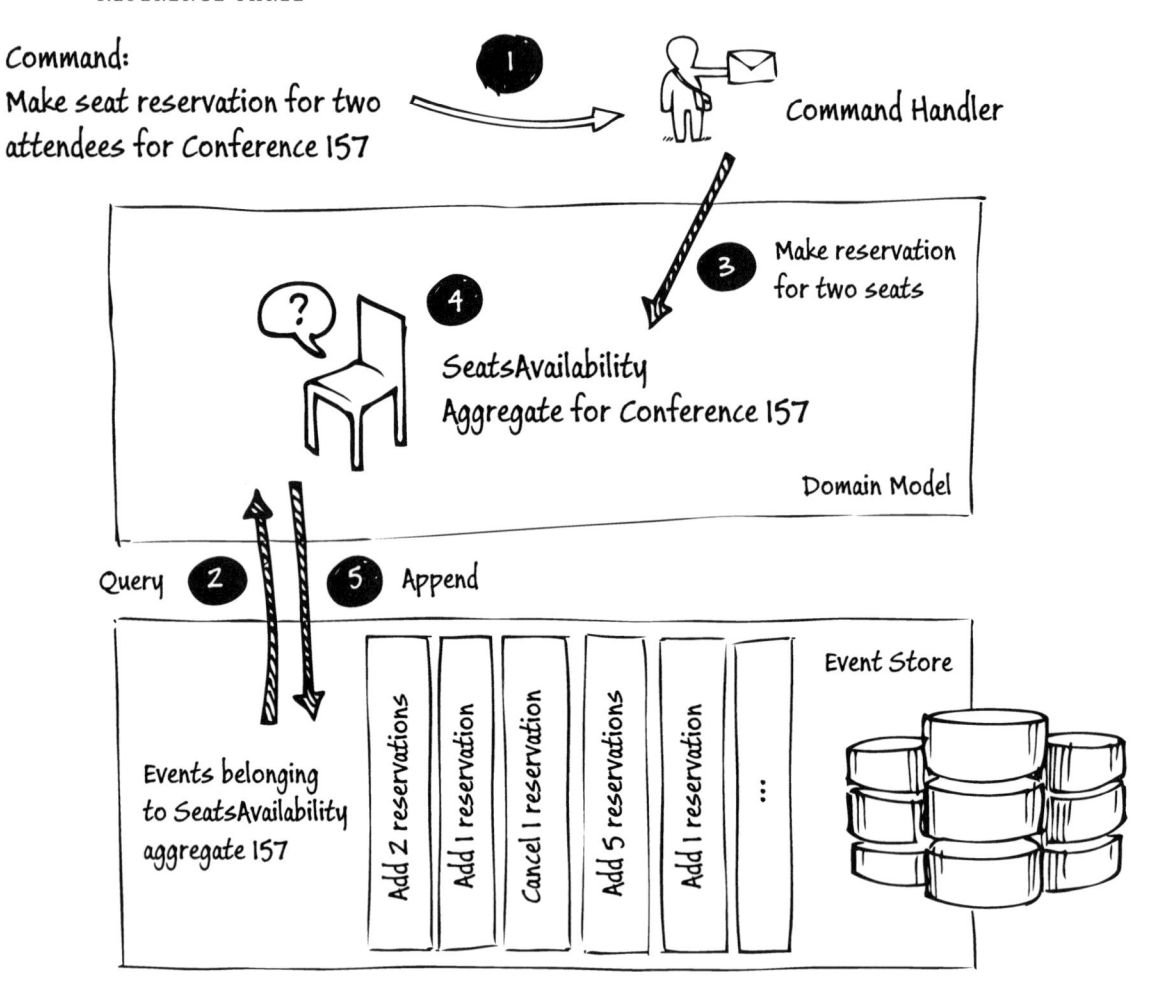

FIGURE 2
Using event sourcing

Figure 2 illustrates the second approach—using event sourcing in place of an ORM layer and a relational database management system (RDBMS).

Note: *You might decide to implement the event store using an RDBMS. The relational schema will be much simpler than the schema used by the ORM layer in the first approach. You can also use a custom event store.*

The following list of steps corresponds to the numbers in Figure 2. Note that steps one, three, and four are the same as for the solution that uses the ORM layer.

1. A process manager or a UI issues a command to reserve seats for two attendees to a conference with an ID of 157. The command is handled by the command handler for the **SeatsAvailability** aggregate type.
2. An aggregate instance is populated by querying for all of the events that belong to **SeatsAvailability** aggregate 157.
3. The command handler invokes the business method on the aggregate instance to make the reservations.
4. The **SeatsAvailability** aggregate performs its domain logic. In this example, this includes calculating the new number of reservations for the conference. The aggregate creates an event to record the effects of the command.
5. The system appends the event that records making two new reservations to the list of events associated with the aggregate in the event store.

This second approach is simpler because it dispenses with the ORM layer, and replaces a complex relational schema in the data store with a much simpler one. The data store only needs to support querying for events by aggregate ID and appending new events. You will still need to consider performance and scalability optimizations for reading from and writing to the store, but the impact of these optimizations on reliability and consistency should be much easier to understand.

> **Note:** *Some optimizations to consider are using snapshots so you don't need to query and replay the full list of events to obtain the current state of the aggregate, and maintaining cached copies of aggregates in memory.*

You must also ensure that you have a mechanism that enables an aggregate to rebuild its state by querying for its list of historical events.

> CQRS/ES makes it easy to change your technologies. For example, you could start with a file-based event store for prototyping and development, and later switch to a Windows Azure table-based store for production.

> For additional insights into using events as a storage mechanism, see *Events as a Storage Mechanism* by Greg Young.

The primary benefit of using event sourcing is a built-in audit mechanism that ensures consistency of transactional data and audit data because these are the same data. Representation via events allows you to reconstruct the state of any object at any moment in time.
—Paweł Wilkosz (Customer Advisory Council)

"Another problem with the having of two models is that it is necessarily more work. One must create the code to save the current state of the objects and one must write the code to generate and publish the events. No matter how you go about doing these things it cannot possibly be easier than only publishing events, even if you had something that made storing current state completely trivial to say a document storage, there is still the effort of bringing that into the project."
—Greg Young - Why use Event Sourcing?

What you have also gained with the second approach is a complete history, or audit trail, of the bookings and cancellations for a conference. Therefore, the event stream becomes your only source of truth. There's no need to persist aggregates in any other form or shape since you can easily replay the events and restore the state of the system to any point in time.

In some domains, such as accounting, event sourcing is the natural, well-established approach: accounting systems store individual transactions from which it is always possible to reconstruct the current state of the system. Event sourcing can bring similar benefits to other domains.

Why should I use event sourcing?

So far, the only justification we have offered for the use of event sourcing is the fact that it stores a complete history of the events associated with the aggregates in your domain. This is a vital feature in some domains, such as accounting, where you need a complete audit trail of the financial transactions, and where events must be immutable. Once a transaction has happened, you cannot delete or change it, although you can create a new corrective or reversing transaction if necessary.

The following list describes some of the additional benefits that you can derive from using event sourcing. The significance of the individual benefits will vary depending on the domain you are working in.

- **Performance**. Because events are immutable, you can use an append-only operation when you save them. Events are also simple, standalone objects. Both these factors can lead to better performance and scalability for the system than approaches that use complex relational storage models.
- **Simplification**. Events are simple objects that describe what has happened in the system. By simply saving events, you are avoiding the complications associated with saving complex domain objects to a relational store; namely, the object-relational impedance mismatch.

- **Audit trail**. Events are immutable and store the full history of the state of the system. As such, they can provide a detailed audit trail of what has taken place within the system.
- **Integration with other subsystems**. Events provide a useful way of communicating with other subsystems. Your event store can publish events to notify other interested subsystems of changes to the application's state. Again, the event store provides a complete record of all the events that it published to other systems.
- **Deriving additional business value from the event history**. By storing events, you have the ability to determine the state of the system at any previous point in time by querying the events associated with a domain object up to that point in time. This enables you to answer historical questions from the business about the system. In addition, you cannot predict what questions the business might want to ask about the information stored in a system. If you store your events, you are not discarding information that may prove to be valuable in the future.
- **Production troubleshooting**. You can use the event store to troubleshoot problems in a production system by taking a copy of the production event store and replaying it in a test environment. If you know the time that an issue occurred in the production system, then you can easily replay the event stream up to that point to observe exactly what was happening.
- **Fixing errors**. You might discover a coding error that results in the system calculating an incorrect value. Rather than fixing the coding error and performing a risky manual adjustment on a stored item of data, you can fix the coding error and replay the event stream so that the system calculates the value correctly based on the new version of the code.
- **Testing**. All of the state changes in your aggregates are recorded as events. Therefore, you can test that a command had the expected effect on an aggregate by simply checking for the event.
- **Flexibility**. A sequence of events can be projected to any desired structural representation.

> *"Event sourcing can also help with complex testing scenarios where you need to verify that a given action triggered a specific result. This is especially relevant for negative results, where you need to verify that an action did not trigger a result; this is frequently not verified when writing tests, but can easily be instrumented when the changes are being recorded through events."*
> —Alberto Población (Customer Advisory Council)

> *"As long as you have a stream of events, you can project it to any form, even a conventional SQL database. For instance, my favorite approach is to project event streams into JSON documents stored in a cloud storage."*
> —Rinat Abdullin, Why Event Sourcing?

"From experience, ORMs lead you down the path of a structural model while ES leads you down the path of a behavioral model. Sometimes one just makes more sense than the other. For example, in my own domain (not model) I get to integrate with other parties that send a lot of really non-interesting information that I need to send out again later when something interesting happens on my end. It's inherently structural. Putting those things into events would be a waste of time, effort, and space. Contrast this with another part of the domain that benefits a lot from knowing what happened, why it happened, when it did or didn't happen, where time and historical data are important to make the next business decision. Putting that into a structural model is asking for a world of pain. It depends, get over it, choose wisely, and above all: make your own mistakes."
—Yves Reynhout (CQRS Advisors Mail List)

Chapter 4, "A CQRS and ES Deep Dive," discusses these benefits in more detail. There are also many illustrations of these benefits in the reference implementation described in the companion guide *Exploring CQRS and Event Sourcing*.

Event sourcing concerns

The previous section described some of the benefits you might realize if you decide to use event sourcing in your system. However, there are some concerns that you may need to address, including:

- **Performance.** Although event sourcing typically improves the performance of updates, you may need to consider the time it takes to load domain object state by querying the event store for all of the events that relate to the state of an aggregate. Using snapshots may enable you to limit the amount of data that you need to load because you can go back to the latest snapshot and replay the events from that point forward. See the chapter "A CQRS and ES Deep Dive," for more information about snapshots.

- **Versioning.** You may find it necessary to change the definition of a particular event type or aggregate at some point in the future. You must consider how your system will be able to handle multiple versions of an event type and aggregates.

- **Querying.** Although it is easy to load the current state of an object by replaying its event stream (or its state at some point in the past), it is difficult or expensive to run a query such as, "find all my orders where the total value is greater than $250." However, if you are implementing the CQRS pattern, you should remember that such queries will typically be executed on the read side where you can ensure that you can build data projections that are specifically designed to answer such questions.

CQRS/ES

The CQRS pattern and event sourcing are frequently combined; each adding benefit to the other.

Chapter 2, "Introducing the Command Query Responsibility Segregation Pattern," suggested that events can form the basis of the push synchronization of the application's state from the data store on the write side to the data store on the read side. Remember that typically the read-side data store contains denormalized data that is optimized for the queries that are run against your data; for example, to display information in your application's UI.

You can use the events you persist in your event store to propagate all the updates made on the write side to the read side. The read side can use the information contained in the events to maintain whatever denormalized data you require on the read side to support your queries.

"ES is a great pattern to use to implement the link between the thing that writes and the thing that reads. It's by no means the only possible way to create that link, but it's a reasonable one and there's plenty of prior art with various forms of logs and log shipping. The major tipping point for whether the link is "ES" seem to be whether the log is ephemeral or a permanent source of truth. The CQRS pattern itself merely mandates a split between the write and the read thing, so ES is strictly complementary."
—*Clemens Vasters (CQRS Advisors Mail List)*

"Event sourcing is about the state of the domain model being persisted as a stream of events rather than as a single snapshot, not about how the command and query sides are kept in sync (usually with a publish/subscribe message-based approach)."
—*Udi Dahan (CQRS Advisors Mail List)*

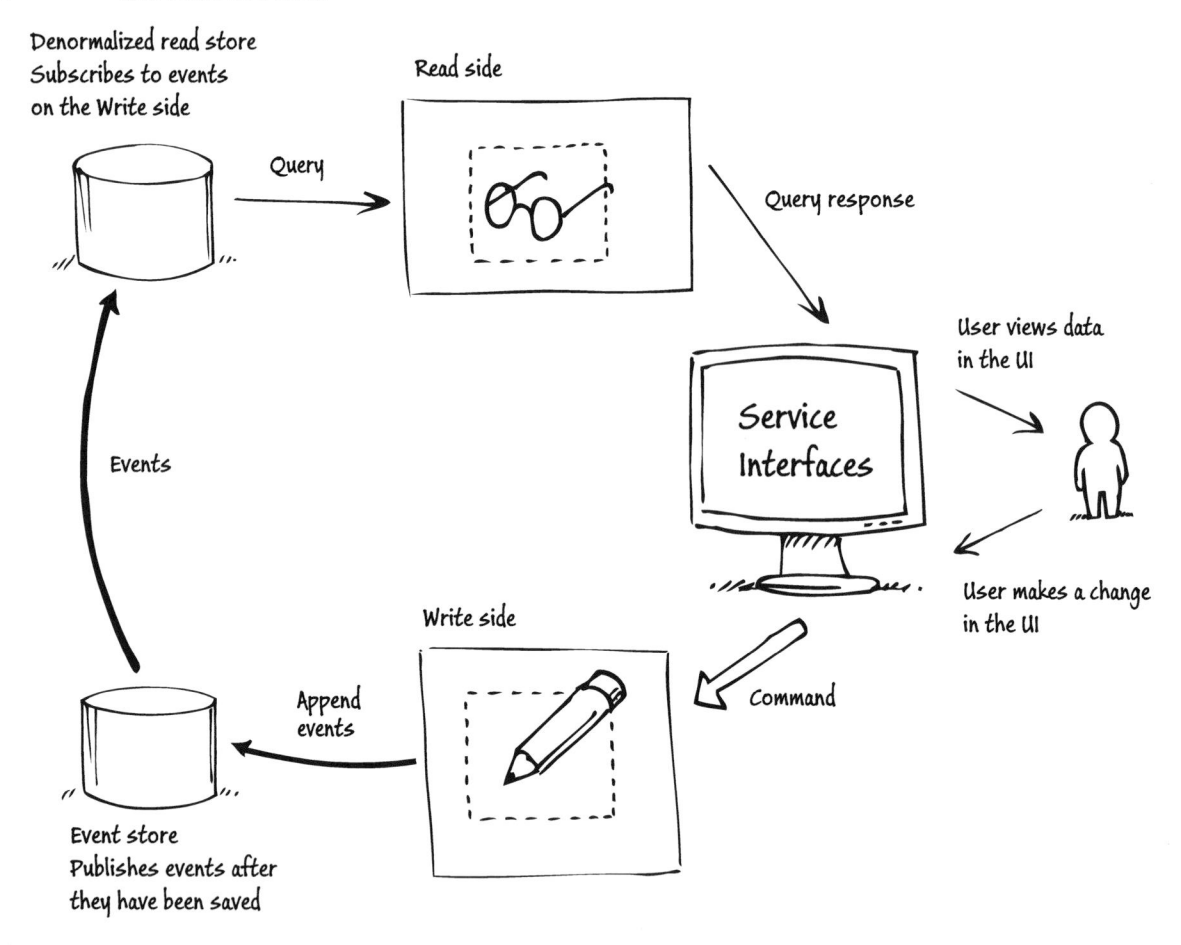

FIGURE 3
CQRS and event sourcing

Notice how the write side publishes events after it persists them to the event store. This avoids the need to use a two-phase commit, which you would need if the aggregate were responsible for saving the event to the event store and publishing the event to the read side.

Normally, these events will enable you to keep the data on the read side up to date practically in real time; there will be some delay due to the transport mechanism, and Chapter 4, "A CQRS and ES Deep Dive" discusses the possible consequences of this delay.

You can also rebuild the data on the read side from scratch at any time by replaying the events from your event store on the write side. You might need to do this if the read side data store got out of synchronization for some reason, or because you needed to modify the structure of the read-side data store to support a new query.

You need to be careful replaying the events from the event store to rebuild the read-side data store if other bounded contexts also subscribe to the same events. It might be easy to empty the read-side data store before replaying the events; it might not be so easy to ensure the consistency of another bounded context if it sees a duplicate stream of events.

Remember that the CQRS pattern does not mandate that you use different stores on the read side and write side. You could decide to use a single relational store with a schema in third normal form and a set of denormalized views over that schema. However, replaying events is a very convenient mechanism for resynchronizing the read-side data store with the write-side data store.

Standalone event sourcing

You can use event sourcing without also applying the CQRS pattern. The ability to rebuild the application state, to mine the event history for new business data, and to simplify the data storage part of the application are all valuable in some scenarios. However, this guide focuses on using event sourcing in the context of the CQRS pattern.

Event stores

If you are using event sourcing, you will need a mechanism to store your events and to return the stream of events associated with an aggregate instance so that you can replay the events to recreate the state of the aggregate. This storage mechanism is typically referred to as an event store.

You may choose to implement your own event store, or use a third-party offering, such as Jonathan Oliver's *EventStore*. Although you can implement a small-scale event store relatively easily, a production quality, scalable one is more of a challenge.

Chapter 8, "Epilogue: Lessons Learned," summarizes the experiences that our team had implementing our own event store.

Basic requirements

Typically, when you implement the CQRS pattern, aggregates raise events to publish information to other interested parties, such as other aggregates, process managers, read models, or other bounded contexts. When you use event sourcing, you persist these same events to an event store. This enables you to use those events to load the state of an aggregate by replaying the sequence of events associated with that aggregate.

Therefore, whenever an aggregate instance raises an event, two things must happen. The system must persist the event to the event store, and the system must publish the event.

> **Note:** *In practice, not all events in a system necessarily have subscribers. You may raise some events solely as a way to persist some properties of an aggregate.*

Whenever the system needs to load the current state of an aggregate, it must query the event store for the list of past events associated with that aggregate instance.

Underlying storage

Events are not complex data structures; typically, they have some standard metadata that includes the ID of the aggregate instance they are associated with and a version number, and a payload with the details of the event itself. You do not need to use a relational database to store your events; you could use a NoSQL store, a document database, or a file system.

Performance, scalability, and consistency

Stored events should be immutable and are always read in the order in which they were saved, so saving an event should be a simple, fast append operation on the underlying store.

When you load the persisted events, you will load them in the order in which they were originally saved. If you are using a relational database, the records should be keyed using the aggregate ID and a field that defines the ordering of events.

If an aggregate instance has a large number of events, this may affect the time that it takes to replay all of the events to reload the state of the aggregate. One option to consider in this scenario is to use a snapshot mechanism. In addition to the full stream of events in the event store, you can store a snapshot of the state of the aggregate at some recent point in time. To reload the state of the aggregate, you first load the most recent snapshot, then replay all of the subsequent events. You could generate the snapshot during the write process; for example, by creating a snapshot every 100 events.

> **Note:** *How frequently you should take snapshots depends on the performance characteristics of your underlying storage. You will need to measure how long it takes to replay different lengths of event streams to determine the optimum time to create your snapshots.*

As an alternative, you could cache heavily used aggregate instances in memory to avoid repeatedly replaying the event stream.

When an event store persists an event, it must also publish that event. To preserve the consistency of the system, both operations must succeed or fail together. The traditional approach to this type of scenario is to use a distributed, two-phase commit transaction that wraps together the data store append operation and the messaging infrastructure publishing operation. In practice, you may find that support for two-phase commit transactions is limited in many data stores and messaging platforms. Using two-phase commit transactions may also limit the performance and scalability of the system.

> **Note:** *For a discussion of two-phase commit transactions and the impact on scalability, see the article "Your Coffee Shop Doesn't Use Two-Phase Commit" by Gregor Hohpe.*

One of the key problems you must solve if you choose to implement your own event store is how to achieve this consistency. For example, an event store built on top of Windows Azure table storage could take the following approach to maintain consistency between persisting and publishing events: use a transaction to write copies of the event to two entities in the same partition in the same table; one entity stores an immutable event that constitutes part of the event stream of the aggregate; the other entity stores an event that is part of a list of events pending publication. You can then have a process that reads the list of events pending publication, guarantees to publish those events at least once, and then after publication removes each event from the pending list.

An additional set of problems related to consistency occurs if you plan to scale out your event store across multiple storage nodes, or use multiple writers to write to the store. In this scenario, you must take steps to ensure the consistency of your data. The data on the write side should be fully consistent, not eventually consistent. For more information about the *CAP theorem* and maintaining consistency in distributed systems, see the next chapter "A CQRS and ES Deep Dive."

More information

All links in this book are accessible from the book's online bibliography available at: *http://msdn.microsoft.com/en-us/library/jj619274.*

Reference 4:

A CQRS and ES Deep Dive

Introduction

This chapter begins with a brief recap of some of the key points from the previous chapters, then explores in more detail the important concepts that relate to the Command Query Responsibility Segregation (CQRS) pattern and event sourcing (ES).

Read models and write models

The CQRS pattern assigns the responsibility for modifying and querying your application data to different sets of objects: a write model and a read model. The immediate benefit of this segregation is to clarify and simplify your code by applying the single-responsibility principle: objects are responsible for either modifying data or querying data.

However, the most important benefit of this segregation of responsibility for reading and writing to different sets of classes is that it is an enabler for making further changes to your application that will provide additional benefits.

Commands and data transfer objects

A typical approach to enabling a user to edit data is to use data transfer objects (DTO): the UI retrieves the data to be edited from the application as a DTO, a user edits the DTO in the UI, the UI sends the modified DTO back to the application, and then the application applies those changes to the data in the database. For an example of implementing a DTO, see *"Implementing Data Transfer Object in .NET with a DataSet."*

This approach is data-centric and tends to use standard create, read, update, delete (CRUD) operations throughout. In the user interface (UI), the user performs operations that are essentially CRUD operations on the data in the DTO.

This is a simple, well understood approach that works effectively for many applications. However, for some applications it is more useful if the UI sends commands instead of DTOs back to the application to make changes to the data. Commands are behavior-centric instead of data-centric, directly represent operations in the domain, may be more intuitive to users, and can capture the user's intent more effectively than DTOs.

In a typical CQRS implementation, the read model returns data to the UI as a DTO. The UI then sends a command (not a DTO) to the write model.

Domain-driven design (DDD) and aggregates

Using commands enables you to build a UI that is more closely aligned with the behaviors associated with your domain. Related to this are the DDD concepts associated with a rich domain model, focusing on aggregates as a way to model consistency boundaries based on domain concepts.

One of the advantages of using commands and aggregates instead of DTOs is that it can simplify locking and concurrency management in your application.

Data and normalization

One of the changes that the CQRS pattern enables in your application is to segregate your data as well as your objects. The write model can use a database that is optimized for writes by being fully normalized. The read model can use a database that is optimized for reads by being denormalized to suit the specific queries that the application must support on the read side.

Several benefits flow from this: better performance because each database is optimized for a particular set of operations, better scalability because you can scale out each side independently, and simpler locking schemes. On the write side you no longer need to worry about how your locks impact queries, and on the read side your database can be read-only.

Events and event sourcing

If you use relational databases on both the read side and write side you will still be performing CRUD operations on the database tables on the write side and you will need a mechanism to push the changes from your normalized tables on the write side to your denormalized tables on the read side.

If you capture changes in your write model as events, you can save all of your changes simply by appending those events to your database or data store on the write side using only **Insert** operations.

You can also use those same events to push your changes to the read side. You can use those events to build projections of the data that contain the data structured to support the queries on the read side.

Eventual consistency

If you use a single database in your application, your locking scheme determines what version of a record is returned by a query. This process can be very complex if a query joins records from multiple tables.

Additionally, in a web application you have to consider that as soon as data is rendered in the UI it is potentially out of date because some other process or user could have since changed it in the data store.

> Think about the complexities of how transaction isolation levels (read uncommitted, read committed, repeatable reads, serializable) determine the locking behavior in a database and the differences between pessimistic and optimistic concurrency behavior.

If you segregate your data into a write-side store and a read-side store, you are now making it explicit in your architecture that when you query data, it may be out of date, but that the data on the read side will be *eventually consistent* with the data on the write side. This helps you to simplify the design of the application and makes it easier to implement collaborative applications where multiple users may be trying to modify the same data simultaneously on the write side.

Defining aggregates in the domain model

In domain-driven design (DDD), an aggregate defines a consistency boundary. Typically, when you implement the CQRS pattern, the classes in the write model define your aggregates. Aggregates are the recipients of commands, and are units of persistence. After an aggregate instance has processed a command and its state has changed, the system must persist the new state of the instance to storage.

An aggregate may consist of multiple related objects; an example is an order and multiple order lines, all of which should be persisted together. However, if you have correctly identified your aggregate boundaries, you should not need to use transactions to persist multiple aggregate instances together.

If an aggregate consists of multiple types, you should identify one type as the aggregate root. You should access all of the objects within the aggregate through the aggregate root, and you should only hold references to the aggregate root. Every aggregate instance should have a unique identifier.

AGGREGATES AND OBJECT-RELATIONAL MAPPING LAYERS

When you are using an object-relational mapping (ORM) layer such as Entity Framework to manage your persistence, persisting your aggregates requires minimal code in your aggregate classes.

The following code sample shows an **IAggregateRoot** interface and a set of classes that define an **Order** aggregate. This illustrates an approach to implementing aggregates that can be persisted using an ORM.

```
public interface IAggregateRoot
{
    Guid Id { get; }
}

public class Order : IAggregateRoot
{
    private List<SeatQuantity> seats;

    public Guid Id { get; private set; }

    public void UpdateSeats(IEnumerable<OrderItem> seats)
    {
        this.seats = ConvertItems(seats);
    }
    ...
}
...

public struct SeatQuantity
{
    ...
}
```

Aggregates and event sourcing

If you are using event sourcing, then your aggregates must create events to record all of the state changes that result from processing commands.

The following code sample shows an **IEventSourced** interface, an **EventSourced** abstract class, and a set of classes that define an **Order** aggregate. This illustrates an approach to implementing aggregates that can be persisted using event sourcing.

```
public interface IEventSourced
{
   Guid Id { get; }

   int Version { get; }

   IEnumerable<IVersionedEvent> Events { get; }
}
...
public abstract class EventSourced : IEventSourced
{
    private readonly Dictionary<Type, Action<IVersionedEvent>> handlers =
        new Dictionary<Type, Action<IVersionedEvent>>();
    private readonly List<IVersionedEvent> pendingEvents =
        new List<IVersionedEvent>();

    private readonly Guid id;
    private int version = -1;

    protected EventSourced(Guid id)
    {
        this.id = id;
    }

    public Guid Id
    {
        get { return this.id; }
    }

    public int Version { get { return this.version; } }

    public IEnumerable<IVersionedEvent> Events
    {
        get { return this.pendingEvents; }
    }

    protected void Handles<TEvent>(Action<TEvent> handler)
        where TEvent : IEvent
```

```csharp
    {
        this.handlers.Add(typeof(TEvent), @event => handler((TEvent)@event));
    }

    protected void LoadFrom(IEnumerable<IVersionedEvent> pastEvents)
    {
        foreach (var e in pastEvents)
        {
            this.handlers[e.GetType()].Invoke(e);
            this.version = e.Version;
        }
    }

    protected void Update(VersionedEvent e)
    {
        e.SourceId = this.Id;
        e.Version = this.version + 1;
        this.handlers[e.GetType()].Invoke(e);
        this.version = e.Version;
        this.pendingEvents.Add(e);
    }
}

...

public class Order : EventSourced
{
    private List<SeatQuantity> seats;

    protected Order(Guid id) : base(id)
    {
        base.Handles<OrderUpdated>(this.OnOrderUpdated);
        ...
    }

    public Order(Guid id, IEnumerable<IVersionedEvent> history) : this(id)
    {
        this.LoadFrom(history);
    }

    public void UpdateSeats(IEnumerable<OrderItem> seats)
    {
        this.Update(new OrderUpdated { Seats = ConvertItems(seats) });
    }
```

```
    private void OnOrderUpdated(OrderUpdated e)
    {
        this.seats = e.Seats.ToList();
    }

    ...
}

...

public struct SeatQuantity
{
    ...
}
```

In this example, the **UpdateSeats** method creates a new **OrderUpdated** event instead of updating the state of the aggregate directly. The **Update** method in the abstract base class is responsible for adding the event to the list of pending events to be appended to the event stream in the store, and for invoking the **OnOrderUpdated** event handler to update the state of the aggregate. Every event that is handled in this way also updates the version of the aggregate.

The constructor in the aggregate class and the **LoadFrom** method in the abstract base class handle replaying the event stream to reload the state of the aggregate.

Commands and command handlers

This section describes the role of commands and command handlers in a CQRS implementation and shows an outline of how they might be implemented in the C# language.

> We tried to avoid polluting the aggregate classes with infrastructure-related code. These aggregate classes should implement the domain model and logic.

COMMANDS

Commands are imperatives; they are requests for the system to perform a task or action. Two examples are: "book two places on conference X" or "allocate speaker Y to room Z." Commands are usually processed just once, by a single recipient.

Both the sender and the receiver of a command should be in the same bounded context. You should not send a command to another bounded context because you would be instructing that other bounded context, which has separate responsibilities in another consistency boundary, to perform some work for you. However, a process manager may not belong to any particular bounded context in the system, but it still sends commands. Some people also take the view that the UI is not a part of the bounded context, but the UI still sends commands.

Example code

The following code sample shows a command and the **ICommand** interface that it implements. Notice that a command is a simple data transfer object (DTO) and that every instance of a command has a unique ID.

```
using System;

public interface ICommand
{
    Guid Id { get; }
}

public class MakeSeatReservation : ICommand
{
    public MakeSeatReservation()
    {
        this.Id = Guid.NewGuid();
    }

    public Guid Id { get; set; }

    public Guid ConferenceId { get; set; }
    public Guid ReservationId { get; set; }
    public int NumberOfSeats { get; set; }
}
```

"I think that in most circumstances (if not all), the command should succeed (and that makes the async story way easier and practical). You can validate against the read model before submitting a command, and this way being almost certain that it will succeed."
—*Julian Dominguez (CQRS Advisors Mail List)*

"When a user issues a command, it'll give the best user experience if it rarely fails. However, from an architectural/implementation point of view, commands will fail once in a while, and the application should be able to handle that."
—*Mark Seemann (CQRS Advisors Mail List)*

Command handlers

Commands are sent to a specific recipient, typically an aggregate instance. The command handler performs the following tasks:

1. It receives a command instance from the messaging infrastructure.
2. It validates that the command is a valid command.
3. It locates the aggregate instance that is the target of the command. This may involve creating a new aggregate instance or locating an existing instance.
4. It invokes the appropriate method on the aggregate instance, passing in any parameters from the command.
5. It persists the new state of the aggregate to storage.

Typically, you will organize your command handlers so that you have a class that contains all of the handlers for a specific aggregate type.

You messaging infrastructure should ensure that it delivers just a single copy of a command to single command handler. Commands should be processed once, by a single recipient.

The following code sample shows a command handler class that handles commands for **Order** instances.

> *"I don't see the reason to retry the command here. When you see that a command could not always be fulfilled due to race conditions, go talk with your business expert and analyze what happens in this case, how to handle compensation, offer an alternate solution, or deal with overbooking. As far as I can see, the only reason to retry is for technical transient failures such as those that could occur when accessing the state storage."*
> —Jérémie Chassaing (CQRS Advisors Mail List)

```
public class OrderCommandHandler :
    ICommandHandler<RegisterToConference>,
    ICommandHandler<MarkSeatsAsReserved>,
    ICommandHandler<RejectOrder>,
    ICommandHandler<AssignRegistrantDetails>,
    ICommandHandler<ConfirmOrder>
{
    private readonly IEventSourcedRepository<Order> repository;

    public OrderCommandHandler(IEventSourcedRepository<Order> repository)
    {
        this.repository = repository;
    }

    public void Handle(RegisterToConference command)
    {
        var items = command.Seats.Select(t => new OrderItem(t.SeatType,
        t.Quantity)).ToList();
        var order = repository.Find(command.OrderId);
        if (order == null)
        {
            order = new Order(command.OrderId, command.ConferenceId, items);
        }
```

```
                else
                {
                        order.UpdateSeats(items);
                }

                repository.Save(order, command.Id.ToString());
        }

        public void Handle(ConfirmOrder command)
        {
                var order = repository.Get(command.OrderId);
                order.Confirm();
                repository.Save(order, command.Id.ToString());
        }

        public void Handle(AssignRegistrantDetails command)
        {
                ...
        }

        public void Handle(MarkSeatsAsReserved command)
        {
                ...
        }

        public void Handle(RejectOrder command)
        {
                ...
        }
}
```

This handler handles five different commands for the **Order** aggregate. The **RegisterToConference** command is an example of a command that creates a new aggregate instance. The **ConfirmOrder** command is an example of a command that locates an existing aggregate instance. Both examples use the **Save** method to persist the instance.

If this bounded context uses an ORM, then the **Find** and **Save** methods in the repository class will locate and persist the aggregate instance in the underlying database.

If this bounded context uses event sourcing, then the **Find** method will replay the aggregate's event stream to recreate the state, and the **Save** method will append the new events to the aggregate's event stream.

> **Note:** *If the aggregate generated any events when it processed the command, then these events are published when the repository saves the aggregate instance.*

COMMANDS AND OPTIMISTIC CONCURRENCY

A common scenario for commands is that some of the information included in the command is provided by the user of the system through the UI, and some of the information is retrieved from the read model. For example, the UI builds a list of orders by querying the read model, the user selects one of those orders, and modifies the list of attendees associated with that order. The UI then sends the command that contains the list of attendees associated with the order to the write model for processing.

However, because of eventual consistency, it is possible that the information that the UI retrieves from the read side is not yet fully consistent with changes that have just been made on the write side (perhaps by another user of the system). This raises the possibility that the command that is sent to update the list of attendees results in an inconsistent change to the write model. For example, someone else could have deleted the order, or already modified the list of attendees.

A solution to this problem is to use version numbers in the read model and the commands. Whenever the write model sends details of a change to the read model, it includes the current version number of the aggregate. When the UI queries the read model, it receives the version number and includes it in the command that it sends to the write model. The write model can compare the version number in the command with the current version number of the aggregate and, if they are different, it can raise a concurrency error and reject the change.

Events and event handlers

Events can play two different roles in a CQRS implementation.
- **Event sourcing.** As described previously, event sourcing is an approach to persisting the state of aggregate instances by saving the stream of events in order to record changes in the state of the aggregate.
- **Communication and Integration.** You can also use events to communicate between aggregates or process managers in the same or in different bounded contexts. Events publish to subscribers information about something that has happened.

One event can play both roles: an aggregate may raise an event to record a state change and to notify an aggregate in another bounded context of the change.

EVENTS AND INTENT

As previously mentioned, events in event sourcing should capture the business intent in addition to the change in state of the aggregate. The concept of intent is hard to pin down, as shown in the following conversation:

Developer 1: One of the claims that I often hear for using event sourcing is that it enables you to capture the user's intent, and that this is valuable data. It may not be valuable right now, but if we capture it, it may turn out to have business value at some point in the future.

Developer 2: Sure. For example, rather than saving just a customer's latest address, we might want to store a history of the addresses the customer has had in the past. It may also be useful to know why a customer's address was changed; perhaps they moved into a new house or you discovered a mistake with the existing address that you have on file.

Developer 1: So in this example, the intent might help you to understand why the customer hadn't responded to offers that you sent, or might indicate that now might be a good time to contact the customer about a particular product. But isn't the information about intent, in the end, just data that you should store. If you do your analysis right, you'd capture the fact that the reason an address changes is an important piece of information to store.

Developer 2: By storing events, we can automatically capture all intent. If we miss something during our analysis, but we have the event history, we can make use of that information later. If we capture events, we don't lose any potentially valuable data.

Developer 1: But what if the event that you stored was just, "the customer address was changed?" That doesn't tell me why the address was changed.

Developer 2: OK. You still need to make sure that you store useful events that capture what is meaningful from the perspective of the business.

Developer 1: So what do events and event sourcing give me that I can't get with a well-designed relational database that captures everything I may need?

Developer 2: It really simplifies things. The schema is simple. With a relational database you have all the problems of versioning if you need to start storing new or different data. With event sourcing, you just need to define a new event type.

Developer 1: So what do events and event sourcing give me that I can't get with a standard database transaction log?

Developer 2: Using events as your primary data model makes it very easy and natural to do time-related analysis of data in your system; for example, "what was the balance on the account at a particular point in time?" or, "what would the customer's status be if we'd introduced the reward program six months earlier?" The transactional data is not hidden away and inaccessible on a tape somewhere, it's there in your system.

Developer 1: So back to this idea of intent. Is it something special that you can capture using events, or is it just some additional data that you save?

Developer 2: I guess in the end, the intent is really there in the commands that originate from the users of the system. The events record the consequences of those commands. If those events record the consequences in business terms then it makes it easier for you to infer the original intent of user.

—Thanks to Clemens Vasters and Adam Dymitruk

How to model intent

This section examines two alternatives for modeling intent with reference to SOAP and REST-style interfaces to help highlight the differences.

> **Note:** *We are using SOAP and REST here as an analogy to help explain the differences between the approaches.*

The following code samples illustrate two slightly different approaches to modeling intent alongside the event data:

Example 1. The Event log or SOAP-style approach.

```
[
    { "reserved": { "seatType": "FullConference", "quantity": "5" } },
    { "reserved": { "seatType": "WorkshopA", "quantity": "3" } },
    { "purchased": { "seatType": "FullConference", "quantity": "5" } },
    { "expired": { "seatType": "WorkshopA", "quantity": "3" } }
]
```

Example 2. The Transaction log or REST-style approach.

```
[
  { "insert" : {
    "resource" : "reservations", "seatType" : "FullConference", "quantity" : "5"
  }},
  { "insert" : {
      "resource" : "reservations", "seatType" : "WorkshopA", "quantity" : "3"
  }},
  { "insert" : {
      "resource" : "orders", "seatType" : "FullConference", "quantity" : "5"
  }},
  { "delete" : {
      "resource" : "reservations", "seatType" : "WorkshopA", "quantity" : "3"
  }},
]
```

The first approach uses an action-based contract that couples the events to a particular aggregate type. The second approach uses a uniform contract that uses a **resource** field as a hint to associate the event with an aggregate type.

> **Note:** *How the events are actually stored is a separate issue. This discussion is focusing on how to model your events.*

The advantages of the first approach are:
- Strong typing.
- More expressive code.
- Better testability.

The advantages of the second approach are:
- Simplicity and a generic approach.
- Easier to use existing internet infrastructure.
- Easier to use with dynamic languages and with changing schemas.

Events

Events report that something has happened. An aggregate or process manager publishes one-way, asynchronous messages that are published to multiple recipients. For example: **SeatsUpdated**, **PaymentCompleted**, and **EmailSent**.

Sample Code

The following code sample shows a possible implementation of an event that is used to communicate between aggregates or process managers. It implements the **IEvent** interface.

> Variable environment state needs to be stored alongside events in order to have an accurate representation of the circumstances at the time when the command resulting in the event was executed, which means that we need to save everything!

```
public interface IEvent
{
    Guid SourceId { get; }
}

...

public class SeatsAdded : IEvent
{
    public Guid ConferenceId { get; set; }

    public Guid SourceId { get; set; }

    public int TotalQuantity { get; set; }

    public int AddedQuantity { get; set; }
}
```

Note: *For simplicity, in C# these classes are implemented as DTOs, but they should be treated as being immutable.*

The following code sample shows a possible implementation of an event that is used in an event sourcing implementation. It extends the **VersionedEvent** abstract class.

```
public abstract class VersionedEvent : IVersionedEvent
{
    public Guid SourceId { get; set; }

    public int Version { get; set; }
}

...

public class AvailableSeatsChanged : VersionedEvent
{
    public IEnumerable<SeatQuantity> Seats { get; set; }
}
```

The **Version** property refers to the version of the aggregate. The version is incremented whenever the aggregate receives a new event.

Event handlers

Events are published to multiple recipients, typically aggregate instances or process managers. The Event handler performs the following tasks:

1. It receives an **Event** instance from the messaging infrastructure.
2. It locates the aggregate or process manager instance that is the target of the event. This may involve creating a new aggregate instance or locating an existing instance.
3. It invokes the appropriate method on the aggregate or process manager instance, passing in any parameters from the event.
4. It persists the new state of the aggregate or process manager to storage.

Sample code

```
public void Handle(SeatsAdded @event)
{
    var availability = this.repository.Find(@event.ConferenceId);
    if (availability == null)
        availability = new SeatsAvailability(@event.ConferenceId);

    availability.AddSeats(@event.SourceId, @event.AddedQuantity);
    this.repository.Save(availability);
}
```

If this bounded context uses an ORM, then the **Find** and **Save** methods in the repository class will locate and persist the aggregate instance in the underlying database.

If this bounded context uses event sourcing, then the **Find** method will replay the aggregate's event stream to recreate the state, and the **Save** method will append the new events to the aggregate's event stream.

Embracing eventual consistency

Maintaining the consistency of business data is a key requirement in all enterprise systems. One of the first things that many developers learn in relation to database systems is the atomicity, consistency, isolation, durability (ACID) properties of transactions: transactions must ensure that the stored data is consistent and be atomic, isolated, and durable. Developers also become familiar with complex concepts such as pessimistic and optimistic concurrency, and their performance characteristics in particular scenarios. They may also need to understand the different isolation levels of transactions: serializable, repeatable reads, read committed, and read uncommitted.

In a distributed computer system, there are some additional factors that are relevant to consistency. The CAP theorem states that it is impossible for a distributed computer system to provide the following three guarantees simultaneously:

- Consistency (C). A guarantee that all the nodes in the system see the same data at the same time.
- Availability (A). A guarantee that the system can continue to operate even if a node is unavailable.
- Partition tolerance (P). A guarantee that the system continues to operate despite the nodes being unable to communicate.

For more information about the CAP theorem, see *CAP theorem* on Wikipedia and the article *CAP Twelve Years Later: How the "Rules" Have Changed* by Eric Brewer on the InfoQ website.

> Cloud providers have broadened the interpretation of the CAP theorem in the sense that they consider a system to be unavailable if the response time exceeds the latency limit.

"In larger distributed-scale systems, network partitions are a given; therefore, consistency and availability cannot be achieved at the same time."
—Werner Vogels, CTO, Amazon in Vogels, E. *Eventually Consistent, Communications of ACM,* 52(1): 40-44, Jan 2009.

"Very often people attempting to introduce eventual consistency into a system run into problems from the business side. A very large part of the reason of this is that they use the word consistent or consistency when talking with domain experts / business stakeholders.

...

Business users hear "consistency" and they tend to think it means that the data will be wrong. That the data will be incoherent and contradictory. This is not actually the case. Instead try using the words stale or old. In discussions when the word stale is used the business people tend to realize that it just means that someone could have changed the data, that they may not have the latest copy of it."
—Greg Young, Quick Thoughts on Eventual Consistency.

The concept of *eventual consistency* offers a way to make it appear from the outside that we are meeting these three guarantees. In the CAP theorem, the consistency guarantee specifies that all the nodes should see the same data *at the same time*; instead, with *eventual consistency* we state that all the nodes will eventually see the same data. It's important that changes are propagated to other nodes in the system at a faster rate than new changes arrive in order to avoid the differences between the nodes continuing to increase. Another way of viewing this is to say that we will accept that, at any given time, some of the data seen by users of the system could be stale. For many business scenarios, this turns out to be perfectly acceptable: a business user will accept that the information they are seeing on a screen may be a few seconds, or even minutes out of date. Depending on the details of the scenario, the business user can refresh the display a bit later on to see what has changed, or simply accept that what they see is always slightly out of date. There are some scenarios where this delay is unacceptable, but they tend to be the exception rather than the rule.

Note: *To better understand the tradeoffs described by the CAP theorem, check out the special issue of IEEE Computer magazine dedicated to it (Vol.45(no.2), Feb 2012).*

> Domain name servers (DNS) use the eventual consistency model to refresh themselves, and that's why DNS propagation delay can occur that results in some, but not all users being able to navigate to a new or updated domain name. The propagation delay is acceptable considering that a coordinated atomic update across all DNS servers globally would not be feasible. Eventually, however, all DNS servers get updated and domain names get resolved properly.

Eventual consistency and CQRS

How does the concept of eventual consistency relate to the CQRS pattern? A typical implementation of the CQRS pattern is a distributed system made up of one node for the write side, and one or more nodes for the read side. Your implementation must provide some mechanism for synchronizing data between these two sides. This is not a complex synchronization task because all of the changes take place on the write side, so the synchronization process only needs to push changes from the write side to the read side.

If you decide that the two sides must always be consistent (the case of strong consistency), then you will need to introduce a distributed transaction that spans both sides, as shown in Figure 1.

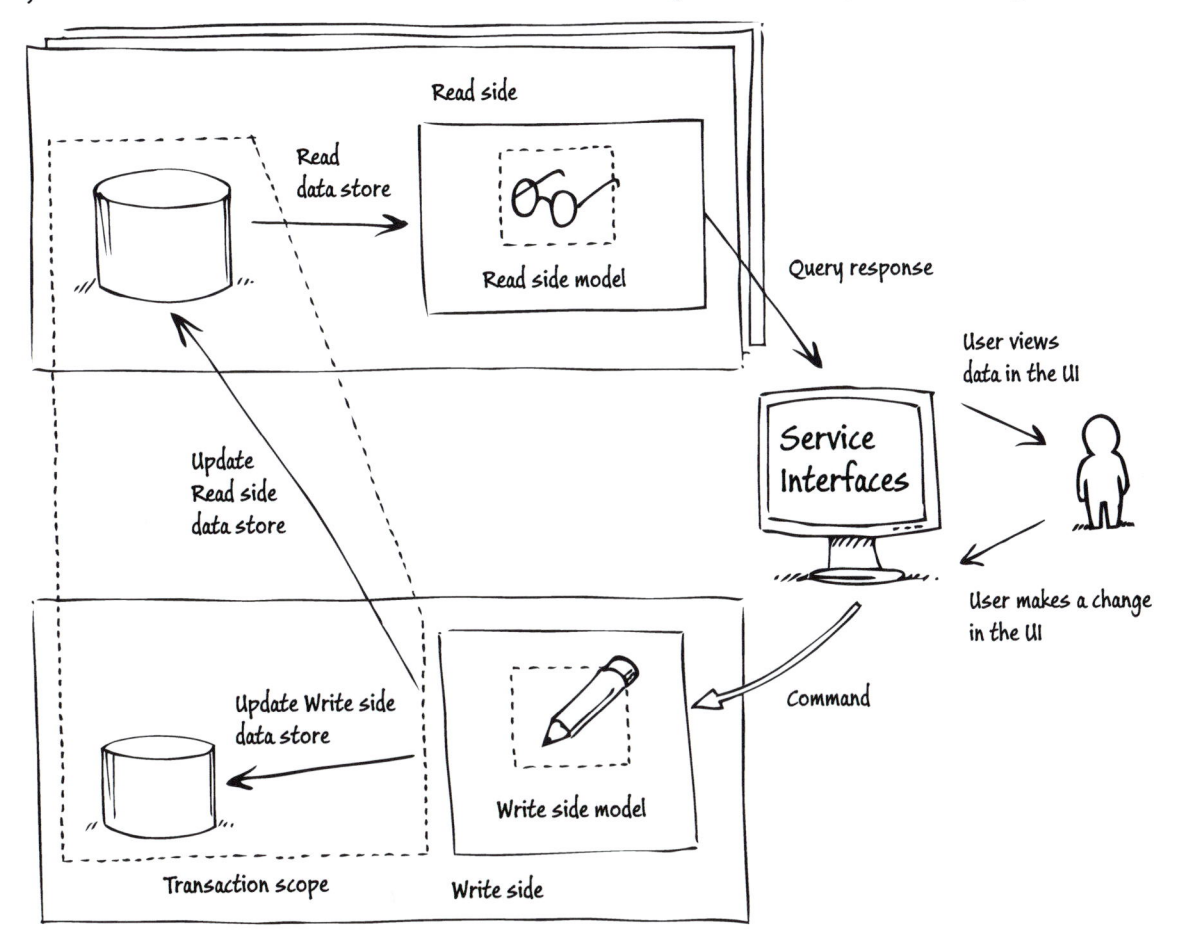

FIGURE 1
Using a distributed transaction to maintain consistency

The problems that may result from this approach relate to performance and availability. Firstly, both sides will need to hold locks until both sides are ready to commit; in other words, the transaction can only complete as fast as the slowest participant can.

This transaction may include more than two participants. If we are scaling the read side by adding multiple instances, the transaction must span all of those instances.

Secondly, if one node fails for any reason or does not complete the transaction, the transaction cannot complete. In terms of the CAP theorem, by guaranteeing consistency, we cannot guarantee the availability of the system.

If you decide to relax your consistency constraint and specify that your read side only needs to be eventually consistent with the write side, you can change the scope of your transaction. Figure 2 shows how you can make the read side eventually consistent with the write side by using a reliable messaging transport to propagate the changes.

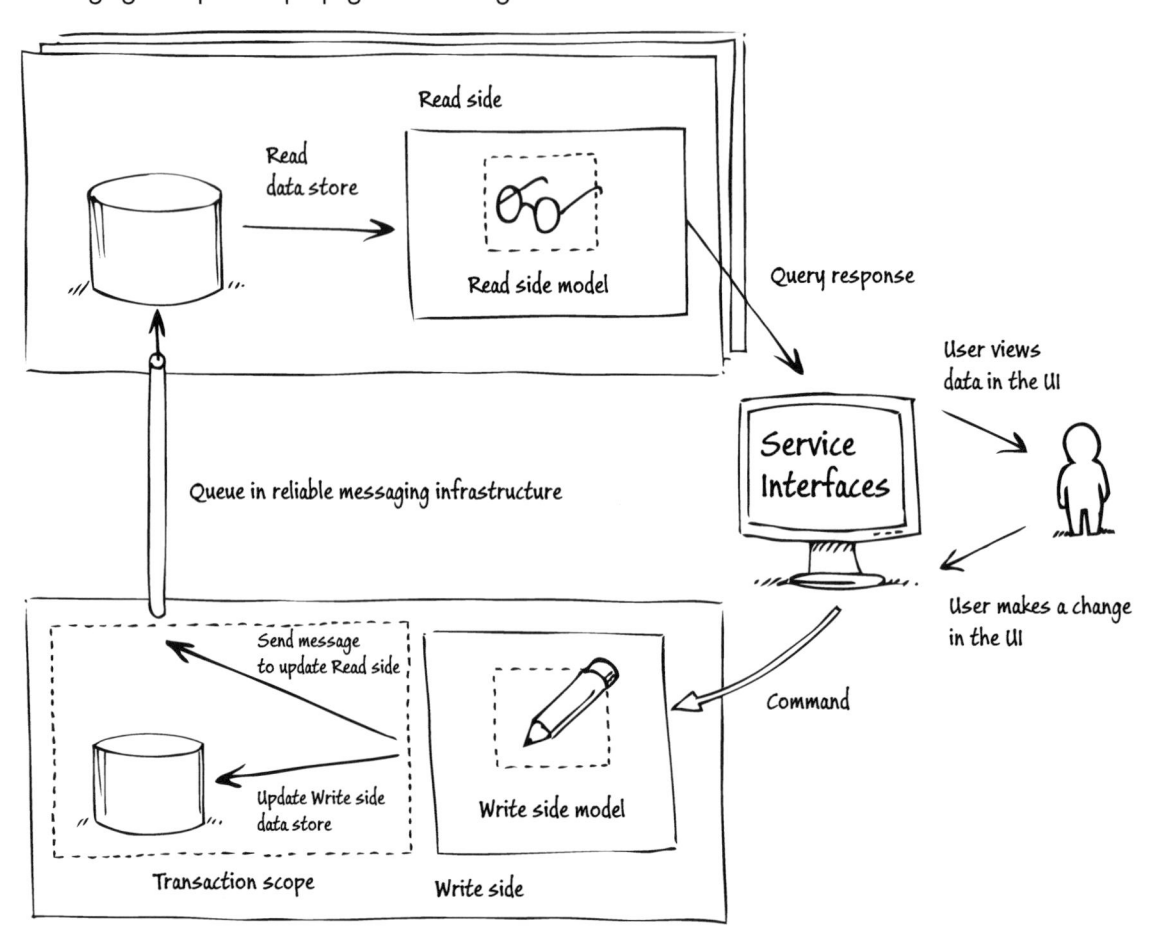

FIGURE 2
Using a reliable message transport

In this example, you can see that there is still a transaction. The scope of this transaction includes saving the changes to the data store on the write side, and placing a copy of the change onto the queue that pushes the change to the read side.

This solution does not suffer from the potential performance problems that you saw in the original solution if you assume that the messaging infrastructure allows you to quickly add messages to a queue. This solution is also no longer dependent on all of the read-side nodes being constantly available because the queue acts as a buffer for the messages addressed to the read-side nodes.

> **Note:** *In practice, the messaging infrastructure is likely to use a publish/subscribe topology rather than a queue to enable multiple read-side nodes to receive the messages.*

This third example (Figure 3) shows a way you can avoid the need for a distributed transaction.

> This eventual consistency might not be able to guarantee the same order of updates on the read side as on the write side.

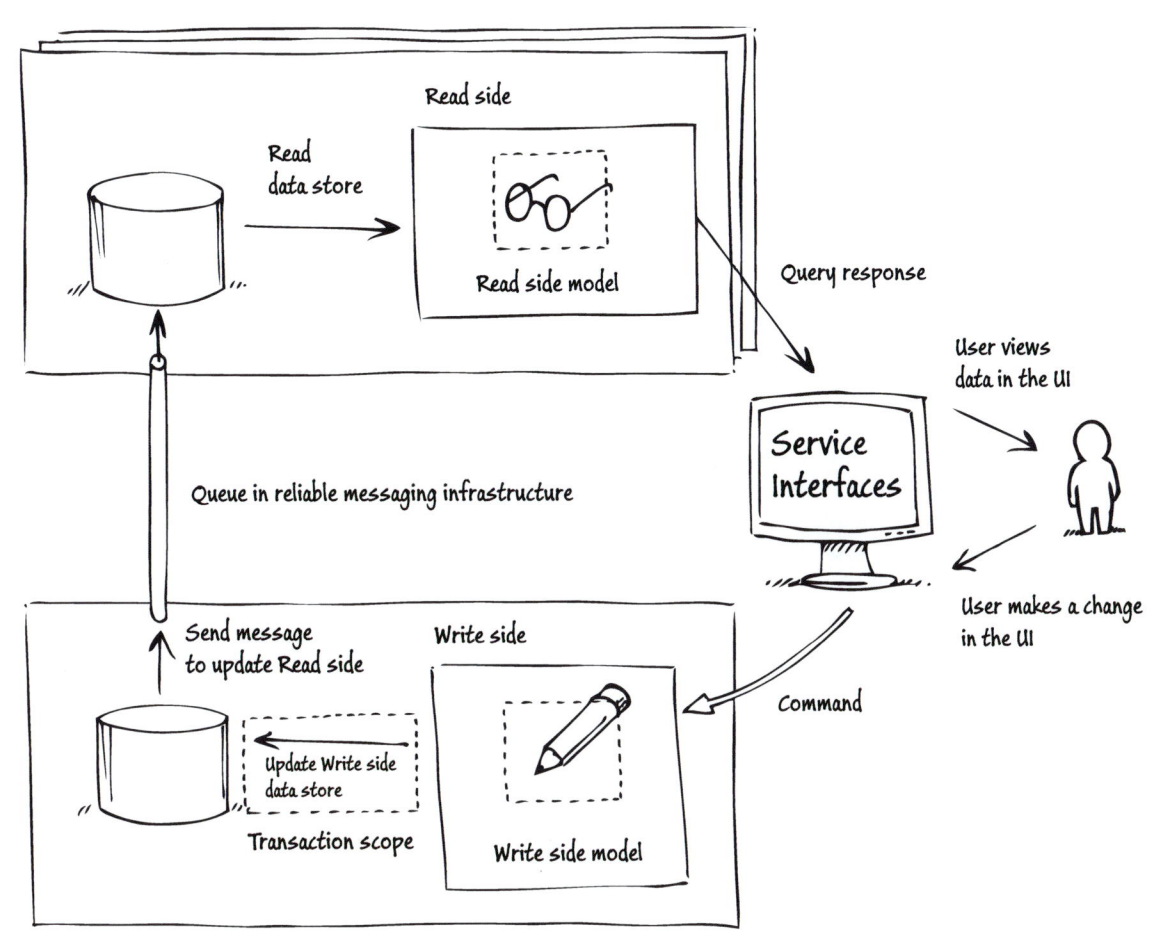

Figure 3
No distributed transactions

This example depends on functionality in the write-side data store: it must be able to send a message in response to every update that the write-side model makes to the data. This approach lends itself particularly well to the scenario in which you combine CQRS with event sourcing. If the event store can send a copy of every event that it saves onto a message queue, then you can make the read side eventually consistent by using this infrastructure feature.

Optimizing the read-side

There are four goals to keep in mind when optimizing the read side. You typically want to:
- Have very fast responses to queries for data.
- Minimize resource utilization.
- Minimize latency.
- Minimize costs.

By separating the read side from the write side, the CQRS pattern enables you to design the read side so that the data store is optimized for reading. You can denormalize your relational tables or choose to store the data in some other format that best suits the part of the application that will use the data. Ideally, the recipient of the data should not need to perform any joins or other complex, resource-intensive operations on the data.

For a discussion of how to discourage any unnecessary operations on the data, see the section, "Querying the read side" in Chapter 4, "Extending and Enhancing the Orders and Registrations Bounded Contexts."

If your system needs to accommodate high volumes of read operations, you can scale out the read side. For example, you could do this in Windows Azure by adding additional role instances. You can also easily scale out your data store on the read side because it is read-only. You should also consider the benefits of caching data on the read side to further speed up response times and reduce processing resource utilization.

For a description of how the team designed the reference implementation for scalability, see Chapter 7, "Adding Resilience and Optimizing Performance."

In the section "Embracing Eventual Consistency" earlier in this chapter, you saw how when you implement the CQRS pattern that you must accept some latency between an update on the write side and that change becoming visible on the read side. However, you will want to keep that delay to a minimum. You can minimize the delay by ensuring that the infrastructure that transports update information to the read side has enough resources, and by ensuring that the updates to your read models happen efficiently.

You should also consider the comparative storage costs for different storage models on the read side such as Windows Azure SQL Database, Windows Azure table storage, and Windows Azure blob storage. This may involve a trade-off between performance and costs.

Optimizing the write side

A key goal in optimizing the write side is to maximize the throughput of commands and events. Typically, the write side performs work when it receives commands from the UI or receives integration events from other bounded contexts. You need to ensure that your messaging infrastructure delivers command and event messages with minimal delay, that the processing in the domain model is efficient, and that interactions with the data store are fast.

Options for optimizing the way that messages are delivered to the write side include:
- Delivering commands in-line without using the messaging infrastructure. If you can host the domain model in the same process as the command sender, you can avoid using the messaging infrastructure. You need to consider the impact this may have on the resilience of your system to failures in this process.
- Handling some commands in parallel. You need to consider whether this will affect the way your system manages concurrency.

If you are using event sourcing, you may be able to reduce the time it takes to load the state of an aggregate by using snapshots. Instead of replaying the complete event stream when you load an aggregate, you load the most recent snapshot of its state and then only play back the events that occurred after the snapshot was taken. You will need to introduce a mechanism that creates snapshots for aggregates on a regular basis. However, given the simplicity of a typical event store schema, loading the state of an aggregate is typically very fast. Using snapshots typically only provides a performance benefit when an aggregate has a very large number of events.

Instead of snapshots, you may be able to optimize the access to an aggregate with a large number of events by caching it in memory. You only need to load the full event stream when it is accessed for the first time after a system start.

CONCURRENCY AND AGGREGATES

A simple implementation of aggregates and command handlers will load an aggregate instance into memory for each command that the aggregate must process. For aggregates that must process a large number of commands, you may decide to cache the aggregate instance in memory to avoid the need to reload it for every command.

If your system only has a single instance of an aggregate loaded into memory, that aggregate may need to process commands that are sent from multiple clients. By arranging for the system to deliver commands to the aggregate instance through a queue, you can ensure that the aggregate processes the commands sequentially. Also, there is no requirement to make the aggregate thread-safe, because it will only process a single command at a time.

In scenarios with an even higher throughput of commands, you may need to have multiple instances of the aggregate loaded into memory, possibly in different processes. To handle the concurrency issues here, you can use event sourcing and versioning. Each aggregate instance must have a version number that is updated whenever the instance persists an event.

"These are technical performance optimizations that can be implemented on case-by-case bases."
—Rinat Abdullin (CQRS Advisors Mail List)

There are two ways to make use of the version number in the aggregate instance:
- **Optimistic:** Append the event to the event-stream if the latest event in the event-stream is the same version as the current, in-memory, instance.
- **Pessimistic:** Load all the events from the event stream that have a version number greater than the version of the current, in-memory, instance.

Messaging and CQRS

CQRS and event sourcing use two types of messages: commands and events. Typically, systems that implement the CQRS pattern are large-scale, distributed systems and therefore you need a reliable, distributed messaging infrastructure to transport the messages between your senders/publishers and receivers/subscribers.

For commands that have a single recipient you will typically use a queue topology. For events, that may have multiple recipients you will typically use a pub/sub topology.

The reference implementation that accompanies this guide uses the Windows Azure Service Bus for messaging. Chapter 7, "Technologies Used in the Reference Implementation" provides additional information about the Windows Azure Service Bus. Windows Azure Service Bus brokered messaging offers a distributed messaging infrastructure in the cloud that supports both queue and pub/sub topologies.

Messaging considerations

Whenever you use messaging, there are a number of issues to consider. This section describes some of the most significant issues when you are working with commands and events in a CQRS implementation.

Duplicate messages

An error in the messaging infrastructure or in the message receiving code may cause a message to be delivered multiple times to its recipient.

There are two potential approaches to handling this scenario.
- Design your messages to be idempotent so that duplicate messages have no impact on the consistency of your data.
- Implement duplicate message detection. Some messaging infrastructures provide a configurable duplicate detection strategy that you can use instead of implementing it yourself.

For a detailed discussion of idempotency in reliable systems, see the article *"Idempotence Is Not a Medical Condition"* by Pat Helland.

> Some messaging infrastructures offer a guarantee of at least once delivery. This implies that you should explicitly handle the duplicate message delivery scenario in your application code.

Lost messages
An error in the messaging infrastructure may cause a message not to be delivered to its recipient.

Many messaging infrastructures offer guarantees that messages are not lost and are delivered at least once to their recipient. Alternative strategies that you could implement to detect when messages have been lost include a handshake process to acknowledge receipt of a message to the sender, or assigning sequence numbers to messages so that the recipient can determine if it has not received a message.

Out-of-order messages
The messaging infrastructure may deliver messages to a recipient in an order different than the order in which the sender sent the messages.

In some scenarios, the order that messages are received in is not significant. If message ordering is important, some messaging infrastructures can guarantee ordering. Otherwise, you can detect out-of-order messages by assigning sequence numbers to messages as they are sent. You could also implement a process manager process in the receiver that can hold out-of-order messages until it can reassemble messages into the correct order.

If messages need to be ordered within a group, you may be able to send the related messages as a single batch.

Unprocessed messages
A client may retrieve a message from a queue and then fail while it is processing the message. When the client restarts, the message has been lost.

Some messaging infrastructures allow you to include the read of the message from the infrastructure as part of a distributed transaction that you can roll back if the message processing fails.

Another approach offered by some messaging infrastructures, is to make reading a message a two-phase operation. First you lock and read the message, then when you have finished processing the message you mark it as complete and it is removed from the queue or topic. If the message does not get marked as complete, the lock on the message times out and it becomes available to read again.

EVENT VERSIONING
As your system evolves, you may find that you need to make changes to the events that your system uses. For example:
- Some events may become redundant in that they are no longer raised by any class in your system.
- You may need to define new events that relate to new features or functionality within in your system.
- You may need to modify existing event definitions.

The following sections discuss each of these scenarios in turn.

> If a message still cannot be processed after a number of retries, it is typically sent to a dead-letter queue for further investigation.

Redundant events

If your system no longer uses a particular event type, you may be able to simply remove it from the system. However, if you are using event sourcing, your event store may hold many instances of this event, and these instances may be used to rebuild the state of your aggregates. Typically, you treat the events in your event store as immutable. In this case, your aggregates must continue to be able to handle these old events when they are replayed from the event store even though the system will no longer raise new instances of this event type.

New event types

If you introduce new event types into your system, this should have no impact on existing behavior. Typically, it is only new features or functionality that use the new event types.

Changing existing event definitions

Handling changes to event type definitions requires more complex changes to your system. For example, your event store may hold many instances of an old version of an event type while the system raises events that are a later version, or different bounded contexts may raise different versions of the same event. Your system must be capable of handling multiple versions of the same event.

An event definition can change in a number of different ways; for example:

- An event gains a new property in the latest version.
- An event loses a property in the latest version.
- A property changes its type or supports a different range of values.

> **Note:** *If the semantic meaning of an event changes, then you should treat that as new event type, and not as a new version of an existing event.*

Where you have multiple versions of an event type, you have two basic choices of how to handle the multiple versions: you can either continue to support multiple versions of the event in your domain classes, or use a mechanism to convert old versions of events to the latest version whenever they are encountered by the system.

The first option may be the quickest and simplest approach to adopt because it typically doesn't require any changes to your infrastructure. However, this approach will eventually pollute your domain classes as they end up supporting more and more versions of your events, but if you don't anticipate many changes to your event definitions this may be acceptable.

The second approach is a cleaner solution: your domain classes only need to support the latest version of each event type. However you do need to make changes to your infrastructure to translate the old event types to the latest type. The issue here is to decide whereabouts in your infrastructure to perform this translation.

One option is to add filtering functionality into your messaging infrastructure so that events are translated as they are delivered to their recipients; you could also add the translation functionality into your event handler classes. If you are using event sourcing, you must also ensure that old versions of events are translated as they are read from the event store when you are rehydrating your aggregates.

Whatever solution you adopt, it must perform the same translation wherever the old version of the event originates from—another bounded context, an event store, or even from the same bounded context if you are in the middle of a system upgrade.

Your choice of serialization format may make it easier to handle different versions of events; for example, JavaScript Object Notation (JSON) deserialization can simply ignore deleted properties, or the class that the object is deserialized to can provide a meaningful default value for any new property.

Task-based UIs

In Figure 3 above, you can see that in a typical implementation of the CQRS pattern, the UI queries the read side and receives a DTO, and sends commands to the write side. This section describes some of the impact this has on the design of your UI.

In a typical three-tier architecture or simple CRUD system, the UI also receives data in the form of DTOs from the service tier. The user then manipulates the DTO through the UI. The UI then sends the modified DTO back to the service tier. The service tier is then responsible for persisting the changes to the data store. This can be a simple, mechanical process of identifying the CRUD operations that the UI performed on the DTO and applying equivalent CRUD operations to the data store. There are several things to notice about this typical architecture:

- It uses CRUD operations throughout.
- If you have a domain model you must translate the CRUD operations from the UI into something that the domain understands.
- It can lead to complexity in the UI if you want to provide a more natural and intuitive UI that uses domain concepts instead of CRUD concepts.
- It does not necessarily capture the user's intent.
- It is simple and well understood.

The following list identifies the changes that occur in your architecture if you implement the CQRS pattern and send commands from the UI to the write side:

- It does not use CRUD-style operations.
- The domain can act directly in response to the commands from the UI.
- You can design the UI to construct the commands directly, making it easier to build a natural and intuitive UI that uses concepts from the domain.
- It is easier to capture the user's intent in a command.
- It is more complex and assumes that you have a domain model in the write side.
- The behavior is typically in one place: the write model.

A task-based UI is a natural, intuitive UI based on domain concepts that the users of the system already understand. It does not impose the CRUD operations on the UI or the user. If you implement the CQRS pattern, your task-based UI can create commands to send to the domain model on the write side. The commands should map very closely onto the mental model that your users have of the domain, and should not require any translation before the domain model receives and processes them.

In many applications, especially where the domain is relatively simple, the costs of implementing the CQRS pattern and adding a task-based UI will outweigh any benefits. Task-based UIs are particularly useful in complex domains.

There is no requirement to use a task-based UI when you implement the CQRS pattern. In some scenarios a simple CRUD-style UI is all that's needed.

Taking advantage of Windows Azure

In Chapter 2, "Introducing the Command Query Responsibility Segregation Pattern," we suggested that the motivations for hosting an application in the cloud were similar to the motivations for implementing the CQRS pattern: scalability, elasticity, and agility. This section describes in more detail how a CQRS implementation might use some of specific features of the Windows Azure platform to provide some of the infrastructure that you typically need when you implement the CQRS pattern.

"Every human-computer interaction (HCI) professional I have worked with has been in favor of task-based UIs. Every user that I have met that has used both styles of UI, task based and grid based, has reported that they were more productive when using the task-based UI for interactive work. Data entry is not interactive work."
—Udi Dahan - Tasks, Messages, & Transactions.

"The concept of a task-based UI is more often than not assumed to be part of CQRS; it is not; it is there so the domain can have verbs, but also capturing the intent of the user is important in general."
—Greg Young - CQRS, Task Based UIs, Event Sourcing agh!

SCALING OUT USING MULTIPLE ROLE INSTANCES

When you deploy an application to Windows Azure, you deploy the application to roles in your Windows Azure environment; a Windows Azure application typically consists of multiple roles. Each role has different code and performs a different function within the application. In CQRS terms, you might have one role for the implementation of the write-side model, one role for the implementation of the read-side model, and another role for the UI elements of the application.

After you deploy the roles that make up your application to Windows Azure, you can specify (and change dynamically) the number of running instances of each role. By adjusting the number of running instances of each role, you can elastically scale your application in response to changes in levels of activity. One of the motivations for using the CQRS pattern is the ability to scale the read side and the write side independently given their typically different usage patterns. For information about how to automatically scale roles in Windows Azure, see *"The Autoscaling Application Block"* on MSDN.

IMPLEMENTING AN EVENT STORE USING WINDOWS AZURE TABLE STORAGE

This section shows an event store implementation using Windows Azure table storage. It is not intended to show production-quality code, but to suggest an approach. An event store should:

- Persist events to a reliable storage medium.
- Enable an individual aggregate to retrieve its stream of events in the order in which they were originally persisted.
- Guarantee to publish each event at least once to a message infrastructure.

Windows Azure tables have two fields that together define the uniqueness of a record: the partition key and the row key.

This implementation uses the value of the aggregate's unique identifier as the partition key, and the event version number as the row key. Partition keys enable you to retrieve all of the records with the same partition key very quickly, and use transactions across rows that share the same partition key.

For more information about Windows Azure table storage see *"Data Storage Offerings in Windows Azure."*

Persisting events

The following code sample shows how the implementation persists an event to Windows Azure table storage.

```csharp
public void Save(string partitionKey, IEnumerable<EventData> events)
{
    var context = this.tableClient.GetDataServiceContext();
    foreach (var eventData in events)
    {
        var formattedVersion = eventData.Version.ToString("D10");
        context.AddObject(
            this.tableName,
            new EventTableServiceEntity
                {
                    PartitionKey = partitionKey,
                    RowKey = formattedVersion,
                    SourceId = eventData.SourceId,
                    SourceType = eventData.SourceType,
                    EventType = eventData.EventType,
                    Payload = eventData.Payload
                });

        ...

    }

    try
    {
        this.eventStoreRetryPolicy.ExecuteAction(() =>
            context.SaveChanges(SaveChangesOptions.Batch));
    }
    catch (DataServiceRequestException ex)
    {
        var inner = ex.InnerException as DataServiceClientException;
        if (inner != null && inner.StatusCode == (int)HttpStatusCode.Conflict)
        {
            throw new ConcurrencyException();
        }

        throw;
    }
}
```

There are two things to note about this code sample:
- An attempt to save a duplicate event (same aggregate ID and same event version) results in a concurrency exception.
- This example uses a retry policy to handle transient faults and to improve the reliability of the save operation. See *The Transient Fault Handling Application Block*.

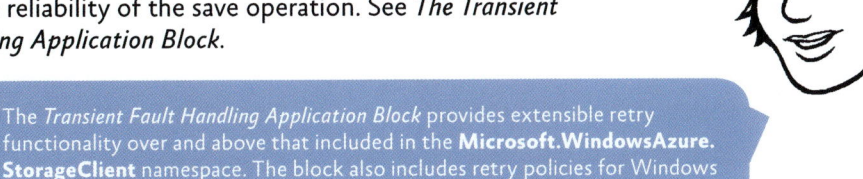

> The *Transient Fault Handling Application Block* provides extensible retry functionality over and above that included in the **Microsoft.WindowsAzure.StorageClient** namespace. The block also includes retry policies for Windows Azure SQL Database, and Windows Azure Service Bus.

Retrieving events
The following code sample shows how to retrieve the list of events associated with an aggregate.

```
public IEnumerable<EventData> Load(string partitionKey, int version)
{
    var minRowKey = version.ToString("D10");
    var query = this.GetEntitiesQuery(partitionKey, minRowKey,
                                     RowKeyVersionUpperLimit);
    var all = this.eventStoreRetryPolicy.ExecuteAction(() => query.Execute());
    return all.Select(x => new EventData
                          {
                              Version = int.Parse(x.RowKey),
                              SourceId = x.SourceId,
                              SourceType = x.SourceType,
                              EventType = x.EventType,
                              Payload = x.Payload
                          });
}
```

The events are returned in the correct order because the version number is used as the row key.

Publishing events

To guarantee that every event is published as well as persisted, you can use the transactional behavior of Windows Azure table partitions. When you save an event, you also add a copy of the event to a virtual queue on the same partition as part of a transaction. The following code sample shows a complete version of the save method that saves two copies of the event.

```
public void Save(string partitionKey, IEnumerable<EventData> events)
{
    var context = this.tableClient.GetDataServiceContext();
    foreach (var eventData in events)
    {
        var formattedVersion = eventData.Version.ToString("D10");
        context.AddObject(
                    this.tableName,
                    new EventTableServiceEntity
                        {
                            PartitionKey = partitionKey,
                            RowKey = formattedVersion,
                            SourceId = eventData.SourceId,
                            SourceType = eventData.SourceType,
                            EventType = eventData.EventType,
                            Payload = eventData.Payload
                        });

        // Add a duplicate of this event to the Unpublished "queue"
        context.AddObject(
                    this.tableName,
                    new EventTableServiceEntity
                        {
                            PartitionKey = partitionKey,
                            RowKey = UnpublishedRowKeyPrefix + formattedVersion,
                            SourceId = eventData.SourceId,
                            SourceType = eventData.SourceType,
                            EventType = eventData.EventType,
                            Payload = eventData.Payload
                        });

    }

    try
    {
        this.eventStoreRetryPolicy.ExecuteAction(() =>
                            context.SaveChanges(SaveChangesOptions.Batch));
    }
```

```
        catch (DataServiceRequestException ex)
        {
            var inner = ex.InnerException as DataServiceClientException;
            if (inner != null && inner.StatusCode == (int)HttpStatusCode.Conflict)
            {
                throw new ConcurrencyException();
            }

            throw;
        }
    }
}
```

You can use a task to process the unpublished events: read the unpublished event from the virtual queue, publish the event on the messaging infrastructure, and delete the copy of the event from the unpublished queue. The following code sample shows a possible implementation of this behavior.

```
private readonly BlockingCollection<string> enqueuedKeys;

public void SendAsync(string partitionKey)
{
    this.enqueuedKeys.Add(partitionKey);
}

public void Start(CancellationToken cancellationToken)
{
    Task.Factory.StartNew(
        () =>
            {
                while (!cancellationToken.IsCancellationRequested)
                {
                    try
                    {
                        this.ProcessNewPartition(cancellationToken);
                    }
                    catch (OperationCanceledException)
                    {
                        return;
                    }
                }
            },
        TaskCreationOptions.LongRunning);
}

private void ProcessNewPartition(CancellationToken cancellationToken)
{
    string key = this.enqueuedKeys.Take(cancellationToken);
    if (key != null)
```

```csharp
{
    try
    {
        var pending = this.queue.GetPending(key).AsCachedAnyEnumerable();
        if (pending.Any())
        {
            foreach (var record in pending)
            {
                var item = record;
                this.sender.Send(() => BuildMessage(item));
                this.queue.DeletePending(item.PartitionKey, item.RowKey);
            }
        }
    }
    catch
    {
        this.enqueuedKeys.Add(key);
        throw;
    }
}
```

There are three points to note about this sample implementation:
- It is not optimized.
- Potentially it could fail between publishing a message and deleting it from the unpublished queue. You could use duplicate message detection in your messaging infrastructure when the message is resent after a restart.
- After a restart, you need code to scan all your partitions for unpublished events.

Implementing a messaging infrastructure using the Windows Azure Service Bus

The Windows Azure Service Bus offers a robust, cloud-based messaging infrastructure that you can use to transport your command and event messages when you implement the CQRS pattern. Its brokered messaging feature enables you to use either a point-to-point topology using queues, or a publish/subscribe topology using topics.

You can design your application to use the Windows Azure Service Bus to guarantee at-least-once delivery of messages, and guarantee message ordering by using message sessions.

The sample application described in *Exploring CQRS and Event Sourcing* uses the Windows Azure Service Bus for delivering both commands and events. The following chapters in *Exploring CQRS and Event Sourcing* contain further information.

- Chapter 3, "Orders and Registrations Bounded Context"
- Chapter 6, "Versioning Our System"
- Chapter 7, "Adding Resilience and Optimizing Performance"

You can find references to additional resources in Chapter 7 "Technologies Used in the Reference Implementation."

A word of warning

For example, a process manager (described in Chapter 6, "A Saga on Sagas") may process a maximum of two messages per second during its busiest periods. Because a process manager must maintain consistency when it persists its state and sends messages, it requires transactional behavior. In Windows Azure, adding this kind of transactional behavior is nontrivial, and you may find yourself writing code to support this behavior: using at-least-once messaging and ensuring that all of the message recipients are idempotent. This is likely to be more complex to implement than a simple distributed transaction.

"Oftentimes when writing software that will be cloud deployed you need to take on a whole slew of non-functional requirements that you don't really have..."
—*Greg Young (CQRS Advisors Mail List)*

More information

All links in this book are accessible from the book's online bibliography available at: *http://msdn.microsoft.com/en-us/library/jj619274*.

Reference 5:

Communicating Between Bounded Contexts

Introduction

Bounded contexts are autonomous components, with their own domain models and their own ubiquitous language. They should not have any dependencies on each other at run time and should be capable of running in isolation. However they are a part of the same overall system and do need to exchange data with one another. If you are implementing the CQRS pattern in a bounded context, you should use events for this type of communication: your bounded context can respond to events that are raised outside of the bounded context, and your bounded context can publish events that other bounded contexts may subscribe to. Events (one-way, asynchronous messages that publish information about something that has already happened), enable you to maintain the loose coupling between your bounded contexts. This guidance uses the term integration event to refer to an event that crosses bounded contexts.

Context maps

A large system, with dozens of bounded contexts, and hundreds of different integration event types, can be difficult to understand. A valuable piece of documentation records which bounded contexts publish which integration events, and which bounded contexts subscribe to which integration events.

The anti-corruption layer

Bounded contexts are independent of each other and may be modified or updated independently of each other. Such modifications may result in changes to the events that a bounded context publishes. These changes might include, introducing a new event, dropping the use of an event, renaming an event, or changing the definition of event by adding or removing information in the payload. A bounded context must be robust in the face of changes that might be made to another bounded context.

A solution to this problem is to introduce an anti-corruption layer to your bounded context. The anti-corruption layer is responsible for verifying that incoming integration events make sense. For example, by verifying that the payload contains the expected types of data for the type of event.

You can also use the anti-corruption layer to translate incoming integration events. This translation might include the following operations:
- Mapping to a different event type when the publishing bounded context has changed the type of an event to one that the receiving bounded context does not recognize.
- Converting to a different version of the event when the publishing bounded context uses a different version to the receiving bounded context.

Integration with legacy systems

Bounded contexts that implement the CQRS pattern will already have much of the infrastructure necessary to publish and receive integration events: a bounded context that contains a legacy system may not. How you choose to implement with a bounded context that uses a legacy implementation depends largely on whether you can modify that legacy system. It may be that it is a black-box with fixed interfaces, or you may have access to the source code and be able to modify it to work with events.

The following sections outline some common approaches to getting data from a legacy system to a bounded context that implements the CQRS pattern.

READING THE DATABASE

Many legacy systems use a relational database to store their data. A simple way to get data from the legacy system to your bounded context that implements the CQRS pattern, is to have your bounded context read the data that it needs directly from the database. This approach may be useful if the legacy system has no APIs that you can use or if you cannot make any changes to the legacy system. However, it does mean that your bounded context is tightly coupled to the database schema in the legacy system.

GENERATING EVENTS FROM THE DATABASE

As an alternative, you can implement a mechanism that monitors the database in the legacy system, and then publishes integration events that describe those changes. This approach decouples the two bounded contexts and can still be done without changing the existing legacy code because you are creating an additional process to monitor the database. However, you now have another program to maintain that is tightly coupled to the legacy system.

MODIFYING THE LEGACY SYSTEMS

If you are able to modify the legacy system, you could modify it to publish integration events directly. With this approach, unless you are careful, you still have a potential consistency problem. You must ensure that the legacy system always saves its data and publishes the event. To ensure consistency, you either need to use a distributed transaction or introduce another mechanism to ensure that both operations complete successfully.

IMPLICATIONS FOR EVENT SOURCING

If the bounded context that implements the CQRS pattern also uses event sourcing, then all of the events published by aggregates in that domain are persisted to the event store. If you have modified your legacy system to publish events, you should consider whether you should persist these integration events as well. For example, you may be using these events to populate a read-model. If you need to be able to rebuild the read-model, you will need a copy of all these integration events.

If you determine that you need to persist your integration events from a legacy bounded context, you also need to decide where to store those events: in the legacy publishing bounded context, or the receiving bounded context. Because you use the integration events in the receiving bounded context, you should probably store them in the receiving bounded context.

Your event store must have a way to store events that are not associated with an aggregate.

> **Note:** *As a practical solution, you could also consider allowing the legacy bounded context to persist events directly into the event store that your CQRS bounded context uses.*

More information

All links in this book are accessible from the book's online bibliography available at: *http://msdn.microsoft.com/en-us/library/jj619274*.

Reference 6:

A Saga on Sagas

Process Managers, Coordinating Workflows, and Sagas

Clarifying the terminology

The term *saga* is commonly used in discussions of CQRS to refer to a piece of code that coordinates and routes messages between bounded contexts and aggregates. However, for the purposes of this guidance we prefer to use the term *process manager* to refer to this type of code artifact. There are two reasons for this:

- There is a well-known, pre-existing definition of the term *saga* that has a different meaning from the one generally understood in relation to CQRS.
- The term *process manager* is a better description of the role performed by this type of code artifact.

The term saga, in relation to distributed systems, was originally defined in the paper *"Sagas"* by Hector Garcia-Molina and Kenneth Salem. This paper proposes a mechanism that it calls a saga as an alternative to using a distributed transaction for managing a long-running business process. The paper recognizes that business processes are often comprised of multiple steps, each of which involves a transaction, and that overall consistency can be achieved by grouping these individual transactions into a distributed transaction. However, in long-running business processes, using distributed transactions can impact on the performance and concurrency of the system because of the locks that must be held for the duration of the distributed transaction.

*Although the term **saga** is often used in the context of the CQRS pattern, it has a pre-existing definition. We have chosen to use the term **process manager** in this guidance to avoid confusion with this pre-existing definition.*

> **Note:** *The saga concept removes the need for a distributed transaction by ensuring that the transaction at each step of the business process has a defined compensating transaction. In this way, if the business process encounters an error condition and is unable to continue, it can execute the compensating transactions for the steps that have already completed. This undoes the work completed so far in the business process and maintains the consistency of the system.*

Although we have chosen to use the term process manager, sagas may still have a part to play in a system that implements the CQRS pattern in some of its bounded contexts. Typically, you would expect to see a process manager routing messages between aggregates within a bounded context, and you would expect to see a saga managing a long-running business process that spans multiple bounded contexts.

The following section describes what we mean by the term process manager. This is the working definition we used during our CQRS journey project.

> **Note:** *For a time the team developing the Reference Implementation used the term coordinating workflow before settling on the term process manager. This pattern is described in the book "Enterprise Integration Patterns" by Gregor Hohpe and Bobby Woolf.*

Process Manager

This section outlines our definition of the term process manager. Before describing the process manager there is a brief recap of how CQRS typically uses messages to communicate between aggregates and bounded contexts.

Messages and CQRS

When you implement the CQRS pattern, you typically think about two types of message to exchange information within your system: commands and events.

Commands are imperatives; they are requests for the system to perform a task or action. For example, "book two places on conference X" or "allocate speaker Y to room Z." Commands are usually processed just once, by a single recipient.

Events are notifications; they inform interested parties that something has happened. For example, "the payment was rejected" or "seat type X was created." Notice how they use the past tense. Events are published and may have multiple subscribers.

Typically, commands are sent within a bounded context. Events may have subscribers in the same bounded context as where they are published, or in other bounded contexts.

The chapter, "A CQRS and ES Deep Dive" in this Reference Guide describes the differences between these two message types in detail.

What is a process manager?

In a complex system that you have modeled using aggregates and bounded contexts, there may be some business processes that involve multiple aggregates, or multiple aggregates in multiple bounded contexts. In these business processes multiple messages of different types are exchanged by the participating aggregates. For example, in a conference management system, the business process of purchasing seats at a conference might involve an order aggregate, a reservation aggregate, and a payment aggregate. They must all cooperate to enable a customer to complete a purchase.

Figure 1 shows a simplified view of the messages that these aggregates might exchange to complete an order. The numbers identify the message sequence.

> **Note:** *This does not illustrate how the Reference Implementation processes orders.*

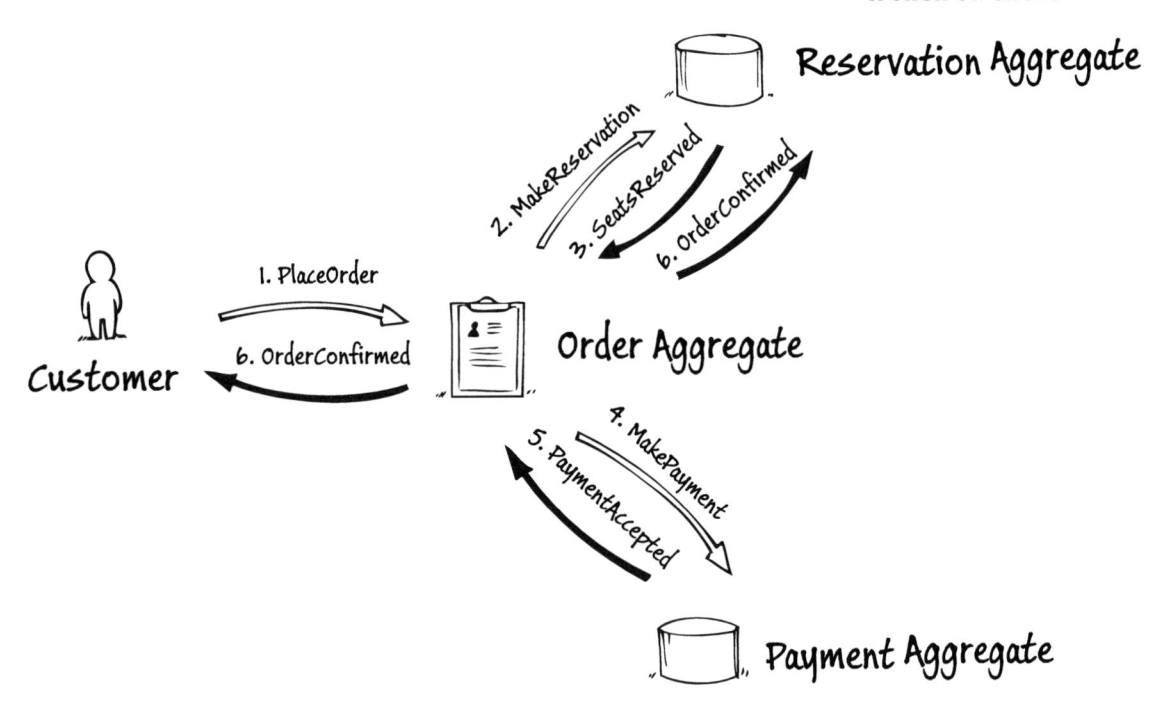

FIGURE 1
Order processing without using a process manager

In the example shown in Figure 1, each aggregate sends the appropriate command to the aggregate that performs the next step in the process. The **Order** aggregate first sends a **MakeReservation** command to the **Reservation** aggregate to reserve the seats requested by the customer. After the seats have been reserved, the **Reservation** aggregate raises a **SeatsReserved** event to notify the **Order** aggregate, and the **Order** aggregate sends a **MakePayment** command to the **Payment** aggregate. If the payment is successful, the **Order** aggregate raises an **OrderConfirmed** event to notify the **Reservation** aggregate that it can confirm the seat reservation, and the customer that the order is now complete.

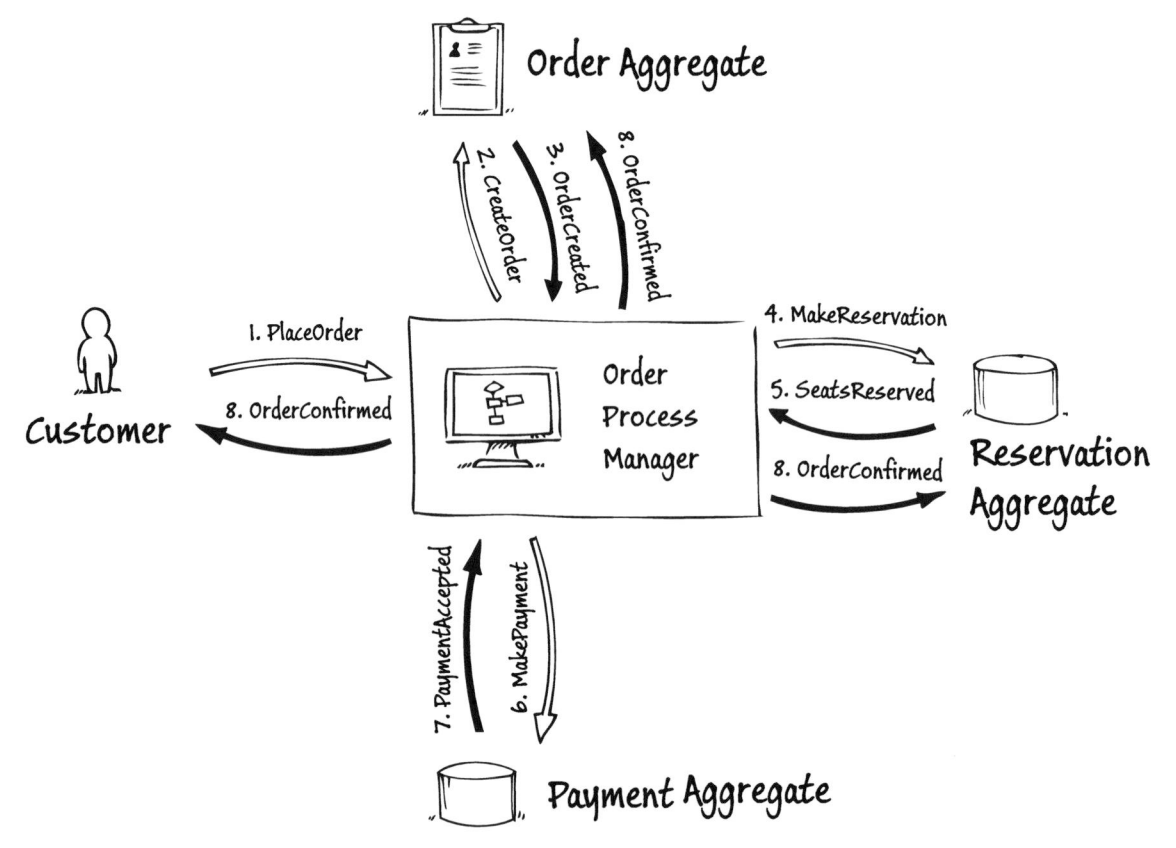

FIGURE 2
Order processing with a process manager

The example shown in Figure 2 illustrates the same business process as that shown in Figure 1, but this time using a process manager. Now, instead of each aggregate sending messages directly to other aggregates, the messages are mediated by the process manager.

This appears to complicate the process: there is an additional object (the process manager) and a few more messages. However, there are benefits to this approach.

Firstly, the aggregates no longer need to know what is the next step in the process. Originally, the **Order** aggregate needed to know that after making a reservation it should try to make a payment by sending a message to the **Payment** aggregate. Now, it simply needs to report that an order has been created.

Secondly, the definition of the message flow is now located in a single place, the process manager, rather than being scattered throughout the aggregates.

In a simple business process such as the one shown in Figure 1 and Figure 2, these benefits are marginal. However, if you have a business process that involves six aggregates and tens of messages, the benefits become more apparent. This is especially true if this is a volatile part of the system where there are frequent changes to the business process: in this scenario, the changes are likely to be localized to a limited number of objects.

In Figure 3, to illustrate this point, we introduce wait listing to the process. If some of the seats requested by the customer cannot be reserved, the system adds these seat requests to a waitlist. To make this change, we modify the **Reservation** aggregate to raise a **SeatsNotReserved** event to report how many seats could not be reserved in addition to the **SeatsReserved** event that reports how many seats could be reserved. The process manager can then send a command to the **WaitList** aggregate to waitlist the unfulfilled part of the request.

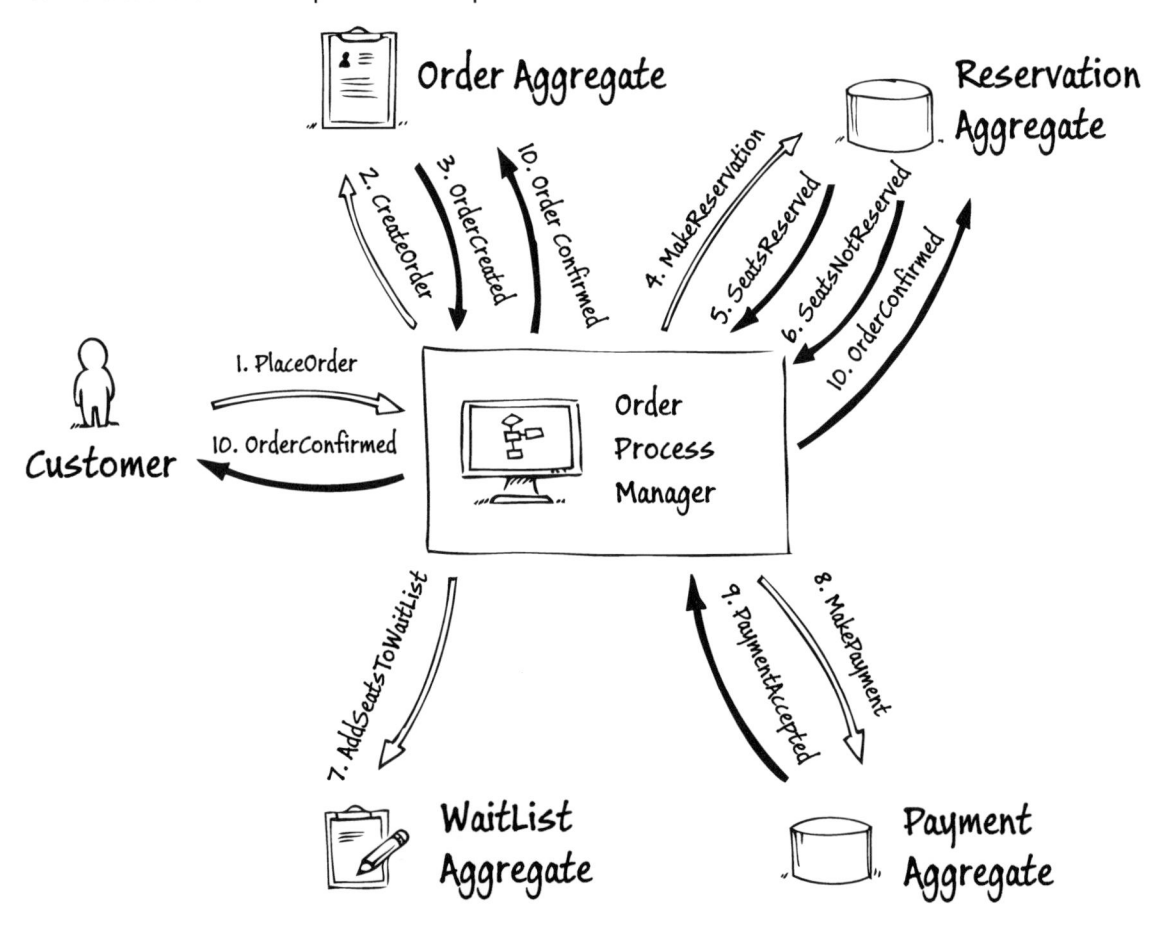

FIGURE 3
Order processing with a process manager and a waitlist

It's important to note that the process manager does not perform any business logic. It only routes messages, and in some cases translates between message types. For example, when it receives a **SeatsNotReserved** event, it sends an **AddToWaitList** command.

When should I use a process manager?

There are two key reasons to use a process manager:
- When your bounded context uses a large number of events and commands that would be difficult to manage as a collection point-to-point interactions between aggregates.
- When you want to make it easier to modify message routing in the bounded context. A process manager gives a single place where the routing is defined.

When should I not use a process manager?

The following list identifies reasons not to use a process manager:
- You should not use a Process manager if your bounded context contains a small number of aggregate types that use a limited number of messages.
- You should not use a process manager to implement any business logic in your domain. Business logic belongs in the aggregate types.

Sagas and CQRS

Although we have chosen to use the term process manager as defined earlier in this chapter, sagas may still have a part to play in a system that implements the CQRS pattern in some of its bounded contexts. Typically, you would expect to see a process manager routing messages between aggregates within a bounded context, and you would expect to see a saga managing a long-running business process that spans multiple bounded contexts.

More information

All links in this book are accessible from the book's online bibliography available at: *http://msdn.microsoft.com/en-us/library/jj619274*.

Reference 7:

Technologies Used in the Reference Implementation

Windows Azure Service Bus

This section is not intended to provide an in-depth description of the Windows Azure Service Bus, rather it is intended to highlight those features that may prove useful in implementing the CQRS pattern and event sourcing. The section "Further Information" below, includes links to additional resources for you to learn more.

The Windows Azure Service Bus provides a cloud-hosted, reliable messaging service. It operates in one of two modes:

- **Relayed**. Relayed messaging provides a direct connection between clients who need to perform request/response messaging, one-way messaging, or peer-to-peer messaging.
- **Brokered**. Brokered messaging provides durable, asynchronous messaging between clients that are not necessarily connected at the same time. Brokered messaging supports both queue and publish/subscribe topologies.

In the context of CQRS and event sourcing, brokered messaging can provide the necessary messaging infrastructure for delivering commands and events reliably between elements of an application. The Windows Azure Service Bus also offers scalability in scenarios that must support high volumes of messages.

Queues

Windows Azure Service Bus queues provide a durable mechanism for senders to send one-way messages for delivery to a single consumer.

Figure 1 shows how a queue delivers messages.

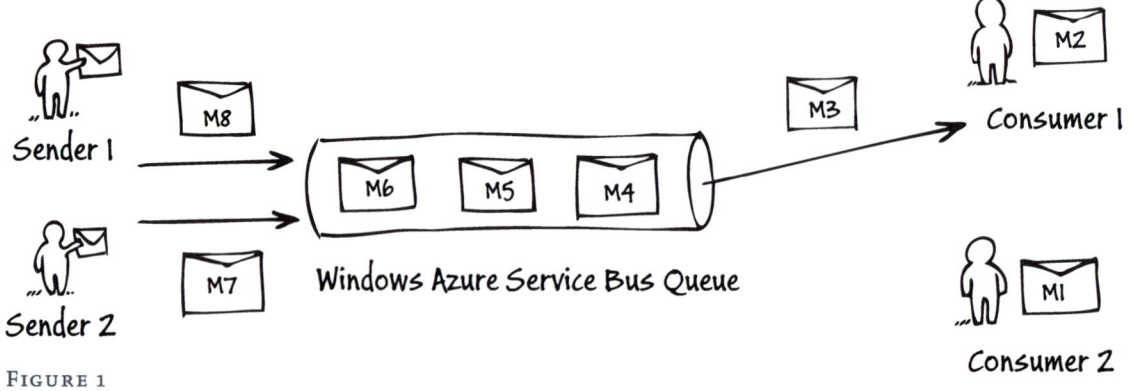

Figure 1
Windows Azure Service Bus Queue

The following list describes some of the key characteristics of queues.
- Queues deliver messages on a First In, First Out (FIFO) basis.
- Multiple senders can send messages on the same queue.
- A queue can have multiple consumers, but an individual message is only consumed by one consumer. Multiple consumers compete for messages on the queue.
- Queues offer "temporal decoupling." Senders and consumer do not need to be connected at the same time.

Topics and Subscriptions

Windows Azure Service Bus topics provide a durable mechanism for senders to send one-way messages for delivery to a multiple consumers.

Figure 2 shows how a topic distributes messages.

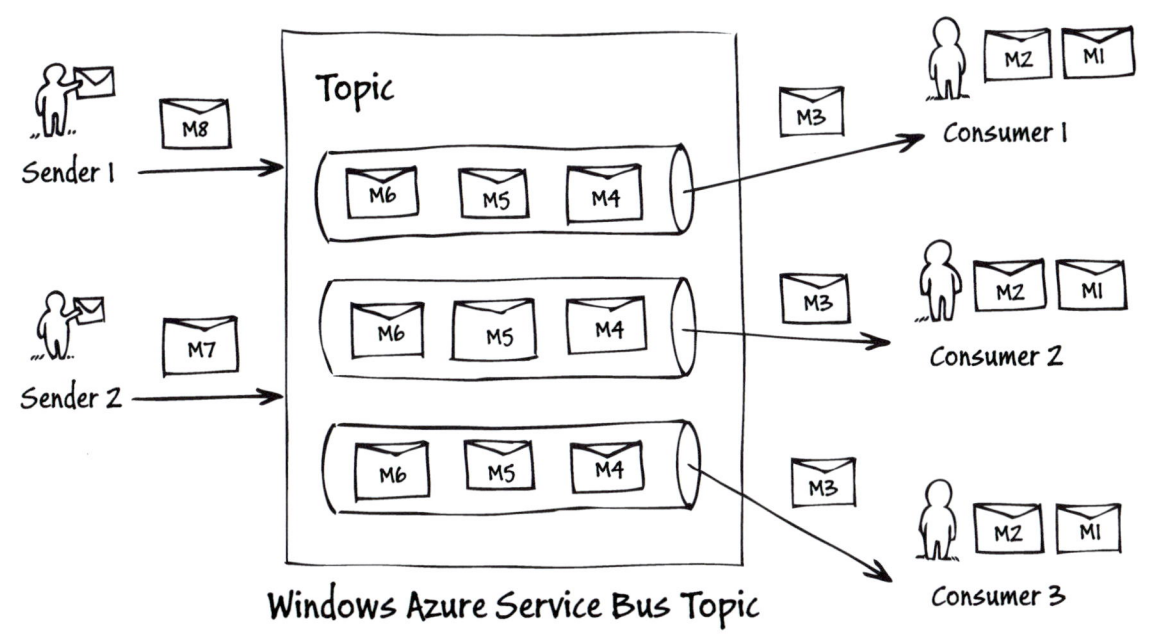

Figure 2
Windows Azure Service Bus Topic

The following list describes some of the key characteristics of topics.
- Topics deliver a copy of each message to each subscription.
- Multiple senders can publish messages to the same topic.
- Each subscription can have multiple consumers, but an individual message in a subscription is only consumed by one consumer. Multiple consumers compete for messages on the subscription.
- Topics offer "temporal decoupling." Senders and consumer do not need to be connected at the same time.
- Individual subscriptions support filters that limit the messages available through that subscription.

Useful API features

The following sections highlight some of the Windows Azure Service Bus API features that are used in the project.

Reading messages

A consumer can use one of two modes to retrieve messages from queues or subscriptions: **ReceiveAndDelete** mode and **PeekLock** mode.

In the **ReceiveAndDelete** mode, a consumer retrieves a message in a single operation: the Service Bus delivers the message to the consumer and marks the message as deleted. This is the simplest mode to use, but there is a risk that a message could be lost if the consumer fails between retrieving the message and processing it.

In the **PeekLock** mode, a consumer retrieves a message in two steps: first, the consumer requests the message, the Service Bus delivers the message to the consumer and marks the message on the queue or subscription as locked. Then, when the consumer has finished processing the message, it informs the Service Bus so that it can mark the message as deleted. In this scenario, if the consumer fails between retrieving the message and completing its processing, the message is re-delivered when the consumer restarts. A timeout ensures that locked messages become available again if the consumer does not complete the second step.

In the **PeekLock** mode, it is possible that a message could be delivered twice in the event of a failure. This is known as at least once delivery. You must ensure that either the messages are idempotent, or add logic to the consumer to detect duplicate messages and ensure exactly once processing. Every message has a unique, unchanging Id which facilitates checking for duplicates.

You can use the **PeekLock** mode to make your application more robust when it receives messages. You can maintain consistency between the messages you receive and a database without using a distributed transaction.

Sending messages

When you create a client to send messages, you can set the **RequiresDuplicateDetection** and **DuplicateDetectionHistoryTimeWindow** properties in the **QueueDescription** or **TopicDescription** class. You can use duplicate detection feature to ensure that a message is sent only once. This is useful if you retry sending a message after a failure and you don't know whether it was previously sent.

You can use the duplicate detection feature to make your application more robust when it receives messages without using a distributed transaction. You can maintain consistency between the messages you send and a database without using a distributed transaction.

Expiring messages

When you create a **BrokeredMessage** object, you can specify an expiry time using the **ExpiresAtUtc** property or a time to live using the **TimeToLive** property. When a message expires you can specify either to send the message to a dead letter queue or discard it.

Delayed message processing

In some scenarios, you may want to send the message now, but to delay delivery until some future time. You can do this by using the **ScheduleEnqueueTimeUtc** property of the **BrokeredMessage** instance.

Serializing messages

You must serialize your **Command** and **Event** objects if you are sending them over the Windows Azure Service Bus.

The Contoso Conference Management System uses Json.NET serializer to serialize command and event messages. The team chose to use this serializer because of its flexibility and resilience to version changes.

The following code sample shows the adapter class in the **Common** project that wraps the Json.NET serializer.

```
public class JsonSerializerAdapter : ISerializer
{
    private JsonSerializer serializer;

    public JsonSerializerAdapter(JsonSerializer serializer)
    {
        this.serializer = serializer;
    }

    public void Serialize(Stream stream, object graph)
    {
        var writer = new JsonTextWriter(new StreamWriter(stream));

        this.serializer.Serialize(writer, graph);

        // We don't close the stream as it's owned by the message.
        writer.Flush();
    }

    public object Deserialize(Stream stream)
    {
        var reader = new JsonTextReader(new StreamReader(stream));

        return this.serializer.Deserialize(reader);
    }
}
```

Further information

For general information about the Windows Azure Service Bus, see *Service Bus* on MSDN.

For more information about Service Bus topologies and patterns, see *Overview of Service Bus Messaging Patterns* on MSDN.

For information about scaling the Windows Azure Service Bus infrastructure, see *Best Practices for Performance Improvements Using Service Bus Brokered Messaging* on MSDN.

For information about Json.NET, see *Json.NET*.

Unity Application Block

The MVC web application in the Contoso Conference Management System uses the Unity Application Block (Unity) dependency injection container. The **Global.asax.cs** file contains the type registrations for the command and event buses, and the repositories. This file also hooks up the MVC infrastructure to the Unity service locator as shown in the following code sample:

```
protected void Application_Start()
{
    this.container = CreateContainer();
    RegisterHandlers(this.container);

    DependencyResolver.SetResolver(new UnityServiceLocator(this.container));

    ...
}
```

The MVC controller classes no longer have parameter-less constructors. The following code sample shows the constructor from the **RegistrationController** class:

```
private ICommandBus commandBus;
private Func<IViewRepository> repositoryFactory;

public RegistrationController(ICommandBus commandBus,
  [Dependency("registration")]Func<IViewRepository> repositoryFactory)
{
    this.commandBus = commandBus;
    this.repositoryFactory = repositoryFactory;
}
```

Further information
For more information about the Unity Application Block, see *Unity Application Block* on MSDN.

More information

All links in this book are accessible from the book's online bibliography available at: *http://msdn.microsoft.com/en-us/library/jj619274*.

Tales from the Trenches

Twilio

Product overview

Twilio provides high-availability voice and SMS APIs, hosted in the cloud, that enable developers to add automated voice and SMS capabilities to a wide range of applications.

Although Twilio did not explicitly implement the CQRS pattern or use event sourcing, many of the fundamental concepts implicit in their designs are very similar to concepts that relate to the CQRS pattern including splitting read and write models and relaxing consistency requirements.

Lessons learned

This section summarizes some of the key lessons learned by Twilio during the development of the Twilio APIs and services.

Separating reads and writes

Rather than separating out the read side and write side explicitly as in the CQRS pattern, Twilio uses a slightly different pair of concepts: in-flight data and post-flight data. In-flight data captures all of the transactional data that is accessed by operations that are currently running through the system. Once an operation completes, any data that needs to be saved becomes immutable post-flight data. In-flight data must be very high performance and support inserts, updates, and reads. Post-flight data is read-only and supports use cases such as analysis and logging. As such, post-flight data has very different performance characteristics.

Typically, there is very little in-flight data in the system, which makes it easy to support no-downtime upgrades that impact in these parts of the system. There is typically a lot more, immutable, post-flight data and any schema change here would be very expensive to implement. Hence, a schema-less data store makes a lot of sense for this post-flight data.

Designing for high availability

One of the key design goals for Twilio was to achieve high availability for their systems in a cloud environment, and some of the specific architectural design principles that help to achieve this are:

This study is contributed by Evan Cooke, CTO, Twilio.

- It's important to understand, for a system, what are the units of failure for the different pieces that make up that system, and then to design the system to be resilient to those failures. Typical units of failure might be an individual host, a datacenter or zone, a geographic region, or a cloud service provider. Identifying units of failure applies both to code deployed by Twilio, and to technologies provided by a vendor, such as data storage or queuing infrastructure. From the perspective of a risk profile, units of failure at the level of a host are to be preferred because it is easier and cheaper to mitigate risk at this level.
- Not all data requires the same level of availability. Twilio gives its developers different primitives to work with that offer three levels of availability for data; a distributed queuing system that is resilient to host and zone failures, a replicated database engine that replicates across regions, and an in-memory distributed data store for high availability. These primitives enable the developers to select a storage option with a specified unit of failure. They can then choose a store with appropriate characteristics for a specific part of the application.

IDEMPOTENCY

An important lesson that Twilio learned in relation to idempotency is the importance of assigning the token that identifies the specific operation or transaction that must be idempotent as early in the processing chain as possible. The later the token is assigned, the harder it is to test for correctness and the more difficult it is to debug. Although Twilio don't currently offer this, they would like to be able to allow their customers to set the idempotency token when they make a call to one of the Twilio APIs.

NO-DOWNTIME DEPLOYMENTS

To enable no-downtime migrations as part of the continuous deployment of their services, Twilio uses risk profiles to determine what process must be followed for specific deployments. For example, a change to the content of a website can be pushed to production with a single click, while a change to a REST API requires continuous integration testing and a human sign-off. Twilio also tries to ensure that changes to data schemas do not break existing code: therefore the application can keep running, without losing requests as the model is updated using a pivoting process.

Some features are also initially deployed in a learning mode. This means that the full processing pipeline is deployed with a no-op at the end so that the feature can be tested with production traffic, but without any impact on the existing system.

PERFORMANCE

Twilio has four different environments: a development environment, an integration environment, a staging environment, and a production environment. Performance testing, which is part of cluster testing, happens automatically in the integration and staging environments. The performance tests that take a long time to run happen in an ongoing basis in the integration environment and may not be repeated in the staging environment.

If load-levels are predictable, there is less of a requirement to use asynchronous service implementations within the application because you can scale your worker pools to handle the demand. However, when you experience big fluctuations in demand and you don't want to use a callback mechanism because you want to keep the request open, then it makes sense to make the service implementation itself asynchronous.

Twilio identified a trade-off in how to effectively instrument their systems to collect performance monitoring data. One option is to use a common protocol for all service interactions that enables the collection of standard performance metrics through a central instrumentation server. However, it's not always desirable to enforce the use of a common protocol and enforce the use of specific interfaces because it may not be the best choice in all circumstances. Different teams at Twilio make their own choices about protocols and instrumentation techniques based on the specific requirements of the pieces of the application they are responsible for.

References

For further information relating to Twilio, see:
- *Twilio.com*
- *High-Availability Infrastructure in the Cloud*
- *Scaling Twilio*
- *Asynchronous Architectures for Implementing Scalable Cloud Services*
- *Why Twilio Wasn't Affected by Today's AWS Issues*

More information

All links in this book are accessible from the book's online bibliography available at: *http://msdn.microsoft.com/en-us/library/jj619274*.

Tales from the Trenches

Lokad Hub

Project overview

Lokad Hub is an infrastructure element that unifies the metered, pay-as-you-go, forecasting subscription offered by Lokad. It also provides an intelligent, self-managing, business backend for Lokad's internal teams.

Lokad requires this piece of infrastructure to be extremely flexible, focused, self-managing, and capable of surviving cloud outages. Key features of Lokad Hub include:

- Multi-tenancy
- Scalability
- Instant data replication to multiple locations
- Deployable to any cloud
- Supports multiple production deployments daily
- Full audit logs and the ability to roll back to any point in time
- Integration with other systems

The current version was developed using the domain-driven design (DDD) approach, implements the CQRS pattern, and uses event sourcing (ES). It is a replacement for a legacy, CRUD-style system.

For Lokad, the two key benefits of the new system are the low development friction that makes it possible to perform multiple deployments per day, and the ability to respond quickly to changes in the system's complex business requirements.

Lessons learned

This section summarizes some of the key lessons learned by Lokad during the development of Lokad Hub.

This case study is based on the original contribution by Rinat Abdullin.

Benefits of DDD
The team at Lokad adopted the DDD approach in the design and development of Lokad Hub. The DDD approach helped to divide the complex domain into multiple bounded contexts. It was then possible to model each bounded context separately and select to most appropriate technologies for that bounded context. In this project, Lokad chose a CQRS/ES implementation for each bounded context.

Lokad captured all the business requirements for the system in the models as code. This code became the foundation of the new system.

However, it did take some time (and multiple iterations) to build these models and correctly capture all of the business requirements.

Reducing dependencies
The core business logic depends only on message contracts and the **Lokad.CQRS** portability interfaces. Therefore, the core business logic does not have any dependencies on specific storage providers, object-relational mappers, specific cloud services, or dependency injection containers. This makes it extremely portable, and simplifies the development process.

Using sagas
Lokad decided not to use sagas in Lokad Hub because they found them to be overly complex and non-transparent. Lokad also found issues with trying to use sagas when migrating data from the legacy CRUD system to the new event sourced system.

Testing and documentation
Lokad uses unit tests as the basis of a mechanism that generates documentation about the system. This is especially valuable in the cases where Lokad uses unit tests to define specifications for complex business behaviors. These specifications are also used to verify the stability of message contracts and to help visualize parts of the domain.

Migration to ES
Lokad developed a custom tool to migrate data from the legacy SQL data stores into event streams for the event-sourced aggregates in the new system.

Using projections
Projections of read-side data, in combination with state of the art UI technologies, made it quicker and easier to build a new UI for the system.

The development process also benefited from the introduction of smart projections that are rebuilt automatically on startup if the system detects any changes in them.

Event sourcing
Event sourcing forms the basis of the cloud failover strategy for the system, by continuously replicating events from the primary system. This strategy has three goals:
- All data should be replicated to multiple clouds and datacenters within one second.
- There should be read-only versions of the UI available immediately if the core system becomes unavailable for any reason.
- A full read/write backup system can be enabled manually if the primary system becomes unavailable.

Although, it would be is possible to push this further and even have a zero downtime strategy, this would bring additional complexity and costs. For this system, a guaranteed recovery within a dozen minutes is more than adequate.

The most important aspect of this strategy is the ability to keep valuable customer data safe and secure even in the face of global cloud outages.

Event sourcing also proved invaluable when a glitch in the code was discovered soon after the initial deployment. It was possible to roll the system back to a point in time before the glitch manifested itself, fix the problem in the code, and then restart the system

INFRASTRUCTURE

When there are multiple bounded contexts to integrate (at least a dozen in the case of Lokad Hub) it's important to have a high-level view of how they integrate with each other. The infrastructure that supports the integration should also make it easy to support and manage the integration in a clean and enabling fashion.

Once you have over 100,000 events to keep and replay, simple file-based or blob-based event stores becoming limiting. With these volumes, it is better to use a dedicated event-streaming server.

References

For further information relating to Lokad Hub, see:
- *Case: Lokad Hub*
- *Lokad.com*
- *Lokad Team*

More information

All links in this book are accessible from the book's online bibliography available at: *http://msdn.microsoft.com/en-us/library/jj619274*.

Tales from the Trenches

DDD/CQRS for large financial company

Project overview

The following is a list of the overall goals of the project. We wanted to:
- Build a sample reference architecture for enterprise level applications with the main emphasis on performance, scalability, reliability, extensibility, testability, and modularity.
- Enforce SOLID (single responsibility, open-closed, Liskov substitution, interface segregation, and dependency inversion) principles.
- Utilize test-driven development and evaluate performance early and often as part of our application lifecycle management (ALM).
- Provide abstraction and interoperability with third-party and legacy systems.
- Address infrastructure concerns such as authentication (by using claims-based, trusted sub systems), and server and client side caching (by using AppFabric for Windows Server).
- Include the capabilities necessary to support various types of clients.

We wanted to use the CQRS pattern to help us to improve the performance, scalability, and reliability of the system.

On the read side, we have a specialized query context that exposes the data in the exact format that the UI clients require which minimizes the amount of processing they must perform. This separation provided great value in terms of a performance boost and enabled us to get very close to the optimal performance of our web server with the given hardware specification.

On the write side, our command service allows us to add queuing for commands if necessary and to add event sourcing to create an audit log of the changes performed, which is a critical component for any financial system. Commands provided a very loosely coupled model to work with our domain. From the ALM perspective, commands provide a useful abstraction for our developers enabling them to work against a concrete interface and with clearly defined contracts. Handlers can be maintained independently and changed on demand through a registration process: this won't break any service contracts, and no code re-complication will be required.

This case study is based on contributions by Alex Dubinkov and Tim Walton.

The initial reference architecture application deals with financial advisor allocation models. The application shows the customers assigned to the financial advisor, and the distribution of their allocations as compared to the modeled distribution that the customer and financial advisor had agreed upon.

Lessons learned

This section summarizes some of the lessons learned during this project

Query performance

During testing of querying de-normalized context for one of the pilot applications, we couldn't get the throughput, measured in requests per second, that we expected even though the CPU and memory counters were all showing in range values. Later on, we observed severe saturation of the network both on the testing clients and on the server. Reviewing the amount of data we were querying for each call, we discovered it to be about 1.6 Mb.

To resolve this issue we:
- Enabled compression on IIS, which significantly reduced amount of data returned from the Open Data Protocol (OData) service.
- Created a highly de-normalized context that invokes a stored procedure that uses pivoting in SQL to return just the final "model layout" back to the client.
- Cached the results in the query service.

Commands

We developed both execute and compensate operations for command handlers and use a technique of batching commands that are wrapped in a transaction scope. It is important to use the correct scope in order to reduce the performance impact.

One-way commands needed a special way to pass error notifications or results back to the caller. Different messaging infrastructures (Windows Azure Service Bus, NServiceBus) support this functionality in different ways, but for our on-premises solution, we had to come up with our own custom approach.

Working with legacy databases

Our initial domain API relied on single GUID key type, but the customer's DBA team has a completely different set of requirements to build normalized databases. They use multiple key types including shorts, integers, and strings. The two solutions we explored that would enable our domain to work with these key types were:
- Allow the use of generic keys.
- Use a mapping mechanism to translate between GUIDs and the legacy keys.

Using an Inversion of Control (IoC) container

Commands help to decouple application services functionality into a loosely coupled, message-driven tier. Our bootstrapping process registers commands and command handlers during the initialization process, and the commands are resolved dynamically using the generic type **ICommandHandler-<CommandType>** from a Unity container. Therefore, the command service itself doesn't have an explicit set of commands to support, it is all initialized through the bootstrapping process.

Because the system is very loosely coupled, it is critical that we have a highly organized bootstrapping mechanism that is generic enough to provide modularity and materialization for the specific container, mapping and logging choices.

Key lessons learned
- There is no one right way to implement CQRS. However, having specific infrastructure elements in place, such as a service bus and a distributed cache, may reduce the overall complexity.
- Have clear performance SLAs on querying throughput and query flexibility.
- Test performance early and often using performance unit tests.
- Choose your serialization format wisely and only return the data that's needed: for OData services prefer JSON serialization over AtomPub.
- Design your application with upfront enforcement of SOLID principals.

More information

All links in this book are accessible from the book's online bibliography available at: *http://msdn.microsoft.com/en-us/library/jj619274*.

Tales from the Trenches

Digital Marketing

Refactoring an existing application has many challenges. Our story is about refactoring an existing application over an extended period of time while still delivering new features. We didn't start with CQRS as the goal, which was a good thing. It became a good fit as we went along. Our product is composed of multiple pieces, of which our customer facing portal (CFP) uses CQRS.

There are many aspects of the DMS that fit well with CQRS, but there were two main problems we were trying to solve: slow reads and bloated View Objects (VO).

The CFP has a very large dataset with many tables containing tens of millions of rows; at the extreme some tables have millions of rows for a single client. Generally, the best practice for this amount of data in SQL Server is highly denormalized tables—ours is no exception. A large portion of our value add is structured and reporting data together, allowing clients to make the most informed decision when altering their structured data. The combination of structured and reporting data required many SQL joins and some of our page load times were over 20 seconds. There was a lot of friction for users to make simple changes.

The combination of structured and reporting data also resulted in bloated View Objects. The CFP suffered from the same woes that many long lived applications do—lots of cooks in the kitchen but a limited set of ingredients. Our application has a very rich UI resulting in the common Get/Modify/Save pattern. A VO started out with a single purpose: we need data on screen A. A few months later we needed a similar screen B that had some of the same data. Fear not, we already had most of that, we just needed to show it on screen B too—after all we wouldn't want to duplicate code. Fast forward a few months and our two screens have evolved independently even though they represented "basically the same data." Worse yet, our VO has been used in two more screens and one of them has already been deprecated. At this point we are lucky if the original developers still remember what values from the VO are used on which screens. Oh wait, it's a few years later and the original developers don't even work here anymore! We would often find ourselves trying to persist a VO from the UI and unable to remember which magical group of properties must be set. It is very easy to violate the Single Responsibility Principle in the name of reuse. There are many solutions to these problems and CQRS is but one tool for making better software.

Before trying to make large architectural changes there are a few things we found to be very successful for the CFP: Dependency Injection (DI) and Bounded Contexts.

This case study is contributed by Scott Brown.

Make your objects injectable and go get a DI Container. Changing a legacy application to be injectable is a very large undertaking and will be painful and difficult. Often the hardest part is sorting out the object dependencies. But this was completely necessary later on. As the CFP became injectable it was possible to write unit tests allowing us to refactor with confidence. Now that our application was modular, injectable, and unit tested we could choose any architecture we wanted.

Since we decided to stick with CQRS, it was a good time to think about bounded contexts. First we needed to figure out the major components of the overall product. The CFP is one bounded context and only a portion of our overall application. It is important to determine bounded contexts because CQRS is best applied within a bounded context and not as an integration strategy.

One of our challenges with CQRS has been physically separating our bounded contexts. Refactoring has to deal with an existing application and the previous decisions that were made. In order to split the CFP into its own bounded context we needed to vastly change the dependency graph. Code that handles cross cutting concerns was factored into reference assemblies; our preference has been NuGet packages built and hosted by TeamCity. All the remaining code that was shared between bounded contexts needed to be split into separate solutions. Long term we would recommend separate repositories to ensure that code is not referenced across the bounded contexts. For the CFP we had too much shared code to be able to completely separate the bounded contexts right away, but having done so would have spared much grief later on.

It is important to start thinking about how your bounded contexts will communicate with each other. Events and event sourcing are often associated with CQRS for good reason. The CFP uses events to keep an auditable change history which results in a very obvious integration strategy of eventing.

At this point the CFP is modular, injectable, testable (not necessarily fully tested), and beginning to be divided by bounded context but we have yet to talk about CQRS. All of this ground work is necessary to change the architecture of a large application—don't be tempted to skip it.

The first piece of CQRS we started with was the commands and queries. This might seem obtusely obvious but I point it out because we did not start with eventing, event sourcing, caching, or even a bus. We created some commands and a bit of wiring to map them to command handlers. If you took our advice earlier and you are using an Inversion of Control (IoC) container, the mapping of command to command handler can be done in less than a day. Since the CFP is now modular and injectable our container can create the command handler dependencies with minimal effort which allowed us to wire our commands into our existing middleware code. Most applications already have a remoting or gateway layer that performs this function of translating UI calls into middleware / VO functions. In the CFP, the commands and queries replaced that layer.

One of our challenges has been to refactor an existing UI to a one-way command model. We have not been able to make a strict one-way contract mainly due to database side ID generation. We are working towards client side ID generation which will allow us to make commands fire and forget. One technique that has helped a bit was to wrap the one way asynchronous bus in a blocking bus. This helped us to minimize the amount of code that depends on the blocking capability. Even with that we have too much code that relies upon command responses simply because the functionality was available, so try not to do this if possible.

Unfortunately we could only do this for so long before we realized it is just the same application with a fancy new façade. The application was easier to work on, but that was more likely due to the DI changes then to the commands and queries. We ran into the problem of where to put certain types of logic. Commands and queries themselves should be very light weight objects with no dependencies on VOs. There were a few occasions we were tempted during a complicated refactor to use an existing VO as part of a query but inevitably we found ourselves back down the path of bloated objects. We also became tempted to use complex properties (getters and setters with code) on commands and queries but this resulted in hidden logic—ultimately we found it better to put the logic in the command handler or better yet in the domain or command validator.

At this point we also began to run into difficulties accomplishing tasks. We were in the middle of a pattern switch and it was difficult to cleanly accomplish a goal. Should command handlers dispatch other commands? How else will they exercise any logic that is now embedded in a command handler? For that matter, what should be a command handler's single responsibility?

We found that these questions could not be answered by writing more commands and queries but rather by flushing out our CQRS implementation. The next logical choice was either the read or the write model. Starting with the cached read model felt like the best choice since it delivers tangible business value. We chose to use events to keep our read model up to date, but where do the events come from? It became obvious that we were forced to create our write model first.

Choose a strategy for the write model that makes sense in your bounded context. That is, after all, what CQRS allows: separating reads and writes to decouple the requirements of each. For the CFP we use domains that expose behavior. We do not practice DDD, but a domain model fits well with CQRS. Creating a domain model is very hard, we spent a lot of time talking about what our aggregate roots are—do not underestimate how hard this will be.

When creating the write model we were very careful about introducing any dependencies to the domain assembly. This will allow the domain to outlive other application specific technologies, but was not without pain points. Our domain started out with a lot of validation that was eventually moved into command validators; dependencies required for validation were not available from within the domain. In the end, the domain simply translates behavior (methods) into events (class instances). Most of our pain points were centered on saving the events without taking dependencies into the domain assembly. The CFP does not use event sourcing, we were able to translate the domain events into our existing SQL tables with objects we call Event Savers. This allows our domain to focus on translating behavior to events and the command handler can publish and save the events. To prevent the command handler from doing too much, we use a repository pattern to get and save a domain. This allows us to switch to event sourcing in a later refactoring of the application if desired with minimal effect on the domain. The Event Savers are simple classes that map an event to a stored procedure call or table(s). We use RabbitMq to publish the events after saving, it is not transactional but that has been ok so far.

As events become more ubiquitous it is possible to keep a read model up to date. We have a separate service that subscribes to events and updates a Redis cache. By keeping this code separate we isolate the dependencies for Redis and make our caching solution more pluggable. The choice of caching technology is difficult and the best solution is likely to change over time. We needed the flexibility to test multiple options and compare the performance vs. maintainability.

Once our cache was in place we discovered the oldest known theorem of caching: That which is cached becomes stale. Invalid cache results can occur many different ways; we found enough that a temporary measure was introduced to update items in the cache on a rolling schedule. The plan was (and still is) to find and eliminate all sources of inconsistency. Database integrations or people/departments that update the write model directly will need to be routed through the domain to prevent the cache from becoming incorrect. Our goal is total elimination of these discrepancies for complete confidence in cached results.

Single Responsibility of Objects

Definitions specific to our implementation:
- Command – carries data
- Command Authorizer – authorizes user to place a command on the bus
- Command Validator – validates a command can be placed on the bus
- Command Handler – maps command to domain call
- Repository Factory – retrieves a repository for specified domain type
- Repository – retrieves/persists domain instance by key
- Domain – maps behavior to domain event
- Domain EventSaver – called by the repository and saves domain events to existing database structure

More information

All links in this book are accessible from the book's online bibliography available at: *http://msdn.microsoft.com/en-us/library/jj619274*.

TALES FROM THE TRENCHES

TOPAZ Technologies

What did we hope to accomplish by using CQRS/ES?

We were looking for a way to radically simplify the development process of our *off-the-shelf* enterprise application. We wanted to minimize unnecessary complexity induced by heavyweight frameworks, middleware, and servers like Oracle and SQL Server RDBMS.

In the past we spent too much time with technical implementation details and as a consequence spent too little time on business relevant activities. Discussions about the business rules, the business processes, and workflows were neglected. We wanted to refocus and to spend significantly more time in discussions with our business analysts and testers. Ideally, we wanted to draft the workflow of a feature with the business analyst, the product manager, and the tester, and then code it without any translation into another language or model. The notions of a bounded context and a ubiquitous language should be natural to all our stakeholders. We also realized that, from a business perspective, verbs (commands, events and more general purpose messages) have a much higher significance than nouns (entities).

Another goal was to get away from the form-over-data type of application and UI, and to develop a more task oriented presentation layer.

Last but not least, we needed an easy way to horizontally scale our application. A short term goal is to self-host the solution on an array inexpensive standard servers but the ultimate goal is to run our software in the cloud.

What were the biggest challenges and how did we overcome them?

One of the biggest challenges was to convince management and other stakeholders in our company to believe in the benefits of this new approach. Initially they were skeptical or even frightened at the thought of not having the data stored in a RDBMS. DBAs, concerned about potential job loss, also tried to influence management in a subtle, negative way regarding this new architecture.

We overcame these objections by implementing just one product using CQRS/ES, then showing the stakeholders how it worked, and demonstrating how much faster we finished the implementation. We also demonstrated the significantly improved quality of the product compared to our other products.

This study is contributed by Gabriel N. Schenker, Chief Software Architect, TOPAZ Technologies LLC

Another challenge was the lack of knowledge in the development team of this area. For everyone CQRS and ES were completely new.

As an architect, I did a lot of teaching in the form of *lunch-and-learns* in which I discussed the fundamental aspects of this new architecture. I also performed live coding in front of the team and developed some end-to-end exercises, which all developers were required to solve. I encouraged our team to watch the various free videos in which Greg Young was presenting various topics related to CQRS and event sourcing.

Yet another challenge is the fact that this type of architecture is still relatively new and not fully established. Thus, finding good guidance or adhering to best practices is not as straightforward as with more traditional architectures. How to do CQRS and ES *right* is still invokes lively discussions, and people have very different opinions about both the overall architecture and individual elements of it.

What were the most important lessons learned?

When we choose the right tool for the job, we can spend much more time discussing the business relevant questions and much less time discussing technical details.

It is more straightforward to implement a user story or a feature as is. Just like in real life, in code, a feature is triggered by an action (command) that results in a sequence of events that might or might not cause side effects.

Issues caused by changing business rules or code defects in the past often did not surface because we could write SQL scripts to correct the wrong data directly in the database. Because the event store is immutable, this is not possible any more—which is good thing. Now we are forced to discuss how to address the issue from a business perspective. Business analysts, product managers and other stakeholders are involved in the process of finding a solution. Often this results in the finding of a previously hidden concept in the business domain.

With hindsight, what would we have done differently?

We started to embrace CQRS and ES for the first time in one of our products, but we were forced to use a hybrid approach due to time constraints and our lack of experience. We were still using an RDBMS for the event store and the read model. We also generated the read model in a synchronous way. These were mistakes. The short-term benefit over a full or pure implementation of CQRS/ES was quickly annihilated by the added complexity and confusion amongst developers. In consequence, we need to refactor this product in the near future.

We will strictly avoid such hybrid implementations in the future. Either we will fully embrace CQRS and ES, or we will stick with a more traditional architecture.

Further information

This *blog series* discusses the details of the implementation.

More information

All links in this book are accessible from the book's online bibliography available at: *http://msdn.microsoft.com/en-us/library/jj619274*.

Tales from the Trenches

eMoney Nexus

eMoney Nexus: Some CQRS lessons

Now that the Microsoft patterns & practices CQRS Journey is coming to a close, I thought it would be a good time to relate some of our experiences with CQRS and Event Sourcing. We have been working with similar patterns for a few years, and our experiences and conclusions are pretty close to the MS p&p team.

About eMoney & the Nexus

eMoney Advisor provides wealth management software to financial advisors and their clients. One of the core features of our product is the ability to aggregate financial account data from multiple financial institutions and use the data from within our client portal and planning products. The front-end application is updated several times a year, and must go through customer and legal review before each deployment, but the data processing system must be updated continuously to respond to daily changes to the data sources. After running our original system for several years, we decided to rebuild the data aggregation portion of our system to solve some performance, maintainability, and complexity issues. In our design of the eMoney Nexus, we used a message-based architecture combined with split read-write duties to solve our core issues.

Since we built the Nexus a few years ago, it is not a pure CQRS/ES implementation, but many of our design choices line up with these patterns and we see the same types of benefits. Now that we can take the learning from CQRS Journey, we will go back and evaluate how these patterns may help us take the next steps to improve our system.

This study is contributed by Jon Wagner, SVP & Chief Architect, eMoney Advisor

System overview
The job of the Nexus is to fetch account data from a number of financial institutions, and publish that data to a number of application servers.

Inputs
- Users – can tell the system to create a subscription to data updates from a source, force an instant refresh of data, or modify processing rules for their accounts.
- Bulk Files – arrive daily with large workloads for account updates
- Timed Updates – arrive scheduled throughout the night to update individual subscriptions.

Subscribers
- Users – user interfaces need to update when operations complete or data changes.
- Planning Applications – multiple application instances need to be notified when data changes.
- Outgoing Bulk Files – enterprise partners need a daily feed of the changes to the account data.

Design Goals
- Decoupled Development – building and upgrading the Nexus should not be constrained by application deployment lifecycles.
- Throughput Resilience – processing load for queries should not affect the throughput of the data updates and vice versa.
- High Availability – processing should be fault tolerant for node outages.
- Continuous Deployment – connections and business logic should be upgradable during business hours and should decouple Nexus changes from other systems.
- Long-Running Processes – data acquisition can take a long time, so an update operation must be decoupled from any read/query operations.
- Re-playable Operations – data acquisition has a high chance of failure due to network errors, timeouts, and so on, so operations must be re-playable for retry scenarios.
- Strong Diagnostics – since updated operations are complex and error-prone, diagnostic tools are a must for the infrastructure.
- Non-Transactional – because our data is not the system of record, there is less of a need for data rollbacks (we can just get a new update), and eventual consistency of the data is acceptable to the end user.

The evolution of the system

The legacy system was a traditional 3-tier architecture with a Web UI Tier, Application Tier, and Database Tier.

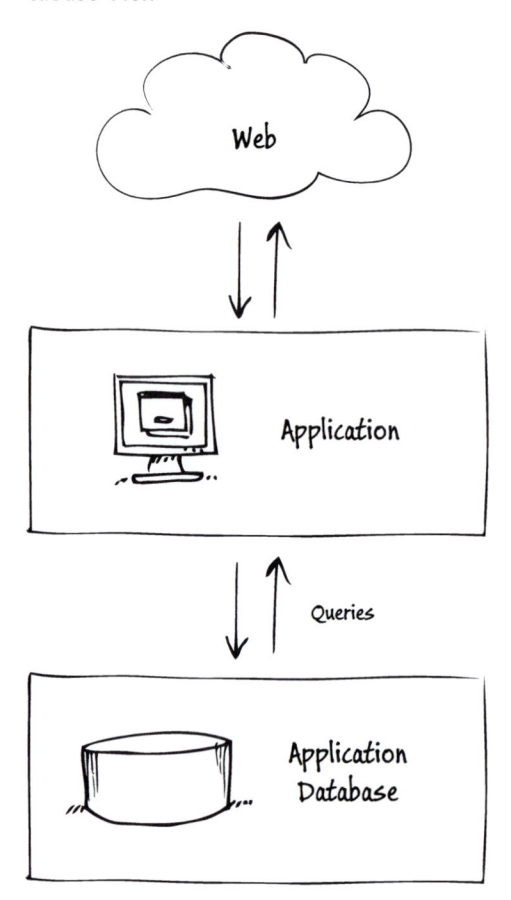

The first step was to decouple the processing engine from the application system. We did that be adding a service layer to accept change requests and a publishing system to send change events back to the application. The application would have its own copy of the account data that is optimized for the planning and search operations for end users. The Nexus could store the data in the best way possible for high-throughput processing.

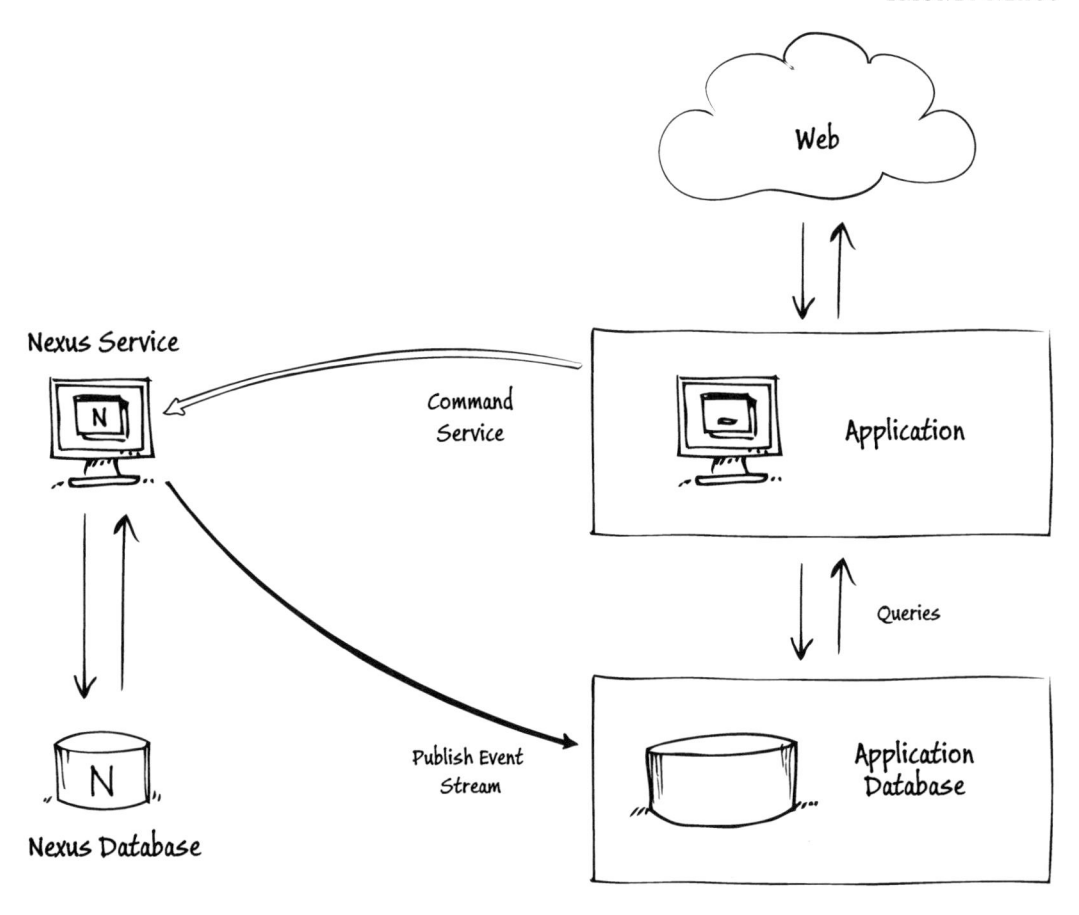

[Diagram: Nexus Service connected to Nexus Database; Application connected to Web and Application Database via Queries; Application sends Command Service to Nexus Service; Nexus Service publishes Event Stream to Application Database.]

Partitioning the system allows us to decouple any changes to the Nexus from the other systems. Like all good Partition / Bounded Context / Service boundaries, the interfaces between the systems are contracts that must be adhered to, but can evolve over time with some coordination between the systems. For example, we have upgraded the publishing interface to the core application 5 or 6 times to add additional data points or optimize the data publishing process. Note that we publish to a SQL Server Service Broker, but this could be another application server in some scenarios.

This allowed us to achieve our first two design goals: **Decoupled Development** and **Throughput Resilience**. Large query loads on the application would be directed at its own database, and bulk load operations on the back end do not slow down the user experience. The Nexus could be deployed on a separate schedule from the application and we could continue to make progress on the system.

Next, we added Windows Load Balancing and WCF services to expose the Command service to consumers.

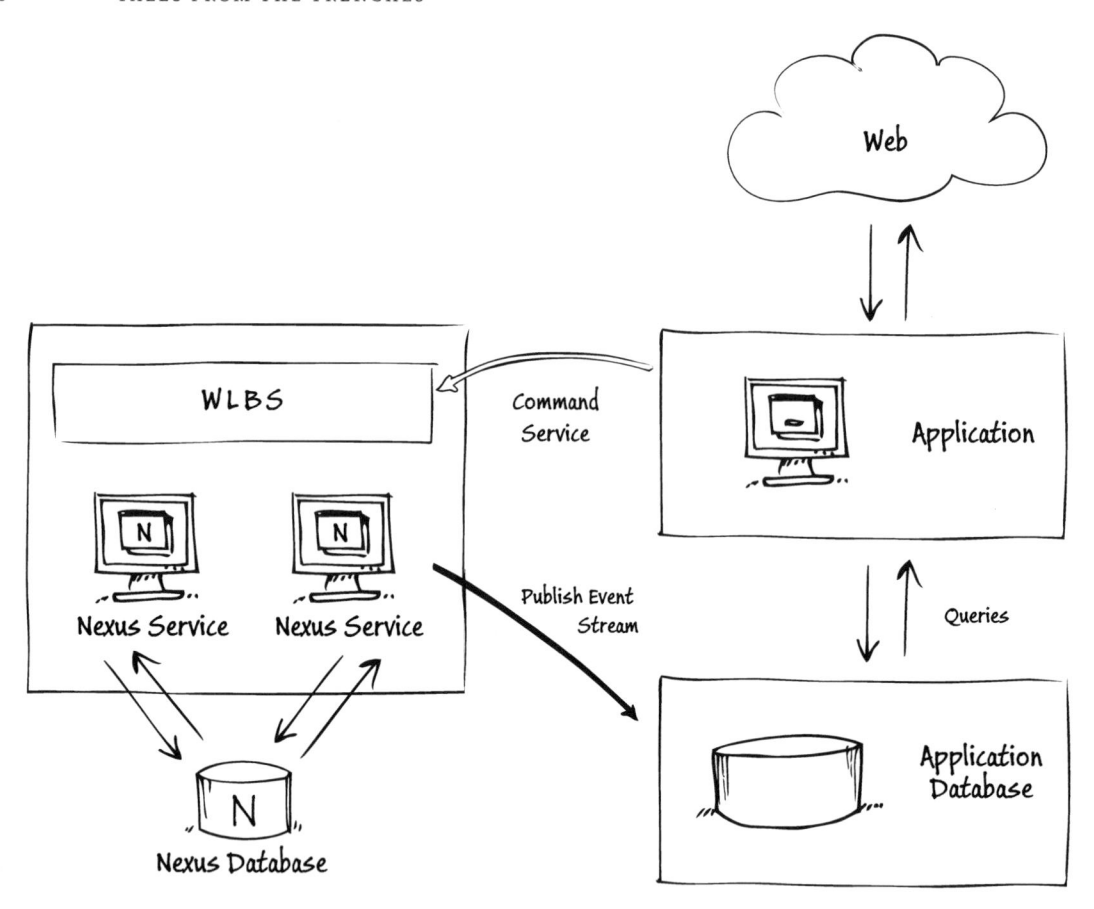

This allows us to add additional processing nodes, as well as remove nodes from the pool in order to upgrade them. This got us to our goal of **High Availability**, as well as **Continuous Deployment**. In most scenarios, we can take a node out of the pool during the day, upgrade it, and return it to the pool to take up work.

For processing, we decided to break up each unit of work into "Messages." Most Messages are Commands that tell the system to perform an operation. Messages can dispatch other messages as part of their processing, causing an entire workflow process to unfold. We don't have a great separation between Sagas (the coordination of Commands) and Commands themselves, and that is something we can improve in future builds.

Whenever a client calls the Command service, if the request cannot be completed immediately, it is placed in a queue for processing. This can be an end user, or one of the automated data load schedulers. We use SQL Server Service Broker for our Message processing Queues. Because each of our data sources have different throughput and latency requirements, we wrote our own thread pooling mechanism to allow us to apportion the right number of threads-per-source at runtime through a configuration screen. We also took advantage of Service Broker's message priority function to allow user requests to jump to the front of the worker queues to keep end users happy. We also separated the Command (API) service from the Worker service so we can scale the workloads differently.

eMoney Nexus

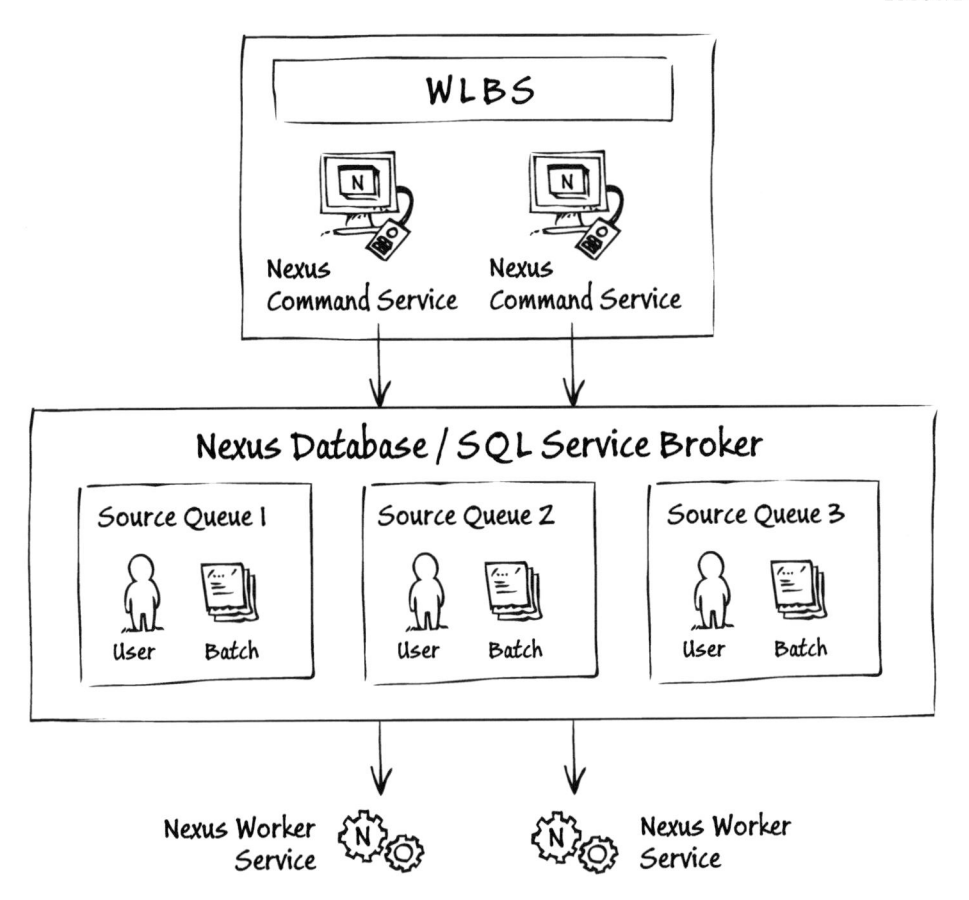

[Diagram: WLBS box containing two Nexus Command Service nodes, both feeding into Nexus Database / SQL Service Broker which contains Source Queue 1, Source Queue 2, and Source Queue 3 (each with User and Batch), feeding into two Nexus Worker Services.]

This message processing design gave us a lot of benefits. First of all, with Command/Query Separation, you are forced to deal with the fact that a Command may not complete immediately. By implementing clients that need to wait for results, you are naturally going to be able to support **Long-Running Processes**. In addition, you can persist the Command messages to a store and easily support **Replayable Operations** to handle retry logic or system restores. The Nexus Service has its own scheduler that sends itself Commands to start jobs at the appropriate time.

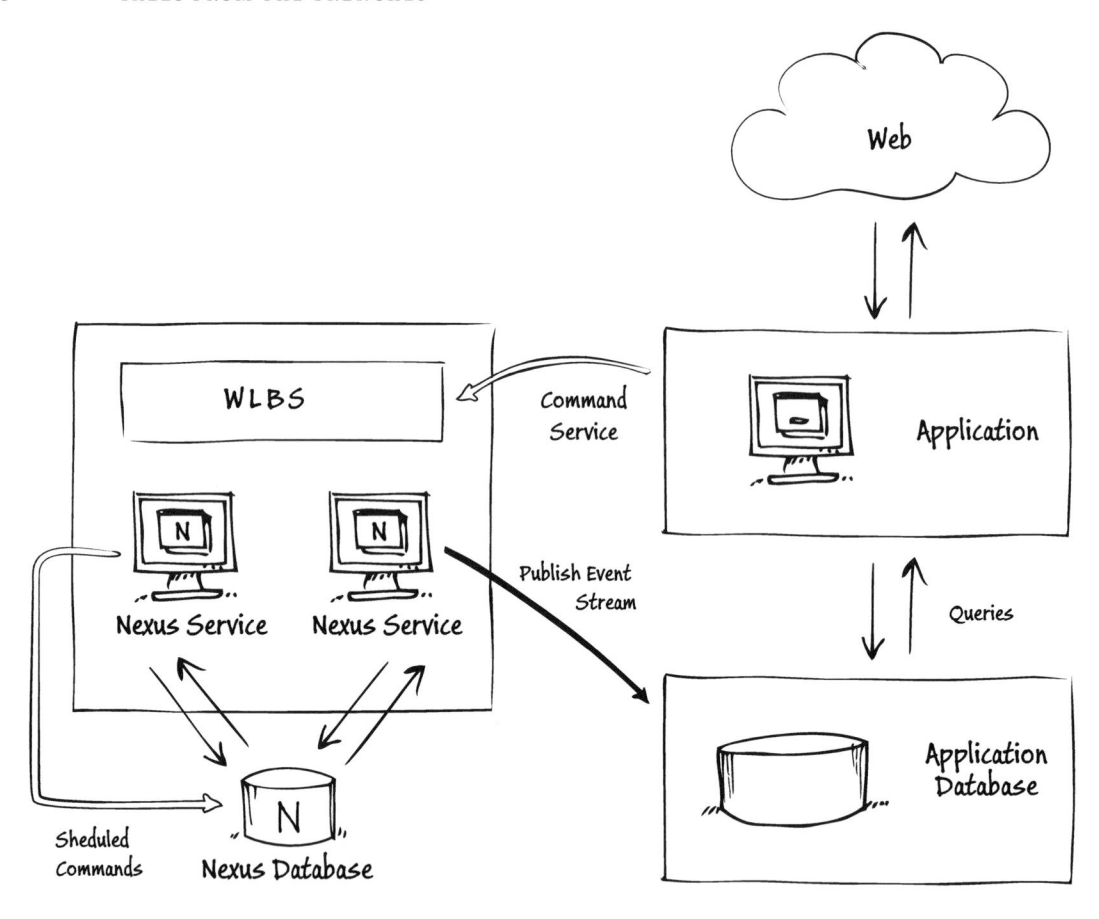

One unexpected benefit of using a queue infrastructure was more scalable performance. Partitioning the workloads (in our case, by data source) allows for more optimal use of resources. When workloads begin to block due to some resource slowness, we can dynamically partition that workload into a separate processing queue so other work can continue.

One of the most important features that we added early on in development was Tracing and Diagnostics. When an operation is started (by a user or by a scheduled process), the system generates a GUID (a "Correlation ID") that is assigned to the message. The Correlation ID is passed throughout the system, and any logging that occurs is tied to the ID. Even if a message dispatches another message to be processed, the Correlation ID is along for the ride. This lets us easily figure out which log events in the system go together (GUIDs are translated to colors for easy visual association). **Strong Diagnostics** was one of our goals. When the processing of a system gets broken into individual asynchronous pieces, it's almost impossible to analyze a production system without this feature.

To drive operations, the application calls the Nexus with Commands such as **CreateSubscription**, **UpdateSubscription**, and **RepublishData**. Some of these operations can take a few minutes to complete, and the user must wait until the operation is finished. To support this, each long-running Command returns an **ActivityID**. The application polls the Nexus periodically to determine whether the activity is still running or if it has completed. An activity is considered completed when the update has completed AND the data has been published to the read replica. This allows the application to immediately perform a query on the read replica to see the data results.

Diagram

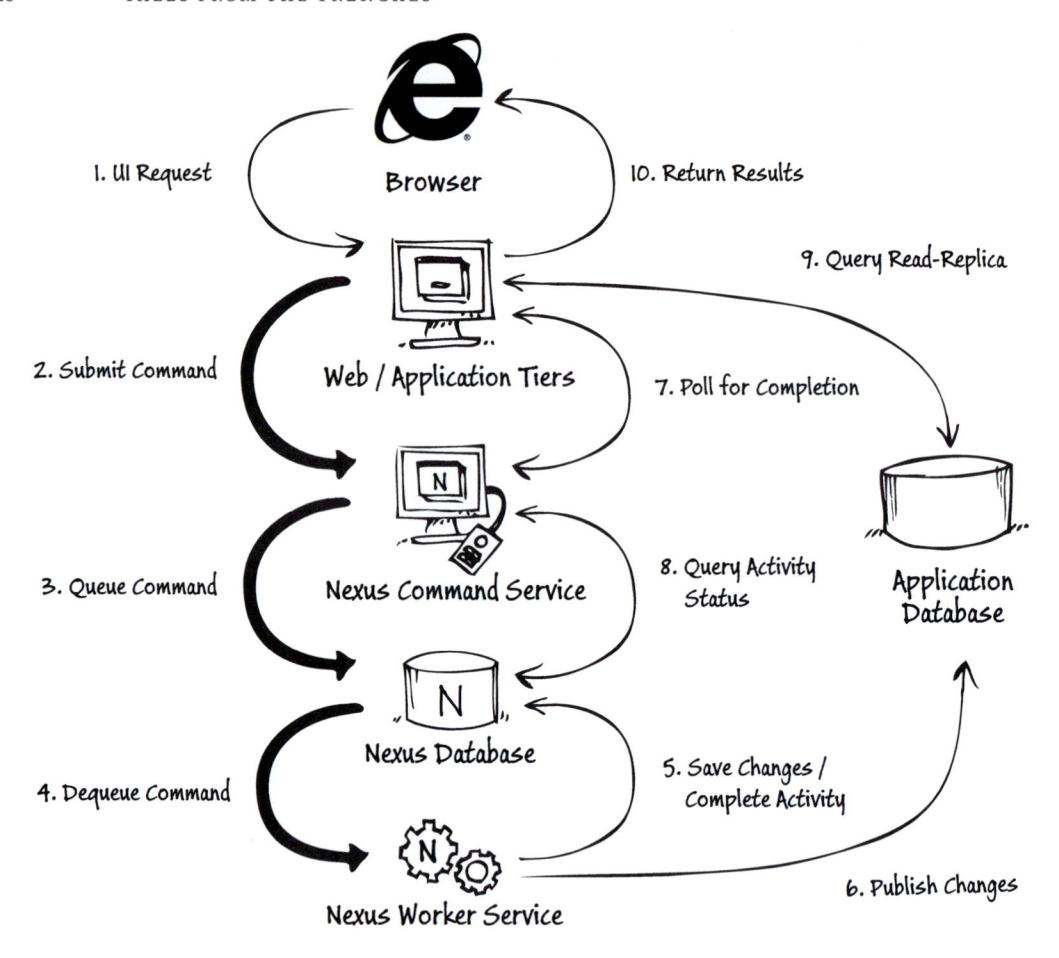

1. UI Request → Browser
2. Submit Command → Web / Application Tiers
3. Queue Command → Nexus Command Service
4. Dequeue Command → Nexus Database → Nexus Worker Service
5. Save Changes / Complete Activity
6. Publish Changes → Application Database
7. Poll for Completion
8. Query Activity Status
9. Query Read-Replica
10. Return Results

Lessons learned

We've been running the Nexus in production for several years now, and for this type of system, the benefits CQRS and ES are evident, at least for the read-write separation and data change events that we use in our system.

- CQRS = Service Boundary + Separation of Concerns – the core of CQRS is creating service boundaries for your inputs and outputs, then realizing that input and output operations are separate concerns and *don't need to have the same (domain) model*.
- Partitions are Important – define your Bounded Context and boundaries carefully. You will have to maintain them over time.
- External systems introduce complexity – particularly when replaying an event stream, managing state against an external system or isolating against external state may be difficult. Martin Fowler has some great thoughts on it here.
- CQRS usually implies async but not always – because you generally want to see the results of your Commands as Query results. It is possible to have Commands complete immediately if it's not a Query. In fact, it's easier that way sometimes. We allow the **CreateSubscription** Command to return a **SubscriptionID** immediately. Then an async process fetches the data and updates the read model.

- User Experience for async is hard – users want to know when their operation completes.
- Build in Diagnostics from the beginning – trust me on this.
- Decomposing work into Commands is good – our **BatchUpdate** message just spawns off a lot of little **SubscriptionUpdate** messages. It makes it easier to extend and reuse workflows over time.
- Queue or Bus + Partitions = Performance Control – this lets you fan out or throttle your workload as needs change.
- Event Sourcing lets you have totally different read systems for your data – we split our event stream and send it to a relational database for user queries and into flat files for bulk delivery to partners.

If you want some more good practical lessons on CQRS, you should read Chapter 8, "Epilogue: Lessons Learned."

Making it better

Like any system, there are many things we would like to do better.
- Workflow Testing is Difficult – we didn't do quite enough work to remove dependencies from our objects and messages, so it is tough to test sequences of events without setting up large test cases. Doing a cleanup pass for DI/IOC would probably make this a lot easier.
- UI code is hard with AJAX and polling – but now that there are push libraries like SignalR, this can be a lot easier.
- Tracking the Duration of an Operation – because our workflows are long, but the user needs to know when they complete, we track each operation with an Activity ID. Client applications poll the server periodically to see if an operation completes. This isn't a scalability issue yet, but we will need to do more work on this at some point.

As you can see, this implementation isn't 100% pure CQRS/ES, but the practical benefits of these patterns are real.

For more information, see Jon Wagner's blog *Zeros, Ones and a Few Twos*.

Appendix 1

Release Notes

The most up-to-date version of the release notes is available online: *http://go.microsoft.com/fwlink/p/?LinkID=258574*.

These release notes apply to the Reference Implementation – Contoso Conference Management System. This RI complements the "Exploring CQRS and Event Sourcing" guide and is for learning purposes only.

System evolution

The system has gone through three pseudo-production releases and additional improvements after V3.

> **Note:** *While the team went through actual deployments to Windows Azure and performed migrations, the releases are referred to as 'pseudo-production' because they lack critical security and other features necessary for a full production release that are not the focus of this guidance.*

The notes apply to the latest version (packaged in this self-extractable zip) unless specified otherwise. To follow the project evolution, please check out specific versions of the entire system tagged **V1-pseudo-prod**, **V2-pseudo-prod** or **V3-pseudo-prod** in the git repository history. Also, see the Migration notes and Chapter 5, "Preparing for the V1 Release," Chapter 6, "Versioning Our System" and Chapter 7, "Adding Resilience and Optimizing Performance" of the Guide.

Building and running the sample code (RI)

This appendix describes how to obtain, build, and run the RI.

These instructions describe five different scenarios for running the RI using the Conference Visual Studio solution:

1. Running the application on a local web server and using a local message bus and event store.
2. Running the application on a local web server and using the Windows Azure Service Bus and an event store that uses Windows Azure table storage.
3. Deploying the application to the local Windows Azure compute emulator and using a local message bus and event store.
4. Deploying the application to the local Windows Azure compute emulator and using the Windows Azure Service Bus and an event store that uses Windows Azure table storage.

5. Deploying the application to Windows Azure and using the Windows Azure Service Bus and an event store that uses Windows Azure table storage.

   Note: *The local message bus and event store use SQL Express and are intended to help you run the application locally for demonstration purposes. They are not intended to illustrate a production-ready scenario.*

   Note: *Scenarios 1, 2, 3 and 4 use SQL Express for other data storage requirements. Scenario 5 requires you to use SQL Database instead of SQL Express.*

   Note: *The source code download for the V3 release also includes a **Conference.NoAzureSDK** solution that enables you to build and run the sample application without installing the Windows Azure SDK. This solution supports scenarios 1 and 2 only.*

Prerequisites

Before you begin, you should install the following pre-requisites:
- Visual Studio 2010 or later
- SQL Server 2008 Express or later
- ASP.NET MVC 3 and MVC 4 for the V1 and V2 releases
- ASP.NET MVC 4 Installer (Visual Studio 2010) for the V3 release
- Windows Azure SDK for .NET - November 2011 for the V1 and V2 releases
- Windows Azure SDK for .NET - June 2012 or later for the V3 release

   Note: *The V1 and V2 releases of the sample application used ASP.NET MVC 3 in addition to ASP.NET MVC 4. As of the V3 release all of the web applications in the project use ASP.NET MVC 4.*

   Note: *The Windows Azure SDK is **not** a pre-requisite if you plan to use the **Conference.NoAzureSDK** solution.*

You can download and install all of these except for Visual Studio by using the Microsoft Web Platform Installer 4.0.

You can install the remaining dependencies from NuGet by running the script **install-packages.ps1** included with the downloadable source.

If you plan to deploy any part of the RI to Windows Azure (scenarios 2, 4, 5), you must have a Windows Azure subscription. You will need to configure a Windows Azure storage account (for blob storage), a Windows Azure Service Bus namespace, and a SQL Database instance (they do not necessarily need to be in the same Windows Azure subscription). You should be aware, that depending on your Windows Azure subscription type, you may incur usage charges when you use the Windows Azure Service Bus, Windows Azure table storage, and when you deploy and run the RI in Windows Azure.

At the time of writing, you can sign-up for a *Windows Azure free trial* that enables you to run the RI in Windows Azure.

   Note: *Scenario 1 enables you to run the RI locally without using the Windows Azure compute and storage emulators.*

Obtaining the code

- You can download the source code from the *Microsoft Download Center* as a self-extractable zip.
- Alternatively, you can get the source code with the full git history from *github*.

Creating the databases

SQL Express Database

For scenarios 1, 2, 3, and 4 you can create a local SQL Express database called **Conference** by running the script **Install-Database.ps1** in the scripts folder.

The projects in the solution use this database to store application data. The SQL-based message bus and event store also use this database.

Windows Azure SQL Database instance

For scenario 5, you must create a SQL Database instance called **Conference** by running the script **Install-Database.ps1** in the scripts folder.

The follow command will populate a SQL Database instance called **Conference** with the tables and views required to support the RI (this script assumes that you have already created the **Conference** database in SQL Database):

```
.\Install-Database.ps1 -ServerName [your-sql-azure-server].database.windows.net
-DoNotCreateDatabase -DoNotAddNetworkServiceUser –UseSqlServerAuthentication
-UserName [your-sql-azure-username]
```

> **Note:** *The command above is displayed in multiple lines for better readability. This command should be entered as a single line.*

You must then modify the **ServiceConfiguration.Cloud.cscfg** file in the Conference.Azure project to use the following connection strings.

SQL Database Connection String:

```
Server=tcp:[your-sql-azure-server].database.windows.net;Database=myDataBase;
User ID=[your-sql-azure-username]@[your-sql-azure-server];
Password=[your-sql-azure-password];Trusted_Connection=False;Encrypt=True;
MultipleActiveResultSets=True;
```

Windows Azure Connection String:

```
DefaultEndpointsProtocol=https;
AccountName=[your-windows-azure-storage-account-name];
AccountKey=[your-windows-azure-storage-account-key]
```

Conference.Azure\ServiceConfiguration.Cloud.cscfg:

```xml
<?xml version="1.0" encoding="utf-8"?>
<ServiceConfiguration serviceName="Conference.Azure" osFamily="1" osVersion="*"
xmlns="http://schemas.microsoft.com/ServiceHosting/2008/10/ServiceConfiguration">
  <Role name="Conference.Web.Admin">
    <Instances count="1" />
    <ConfigurationSettings>
      <Setting name="Microsoft.WindowsAzure.Plugins.Diagnostics.ConnectionString"
            value="[your-windows-azure-connection-string]" />
      <Setting name="Diagnostics.ScheduledTransferPeriod" value="00:02:00" />
      <Setting name="Diagnostics.LogLevelFilter" value="Warning" />
      <Setting name="Diagnostics.PerformanceCounterSampleRate" value="00:00:30" />
      <Setting name="DbContext.ConferenceManagement"
            value="[your-sql-azure-connection-string]" />
      <Setting name="DbContext.SqlBus"
            value="[your-sql-azure-connection-string]" />
    </ConfigurationSettings>
  </Role>
  <Role name="Conference.Web.Public">
    <Instances count="1" />
    <ConfigurationSettings>
      <Setting name="Microsoft.WindowsAzure.Plugins.Diagnostics.ConnectionString"
            value="[your-windows-azure-connection-string]" />
      <Setting name="Diagnostics.ScheduledTransferPeriod" value="00:02:00" />
      <Setting name="Diagnostics.LogLevelFilter" value="Warning" />
      <Setting name="Diagnostics.PerformanceCounterSampleRate" value="00:00:30" />
      <Setting name="DbContext.Payments"
            value="[your-sql-azure-connection-string]" />
      <Setting name="DbContext.ConferenceRegistration"
            value="[your-sql-azure-connection-string]" />
      <Setting name="DbContext.SqlBus"
            value="[your-sql-azure-connection-string]" />
      <Setting name="DbContext.BlobStorage"
            value="[your-sql-azure-connection-string]" />
    </ConfigurationSettings>
  </Role>
  <Role name="WorkerRoleCommandProcessor">
    <Instances count="1" />
    <ConfigurationSettings>
      <Setting name="Microsoft.WindowsAzure.Plugins.Diagnostics.ConnectionString"
            value="[your-windows-azure-connection-string]" />
      <Setting name="Diagnostics.ScheduledTransferPeriod" value="00:02:00" />
      <Setting name="Diagnostics.LogLevelFilter" value="Information" />
      <Setting name="Diagnostics.PerformanceCounterSampleRate" value="00:00:30" />
```

```xml
    <Setting name="DbContext.Payments"
             value="[your-sql-azure-connection-string]" />
    <Setting name="DbContext.EventStore"
             value="[your-sql-azure-connection-string]" />
    <Setting name="DbContext.ConferenceRegistrationProcesses"
             value="[your-sql-azure-connection-string]" />
    <Setting name="DbContext.ConferenceRegistration"
             value="[your-sql-azure-connection-string]" />
    <Setting name="DbContext.SqlBus"
             value="[your-sql-azure-connection-string]" />
    <Setting name="DbContext.BlobStorage"
             value="[your-sql-azure-connection-string]" />
    <Setting name="DbContext.ConferenceManagement"
             value="your-sql-azure-connection-string]" />
  </ConfigurationSettings>
 </Role>
</ServiceConfiguration>
```

> **Note:** *The **LogLevelFilter** values for these roles is set to either **Warning** or **Information**. If you want to capture logs from the application into the **WADLogsTable**, you should change these values to **Verbose**.*

Creating the Settings.xml File

Before you can build the solution, you must create a **Settings.xml** file in the **Infrastructure Projects\Azure** solution folder. You can copy the **Settings.Template.xml** in this solution folder to create a **Settings.xml** file.

> **Note:** *You only need to create the **Settings.xml** file if you plan to use either the **Debug** or **Release** build configurations.*

If you plan to use the Windows Azure Service Bus and the Windows Azure table storage based event store then you must edit the **Settings.xml** file in the **Infrastructure Projects\Azure** solution folder to include details of your Windows Azure storage account and a Windows Azure Service Bus namespace.

> **Note:** *See the contents of the **Settings.Template.xml** for details of the configuration information that is required.*

> **Note:** *You cannot currently use the Windows Azure storage emulator for the event store. You must use a real Windows Azure storage account.*

Building the RI

Open the **Conference** Visual Studio solution file in the code repository that you downloaded and un-zipped.

You can use NuGet to download and install all of the dependencies by running the script **install-packages.ps1** before building the solution.

Build Configurations

The solution includes a number of build configurations. These are described in the following sections:

Release

Use the **Release** build configuration if you plan to deploy your application to Windows Azure.
This solution uses the Windows Azure Service Bus to provide the messaging infrastructure.
Use this build configuration if you plan to deploy the RI to Windows Azure (scenario 5).

Debug

Use the **Debug** build configuration if you plan either to deploy your application locally to the Windows Azure compute emulator or to run the application locally and stand-alone without using the Windows Azure compute emulator.
This solution uses the Windows Azure Service Bus to provide the messaging infrastructure and the event store based on Windows Azure table storage (scenarios 2 and 4).

DebugLocal

Use the **DebugLocal** build configuration if you plan to either deploy your application locally to the Windows Azure compute emulator or run the application on a local web server without using the Windows Azure compute emulator.
This solution uses a local messaging infrastructure and event store built using SQL Server (scenarios 1 and 3).

Running the RI

When you run the RI, you should first create a conference, add at least one seat type, and then publish the conference using the **Conference.Web.Admin** site.
After you have published the conference, you will then be able to use the site to order seats and use the simulated the payment process using the **Conference.Web** site.
The following sections describe how to run the RI using in the different scenarios.

Scenario 1. Local Web Server, SQL Event Bus, SQL Event Store

To run this scenario you should build the application using the **DebugLocal** configuration.
Run the **WorkerRoleCommandProcessor** project as a console application.
Run the **Conference.Web.Public** and **Conference.Web.Admin** (located in the **Conference-Management** folder) as web applications.

Scenario 2. Local Web Server, Windows Azure Service Bus, Table Storage Event Store

To run this scenario you should build the application using the **Debug** configuration.

Run the **WorkerRoleCommandProcessor** project as a console application.

Run the **Conference.Web.Public** and **Conference.Web.Admin** (located in the **Conference-Management** folder) as web applications.

Scenario 3. Compute Emulator, SQL Event Bus, SQL Event Store

To run this scenario you should build the application using the **DebugLocal** configuration.
Run the **Conference.Azure** Windows Azure project.

> **Note:** *To use the Windows Azure compute emulator you must launch Visual Studio as an administrator.*

Scenario 4. Compute Emulator, Windows Azure Service Bus, Table Storage Event Store

To run this scenario you should build the application using the **Debug** configuration.
Run the **Conference.Azure** Windows Azure project.

> **Note:** *To use the Windows Azure compute emulator you must launch Visual Studio as an administrator.*

Scenario 5. Windows Azure, Windows Azure Service Bus, Table Storage Event Store

Deploy the **Conference.Azure** Windows Azure project to your Windows Azure account.

> **Note:** *You must also ensure that you have created **Conference** database in SQL Database using the **Install-Database.ps1** in the scripts folder as described above. You must also ensure that you have modified the connection strings in the configuration files in the solution to point to your SQL Database **Conference** database instead of your local SQL Express **Conference** database as described above.*

Running the Tests

The following sections describe how to run the unit, integration, and acceptance tests.

Running the Unit and Integration Tests

The unit and integration tests in the **Conference** solution are created using **xUnit.net**.

For more information about how you can run these tests, please visit the *xUnit.net* site on Codeplex.

RUNNING THE ACCEPTANCE TESTS

The acceptance tests are located in the Visual Studio solution in the **Conference.AcceptanceTests** folder.

You can use NuGet to download and install all of the dependencies by running the script **install-packages.ps1** before building this solution.

The acceptance tests are created using SpecFlow. For more information about SpecFlow, please visit *SpecFlow*.

The SpecFlow tests are implemented using **xUnit.net**.

The **Conference.AcceptanceTests** solution uses the same build configurations as the **Conference** solution to control whether you run the acceptance tests against either the local SQL-based messaging infrastructure and event store or the Windows Azure Service Bus messaging infrastructure and Windows Azure table storage based event store.

You can use the xUnit console runner or a third-party tool with Visual Studio integration and xUnit support (for example TDD.net) to run the tests. The xUnit GUI tool is not supported.

Known issues

The list of known issues attached and is available *online*.

More information

All links in this book are accessible from the book's online bibliography available at: *http://msdn.microsoft.com/en-us/library/jj619274*.

Appendix 2

Migrations

Migrating from the V1 to the V2 release

If you have been running the V1 release and have data that you would like to preserve as you migrate to the V2 release, the following steps describe how you can perform this migration if you are hosting the V1 release in Windows Azure.

> **Note:** *You should create a backup of the Conference database before you begin the migration.*

1. Make sure that the V1 release is running in your Windows Azure production environment.
2. Deploy the V2 release to your Windows Azure staging environment. The V2 release has a global **MaintenanceMode** property that is initially set to **true**. In this mode, the application displays a message to the user that site is currently undergoing maintenance.
3. When you are ready, swap the V2 release (still in maintenance mode) into your Windows Azure production environment.
4. Leave the V1 release (now running in the staging environment) to run for a few minutes to ensure that all in-flight messages complete their processing.
5. Run the migration program to migrate the data (see below).
6. After the data migration completes successfully, change the **MaintenanceMode** property to **false**.
7. The V2 release is now live in Windows Azure.

> **Note:** *You can change the value of the **MaintenanceMode** property in the Windows Azure management portal.*

Running the migration program to migrate the data

Before beginning the data migration process, ensure that you have a backup of the data from your SQL Database instance.

The **MigrationToV2** utility uses the same **Settings.xml** file as the other projects in the **Conference** solution in addition to its own **App.config** file to specify the Windows Azure storage account and SQL connection strings.

The **Settings.xml** file contains the names of the new Windows Azure tables that the V2 release uses. If you are migrating data from V1 to V2 ensure that the name of the **EventSourcing** table is different from the name of the table used by the V1 release. The name of the table used by the V1 release is hardcoded in the **Program.cs** file in the MigrationToV2 project:

```
var originalEventStoreName = "ConferenceEventStore";
```

The name of the new table for V2 is in the **Settings.xml** file:

```xml
<EventSourcing>
    <ConnectionString>...</ConnectionString>
    <TableName>ConferenceEventStoreApplicationDemoV2</TableName>
</EventSourcing>
```

> **Note:** *The migration utility assumes that the V2 event sourcing table is in the same Windows Azure storage account as the V1 event sourcing table. If this is not the case, you will need to modify the MigrationToV2 application code.*

The **App.config** file contains the **DbContext.ConferenceManagement** connection string. The migration utility uses this connection string to connect to the SQL Database instance that contains the SQL tables used by the application. Ensure that this connection string points to the Windows Azure SQL Database that contains your production data. You can verify which SQL Database instance your production environment uses by looking in the active **ServiceConfiguration.csfg** file.

> **Note:** *If you are running the application locally using the **Debug** configuration, the **DbContext.ConferenceManagement** connection string will point to local SQL Express database.*

> **Note:** *To avoid data transfer charges, you should run the migration utility inside a Windows Azure worker role instead of on-premise. The solution includes an empty, configured Windows Azure worker role in the **MigrationToV2.Azure** with diagnostics that you can use for this purpose. For information about how to run an application inside a Windows Azure role instance, see Using Remote Desktop with Windows Azure Roles.*

> **Note:** *Migration from V1 to V2 is not supported if you are using the **DebugLocal** configuration.*

If the data migration fails

If the data migration process fails for any reason, then before you retry the migration you should:
1. Restore the SQL database back to its state before you ran the migration utility.
2. Delete the two new Windows Azure tables defined in **Settings.xml** in the **EventSourcing** and **MessageLog** sections.

Migrating from the V2 to the V3 Release

If you have been running the V2 release and have data that you would like to preserve as you migrate to the V3 release, the following steps describe how you can perform this migration if you are hosting the V2 release in Windows Azure.

> **Note:** *You should create a backup of the Conference database before you begin the migration.*

1. Make sure that the V2 release is running in your Windows Azure production environment.
2. Deploy the V3 release to your Windows Azure staging environment. In the V3 release, the command processor worker role has a **MaintenanceMode** property that is initially set to **true**.
3. Start the ad-hoc MigrationToV3.InHouseProcessor utility to rebuild the read models for the V3 deployment.
4. Change the **MaintenanceMode** property of the command processor worker role in the V2 release (running in the production slot) to **true**. At this point, the application is still running, but the registrations cannot progress. You should wait until the status of the worker role instance shows as **Ready** in the Windows Azure portal (this may take some time).
5. Change the **MaintenanceMode** property of the command processor worker role in the V3 release (running in the staging slot) to **false** and allow the MigrationToV3.InHouseProcessor utility to start handling the V2 events. The migration utility prompts you to start handling these V2 events when you are ready. This change is faster than changing the value of the **MaintenanceMode** property in the V2 release. When this change is complete, the V2 release web roles are using the data processed by the V3 version of the worker role. This configuration change also triggers the database migration.
6. In the Windows Azure Management Portal, perform a VIP swap to make the V3 web roles visible externally.
7. Shutdown the V2 deployment that is now running in the staging slot.
8. The V3 release is now live in Windows Azure.

> **Note:** *You can change the value of the **MaintenanceMode** property in the Windows Azure management portal.*

More information

All links in this book are accessible from the book's online bibliography available at:
http://msdn.microsoft.com/en-us/library/jj619274.